THOMAS BULFINCH (1796–1867) was a native of Boston, and a professor at Harvard College. He saw the need in his teaching for a source book on the myths and legends which lend so much color and meaning to the classical civilizations. *The Age of Fable* was completed in 1855, *The Age of Chivalry* three years later, and *Legends of Charlemagne* in 1863. In the course of a century the *Mythology,* made up of these three books, has become so famous that the very word automatically calls to mind the name of its author.

EDMUND FULLER teaches English and Classics at Kent School. He is the author of two novels, *A Star Pointed North* and *Brothers Divided,* and a book of critical essays, *Man in Modern Fiction,* as well as the editor of *Mark Twain: A Laurel Reader* (LC–111, 50c). His abridgment of *Mythology* is designed for the student and general reader, and retains the original language throughout.

LAUREL
EDITIONS

Mythology

by

Thomas Bulfinch

A Modern Abridgment
by Edmund Fuller

A LAUREL CLASSIC

Published by
DELL PUBLISHING CO., INC.
750 Third Avenue
New York 17, N.Y.

© Copyright, 1959, by Edmund Fuller

Laurel ® TM 674623, Dell Publishing Co., Inc.

First printing—June, 1959
Second printing—November, 1960
Third printing—January, 1962
Fourth printing—December, 1962

Printed in U.S.A.

EDITOR'S NOTE

Considerable experience in classrooms with both the classical and later myths has given me a heightened sense of the importance of this rich heritage. Ours tends to be a literal-minded age, in spite of the scientific marvels it boasts. The myths have never been a more important part of our cultural equipment. They cultivate the sense of wonder and accustom the mind to symbolic language. Students need to learn that "myth" does not mean "something that is not real or true," but that it means a kind of truth and a kind of reality not communicable by any means other than the symbolic story.

Arnold Toynbee, speaking as historian, has said: "History grew out of mythology. . . . It has been said of the *Iliad* that anyone who starts reading it as history will find that it is full of fiction but, equally, anyone who starts reading it as fiction will find that it is full of history."

Gilbert Highet, speaking as classical scholar, has said: ". . . the myths are permanent. They deal with the greatest of all problems, the problems which do not change, because men and women do not change. They deal with love; with war; with sin; with tyranny; with courage; with fate: and all in some way or other deal with the relation of man to those divine powers which are sometimes felt to be irrational, sometimes to be cruel, and sometimes, alas, to be just."

The three separate volumes which are combined in this book long ago ceased to be thought of individually as "The Age of Fable," "The Age of Chivalry," and "Legends of Charlemagne" and became together that household word: *Bulfinch's Mythology*. In this one-volume, paperbound edition for the modern reader and student, we have sought to preserve both the scope and unity of the work.

The great foundation, "The Age of Fable," is only slightly abridged. Most of the deletions are examples of poetic allusions from the work of long-forgotten early Victorian poets. Many useful citations from Shakespeare, Spenser, Milton, and other writers, remain. This is the oldest, best loved, standard handbook of the classical myths. Yet this present edition also contains the central frame and substance of the Arthurian chronicles in "The Age of Chivalry," as well as a representative selection from medieval romance in "Legends of Charlemagne."

The basic patterns of the legends of Charlemagne are repetitious to a high degree. It is neither practical nor desirable, here, to give more than a substantial selection indicative of their character and quality. We meet the major heroes and see the varieties of fanciful events and creatures that fill the tales, with their many borrowings from classical myths. Our selections culminate with the climax—the greatest episode of the whole tradition—the battle of Roncesvalles and the sounding of the great horn of Roland.

The general reader, with the student, will enter a realm of adventure, color, and magic in all the sections of this book.

EDMUND FULLER
June, 1959

CONTENTS

The Age of Fable
or
Stories of
Gods and Heroes

PREFACE

If no other knowledge deserves to be called useful but that which helps to enlarge our possessions or to raise our station in society, then mythology has no claim to the appellation. But if that which tends to make us happier and better can be called useful then we claim that epithet for our subject. For mythology is the handmaid of literature; and literature is one of the best allies of virtue and promoters of happiness.

Without a knowledge of mythology much of the elegant literature of our own language cannot be understood and appreciated. When Byron calls Rome "the Niobe of nations," or says of Venice, "She looks a Sea-Cybele fresh from ocean," he calls up to the mind of one familiar with our subject, illustrations more vivid and striking than the pencil could furnish, but which are lost to the reader ignorant of mythology. Milton abounds in similar allusions. The short poem "Comus" contains more than thirty such, and the ode "On the Morning of the Nativity" half as many. Through "Paradise Lost" they are scattered profusely. This is one reason why we often hear persons by no means illiterate say that they cannot enjoy Milton. But were these persons to add to their more solid acquirements the easy learning of this little volume, much of the poetry of Milton which has appeared to them "harsh and crabbed" would be found "musical as is Apollo's lute."

But how is mythology to be taught to one who does not learn it through the medium of the languages of Greece and Rome? To devote study to a species of learning which relates wholly to false marvels and obsolete faiths is not to be expected of the general reader in a practical age like this. The time even of the young is claimed by so many sciences of facts and things that little can be spared for set treatises on a science of mere fancy.

But may not the requisite knowledge of the subject be acquired by reading the ancient poets in translations? We reply, the field is too extensive for a preparatory course; and these very translations require some previous knowledge of the subject to make them intelligible. Let any one who doubts it read the first page of the "Aeneid," and see what he can make of "the hatred of Juno," the "decree of the Parcae," the "judgment of Paris," and the "honours of Ganymede," without this knowledge.

Shall we be told that answers to such queries may be found in notes, or by a reference to the Classical Dictionary? We reply, the interruption of one's reading by either process is so annoying that most readers prefer to let an allusion pass unapprehended rather than submit to it. Moreover, such sources give us only the dry facts without any of the charm of the original narrative; and what is a poetical myth when stripped of its poetry?

Our book is an attempt to solve this problem, by telling the stories of mythology in such a manner as to make them a source of amusement. We have endeavoured to tell them correctly, according to the ancient authorities, so that when the reader finds them referred to he may not be at a loss to recognize the reference. Thus we hope to teach mythology not as a study, but as a relaxation from study; to give our work the charm of a story-book, yet by means of it to impart a knowledge of an important branch of education.

Most of the classical legends in this book are derived from Ovid and Virgil. They are not literally translated, for, in the author's opinion, poetry translated into literal prose is very unattractive reading. Neither are they in verse, as well for other reasons as from a conviction that to translate faithfully under all the embarrassments of rhyme and measure is impossible. The attempt has been made to tell the stories in prose, preserving so much of the poetry as resides in the thoughts and is separable from the language itself, and omitting those amplifications which are not suited to the altered form.

The Northern mythological stories are copied with some abridgement from Mallet's "Northern Antiquities."

1. INTRODUCTION

The religions of ancient Greece and Rome are extinct. The so-called divinities of Olympus have not a single worshipper among living men. They belong now not to the department of theology, but to those of literature and taste. There they still hold their place, and will continue to hold it, for they are too closely connected with the finest productions of poetry and art, both ancient and modern, to pass into oblivion.

We propose to tell the stories relating to them which have come down to us from the ancients, and which are alluded to by modern poets, essayists, and orators. Our readers may thus at the same time be entertained by the most charming fictions which fancy has ever created, and put in possession of information indispensable to every one who would read with intelligence the elegant literature of his own day.

In order to understand these stories, it will be necessary to acquaint ourselves with the ideas of the structure of the universe which prevailed among the Greeks—the people from whom the Romans, and other nations through them, received their science and religion.

The Greeks believed the earth to be flat and circular, their own country occupying the middle of it, the central point being either Mount Olympus, the abode of the gods, or Delphi, so famous for its oracle.

The circular disk of the earth was crossed from west to east and divided into two equal parts by the *Sea*, as they called the Mediterranean, and its continuation the Euxine, the only seas with which they were acquainted.

Around the earth flowed the *River Ocean*, its course being from south to north on the western side of the earth, and in a contrary direction on the eastern side. It flowed in a steady, equable current, unvexed by storm or tempest. The sea, and all the rivers on earth, received their waters from it.

The northern portion of the earth was supposed to be inhabited by a happy race named the Hyperboreans, dwelling in everlasting bliss and spring beyond the lofty mountains whose caverns were supposed to send forth the piercing blasts of the north wind, which chilled the people of Hellas (Greece). Their country was inaccessible by land or sea. They lived exempt from disease or old age, from toils and warfare.

On the south side of the earth, close to the stream of Ocean, dwelt a people happy and virtuous as the Hyperboreans. They were named the Aethiopians. The gods favoured them so highly that they were wont to leave at times their Olympian abodes and go to share their sacrifices and banquets.

On the western margin of the earth, by the stream of Ocean, lay a happy place named the Elysian Plain, whither mortals favoured by the gods were transported without tasting of death, to enjoy an immortality of bliss. This happy region was also called the "Fortunate Fields," and the "Isles of the Blessed."

We thus see that the Greeks of the early ages knew little of any real people except those to the east and south of their own country, or near the coast of the Mediterranean. Their imagination meantime peopled the western portion of this sea with giants, monsters, and enchantresses; while they placed around the disk of the earth, which they probably regarded as of no great width, nations enjoying the peculiar favour of the gods, and blessed with happiness and longevity.

The Dawn, the Sun, and the Moon were supposed to rise out of the Ocean, on the eastern side, and to drive through the air, giving light to gods and men. The stars, also, except those forming the Wain or Bear, and others near them, rose out of and sank into the stream of Ocean. There the sun-god embarked in a winged boat, which conveyed him round by the northern part of the earth, back to his place of rising in the east.

The abode of the gods was on the summit of Mount Olympus, in Thessaly. A gate of clouds, kept by the goddesses named the Seasons, opened to permit the passage of the Celestials to earth, and to receive them on their return. The gods had their separate dwellings; but all, when summoned, repaired to the palace of Jupiter, as did also those deities whose usual abode was the earth, the waters, or the underworld. It was also in the great hall of the palace of the Olympian king that the gods feasted each day on ambrosia and nectar, their food and drink, the latter being handed round by the lovely goddess Hebe. Here they conversed of the affairs of heaven and earth; and as they quaffed their nectar, Apollo, the god of music, delighted them with the tones of his lyre, to which the Muses sang in responsive strains. When the sun was set, the gods retired to sleep in their respective dwellings.

The robes and other parts of the dress of the goddesses were woven by Minerva and the Graces, and everything of a more solid nature was formed of the various metals. Vulcan was architect, smith, armourer, chariot builder, and artist of all work in Olympus. He built of brass the houses of the gods; he made for them the golden shoes with which they trod the air or the water, and moved from place to place with the speed of the wind, or even of thought. He also shod with brass the celestial steeds, which whirled the chariots of the gods through the air, or along the surface of the sea. He was able to bestow on his workmanship self-motion, so that the tripods (chairs and tables) could move of themselves in and out of the celestial hall. He even endowed with intelligence the golden handmaidens whom he made to wait on himself.

Jupiter, or Jove (Zeus [1]), though called the father of gods and men, had himself a beginning. Saturn (Cronos) was his father, and Rhea (Ops) his mother. Saturn and Rhea were of the race of Titans, who were the children of Earth and Heaven, which sprang from Chaos, of which we shall give a further account in our next chapter.

There is another cosmogony, or account of the creation, according to which Earth, Erebus, and Love were the first of beings. Love (Eros) issued from the egg of Night, which

---

[1] The names included in parentheses are the Greek, the others being the Roman or Latin names.

floated on Chaos. By his arrows and torch he pierced and vivified all things, producing life and joy.

Saturn and Rhea were not the only Titans. There were others, whose names were Oceanus, Hyperion, Iapetus, and Ophion, males; and Themis, Mnemosyne, Eurynome, females. They are spoken of as the elder gods, whose dominion was afterwards transferred to others. Saturn yielded to Jupiter, Oceanus to Neptune, Hyperion to Apollo. Hyperion was the father of the Sun, Moon, and Dawn. He is therefore the original sun-god, and is painted with the splendour and beauty which were afterwards bestowed on Apollo. Ophion and Eurynome ruled over Olympus till they were dethroned by Saturn and Rhea.

The representations given of Saturn are not very consistent; for on the one hand his reign is said to have been the golden age of innocence and purity, and on the other he is described as a monster who devoured his children.[1] Jupiter, however, escaped this fate, and when grown up espoused Metis (Prudence), who administered a draught to Saturn which caused him to disgorge his children. Jupiter, with his brothers and sisters, now rebelled against their father Saturn and his brothers the Titans; vanquished them, and imprisoned some of them in Tartarus, inflicting other penalties on others. Atlas was condemned to bear up the heavens on his shoulders.

On the dethronement of Saturn, Jupiter with his brothers Neptune (Poseidon) and Pluto (Dis) divided his dominions. Jupiter's portion was the heavens, Neptune's the ocean, and Pluto's the realms of the dead. Earth and Olympus were common property. Jupiter was king of gods and men. The thunder was his weapon, and he bore a shield called Aegis, made for him by Vulcan. The eagle was his favourite bird, and bore his thunderbolts.

Juno (Hera) was the wife of Jupiter, and queen of the gods. Iris, the goddess of the rainbow, was her attendant and messenger. The peacock was her favourite bird.

Vulcan (Hephaestos), the celestial artist, was the son of Jupiter and Juno. He was born lame, and his mother was so

[1] This inconsistency arises from considering the Saturn of the Romans the same with the Grecian deity Cronos (Time), which, as it brings an end to all things which have had a beginning, may be said to devour its own offspring.

displeased at the sight of him that she flung him out of heaven. Other accounts say that Jupiter kicked him out for taking part with his mother in a quarrel which occurred between them. Vulcan's lameness, according to this account, was the consequence of his fall. He was a whole day falling, and at last alighted in the Island of Lemnos, which was thenceforth sacred to him. Milton alludes to this story in "Paradise Lost," Book I.:

> "... From morn
> To noon he fell, from noon to dewy eve,
> A summer's day; and with the setting sun
> Dropped from the zenith, like a falling star,
> On Lemnos, the Aegean isle."

Mars (Ares), the god of war, was the son of Jupiter and Juno.

Phoebus Apollo, the god of archery, prophecy, and music, was the son of Jupiter and Latona, and brother of Diana (Artemis). He was god of the sun, as Diana, his sister, was the goddess of the moon.

Venus (Aphrodite), the goddess of love and beauty, was the daughter of Jupiter and Dione. Others say that Venus sprang from the foam of the sea. The zephyr wafted her along the waves to the Isle of Cyprus, where she was received and attired by the Seasons, and then led to the assembly of the gods. All were charmed with her beauty, and each one demanded her for his wife. Jupiter gave her to Vulcan, in gratitude for the service he had rendered in forging thunderbolts. So the most beautiful of the goddesses became the wife of the most ill-favoured of gods. Venus possessed an embroidered girdle called Cestus, which had the power of inspiring love. Her favourite birds were swans and doves, and the plants sacred to her were the rose and the myrtle.

Cupid (Eros), the god of love, was the son of Venus. He was her constant companion; and, armed with bow and arrows, he shot the darts of desire into the bosoms of both gods and men. There was a deity named Anteros, who was sometimes represented as the avenger of slighted love, and sometimes as the symbol of reciprocal affection. The following legend is told of him:

Venus, complaining to Themis that her son Eros continued always a child, was told by her that it was because he was solitary, and that if he had a brother he would grow apace. Anteros was soon afterwards born, and Eros immediately was seen to increase rapidly in size and strength.

Minerva (Pallas, Athene, the goddess of wisdom) was the offspring of Jupiter, without a mother. She sprang forth from his head completely armed. Her favourite bird was the owl, and the plant sacred to her the olive.

Mercury (Hermes) was the son of Jupiter and Maia. He presided over commerce, wrestling, and other gymnastic exercises, even over thieving, and everything, in short, which required skill and dexterity. He was the messenger of Jupiter, and wore a winged cap and winged shoes. He bore in his hand a rod entwined with two serpents, called the caduceus.

Mercury is said to have invented the lyre. He found, one day, a tortoise, of which he took the shell, made holes in the opposite edges of it, and drew cords of linen through them, and the instrument was complete. The cords were nine, in honour of the nine Muses. Mercury gave the lyre to Apollo, and received from him in exchange the caduceus.

Ceres (Demeter) was the daughter of Saturn and Rhea. She had a daughter named Proserpine (Persephone), who became the wife of Pluto, and queen of the realms of the dead. Ceres presided over agriculture.

Bacchus (Dionysus), the god of wine, was the son of Jupiter and Semele. He represents not only the intoxicating power of wine, but its social and beneficent influences likewise, so that he is viewed as the promoter of civilization, and a lawgiver and lover of peace.

The Muses were the daughters of Jupiter and Mnemosyne (Memory). They presided over song, and prompted the memory. They were nine in number, to each of whom was assigned the presidence over some particular department of literature, art, or science. Calliope was the muse of epic poetry, Clio of history, Euterpe of lyric poetry, Melpomene of tragedy, Terpsichore of choral dance and song, Erato of love poetry, Polyhymnia of sacred poetry, Urania of astronomy, Thalia of comedy.

The Graces were goddesses presiding over the banquet, the dance, and all social enjoyments and elegant arts. They were three in number. Their names were Euphrosyne, Aglaia, and Thalia.

Spenser describes the office of the Graces thus:

"These three on men all gracious gifts bestow
   Which deck the body or adorn the mind,
To make them lovely or well-favoured show;
   As comely carriage, entertainment kind,
   Sweet semblance, friendly offices that bind,
And all the complements of courtesy;
   They teach us how to each degree and kind
   We should ourselves demean, to low, to high,
To friends, to foes; which skill men call Civility."

The Fates were also three—Clotho, Lachesis, and Atropos. Their office was to spin the thread of human destiny, and they were armed with shears, with which they cut it off when they pleased. They were the daughters of Themis (Law), who sits by Jove on his throne to give him counsel.

The Erinnyes, or Furies, were three goddesses who punished by their secret stings the crimes of those who escaped or defied public justice. The heads of the Furies were wreathed with serpents, and their whole appearance was terrific and appalling. Their names were Alecto, Tisiphone, and Megaera. They were also called Eumenides.[1]

Nemesis was also an avenging goddess. She represents the righteous anger of the gods, particularly towards the proud and insolent.

Pan was the god of flocks and shepherds. His favourite residence was in Arcadia.

The Satyrs were deities of the woods and fields. They were conceived to be covered with bristly hair, their heads decorated with short, sprouting horns, and their feet like goats' feet.

Momus was the god of laughter, and Plutus the god of wealth.

Roman Divinities

The preceding are Grecian divinities, though received also by the Romans. Those which follow are peculiar to Roman mythology:

Saturn was an ancient Italian deity. It was attempted to

[1] Meaning "kindly spirits," a euphemism.

identify him with the Grecian god Cronos, and fabled that after his dethronement by Jupiter he fled to Italy, where he reigned during what was called the Golden Age. In memory of his beneficent dominion, the feast of Saturnalia was held every year in the winter season. Then all public business was suspended, declarations of war and criminal executions were postponed, friends made presents to one another, and the slaves were indulged with great liberties. A feast was given them at which they sat at table, while their masters served them, to show the natural equality of men, and that all things belonged equally to all, in the reign of Saturn.

Faunus,[1] the grandson of Saturn, was worshipped as the god of fields and shepherds, and also as a prophetic god. His name in the plural, Fauns, expressed a class of game- some deities, like the Satyrs of the Greeks.

Quirinus was a war god, said to be no other than Romu- lus, the founder of Rome, exalted after his death to a place among the gods.

Bellona, a war goddess.

Terminus, the god of landmarks. His statue was a rude stone or post, set in the ground to mark the boundaries of fields.

Pales, the goddess presiding over cattle and pastures.

Pomona presided over fruit trees.

Flora, the goddess of flowers.

Lucina, the goddess of childbirth.

Vesta (the Hestia of the Greeks) was a deity presiding over the public and private hearth. A sacred fire, tended by six virgin priestesses called Vestals, flamed in her temple. As the safety of the city was held to be connected with its conservation, the neglect of the virgins, if they let it go out, was severely punished, and the fire was rekindled from the rays of the sun.

Liber is the Latin name of Bacchus; and Mulciber of Vul- can.

Janus was the porter of heaven. He opens the year, the first month being named after him. He is the guardian deity of gates, on which account he is commonly represented with two heads, because every door looks two ways. His temples

---

[1] There was also a goddess called Fauna, or Bona Dea.

at Rome were numerous. In war time the gates of the principal one were always open. In peace they were closed; but they were shut only once between the reign of Numa and that of Augustus.

The Penates were the gods who were supposed to attend to the welfare and prosperity of the family. Their name is derived from Penus, the pantry, which was sacred to them. Every master of a family was the priest of the Penates of his own house.

The Lares, or Lars, were also household gods, but differed from the Penates in being regarded as the deified spirits of mortals. The family Lars were held to be the souls of the ancestors, who watched over and protected their descendants. The words Lemur and Larva more nearly correspond to our word Ghost.

The Romans believed that every man had his Genius, and every woman her Juno: that is, a spirit who had given them being, and was regarded as their protector through life. On their birthdays men made offerings to their Genius, women to their Juno.

N.B.—It is to be observed that in proper names the final *e* and *es* are to be sounded. Thus Cybele and Penates are words of three syllables. But Proserpine and Thebes are exceptions, and to be pronounced as English words.

2. PROMETHEUS AND PANDORA

The creation of the world is a problem naturally fitted to excite the liveliest interest of man, its inhabitant. The ancient pagans had their own way of telling the story, which is as follows:

Before earth and sea and heaven were created, all things wore one aspect, to which we give the name of Chaos—a confused and shapeless mass, nothing but dead weight, in which, however, slumbered the seeds of things. Earth, sea, and air were all mixed up together; so the earth was not solid, the sea was not fluid, and the air was not transparent.

God and Nature at last interposed, and put an end to this discord, separating earth from sea, and heaven from both. The fiery part, being the lightest, sprang up, and formed the skies; the air was next in weight and place. The earth, being heavier, sank below; and the water took the lowest place, and buoyed up the earth.

Here some god—it is not known which—gave his good offices in arranging and disposing the earth. He appointed rivers and bays their places, raised mountains, scooped out valleys, distributed woods, fountains, fertile fields, and stony plains. The air being cleared, the stars began to appear, fishes took possession of the sea, birds of the air, and four-footed beasts of the land.

But a nobler animal was wanted, and Man was made. It is not known whether the creator made him of divine materials, or whether in the earth, so lately separated from heaven, there lurked still some heavenly seeds. Prometheus took some of this earth, and kneading it up with water, made man in the image of the gods. He gave him an upright stature, so that while all other animals turn their faces downward, and look to the earth, he raises his to heaven, and gazes on the stars.

Prometheus was one of the Titans, a gigantic race, who inhabited the earth before the creation of man. To him and his brother Epimetheus was committed the office of making man, and providing him and all other animals with the faculties necessary for their preservation. Epimetheus undertook to do this, and Prometheus was to overlook his work, when it was done. Epimetheus accordingly proceeded to bestow upon the different animals the various gifts of courage, strength, swiftness, sagacity; wings to one, claws to another, a shelly covering to a third, etc. But when man came to be provided for, who was to be superior to all other animals, Epimetheus had been so prodigal of his resources that he had nothing left to bestow upon him. In his perplexity he resorted to his brother Prometheus, who, with the aid of Minerva, went up to heaven, and lighted his torch at the chariot of the sun, and brought down fire to man. With this gift man was more than a match for all other animals. It enabled him to make weapons wherewith to subdue them; tools with which to cultivate the earth; to warm his dwelling, so as to be comparatively independent of climate; and finally to introduce the arts and to coin money, the means of trade and commerce.

Woman was not yet made. The story is that Jupiter made her, and sent her to Prometheus and his brother, to punish them for their presumption in stealing fire from heaven; and man, for accepting the gift. The first woman was named Pandora. She was made in heaven, every god contributing something to perfect her. Venus gave her beauty, Mercury persuasion, Apollo music, etc. Thus equipped, she was conveyed to earth, and presented to Epimetheus, who gladly accepted her, though cautioned by his brother to beware of Jupiter and his gifts. Epimetheus had in his house a jar, in which were kept certain noxious articles for which, in fitting man for his new abode, he had had no occasion. Pandora was seized with an eager curiosity to know what this jar contained; and one day she slipped off the cover and looked in. Forthwith there escaped a multitude of plagues for hapless man,—such as gout, rheumatism, and colic for his body, and envy, spite, and revenge for his mind,—and scattered themselves far and wide. Pandora hastened to replace the lid! but, alas! the whole contents of the jar had escaped, one thing only excepted, which lay at the bottom, and that was *hope.* So we see at this day, whatever evils are abroad, hope never entirely leaves us; and while we have *that,* no amount of other ills can make us completely wretched.

Another story is that Pandora was sent in good faith, by Jupiter, to bless man; that she was furnished with a box containing her marriage presents, into which every god had put some blessing. She opened the box incautiously, and the blessings all escaped, *hope* only excepted. This story seems more probable than the former; for how could *hope,* so precious a jewel as it is, have been kept in a jar full of all manner of evils, as in the former statement?

The world being thus furnished with inhabitants, the first age was an age of innocence and happiness, called the *Golden Age.* Truth and right prevailed, though not enforced by law, nor was there any magistrate to threaten or punish. The forest had not yet been robbed of its trees to furnish timbers for vessels, nor had men built fortifications round their towns. There were no such things as swords, spears, or helmets. The earth brought forth all things necessary for man, without his labour in ploughing or sowing. Perpetual spring reigned, flowers sprang up without seed, the rivers flowed with milk and wine, and yellow honey distilled from the oaks.

Then succeeded the *Silver Age,* inferior to the golden, but better than that of brass. Jupiter shortened the spring, and divided the year into seasons. Then, first, men had to endure the extremes of heat and cold, and houses became necessary. Caves were the first dwellings, and leafy coverts of the woods, and huts woven of twigs. Crops would no longer grow without planting. The farmer was obliged to sow the seed, and the toiling ox to draw the plough.

Next came the *Brazen Age,* more savage of temper, and readier to the strife of arms, yet not altogether wicked. The hardest and worst was the *Iron Age.* Crime burst in like a flood; modesty, truth, and honour fled. In their places came fraud and cunning, violence, and the wicked love of gain. Then seamen spread sails to the wind, and the trees were torn from the mountains to serve for keels to ships, and vex the face of the ocean. The earth, which till now had been cultivated in common, began to be divided off into possessions. Men were not satisfied with what the surface produced, but must dig into its bowels, and draw forth from thence the ores of metals. Mischievous *iron,* and more mischievous *gold,* were produced. War sprang up, using both as weapons; the guest was not safe in his friend's house; and sons-in-law and fathers-in-law, brothers and sisters, husbands and wives, could not trust one another. Sons wished their fathers dead, that they might come to the inheritance; family love lay prostrate. The earth was wet with slaughter, and the gods abandoned it, one by one, till Astraea [1] alone was left, and finally she also took her departure.

---

[1] The goddess of innocence and purity. After leaving earth, she was placed among the stars, where she became the constellation Virgo—the Virgin. Themis (Justice) was the mother of Astraea. She is represented as holding aloft a pair of scales, in which she weighs the claims of opposing parties.

It was a favourite idea of the old poets that these goddesses would one day return, and bring back the Golden Age. Even in a Christian hymn, the "Messiah" of Pope, this idea occurs:

> "All crimes shall cease, and ancient fraud shall fail,
>   Returning Justice lift aloft her scale,

Jupiter, seeing this state of things, burned with anger. He summoned the gods to council. They obeyed the call, and took the road to the palace of heaven. The road, which any one may see in a clear night, stretches across the face of the sky, and is called the Milky Way. Along the road stand the palaces of the illustrious gods; the common people of the skies live apart, on either side. Jupiter addressed the assembly. He set forth the frightful condition of things on the earth, and closed by announcing his intention to destroy the whole of its inhabitants, and provide a new race, unlike the first, who would be more worthy of life, and much better worshippers of the gods. So saying he took a thunderbolt, and was about to launch it at the world, and destroy it by burning; but recollecting the danger that such a conflagration might set heaven itself on fire, he changed his plan, and resolved to drown it. The north wind, which scatters the clouds, was chained up; the south was sent out, and soon covered all the face of heaven with a cloak of pitchy darkness. The clouds, driven together, resound with a crash; torrents of rain fall; the crops are laid low; the year's labour of the husbandman perishes in an hour. Jupiter, not satisfied with his own waters, calls on his brother Neptune to aid him with his. He lets loose the rivers, and pours them over the land. At the same time, he heaves the land with an earthquake, and brings in the reflux of the ocean over the shores. Flocks, herds, men, and houses are swept away, and temples, with their sacred enclosures, profaned. If any edifice remained standing, it was overwhelmed, and its turrets lay hid beneath the waves. Now all was sea, sea without shore. Here and there an individual remained on a projecting hilltop, and a few, in boats, pulled the oar where they had lately driven the plough. The fishes swim among the treetops; the anchor is let down into a garden. Where the graceful lambs played but now, unwieldy sea calves gambol. The wolf swims among the sheep, the yellow lions and tigers struggle in the water. The strength of the wild boar serves him not, nor his swiftness the stag. The birds fall with weary wing into the water, having found no land for a

Peace o'er the world her olive wand extend,
And white-robed Innocence from heaven descend."

See, also, Milton's "Hymn on the Nativity," stanzas xiv. and xv.

resting-place. Those living beings whom the water spared fell a prey to hunger.

Parnassus alone, of all the mountains, overtopped the waves; and there Deucalion, and his wife Pyrrha, of the race of Prometheus, found refuge—he a just man, and she a faithful worshipper of the gods. Jupiter, when he saw none left alive but this pair, and remembered their harmless lives and pious demeanour, ordered the north winds to drive away the clouds, and disclose the skies to earth, and earth to the skies. Neptune also directed Triton to blow on his shell, and sound a retreat to the waters. The waters obeyed, and the sea returned to its shores, and the rivers to their channels. Then Deucalion thus addressed Pyrrha: "O wife, only surviving woman, joined to me first by the ties of kindred and marriage, and now by a common danger, would that we possessed the power of our ancestor Prometheus, and could renew the race as he at first made it! But as we cannot, let us seek yonder temple, and inquire of the gods what remains for us to do." They entered the temple, deformed as it was with slime, and approached the altar, where no fire burned. There they fell prostrate on the earth, and prayed the goddess to inform them how they might retrieve their miserable affairs. The oracle answered, "Depart from the temple with head veiled and garments unbound, and cast behind you the bones of your mother." They heard the words with astonishment. Pyrrha first broke silence: "We cannot obey; we dare not profane the remains of our parents." They sought the thickest shades of the wood, and revolved the oracle in their minds. At length Deucalion spoke: "Either my sagacity deceives me, or the command is one we may obey without impiety. The earth is the great parent of all; the stones are her bones; these we may cast behind us; and I think this is what the oracle means. At least, it will do no harm to try." They veiled their faces, unbound their garments, and picked up stones, and cast them behind them. The stones (wonderful to relate) began to grow soft, and assume shape. By degrees, they put on a rude resemblance to the human form, like a block half finished in the hands of the sculptor. The moisture and slime that were about them became flesh; the stony part became bones; the veins remained veins, retaining their name, only changing their use. Those thrown by the hand of the man became men, and those by the woman became women. It was a hard race, and well adapted to labour, as we find ourselves to be at this day, giving plain indications of our origin.

The comparison of Eve to Pandora is too obvious to have escaped Milton, who introduces it in Book IV. of "Paradise Lost":

> "More lovely than Pandora, whom the gods
> Endowed with all their gifts; and O, too like
> In sad event . . ."

Prometheus has been a favourite subject with the poets. He is represented as the friend of mankind, who interposed in their behalf when Jove was incensed against them, and who taught them civilization and the arts. But as, in so doing, he transgressed the will of Jupiter, he drew down on himself the anger of the ruler of gods and men. Jupiter had him chained to a rock on Mount Caucasus, where a vulture preyed on his liver, which was renewed as fast as devoured. This state of torment might have been brought to an end at any time by Prometheus, if he had been willing to submit to his oppressor; for he possessed a secret which involved the stability of Jove's throne, and if he would have revealed it, he might have been at once taken into favour. But that he disdained to do. He has therefore become the symbol of magnanimous endurance of unmerited suffering, and strength of will resisting oppression.

3. APOLLO AND DAPHNE — PYRAMUS AND THISBE — CEPHALUS AND PROCRIS

The slime with which the earth was covered by the waters of the flood produced an excessive fertility, which called forth every variety of production, both bad and good. Among the rest, Python, an enormous serpent, crept forth, the terror of the people, and lurked in the caves of Mount Parnassus. Apollo slew him with his arrows—weapons which he had not before used against any but feeble animals, hares, wild goats, and such game. In commemoration of this illustrious conquest he instituted the Pythian games, in which the victor in feats of strength, swiftness of foot, or in the chariot race was crowned with a wreath of beech leaves; for the laurel was not yet adopted by Apollo as his own tree.

The famous statue of Apollo called the Belvedere represents the god after this victory over the serpent Python.

Apollo and Daphne

Daphne was Apollo's first love. It was not brought about by accident, but by the malice of Cupid. Apollo saw the boy playing with his bow and arrows; and being himself elated with his recent victory over Python, he said to him, "What have you to do with warlike weapons, saucy boy? Leave them for hands worthy of them. Behold the conquest I have won by means of them over the vast serpent who stretched his poisonous body over acres of the plain! Be content with your torch, child, and kindle up your flames, as you call them, where you will, but presume not to meddle with my weapons." Venus's boy heard these words, and rejoined, "Your arrows may strike all things else, Apollo, but mine shall strike you." So saying, he took his stand on a rock of Parnassus, and drew from his quiver two arrows of different workmanship, one to excite love, the other to repel it. The former was of gold and sharp pointed, the latter blunt and tipped with lead. With the leaden shaft he struck the nymph Daphne, the daughter of the river god Peneus, and with the golden one Apollo, through the heart. Forthwith the god was seized with love for the maiden, and she abhorred the thought of loving. Her delight was in woodland sports and in the spoils of the chase. Many lovers sought her, but she spurned them all, ranging the woods, and taking no thought of Cupid nor of Hymen. Her father often said to her, "Daughter, you owe me a son-in-law; you owe me grandchildren." She, hating the thought of marriage as a crime, with her beautiful face tinged all over with blushes, threw her arms around her father's neck, and said, "Dearest fa-

ther, grant me this favour, that I may always remain unmarried, like Diana." He consented, but at the same time said,
"Your own face will forbid it."

Apollo loved her, and longed to obtain her; and he who
gives oracles to all the world was not wise enough to look
into his own fortunes. He saw her hair flung loose over her
shoulders, and said, "If so charming in disorder, what would
it be if arranged?" He saw her eyes bright as stars; he saw
her lips, and was not satisfied with only seeing them. He admired her hands and arms, naked to the shoulder, and whatever was hidden from view he imagined more beautiful still.
He followed her; she fled, swifter than the wind, and delayed not a moment at his entreaties. "Stay," said he,
"daughter of Peneus; I am not a foe. Do not fly me as a
lamb flies the wolf, or a dove the hawk. It is for love I pursue you. You make me miserable, for fear you should fall
and hurt yourself on these stones, and I should be the cause.
Pray run slower, and I will follow slower. I am no clown, no
rude peasant. Jupiter is my father, and I am lord of Delphos
and Tenedos, and know all things, present and future. I am
the god of song and the lyre. My arrows fly true to the
mark; but, alas! an arrow more fatal than mine has pierced
my heart! I am the god of medicine, and know the virtues
of all healing plants. Alas! I suffer a malady that no balm
can cure!"

The nymph continued her flight, and left his plea half
uttered. And even as she fled she charmed him. The wind
blew her garments, and her unbound hair streamed loose
behind her. The god grew impatient to find his wooings
thrown away, and, sped by Cupid, gained upon her in the
race. It was like a hound pursuing a hare, with open jaws
ready to seize, while the feebler animal darts forward, slipping from the very grasp. So flew the god and the virgin—
he on the wings of love, and she on those of fear. The pursuer is the more rapid, however, and gains upon her, and his
panting breath blows upon her hair. Her strength begins to
fail, and, ready to sink, she calls upon her father, the river
god: "Help me, Peneus! open the earth to enclose me, or
change my form, which has brought me into this danger!"
Scarcely had she spoken, when a stiffness seized all her
limbs; her bosom began to be enclosed in a tender bark;
her hair became leaves; her arms became branches; her foot

stuck fast in the ground, as a root; her face became a tree-top, retaining nothing of its former self but its beauty. Apollo stood amazed. He touched the stem, and felt the flesh tremble under the new bark. He embraced the branches, and lavished kisses on the wood. The branches shrank from his lips. "Since you cannot be my wife," said he, "you shall assuredly be my tree. I will wear you for my crown; I will decorate with you my harp and my quiver; and when the great Roman conquerors lead up the trium-phal pomp to the Capitol, you shall be woven into wreaths for their brows. And, as eternal youth is mine, you also shall be always green, and your leaf know no decay." The nymph, now changed into a Laurel tree, bowed its head in grateful acknowledgment.

Pyramus and Thisbe

Pyramus was the handsomest youth, and Thisbe the fair-est maiden, in all Babylonia, where Semiramis reigned. Their parents occupied adjoining houses; and neighbour-hood brought the young people together, and acquaintance ripened into love. They would gladly have married, but their parents forbade. One thing, however, they could not forbid—that love should glow with equal ardour in the bosoms of both. They conversed by signs and glances, and the fire burned more intensely for being covered up. In the wall that parted the two houses there was a crack, caused by some fault in the structure. No one had remarked it before, but the lovers discovered it. What will not love discover! It afforded a passage to the voice; and tender messages used to pass backward and forward through the gap. As they stood, Pyramus on this side, Thisbe on that, their breaths would mingle. "Cruel wall," they said, "why do you keep two lovers apart? But we will not be ungrateful. We owe you, we confess, the privilege of transmitting loving words to willing ears." Such words they uttered on different sides of the wall; and when night came and they must say fare-well, they pressed their lips upon the wall, she on her side, he on his, as they could come no nearer.

Next morning, when Aurora had put out the stars, and the sun had melted the frost from the grass, they met at the accustomed spot. Then, after lamenting their hard fate, they

agreed that next night, when all was still, they would slip
away from the watchful eyes, leave their dwellings and walk
out into the fields; and to insure a meeting, repair to a well-
known edifice standing without the city's bounds, called the
Tomb of Ninus, and that the one who came first should
await the other at the foot of a certain tree. It was a white
mulberry tree, and stood near a cool spring. All was agreed
on, and they waited impatiently for the sun to go down beneath the waters and night to rise up from them. Then cautiously Thisbe stole forth, unobserved by the family, her
head covered with a veil, made her way to the monument
and sat down under the tree. As she sat alone in the dim
light of the evening she descried a lioness, her jaws reeking
with recent slaughter, approaching the fountain to slake her
thirst. Thisbe fled at the sight, and sought refuge in the hollow of a rock. As she fled she dropped her veil. The lioness
after drinking at the spring turned to retreat to the woods,
and seeing the veil on the ground, tossed and rent it with her
bloody mouth.

Pyramus, having been delayed, now approached the place
of meeting. He saw in the sand the footsteps of the lion, and
the colour fled from his cheeks at the sight. Presently he
found the veil all rent and bloody. "O hapless girl," said he,
"I have been the cause of thy death! Thou, more worthy of
life than I, hast fallen the first victim. I will follow. I am the
guilty cause, in tempting thee forth to a place of such peril,
and not being myself on the spot to guard thee. Come forth,
ye lions, from the rocks, and tear this guilty body with your
teeth." He took up the veil, carried it with him to the appointed tree, and covered it with kisses and with tears. "*My*
blood also shall stain your texture," said he, and drawing his
sword plunged it into his heart. The blood spurted from the
wound, and tinged the white mulberries of the tree all red;
and sinking into the earth reached the roots, so that the red
colour mounted through the trunk to the fruit.

By this time Thisbe, still trembling with fear, yet wishing
not to disappoint her lover, stepped cautiously forth, looking anxiously for the youth, eager to tell him the danger she
had escaped. When she came to the spot and saw the
changed colour of the mulberries she doubted whether it
was the same place. While she hesitated she saw the form of
one struggling in the agonies of death. She started back, a

shudder ran through her frame as a ripple on the face of
the still water when a sudden breeze sweeps over it. But as
soon as she recognized her lover, she screamed and beat her
breast, embracing the lifeless body, pouring tears into its
wounds, and imprinting kisses on the cold lips. "O Pyramus,"
she cried, "what has done this? Answer me, Pyramus; it is
your own Thisbe that speaks. Hear me, dearest, and lift
that drooping head!" At the name of Thisbe Pyramus
opened his eyes, then closed them again. She saw her veil
stained blood and the scabbard empty of its sword. "Thy
own hand has slain thee, and for my sake," she said. "I too
can be brave for once, and my love is as strong as thine. I
will follow thee in death, for I have been the cause; and
death which alone could part us shall not prevent my joining thee. And ye, unhappy parents of us both, deny us not
our united request. As love and death have joined us, let
one tomb contain us. And thou, tree, retain the marks of
slaughter. Let thy berries still serve for memorials of our
blood." So saying she plunged the sword into her breast.
Her parents ratified her wish, the gods also ratified it. The
two bodies were buried in one sepulchre, and the tree ever
after brought forth purple berries, as it does to this day.

Cephalus and Procris

Cephalus was a beautiful youth and fond of manly sports.
He would rise before the dawn to pursue the chase. Aurora
saw him when she first looked forth, fell in love with him,
and stole him away. But Cephalus was just married to a
charming wife whom he devotedly loved. Her name was
Procris. She was a favourite of Diana, the goddess of hunting, who had given her a dog which could outrun every
rival, and a javelin which would never fail of its mark; and
Procris gave these presents to her husband. Cephalus was so
happy in his wife that he resisted all the entreaties of Aurora, and she finally dismissed him in displeasure, saying,
"Go, ungrateful mortal, keep your wife, whom, if I am
not much mistaken, you will one day be very sorry you ever
saw again."

Cephalus would go out at early morning, ranging the
woods and hills unaccompanied by any one, needing no
help, for his javelin was a sure weapon in all cases. Fatigued

with hunting, when the sun got high he would seek a shady nook where a cool stream flowed, and, stretched on the grass, with his garments thrown aside, would enjoy the breeze. Sometimes he would say aloud, "Come, sweet breeze, come and fan my breast, come and allay the heat that burns me." Some one passing by one day heard him talking in this way to the air, and, foolishly believing that he was talking to some maiden, went and told the secret to Procris, Cephalus's wife. Love is credulous. Procris, at the sudden shock, fainted away. Presently recovering, she said, "It cannot be true; I will not believe it unless I myself am a witness to it." So she waited, with anxious heart, till the next morning, when Cephalus went to hunt as usual. Then she stole out after him, and concealed herself in the place where the informer directed her. Cephalus came as he was wont when tired with sport, and stretched himself on the green bank, saying, "Come, sweet breeze, come and fan me; you know how I love you! you make the groves and my solitary rambles delightful." He was running on in this way when he heard, or thought he heard, a sound as of a sob in the bushes. Supposing it some wild animal, he threw his javelin at the spot. A cry from his beloved Procris told him that the weapon had too surely met its mark. He rushed to the place, and found her bleeding, and with sinking strength endeavouring to draw forth from the wound the javelin, her own gift. Cephalus raised her from the earth, strove to stanch the blood, and called her to revive and not to leave him miserable, to reproach himself with her death. She opened her feeble eyes, and forced herself to utter these few words: "I implore you, if you have ever loved me, if I have ever deserved kindness at your hands, my husband, grant me this last request; do not marry that odious Breeze!" This disclosed the whole mystery: but alas! what advantage to disclose it now? She died; but her face wore a calm expression, and she looked pityingly and forgivingly on her husband when he made her understand the truth.

4. JUNO AND HER RIVALS, IO AND
CALLISTO — LATONA — DIANA
AND ACTAEON

Juno one day perceived it suddenly grow dark, and immediately suspected that her husband had raised a cloud to hide some of his doings that would not bear the light. She brushed away the cloud, and saw her husband on the banks of a glassy river, with a beautiful heifer standing near him. Juno suspected the heifer's form concealed some fair nymph of mortal mould—as was, indeed, the case; for it was Io, the daughter of the river god Inachus, whom Jupiter had been flirting with, and, when he became aware of the approach of his wife, had changed into that form.

Juno joined her husband, and noticing the heifer praised its beauty, and asked whose it was, and of what herd. Jupiter, to stop questions, replied that it was a fresh creation from the earth. Juno asked to have it as a gift. What could Jupiter do? He was loath to give his mistress to his wife; yet how refuse so trifling a present as a simple heifer? He could not, without exciting suspicion; so he consented. The goddess was not yet relieved of her suspicions; so she delivered the heifer to Argus, to be strictly watched.

Now Argus had a hundred eyes in his head, and never went to sleep with more than two at a time, so that he kept watch of Io constantly. He suffered her to feed through the day, and at night tied her up with a vile rope round her neck. She would have stretched out her arms to implore freedom of Argus, but she had no arms to stretch out, and her voice was a bellow that frightened even herself. She saw her father and her sisters, went near them, and suffered them to pat her back, and heard them admire her beauty. Her father reached her a tuft of grass, and she licked the outstretched hand. She longed to make herself known to him,

and would have uttered her wish; but, alas! words were
wanting. At length she bethought herself of writing, and inscribed her name—it was a short one—with her hoof on the
sand. Inachus recognized it, and discovering that his daughter, whom he had long sought in vain, was hidden under
this disguise, mourned over her, and, embracing her white
neck, exclaimed, "Alas! my daughter, it would have been
a less grief to have lost you altogether!" While he thus lamented, Argus, observing, came and drove her away, and
took his seat on a high bank, from whence he could see all
round in every direction.

Jupiter was troubled at beholding the sufferings of his
mistress, and calling Mercury told him to go and despatch
Argus. Mercury made haste, put his winged slippers on his
feet, and cap on his head, took his sleep-producing wand,
and leaped down from the heavenly towers to the earth.
There he laid aside his wings, and kept only his wand, with
which he presented himself as a shepherd driving his flock.
As he strolled on he blew upon his pipes. These were what
are called the Syrinx or Pandean pipes. Argus listened with
delight, for he had never seen the instrument before.
"Young man," said he, "come and take a seat by me on this
stone. There is no better place for your flocks to graze in than
hereabouts, and here is a pleasant shade such as shepherds
love." Mercury sat down, talked, and told stories till it grew
late, and played upon his pipes his most soothing strains,
hoping to lull the watchful eyes to sleep, but all in vain; for
Argus still contrived to keep some of his eyes open though
he shut the rest.

Among other stories, Mercury told him how the instrument on which he played was invented. "There was a certain
nymph, whose name was Syrinx, who was much beloved by
the satyrs and spirits of the wood; but she would have none
of them, but was a faithful worshipper of Diana, and followed the chase. You would have thought it was Diana herself, had you seen her in her hunting dress, only that her
bow was of horn and Diana's of silver. One day, as she was
returning from the chase, Pan met her, told her just this,
and added more of the same sort. She ran away, without
stopping to hear his compliments, and he pursued till she
came to the bank of the river, where he overtook her, and

she had only time to call for help on her friends the water nymphs. They heard and consented. Pan threw his arms around what he supposed to be the form of the nymph, and found he embraced only a tuft of reeds! As he breathed a sigh, the air sounded through the reeds, and produced a plaintive melody. The god, charmed with the novelty and with the sweetness of the music, said, 'Thus, then, at least, you shall be mine.' And he took some of the reeds, and placing them together, of unequal lengths, side by side, made an instrument which he called Syrinx, in honour of the nymph." Before Mercury had finished his story he saw Argus's eyes all asleep. As his head nodded forward on his breast, Mercury with one stroke cut his neck through, and tumbled his head down the rocks. O hapless Argus! the light of your hundred eyes is quenched at once! Juno took them and put them as ornaments on the tail of her peacock, where they remain to this day.

But the vengeance of Juno was not yet satiated. She sent a gadfly to torment Io, who fled over the whole world from its pursuit. She swam through the Ionian sea, which derived its name from her, then roamed over the plains of Illyria, ascended Mount Haemus, and crossed the Thracian strait, thence named the Bosphorus (cowford), rambled on through Scythia, and the country of the Cimmerians, and arrived at last on the banks of the Nile. At length Jupiter interceded for her, and upon his promising not to pay her any more attentions Juno consented to restore her to her form. It was curious to see her gradually recover her former self. The coarse hairs fell from her body, her horns shrank up, her eyes grew narrower, her mouth shorter; hands and fingers came instead of hoofs to her forefeet; in fine there was nothing left of the heifer, except her beauty. At first she was afraid to speak, for fear she should low, but gradually she recovered her confidence and was restored to her father and sisters.

Callisto

Callisto was another maiden who excited the jealousy of Juno, and the goddess changed her into a bear. "I will take away," said she, "that beauty with which you have captivated my husband." Down fell Callisto on her hands and

knees; she tried to stretch out her arms in supplication—
they were already beginning to be covered with black hair.
Her hands grew rounded, became armed with crooked
claws, and served for feet; her mouth, which Jove used to
praise for its beauty, became a horrid pair of jaws; her
voice, which if unchanged would have moved the heart to
pity, became a growl, more fit to inspire terror. Yet her
former disposition remained, and with continual groaning,
she bemoaned her fate, and stood upright as well as she
could, lifting up her paws to beg for mercy, and felt that
Jove was unkind, though she could not tell him so. Ah, how
often, afraid to stay in the woods all night alone, she wandered about the neighbourhood of her former haunts; how
often, frightened by the dogs, did she, so lately a huntress,
fly in terror from the hunters! Often she fled from the wild
beasts, forgetting that she was now a wild beast herself; and,
bear as she was, was afraid of the bears.

One day a youth espied her as he was hunting. She saw
him and recognized him as her own son, now grown a young
man. She stopped and felt inclined to embrace him. As she
was about to approach, he, alarmed, raised his hunting spear,
and was on the point of transfixing her, when Jupiter, beholding, arrested the crime, and snatching away both of
them, placed them in the heavens as the Great and Little
Bear.

Juno was in a rage to see her rival so set in honour, and
hastened to ancient Tethys and Oceanus, the powers of
ocean, and in answer to their inquiries thus told the cause
of her coming: "Do you ask why I, the queen of the gods,
have left the heavenly plains and sought your depths? Learn
that I am supplanted in heaven—my place is given to another. You will hardly believe me; but look when night
darkens the world, and you shall see the two of whom I
have so much reason to complain exalted to the heavens, in
that part where the circle is the smallest, in the neighbour-
hood of the pole. You, my foster-parents, if you feel for
me, and see with displeasure this unworthy treatment of me,
show it, I beseech you, by forbidding this couple from coming into your waters." The powers of the ocean assented,
and consequently the two constellations of the Great and
Little Bear move round and round in heaven, but never
sink, as the other stars do, beneath the ocean.

Latona

Latona (Leto) was another of Jupiter's loves to bear the
jealous rage of Juno. The tradition was that the future
mother of Apollo and Diana, flying from the wrath of Juno,
besought all the islands of the Aegean to afford her a place
of rest, but all feared too much the potent queen of heaven
to assist her rival. Delos alone consented to become the
birthplace of the future deities. Delos was then a floating
island; but when Latona arrived there, Jupiter fastened it
with adamantine chains to the bottom of the sea, that it
might be a secure resting-place for his beloved.

Diana and Actaeon

Thus in three instances we have seen Juno's severity to
her rivals; now let us learn how a virgin goddess punished
an invader of her privacy.

It was midday, and the sun stood equally distant from
either goal, when young Actaeon, son of King Cadmus,
thus addressed the youths who with him were hunting the
stag in the mountains:

"Friends, our nets and our weapons are wet with the
blood of our victims; we have had sport enough for one day,
and to-morrow we can renew our labours. Now, while
Phoebus parches the earth, let us put by our implements
and indulge ourselves with rest."

There was a valley thick enclosed with cypresses and
pines, sacred to the huntress queen, Diana. In the extremity
of the valley was a cave, not adorned with art, but nature
had counterfeited art in its construction, for she had turned
the arch of its roof with stones, as delicately fitted as if by
the hand of man. A fountain burst out from one side, whose
open basin was bounded by a grassy rim. Here the goddess
of the woods used to come when weary with hunting and
lave her virgin limbs in the sparkling water.

One day, having repaired thither with her nymphs, she
handed her javelin, her quiver, and her bow to one, her
robe to another, while a third unbound the sandals from
her feet. Then Crocale, the most skilful of them, arranged
her hair, and Nephele, Hyale, and the rest drew water in

capacious urns. While the goddess was thus employed in the labours of the toilet, behold Actaeon, having quitted his companions, and rambling without any especial object, came to the place, led thither by his destiny. As he presented himself at the entrance of the cave, the nymphs, seeing a man, screamed and rushed towards the goddess to hide her with their bodies. But she was taller than the rest and overtopped them all by a head. Such a colour as tinges the clouds at sunset or at dawn came over the countenance of Diana thus taken by surprise. Surrounded as she was by her nymphs, she yet turned half away, and sought with a sudden impulse for her arrows. As they were not at hand, she dashed the water into the face of the intruder, adding these words: "Now go and tell, if you can, that you have seen Diana unapparelled." Immediately a pair of branching stag's horns grew out of his head, his neck gained in length, his ears grew sharp-pointed, his hands became feet, his arms long legs, his body was covered with a hairy spotted hide. Fear took the place of his former boldness, and the hero fled. He could not but admire his own speed; but when he saw his horns in the water, "Ah, wretched me!" he would have said, but no sound followed the effort. He groaned, and tears flowed down the face which had taken the place of his own. Yet his consciousness remained. What shall he do?—go home to seek the palace, or lie hid in the woods? The latter he was afraid, the former he was ashamed, to do. While he hesitated the dogs saw him. First Melampus, a Spartan dog, gave the signal with his bark, then Pamphagus, Dorceus, Lelaps, Theron, Nape, Tigris, and all the rest, rushed after him swifter than the wind. Over rocks and cliffs, through mountain gorges that seemed impracticable, he fled and they followed. Where he had often chased the stag and cheered on his pack, his pack now chased him, cheered on by his huntsmen. He longed to cry out, "I am Actaeon; recognize your master!" but the words came not at his will. The air resounded with the bark of the dogs. Presently one fastened on his back, another seized his shoulder. While they held their master, the rest of the pack came up and buried their teeth in his flesh. He groaned,—not in a human voice, yet certainly not in a stag's,—and falling on his knees, raised his eyes, and would have raised his arms in supplication, if he had had them. His friends and fellow-huntsmen cheered on the dogs, and looked everywhere for Actaeon, calling on him to join the sport. At the sound of his name he turned his head, and heard them regret that he should be away. He earnestly wished he was. He would have been well pleased to see the exploits of his dogs, but to feel them was too much. They were all around him, rending and tearing; and it was not till they had torn his life out that the anger of Diana was satisfied.

5. PHAETON

Phaëton was the son of Apollo and the nymph Clymene. One day a schoolfellow laughed at the idea of his being the son of the god, and Phaëton went in rage and shame and reported it to his mother. "If," said he, "I am indeed of heavenly birth, give me, mother, some proof of it, and establish my claim to the honour." Clymene stretched forth her hands towards the skies, and said, "I call to witness the Sun which looks down upon us, that I have told you the truth. If I speak falsely, let this be the last time I behold his light. But it needs not much labour to go and inquire for yourself; the land whence the Sun rises lies next to ours. Go and demand of him whether he will own you as a son." Phaëton heard with delight. He travelled to India, which lies directly in the regions of sunrise; and, full of hope and pride, approached the goal whence his parent begins his course.

Clymene's son advanced up the steep ascent, and entered the halls of his disputed father. He approached the paternal presence, but stopped at a distance, for the light was more than he could bear. Phoebus, arrayed in a purple vesture, sat on a throne, which glittered as with diamonds. On his right hand and his left stood the Day, the Month, and the Year, and, at regular intervals, the Hours. Spring stood with her head crowned with flowers, and Summer, with garment cast aside, and a garland formed of spears of ripened grain, and Autumn, with his feet stained with grape-juice, and icy Winter, with his hair stiffened with hoar frost. Surrounded by these attendants, the Sun, with the eye that sees everything, beheld the youth dazzled with the novelty and splen-

dour of the scene, and inquired the purpose of his errand.
The youth replied, "O light of the boundless world, Phoebus, my father,—if you permit me to use that name,—give
me some proof, I beseech you, by which I may be known as
yours." He ceased; and his father, laying aside the beams
that shone all around his head, bade him approach, and embracing him, said, "My son, you deserve not to be disowned,
and I confirm what your mother has told you. To put an
end to your doubts, ask what you will, the gift shall be
yours. I call to witness that dreadful lake, which I never
saw, but which we gods swear by in our most solemn engagements." [1] Phaëton immediately asked to be permitted
for one day to drive the chariot of the sun. The father repented of his promise; thrice and four times he shook his
radiant head in warning. "I have spoken rashly," said he;
"this only request I would fain deny. I beg you to withdraw
it. It is not a safe boon, nor one, my Phaëton, suited to your
youth and strength. Your lot is mortal, and you ask what is
beyond a mortal's power. In your ignorance you aspire to do
that which not even the gods themselves may do. None but
myself may drive the flaming car of day. Not even Jupiter,
whose terrible right arm hurls the thunderbolts. The first
part of the way is steep, and such as the horses when fresh
in the morning can hardly climb; the middle is high up in
the heavens, whence I myself can scarcely, without alarm,
look down and behold the earth and sea stretched beneath
me. The last part of the road descends rapidly, and requires
most careful driving. Tethys, who is waiting to receive me,
often trembles for me lest I should fall headlong. Add to
all this, the heaven is all the time turning round and carrying the stars with it. I have to be perpetually on my guard
lest that movement, which sweeps everything else along,
should hurry me also away. Suppose I should lend you the
chariot, what would you do? Could you keep your course
while the sphere was revolving under you? Perhaps you
think that there are forests and cities, the abodes of gods,
and palaces and temples on the way. On the contrary, the
road is through the midst of frightful monsters. You pass by
the horns of the Bull, in front of the Archer, and near the
Lion's jaws, and where the Scorpion stretches its arms in one

[1] This was the oath on the River Styx.

direction and the Crab in another. Nor will you find it easy
to guide those horses, with their breasts full of fire that they
breathe forth from their mouths and nostrils. I can scarcely
govern them myself, when they are unruly and resist the
reins. Beware, my son, lest I be the donor of a fatal gift; recall your request while yet you may. Do you ask me for a
proof that you are sprung from my blood? I give you a
proof in my fears for you. Look at my face—I would that
you could look into my breast, you would there see all a father's anxiety. Finally," he continued, "look round the world
and choose whatever you will of what earth or sea contains
most precious—ask it and fear no refusal. This only I pray
you not to urge. It is not honour, but destruction you seek.
Why do you hang round my neck and still entreat me? You
shall have it if you persist,—the oath is sworn and must be
kept,—but I beg you to choose more wisely."

He ended; but the youth rejected all admonition and held
to his demand. So, having resisted as long as he could,
Phoebus at last led the way to where stood the lofty chariot.

It was of gold, the gift of Vulcan; the axle was of gold,
the pole and wheels of gold, the spokes of silver. Along the
seat were rows of chrysolites and diamonds which reflected
all around the brightness of the sun. While the daring youth
gazed in admiration, the early Dawn threw open the purple
doors of the east, and showed the pathway strewn with
roses. The stars withdrew, marshalled by the Day-star,
which last of all retired also. The father, when he saw the
earth beginning to glow, and the Moon preparing to retire,
ordered the Hours to harness up the horses. They obeyed,
and led forth from the lofty stalls the steeds full fed with
ambrosia, and attached the reins. Then the father bathed the
face of his son with a powerful unguent, and made him capable of enduring the brightness of the flame. He set the rays
on his head, and, with a foreboding sigh, said, "If, my son,
you will in this at least heed my advice, spare the whip and
hold tight the reins. They go fast enough of their own accord; the labour is to hold them in. You are not to take the
straight road directly between the five circles, but turn off
to the left. Keep within the limit of the middle zone, and
avoid the northern and the southern alike. You will see the
marks of the wheels, and they will serve to guide you. And,
that the skies and the earth may each receive their due share

of heat, go not too high, or you will burn the heavenly dwellings, nor too low, or you will set the earth on fire; the middle course is safest and best.[1] And now I leave you to your chance, which I hope will plan better for you than you have done for yourself. Night is passing out of the western gates and we can delay no longer. Take the reins; but if at last your heart fails you, and you will benefit by my advice, stay where you are in safety, and suffer me to light and warm the earth." The agile youth sprang into the chariot, stood erect, and grasped the reins with delight, pouring out thanks to his reluctant parent.

Meanwhile the horses fill the air with their snortings and fiery breath, and stamp the ground impatient. Now the bars are let down, and the boundless plain of the universe lies open before them. They dart forward and cleave the opposing clouds, and outrun the morning breezes which started from the same eastern goal. The steeds soon perceived that the load they drew was lighter than usual; and as a ship without ballast is tossed hither and thither on the sea, so the chariot, without its accustomed weight, was dashed about as if empty. They rush headlong and leave the travelled road. He is alarmed, and knows not how to guide them; nor, if he knew, has he the power. Then, for the first time, the Great and Little Bear were scorched with heat, and would fain, if it were possible, have plunged into the water; and the Serpent which lies coiled up round the north pole, torpid and harmless, grew warm, and with warmth felt its rage revive. Boötes, they say, fled away, though encumbered with his plough, and all unused to rapid motion.

When hapless Phaëton looked down upon the earth, now spreading in vast extent beneath him, he grew pale and his knees shook with terror. In spite of the glare all around him, the sight of his eyes grew dim. He wished he had never touched his father's horses, never learned his parentage, never prevailed in his request. He is borne along like a vessel that flies before a tempest, when the pilot can do no more and betakes himself to his prayers. What shall he do? Much of the heavenly road is left behind, but more remains before. He turns his eyes from one direction to the

---

[1] See Proverbial Expressions, page 268.

other; now to the goal whence he began his course, now to
the realms of sunset which he is not destined to reach. He
loses his self-command, and knows not what to do,—
whether to draw tight the reins or throw them loose; he for-
gets the names of the horses. He sees with terror the monstrous forms scattered over the surface of heaven. Here the
Scorpion extended his two great arms, with his tail and
crooked claws stretching over two signs of the zodiac.
When the boy beheld him, reeking with poison and menac-
ing with his fangs, his courage failed, and the reins fell from
his hands. The horses, when they felt them loose on their
backs, dashed headlong, and unrestrained went off into
unknown regions of the sky, in among the stars, hurling the
chariot over pathless places, now up in high heaven, now
down almost to the earth. The moon saw with astonishment
her brother's chariot running beneath her own. The clouds
begin to smoke, and the mountain tops take fire; the fields
are parched with heat, the plants wither, the trees with
their leafy branches burn, the harvest is ablaze! But these
are small things. Great cities perished, with their walls and
towers; whole nations with their people were consumed to
ashes! The forest-clad mountains burned, Athos and Taurus
and Tmolus and Oete; Ida, once celebrated for fountains,
but now all dry; the Muses' mountain Helicon, and Haemus;
Aetna, with fires within and without, and Parnassus, with his
two peaks, and Rhodope, forced at last to part with his
snowy crown. Her cold climate was no protection to Scythia, Caucasus burned, and Ossa and Pindus, and greater
than both, Olympus; the Alps high in air, and the Apen-
nines crowned with clouds.

Then Phaëton beheld the world on fire, and felt the heat
intolerable. The air he breathed was like the air of a furnace and full of burning ashes, and the smoke was of a
pitchy darkness. He dashed forward he knew not whither.
Then, it is believed, the people of Aethiopia became black by
the blood being forced so suddenly to the surface, and the
Libyan desert was dried up to the condition in which it remains to this day. The Nymphs of the fountains, with dishevelled hair, mourned their waters, nor were the rivers
safe beneath their banks. The earth cracked open, and
through the chinks light broke into Tartarus, and fright-

ened the king of shadows and his queen. The sea shrank up. Where before was water, it became a dry plain; and the mountains that lie beneath the waves lifted up their heads and became islands. The fishes sought the lowest depths, and the dolphins no longer ventured as usual to sport on the surface. Even Nereus, and his wife Doris, with the Nereids, their daughters, sought the deepest caves for refuge. Thrice Neptune essayed to raise his head above the surface, and thrice was driven back by the heat. Earth, surrounded as she was by waters, yet with head and shoulders bare, screening her face with her hand, looked up to heaven, and with a husky voice called on Jupiter:

"O ruler of the gods, if I have deserved this treatment, and it is your will that I perish with fire, why withhold your thunderbolts? Let me at least fall by your hand. Is this the reward of my fertility, of my obedient service? Is it for this that I have supplied herbage for cattle, and fruits for men, and frankincense for your altars? But if I am unworthy of regard, what has my brother Ocean done to deserve such a fate? If neither of us can excite your pity, think, I pray you, of your own heaven, and behold how both the poles are smoking which sustain your palace, which must fall if they be destroyed. Atlas faints, and scarce holds up his burden. If sea, earth, and heaven perish, we fall into ancient Chaos. Save what yet remains to us from the devouring flame. O, take thought for our deliverance in this awful moment!"

Thus spoke Earth, and overcome with heat and thirst, could say no more. Then Jupiter omnipotent, calling to witness all the gods, including him who had lent the chariot, and showing them that all was lost unless some speedy remedy were applied, mounted the lofty tower from whence he diffuses clouds over the earth, and hurls the forked lightnings. But at that time not a cloud was to be found to interpose for a screen to earth, nor was a shower remaining unexhausted. He thundered, and brandishing a lightning bolt in his right hand launched it against the charioteer, and struck him at the same moment from his seat and from existence! Phaëton, with his hair on fire, fell headlong, like a shooting star which marks the heavens with its brightness as it falls, and Eridanus, the great river, received him and

cooled his burning frame.[1] The Italian Naiads reared a
tomb for him, and inscribed these words upon the stone:

> "Driver of Phoebus' chariot, Phaëton,
> Struck by Jove's thunder, rests beneath this stone.
> He could not rule his father's car of fire,
> Yet was it much so nobly to aspire."

His sisters, the Heliades, as they lamented his fate, were
turned into poplar trees, on the banks of the river, and their
tears, which continued to flow, became amber as they
dropped into the stream.

6. MIDAS — BAUCIS AND PHILEMON

Bacchus, on a certain occasion, found his old schoolmaster
and foster-father, Silenus, missing. The old man had been
drinking, and in that state wandered away, and was found
by some peasants, who carried him to their king, Midas.
Midas recognized him, and treated him hospitably, entertaining him for ten days and nights with an unceasing round
of jollity. On the eleventh day he brought Silenus back, and
restored him in safety to his pupil. Whereupon Bacchus
offered Midas his choice of a reward, whatever he might
wish. He asked that whatever he might touch should be
changed into *gold*. Bacchus consented, though sorry that
he had not made a better choice. Midas went his way, rejoicing in his new-acquired power, which he hastened to
put to the test. He could scarce believe his eyes when he
found a twig of an oak, which he plucked from the branch,
become gold in his hand. He took up a stone; it changed to
gold. He touched a sod; it did the same. He took an apple
from the tree; you would have thought he had robbed the
garden of the Hesperides. His joy knew no bounds, and as
soon as he got home, he ordered the servants to set a splendid repast on the table. Then he found to his dismay that
whether he touched bread, it hardened in his hand; or put

---

[1] See Proverbial Expressions, page 268.

a morsel to his lip, it defied his teeth. He took a glass of
wine, but it flowed down his throat like melted gold.

In consternation at the unprecedented affliction, he strove
to divest himself of his power; he hated the gift he had
lately coveted. But all in vain; starvation seemed to await
him. He raised his arms, all shining with gold, in prayer
to Bacchus, begging to be delivered from his glittering destruction. Bacchus, merciful deity, heard and consented.
"Go," said he, "to the River Pactolus, trace the stream
to its fountain-head, there plunge your head and body in,
and wash away your fault and its punishment." He did so,
and scarce had he touched the waters before the gold-creat-
ing power passed into them, and the river sands became
changed into *gold,* as they remain to this day.

Thenceforth Midas, hating wealth and splendour, dwelt
in the country, and became a worshipper of Pan, the god
of the fields. On a certain occasion Pan had the temerity to
compare his music with that of Apollo, and to challenge
the god of the lyre to a trial of skill. The challenge was
accepted, and Tmolus, the mountain god, was chosen umpire. The senior took his seat, and cleared away the trees
from his ears to listen. At a given signal Pan blew on his
pipes, and with his rustic melody gave great satisfaction to
himself and his faithful follower Midas, who happened to
be present. Then Tmolus turned his head toward the Sun-
god, and all his trees turned with him. Apollo rose, his brow
wreathed with Parnassian laurel, while his robe of Tyrian
purple swept the ground. In his left hand he held the lyre,
and with his right hand struck the strings. Ravished with
the harmony, Tmolus at once awarded the victory to the
god of the lyre, and all but Midas acquiesced in the judgment. He dissented, and questioned the justice of the award.
Apollo would not suffer such a depraved pair of ears any
longer to wear the human form, but caused them to increase
in length, grow hairy, within and without, and movable on
their roots; in short, to be on the perfect pattern of those of
an ass.

Mortified enough was King Midas at this mishap; but he
consoled himself with the thought that it was possible to
hide his misfortune, which he attempted to do by means of
an ample turban or head-dress. But his hair-dresser of
course knew the secret. He was charged not to mention it,

and threatened with dire punishment if he presumed to disobey. But he found it too much for his discretion to keep
such a secret; so he went out into the meadow, dug a hole
in the ground, and stooping down, whispered the story, and
covered it up. Before long a thick bed of reeds sprang up
in the meadow, and as soon as it had gained its growth,
began whispering the story, and has continued to do so,
from that day to this, every time a breeze passes over the
place.

Midas was king of Phrygia. He was the son of Gordius, a
poor countryman, who was taken by the people and made
king, in obedience to the command of the oracle, which
had said that their future king should come in a wagon.
While the people were deliberating, Gordius with his wife
and son came driving his wagon into the public square.

Gordius, being made king, dedicated his wagon to the
deity of the oracle, and tied it up in its place with a fast
knot. This was the celebrated *Gordian knot,* which, in after
times it was said, whoever should untie should become lord
of all Asia. Many tried to untie it, but none succeeded, till
Alexander the Great, in his career of conquest, came to
Phrygia. He tried his skill with as ill success as others, till
growing impatient he drew his sword and cut the knot.
When he afterwards succeeded in subjecting all Asia to his
sway, people began to think that he had complied with the
terms of the oracle according to its true meaning.

Baucis and Philemon

On a certain hill in Phrygia stands a linden tree and an
oak, enclosed by a low wall. Not far from the spot is a
marsh, formerly good habitable land, but now indented
with pools, the resort of fen-birds and cormorants. Once
on a time Jupiter, in human shape, visited this country, and
with him his son Mercury (he of the caduceus), without
his wings. They presented themselves, as weary travellers,
at many a door, seeking rest and shelter, but found all
closed, for it was late, and the inhospitable inhabitants
would not rouse themselves to open for their reception. At
last a humble mansion received them, a small thatched cottage, where Baucis, a pious old dame, and her husband

Philemon, united when young, had grown old together. Not ashamed of their poverty, they made it endurable by moderate desires and kind dispositions. One need not look there for master or for servant; they two were the whole household, master and servant alike. When the two heavenly guests crossed the humble threshold, and bowed their heads to pass under the low door, the old man placed a seat, on which Baucis, bustling and attentive, spread a cloth, and begged them to sit down. Then she raked out the coals from the ashes, and kindled up a fire, fed it with leaves and dry bark, and with her scanty breath blew it into a flame. She brought out of a corner split sticks and dry branches, broke them up, and placed them under the small kettle. Her husband collected some pot-herbs in the garden, and she shred them from the stalks, and prepared them for the pot. He reached down with a forked stick a flitch of bacon hanging in the chimney, cut a small piece, and put it in the pot to boil with the herbs, setting away the rest for another time. A beechen bowl was filled with warm water, that their guests might wash. While all was doing, they beguiled the time with conversation.

On the bench designed for the guests was laid a cushion stuffed with sea-weed; and a cloth, only produced on great occasions, but ancient and coarse enough, was spread over that. The old lady, with her apron on, with trembling hand set the table. One leg was shorter than the rest, but a piece of slate put under restored the level. When fixed, she rubbed the table down with some sweet-smelling herbs. Upon it she set some of chaste Minerva's olives, some cornel berries preserved in vinegar, and added radishes and cheese, with eggs lightly cooked in the ashes. All were served in earthen dishes, and an earthenware pitcher, with wooden cups, stood beside them. When all was ready, the stew, smoking hot, was set on the table. Some wine, not of the oldest, was added; and for dessert, apples and wild honey; and over and above all, friendly faces, and simple but hearty welcome.

Now while the repast proceeded, the old folks were astonished to see that the wine, as fast as it was poured out, renewed itself in the pitcher, of its own accord. Struck with terror, Baucis and Philemon recognized their heavenly guests, fell on their knees, and with clasped hands implored forgiveness for their poor entertainment. There was an old goose, which they kept as the guardian of their humble cottage; and they bethought them to make this a sacrifice in honour of their guests. But the goose, too nimble, with the aid of feet and wings, for the old folks, eluded their pursuit, and at last took shelter between the gods themselves. They forbade it to be slain; and spoke in these words: "We are gods. This inhospitable village shall pay the penalty of its impiety; you alone shall go free from the chastisement. Quit your house, and come with us to the top of yonder hill." They hastened to obey, and, staff in hand, laboured up the steep ascent. They had reached to within an arrow's flight of the top, when, turning their eyes below, they beheld all the country sunk in a lake, only their own house left standing. While they gazed with wonder at the sight, and lamented the fate of their neighbours, that old house of theirs was changed into a temple. Columns took the place of the corner posts, the thatch grew yellow and appeared a gilded roof, the floors became marble, the doors were enriched with carving and ornaments of gold. Then spoke Jupiter in benignant accents: "Excellent old man, and woman worthy of such a husband, speak, tell us your wishes; what favour have you to ask of us?" Philemon took counsel with Baucis a few moments; then declared to the gods their united wish. "We ask to be priests and guardians of this your temple; and since here we have passed our lives in love and concord, we wish that one and the same hour may take us both from life, that I may not live to see her grave, nor be laid in my own by her." Their prayer was granted. They were the keepers of the temple as long as they lived. When grown very old, as they stood one day before the steps of the sacred edifice, and were telling the story of the place, Baucis saw Philemon begin to put forth leaves, and old Philemon saw Baucis changing in like manner. And now a leafy crown had grown over their heads, while exchanging parting words, as long as they could speak. "Farewell, dear spouse," they said, together, and at the same moment the bark closed over their mouths.

When Jupiter and his brothers had defeated the Titans and banished them to Tartarus, a new enemy rose up against the gods. They were the giants Typhon, Briareus, Enceladus, and others. Some of them had a hundred arms, others breathed out fire. They were finally subdued and buried alive under Mount Aetna, where they still sometimes struggle to get loose, and shake the whole island with earthquakes. Their breath comes up through the mountain, and is what men call the eruption of the volcano.

The fall of these monsters shook the earth, so that Pluto was alarmed, and feared that his kingdom would be laid open to the light of day. Under this apprehension, he mounted his chariot, drawn by black horses, and took a circuit of inspection to satisfy himself of the extent of the damage. While he was thus engaged, Venus, who was sitting on Mount Eryx playing with her boy Cupid, espied him, and said, "My son, take your darts with which you conquer all, even Jove himself, and send one into the breast of yonder dark monarch, who rules the realm of Tartarus. Why should he alone escape? Seize the opportunity to extend your empire and mine. Do you not see that even in heaven some despise our power? Minerva the wise, and Diana the huntress, defy us; and there is that daughter of Ceres, who threatens to follow their example. Now do you, if you have any regard for your own interest or mine, join these two in one." The boy unbound his quiver, and selected his sharpest and truest arrow; then straining the bow against his knee, he attached the string, and, having made ready, shot the arrow with its barbed point right into the heart of Pluto.

In the vale of Enna there is a lake embowered in woods, which screen it from the fervid rays of the sun, while the moist ground is covered with flowers, and Spring reigns perpetual. Here Proserpine was playing with her companions, gathering lilies and violets, and filling her basket and

her apron with them, when Pluto saw her, loved her, and
carried her off. She screamed for help to her mother and
companions; and when in her fright she dropped the corners
of her apron and let the flowers fall, childlike she felt the
loss of them as an addition to her grief. The ravisher urged
on his steeds, calling them each by name, and throwing
loose over their heads and necks his iron-coloured reins.
When he reached the River Cyane, and it opposed his passage, he struck the river-bank with his trident, and the
earth opened and gave him a passage to Tartarus.

Ceres sought her daughter all the world over. Bright-
haired Aurora, when she came forth in the morning, and
Hesperus when he led out the stars in the evening, found
her still busy in the search. But it was all unavailing. At
length, weary and sad, she sat down upon a stone, and
continued sitting nine days and nights, in the open air, under the sunlight and moonlight and falling showers. It was
where now stands the city of Eleusis, then the home of an
old man named Celeus. He was out on the field, gathering
acorns and blackberries, and sticks for his fire. His little
girl was driving home their two goats, and as she passed the
goddess, who appeared in the guise of an old woman, she
said to her, "Mother,"—and the name was sweet to the
ears of Ceres,—"why do you sit here alone upon the rocks?"
The old man also stopped, though his load was heavy, and
begged her to come into his cottage, such as it was. She
declined, and he urged her. "Go in peace," she replied, "and
be happy in your daughter; I have lost mine." As she spoke,
tears—or something like tears, for the gods never weep—
fell down her cheeks upon her bosom. The compassionate
old man and his child wept with her. Then said he, "Come
with us, and despise not our humble roof; so may your
daughter be restored to you in safety." "Lead on," said she,
"I cannot resist that appeal!" So she rose from the stone and
went with them. As they walked he told her that his only
son, a little boy, lay very sick, feverish, and sleepless. She
stooped and gathered some poppies. As they entered the
cottage, they found all in great distress, for the boy seemed
past hope of recovery. Metanira, his mother, received her
kindly, and the goddess stooped and kissed the lips of the
sick child. Instantly the paleness left his face, and healthy
vigour returned to his body. The whole family were de-

lighted—that is, the father, mother, and little girl, for they
were all; they had no servants. They spread the table, and
put upon it curds and cream, apples, and honey in the comb.
While they ate, Ceres mingled poppy juice in the milk of
the boy. When night came and all was still, she arose, and
taking the sleeping boy, moulded his limbs with her hands,
and uttered over him three times a solemn charm, then
went and laid him in the ashes. His mother, who had been
watching what her guest was doing, sprang forward with
a cry and snatched the child from the fire. Then Ceres assumed her own form, and a divine splendour shone all
around. While they were overcome with astonishment, she
said, "Mother, you have been cruel in your fondness to your
son. I would have made him immortal, but you have frus-
trated my attempt. Nevertheless, he shall be great and useful. He shall teach men the use of the plough, and the rewards which labour can win from the cultivated soil." So
saying, she wrapped a cloud about her, and mounting her
chariot rode away.

Ceres continued her search for her daughter, passing
from land to land, and across seas and rivers, till at length
she returned to Sicily, whence she at first set out, and stood
by the banks of the River Cyane, where Pluto made himself a passage with his prize to his own dominions. The
river nymph would have told the goddess all she had witnessed, but dared not, for fear of Pluto; so she only ventured to take up the girdle which Proserpine had dropped
in her flight, and waft it to the feet of the mother. Ceres,
seeing this, was no longer in doubt of her loss, but she did
not yet know the cause, and laid the blame on the innocent
land. "Ungrateful soil," said she, "which I have endowed
with fertility and clothed with herbage and nourishing grain,
no more shall you enjoy my favours." Then the cattle died,
the plough broke in the furrow, the seed failed to come up;
there was too much sun, there was too much rain; the birds
stole the seeds—thistles and brambles were the only growth.
Seeing this, the fountain Arethusa interceded for the land.
"Goddess," said she, "blame not the land; it opened unwillingly to yield a passage to your daughter. I can tell you of
her fate, for I have seen her. This is not my native country;
I came hither from Elis. I was a woodland nymph, and delighted in the chase. They praised my beauty, but I cared

nothing for it, and rather boasted of my hunting exploits. One day I was returning from the wood, heated with exercise, when I came to a stream silently flowing, so clear that you might count the pebbles on the bottom. The willows shaded it, and the grassy bank sloped down to the water's edge. I approached, I touched the water with my foot. I stepped in knee-deep, and not content with that, I laid my garments on the willows and went in. While I sported in the water, I heard an indistinct murmur coming up as out of the depths of the stream; and made haste to escape to the nearest bank. The voice said, 'Why do you fly, Arethusa? I am Alpheus, the god of this stream.' I ran, he pursued; he was not more swift than I, but he was stronger, and gained upon me, as my strength failed. At last, exhausted, I cried for help to Diana. 'Help me, goddess! help your votary!' The goddess heard, and wrapped me suddenly in a thick cloud. The river god looked now this way and now that, and twice came close to me, but could not find me. 'Arethusa! Arethusa!' he cried. Oh, how I trembled,—like a lamb that hears the wolf growling outside the fold. A cold sweat came over me, my hair flowed down in streams; where my foot stood there was a pool. In short, in less time than it takes to tell it, I became a fountain. But in this form Alpheus knew me and attempted to mingle his stream with mine. Diana cleft the ground, and I, endeavouring to escape him, plunged into the cavern, and through the bowels of the earth came out here in Sicily. While I passed through the lower parts of the earth, I saw your Proserpine. She was sad, but no longer showing alarm in her countenance. Her look was such as became a queen—the queen of Erebus; the powerful bride of the monarch of the realms of the dead."

When Ceres heard this, she stood for a while like one stupefied; then turned her chariot towards heaven, and hastened to present herself before the throne of Jove. She told the story of her bereavement, and implored Jupiter to interfere to procure the restitution of her daughter. Jupiter consented on one condition, namely, that Proserpine should not during her stay in the lower world have taken any food; otherwise, the Fates forbade her release. Accordingly, Mercury was sent, accompanied by Spring, to demand Proserpine of Pluto. The wily monarch consented; but, alas! the maiden had taken a pomegranate which Pluto offered her, and had sucked the sweet pulp from a few of the seeds. This was enough to prevent her complete release; but a compromise was made, by which she was to pass half the time with her mother, and the rest with her husband Pluto.

Ceres allowed herself to be pacified with this arrangement, and restored the earth to her favour. Now she remembered Celeus and his family, and her promise to his infant son Triptolemus. When the boy grew up, she taught him the use of the plough, and how to sow the seed. She took him in her chariot, drawn by winged dragons, through all the countries of the earth, imparting to mankind valuable grains, and the knowledge of agriculture. After his return, Triptolemus built a magnificent temple to Ceres in Eleusis, and established the worship of the goddess, under the name of the Eleusinian mysteries, which, in the splendour and solemnity of their observance, surpassed all other religious celebrations among the Greeks.

There can be little doubt of this story of Ceres and Proserpine being an allegory. Proserpine signifies the seed-corn which when cast into the ground lies there concealed—that is, she is carried off by the god of the underworld. It reappears—that is, Proserpine is restored to her mother. Spring leads her back to the light of day.

Milton alludes to the story of Proserpine in "Paradise Lost," Book IV.:

"... Not that fair field
Of Enna where Proserpine gathering flowers,
Herself a fairer flower, by gloomy Dis
Was gathered, which cost Ceres all that pain
To seek her through the world,—
... might with this Paradise
Of Eden strive."

The River Alpheus does in fact disappear underground, in part of its course, finding its way through subterranean channels till it again appears on the surface. It was said that the Sicilian fountain Arethusa was the same stream, which, after passing under the sea, came up again in Sicily. Hence the story ran that a cup thrown into the Alpheus appeared again in Arethusa. It is this fable of the underground course of Alpheus that Coleridge alludes to in his poem of "Kubla Khan":

> "In Xanadu did Kubla Khan
>   A stately pleasure-dome decree,
> Where Alph, the sacred river, ran
> Through caverns measureless to man,
>   Down to a sunless sea."

Glaucus and Scylla

Glaucus was a fisherman. One day he had drawn his nets to land, and had taken a great many fishes of various kinds. So he emptied his net, and proceeded to sort the fishes on the grass. The place where he stood was a beautiful island in the river, a solitary spot, uninhabited, and not used for pasturage of cattle, not ever visited by any but himself. On a sudden, the fishes, which had been laid on the grass, began to revive and move their fins as if they were in the water; and while he looked on astonished, they one and all moved off to the water, plunged in, and swam away. He did not know what to make of this, whether some god had done it or some secret power in the herbage. "What herb has such a power?" he exclaimed; and gathering some of it, he tasted it. Scarce had the juices of the plant reached his palate when he found himself agitated with a longing desire for the water. He could no longer restrain himself, but bidding farewell to earth, he plunged into the stream. The gods of the water received him graciously, and admitted him to the honour of their society. They obtained the consent of Oceanus and Tethys, the sovereigns of the sea, that all that was mortal in him should be washed away. A hundred rivers poured their waters over him. Then he lost all sense of his former nature and all consciousness. When he recovered, he found himself changed in form and mind. His hair was sea-green, and trailed behind him on the water; his shoulders grew broad, and what had been thighs and legs assumed the form of a fish's tail. The sea-gods complimented him on the change of his appearance, and he fancied himself rather a good-looking personage.

One day Glaucus saw the beautiful maiden Scylla, the

favourite of the water-nymphs, rambling on the shore, and when she had found a sheltered nook, laving her limbs in the clear water. He fell in love with her, and showing himself on the surface, spoke to her, saying such things as he thought most likely to win her to stay; for she turned to run immediately on the sight of him, and ran till she had gained a cliff overlooking the sea. Here she stopped and turned round to see whether it was a god or a sea animal, and observed with wonder his shape and colour. Glaucus partly emerging from the water, and supporting himself against a rock, said, "Maiden, I am no monster, nor a sea animal, but a god; and neither Proteus nor Triton ranks higher than I. Once I was a mortal, and followed the sea for a living; but now I belong wholly to it." Then he told the story of his metamorphosis, and how he had been promoted to his present dignity, and added, "But what avails all this if it fails to move your heart?" He was going on in this strain, but Scylla turned and hastened away.

Glaucus was in despair, but it occurred to him to consult the enchantress Circe. Accordingly he repaired to her island—the same where afterwards Ulysses landed, as we shall see in one of our later stories. After mutual salutations, he said, "Goddess, I entreat your pity; you alone can relieve the pain I suffer. The power of herbs I know as well as any one, for it is to them I owe my change of form. I love Scylla. I am ashamed to tell you how I have sued and promised to her, and how scornfully she has treated me. I beseech you to use your incantations, or potent herbs, if they are more prevailing, not to cure me of my love,—for that I do not wish,—but to make her share it and yield me a like return." To which Circe replied, for she was not insensible to the attractions of the sea-green deity, "You had better pursue a willing object; you are worthy to be sought, instead of having to seek in vain. Be not diffident, know your own worth. I protest to you that even I, goddess though I be, and learned in the virtues of plants and spells, should not know how to refuse you. If she scorns you scorn her; meet one who is ready to meet you half way, and thus make a due return to both at once." To these words Glaucus replied, "Sooner shall trees grow at the bottom of the ocean, and sea-weed on the top of the mountains, than I will cease to love Scylla, and her alone."

The goddess was indignant, but she could not punish him, neither did she wish to do so, for she liked him too well; so she turned all her wrath against her rival, poor Scylla. She took plants of poisonous powers and mixed them together, with incantations and charms. Then she passed through the crowd of gamboling beasts, the victims of her art, and proceeded to the coast of Sicily, where Scylla lived. There was a little bay on the shore to which Scylla used to resort, in the heat of the day, to breathe the air of the sea, and to bathe in its waters. Here the goddess poured her poisonous mixture, and muttered over it incantations of mighty power. Scylla came as usual and plunged into the water up to her waist. What was her horror to perceive a brood of serpents and barking monsters surrounding her! At first she could not imagine they were a part of herself, and tried to run from them, and to drive them away; but as she ran she carried them with her, and when she tried to touch her limbs, she found her hands touch only the yawning jaws of monsters. Scylla remained rooted to the spot. Her temper grew as ugly as her form, and she took pleasure in devouring hapless mariners who came within her grasp. Thus she destroyed six of the companions of Ulysses, and tried to wreck the ships of Aeneas, till at last she was turned into a rock, and as such still continues to be a terror to mariners.

8. PYGMALION — DRYOPE — VENUS AND ADONIS — APOLLO AND HYACINTHUS

Pygmalion saw so much to blame in women that he came at last to abhor the sex, and resolved to live unmarried. He was a sculptor, and had made with wonderful skill a statue of ivory, so beautiful that no living woman came anywhere near it. It was indeed the perfect semblance of a maiden that seemed to be alive, and only prevented from moving by modesty. His art was so perfect that it concealed itself and its product looked like the workmanship of nature. Pygmalion admired his own work, and at last fell in love with the counterfeit creation. Oftentimes he laid his hand upon it as if to assure himself whether it were living or not, and could not even then believe that it was only ivory. He laid her on a couch spread with cloths of Tyrian dye, and called her his wife, and put her head upon a pillow of the softest feathers, as if she could enjoy their softness.

The festival of Venus was at hand—a festival celebrated with great pomp at Cyprus. Victims were offered, the altars smoked, and the odour of incense filled the air. When Pygmalion had performed his part in the solemnities, he stood before the altar and timidly said, "Ye gods, who can do all things, give me, I pray you, for my wife"—he dared not say "my ivory virgin," but said instead—"one like my ivory virgin." Venus, who was present at the festival, heard him and knew the thought he would have uttered; and as an omen of her favour, caused the flame on the altar to shoot up thrice in a fiery point into the air. When he returned home, he went to see his statue, and leaning over the couch, gave a kiss to the mouth. It seemed to be warm. He pressed its lips again, he laid his hand upon the limbs; the ivory felt soft to his touch and yielded to his fingers like the wax of Hymettus. It was indeed alive! Then at last the votary of Venus found words to thank the goddess, and pressed his lips upon lips as real as his own. The virgin felt the kisses and blushed, and opening her timid eyes to the light, fixed them at the same moment on her lover. Venus blessed the nuptials she had formed, and from this union Paphos was born, from whom the city, sacred to Venus, received its name.

Dryope

Dryope and Iole were sisters. The former was the wife of Andraemon, beloved by her husband, and happy in the birth of her first child. One day the sisters strolled to the bank of a stream that sloped gradually down to the water's edge, while the upland was overgrown with myrtles. They were intending to gather flowers for forming garlands for the altars of the nymphs, and Dryope carried her child at her bosom, precious burden, and nursed him as she walked. Near the water grew a lotus plant, full of purple flowers. Dryope gathered some and offered them to the baby, and

Iole was about to do the same, when she perceived blood dropping from the places where her sister had broken them off the stem. The plant was no other than the nymph Lotis, who, running from a base pursuer, had been changed into this form. This they learned from the country people when it was too late.

Dryope, horror-struck when she perceived what she had done, would gladly have hastened from the spot, but found her feet rooted to the ground. She tried to pull them away, but moved nothing but her upper limbs. The woodiness crept upward and by degrees invested her body. In anguish she attempted to tear her hair, but found her hands filled with leaves. The infant felt his mother's bosom begin to harden, and the milk cease to flow. Iole looked on at the sad fate of her sister, and could render no assistance. She embraced the growing trunk, as if she would hold back the advancing wood, and would gladly have been enveloped in the same bark. At this moment Andraemon, the husband of Dryope, with her father, approached; and when they asked for Dryope, Iole pointed them to the new-formed lotus. They embraced the trunk of the yet warm tree, and showered their kisses on its leaves.

Now there was nothing left of Dryope but her face. Her tears still flowed and fell on her leaves, and while she could she spoke. "I am not guilty. I deserve not this fate. I have injured no one. If I speak falsely, may my foliage perish with drought and my trunk be cut down and burned. Take this infant and give it to a nurse. Let it often be brought and nursed under my branches, and play in my shade; and when he is old enough to talk, let him be taught to call me mother, and to say with sadness, 'My mother lies hid under this bark.' But bid him be careful of river banks, and beware how he plucks flowers, remembering that every bush he sees may be a goddess in disguise. Farewell, dear husband, and sister, and father. If you retain any love for me, let not the axe wound me, nor the flocks bite and tear my branches. Since I cannot stoop to you, climb up hither and kiss me; and while my lips continue to feel, lift up my child that I may kiss him. I can speak no more, for already the bark advances up my neck, and will soon shoot over me. You need not close my eyes, the bark will close them without your aid." Then the lips ceased to move, and life was extinct; but the branches retained for some time longer the vital heat.

Venus and Adonis

Venus, playing one day with her boy Cupid, wounded her bosom with one of his arrows. She pushed him away, but the wound was deeper than she thought. Before it healed she beheld Adonis, and was captivated with him. She no longer took any interest in her favourite resorts—Paphos, and Cnidos, and Amathos, rich in metals. She absented herself even from heaven, for Adonis was dearer to her than heaven. Him she followed and bore him company. She who used to love to recline in the shade, with no care but to cultivate her charms, now rambles through the woods and over the hills, dressed like the huntress Diana; and calls her dogs, and chases hares and stags, or other game that it is safe to hunt, but keeps clear of the wolves and bears, reeking with the slaughter of the herd. She charged Adonis, too, to beware of such dangerous animals.

Having given him this warning, she mounted her chariot drawn by swans, and drove away through the air. But Adonis was too noble to heed such counsels. The dogs had roused a wild boar from his lair, and the youth threw his spear and wounded the animal with a sidelong stroke. The beast drew out the weapon with his jaws, and rushed after Adonis, who turned and ran; but the boar overtook him, and buried his tusks in his side, and stretched him dying upon the plain.

Venus, in her swan-drawn chariot, had not yet reached Cyprus, when she heard coming up through mid-air the groans of her beloved, and turned her white-winged coursers back to earth. As she drew near and saw from on high his lifeless body bathed in blood, she alighted, and, bending over it, beat her breast and tore her hair. Reproaching the Fates, she said, "Yet theirs shall be but a partial triumph; memorials of my grief shall endure, and the spectacle of your death, my Adonis, and of my lamentation shall be annually renewed. Your blood shall be changed into a flower; that consolation none can envy me." Thus speaking, she sprinkled nectar on the blood; and as they mingled, bubbles rose as in a pool on which raindrops fall, and in an hour's time there sprang up a flower of bloody hue like that of the pomegranate. But it is short-lived. It is said the wind blows the blossoms open, and afterwards blows the petals away; so it is called Anemone, or Wind Flower, from the cause which assists equally in its production and its decay.

Apollo and Hyacinthus

Apollo was passionately fond of a youth named Hyacinthus. He accompanied him in his sports, carried the nets when he went fishing, led the dogs when he went to hunt, followed him in his excursions in the mountains, and neglected for him his lyre and his arrows. One day they played a game of quoits together, and Apollo, heaving aloft the discus, with strength mingled with skill, sent it high and far. Hyacinthus watched it as it flew, and excited with the sport ran forward to seize it, eager to make his throw, when the quoit bounded from the earth and struck him in the forehead. He fainted and fell. The god, as pale as himself, raised him and tried all his art to stanch the wound and retain the flitting life, but all in vain; the hurt was past the power of medicine. As when one has broken the stem of a lily in the garden it hangs its head and turns its flowers to the earth, so the head of the dying boy, as if too heavy for his neck, fell over on his shoulder. "Thou diest, Hyacinth," so spoke Phoebus, "robbed of thy youth by me. Thine is the suffering, mine the crime. Would that I could die for thee! But since that may not be, thou shalt live with me in memory and in song. My lyre shall celebrate thee, my song shall tell thy fate, and thou shalt become a flower inscribed with my regrets." While Apollo spoke, behold the blood which had flowed on the ground and stained the herbage ceased to be blood; but a flower of hue more beautiful than the Tyrian sprang up, resembling the lily, if it were not that this is purple and that silvery white.[1] And this was not enough for Phoebus; but to confer still greater honour, he marked the petals with his sorrow, and inscribed "Ah! ah!" upon them, as we see to this day. The flower bears the name of Hyacinthus, and with every returning spring revives the memory of his fate.

[1] It is evidently not our modern hyacinth that is here described. It is perhaps some species of iris, or perhaps of larkspur or of pansy.

It was said that Zephyrus (the West wind), who was also fond of Hyacinthus and jealous of his preference of Apollo, blew the quoit out of its course to make it strike Hyacinthus.

9. CEYX AND HALCYONE:
OR, THE HALCYON BIRDS

Ceyx was king of Thessaly, where he reigned in peace, without violence or wrong. He was son of Hesperus, the Daystar, and the glow of his beauty reminded one of his father. Halcyone, the daughter of Aeolus, was his wife, and devotedly attached to him. Now Ceyx was in deep affliction for the loss of his brother, and direful prodigies following his brother's death made him feel as if the gods were hostile to him. He thought best, therefore, to make a voyage to Carlos in Ionia, to consult the oracle of Apollo. But as soon as he disclosed his intention to his wife Halcyone, a shudder ran through her frame, and her face grew deadly pale. "What fault of mine, dearest husband, has turned your affection from me? Where is that love of me that used to be uppermost in your thoughts? Have you learned to feel easy in the absence of Halcyone? Would you rather have me away?" She also endeavoured to discourage him, by describing the violence of the winds, which she had known familiarly when she lived at home in her father's house,— Aeolus being the god of the winds, and having as much as he could do to restrain them. "They rush together," said she, "with such fury that fire flashes from the conflict. But if you must go," she added, "dear husband, let me go with you, otherwise I shall suffer not only the real evils which you must encounter, but those also which my fears suggest."

These words weighed heavily on the mind of King Ceyx, and it was no less his own wish than hers to take her with him, but he could not bear to expose her to the dangers of the sea. He answered, therefore, consoling her as well as he could, and finished with these words: "I promise, by the rays of my father the Day-star, that if fate permits I will return before the moon shall have twice rounded her orb." When he had thus spoken, he ordered the vessel to be drawn out of the shiphouse, and the oars and sails to be put aboard. When Halcyone saw these preparations she shuddered, as if with a presentiment of evil. With tears and sobs she said farewell, and then fell senseless to the ground.

Ceyx would still have lingered, but now the young men grasped their oars and pulled vigorously through the waves, with long and measured strokes. Halcyone raised her streaming eyes, and saw her husband standing on the deck, waving his hand to her. She answered his signal till the vessel had receded so far that she could no longer distinguish his form from the rest. When the vessel itself could no more be seen, she strained her eyes to catch the last glimmer of the sail, till that too disappeared. Then, retiring to her chamber, she threw herself on her solitary couch.

Meanwhile they glide out of the harbour, and the breeze plays among the ropes. The seamen draw in their oars, and hoist their sails. When half or less of their course was passed, as night drew on, the sea began to whiten with swelling waves, and the east wind to blow a gale. The master gave the word to take in sail, but the storm forbade obedience, for such is the roar of the winds and waves his orders are unheard. The men, of their own accord, busy themselves to secure the oars, to strengthen the ship, to reef the sail. While they thus do what to each one seems best, the storm increases.

The vessel seems like a wild beast that rushes on the spears of the hunters. The men are stupefied with terror. The thought of parents, and kindred, and pledges left at home, comes over their minds. Ceyx thinks of Halcyone. No name but hers is on his lips, and while he yearns for her, he yet rejoices in her absence. Presently the mast is shattered by a stroke of lightning, the rudder broken, and the triumphant surge curling over looks down upon the wreck, then falls, and crushes it to fragments. Some of the seamen, stunned by the stroke, sink, and rise no more; others cling to fragments of the wreck. Ceyx, with the hand that used to grasp the sceptre, holds fast to a plank, calling for help,— alas, in vain,—upon his father and his father-in-law. But oftenest on his lips was the name of Halcyone. To her his thoughts cling. He prays that the waves may bear his body to her sight, and that it may receive burial at her hands. At length the waters overwhelm him, and he sinks. The Day-star looked dim that night. Since it could not leave the heavens, it shrouded its face with clouds.

In the meanwhile Halcyone, ignorant of all these horrors, counted the days till her husband's promised return. To all the gods she offers frequent incense, but more than all to Juno. The goddess, at length, could not bear any longer to be pleaded with for one already dead, and to have hands raised to her altars that ought rather to be offering funeral rites. So, calling Iris, she said, "Iris, my faithful messenger, go to the drowsy dwelling of Somnus, and tell him to send a vision to Halcyone in the form of Ceyx, to make known to her the event."

Iris puts on her robe of many colours, and tinging the sky with her bow, seeks the palace of the King of Sleep. Near the Cimmerian country, a mountain cave is the abode of the dull god Somnus. Here Phoebus dares not come, either rising, at midday, or setting. Clouds and shadows are exhaled from the ground, and the light glimmers faintly. The bird of dawning, with crested head, never there calls aloud to Aurora, nor watchful dog, nor more sagacious goose disturbs the silence. No wild beast, nor cattle, nor branch moved with the wind, nor sound of human conversation, breaks the stillness. Silence reigns there; but from the bottom of the rock the River Lethe flows, and by its murmur invites to sleep. Poppies grow abundantly before the door of the cave, and other herbs, from whose juices Night collects slumbers, which she scatters over the darkened earth. There is no gate to the mansion, to creak on its hinges, nor any watchman; but in the midst a couch of black ebony, adorned with black plumes and black curtains. There the god reclines, his limbs relaxed with sleep. Around him lie dreams, resembling all various forms, as many as the harvest bears stalks, or the forest leaves, or the seashore sand grains.

As soon as the goddess entered and brushed away the dreams that hovered around her, her brightness lit up all the cave. The god, scarce opening his eyes, and ever and anon dropping his beard upon his breast, at last shook himself free from himself, and leaning on his arm, inquired her errand,—for he knew who she was. She answered, "Somnus, gentlest of the gods, tranquillizer of minds and soother of care-worn hearts, Juno sends you her commands that you despatch a dream to Halcyone, in the city of Trachine, representing her lost husband and all the events of the wreck."

Then Somnus called one of his numerous sons,—Morpheus,—the most expert in counterfeiting forms, and in imitating the walk, the countenance, and mode of speaking, even the clothes and attitudes most characteristic of each. But he only imitates men, leaving it to another to personate birds, beasts, and serpents. Him they call Icelos; and Phantasos is a third, who turns himself into rocks, waters, woods, and other things without life. These wait upon kings and great personages in their sleeping hours, while others move among the common people. Somnus chose, from all the brothers, Morpheus, to perform the command of Iris; then laid his head on his pillow and yielded himself to grateful repose.

Morpheus flew, making no noise with his wings, and soon came to the Haemonian city, where, laying aside his wings, he assumed the form of Ceyx. Under that form, but pale like a dead man, naked, he stood before the couch of the wretched wife. His beard seemed soaked with water, and water trickled from his drowned locks. Leaning over the bed, tears streaming from his eyes, he said, "Do you recognize your Ceyx, unhappy wife, or has death too much changed my visage? Behold me, know me, your husband's shade, instead of himself. Your prayers, Halcyone, availed me nothing. I am dead. No more deceive yourself with vain hopes of my return. The stormy winds sunk my ship in the Aegean Sea, waves filled my mouth while it called aloud on you. No uncertain messenger tells you this, no vague rumour brings it to your ears. I come in person, a shipwrecked man, to tell you my fate. Arise! give me tears, give me lamentations, let me not go down to Tartarus unwept." To these words Morpheus added the voice, which seemed to be that of her husband; he seemed to pour forth genuine tears; his hands had the gestures of Ceyx.

Halcyone, weeping, groaned, and stretched out her arms in her sleep, striving to embrace his body, but grasping only the air. "Stay!" she cried; "whither do you fly? let us go together." Her own voice awakened her. Starting up, she gazed eagerly around, to see if he was still present, for the servants, alarmed by her cries, had brought a light. When she found him not, she smote her breast and rent her garments. She cares not to unbind her hair, but tears it wildly. Her nurse asks what is the cause of her grief. "Halcyone is no more," she answers, "she perished with her Ceyx. Utter not words of comfort, he is shipwrecked and dead. I have seen him, I have recognized him. I stretched out my hands to seize him and detain him. His shade vanished, but it was the true shade of my husband. Not with the accustomed features, not with the beauty that was his, but pale, naked, and with his hair wet with sea water, he appeared to wretched me. Here, in this very spot, the sad vision stood," —and she looked to find the mark of his footsteps.

It was now morning. She went to the seashore, and sought the spot where she last saw him, on his departure. Looking out over the sea, she descries an indistinct object floating in the water. At first she was in doubt what it was, but by degrees the waves bore it nearer, and it was plainly the body of a man. Though unknowing of whom, yet, as it was of some shipwrecked one, she was deeply moved, and gave it her tears, saying, "Alas! unhappy one, and unhappy, if such there be, thy wife!" Borne by the waves, it came nearer. As she more and more nearly views it, she trembles more and more. Now, now it approaches the shore. Now marks that she recognizes appear. It is her husband! Stretching out her trembling hands towards it, she exclaims, "O dearest husband, is it thus you return to me?"

There was built out from the shore a mole, constructed to break the assaults of the sea, and stem its violent ingress. She leaped upon this barrier and (it was wonderful she could do so) she flew, and striking the air with wings produced on the instant, skimmed along the surface of the water, an unhappy bird. As she flew, her throat poured forth sounds full of grief, and like the voice of one lamenting. When she touched the mute and bloodless body, she enfolded its beloved limbs with her new-formed wings, and tried to give kisses with her horny beak. Whether Ceyx felt it, or whether it was only the action of the waves, those who looked on doubted, but the body seemed to raise its head. But indeed he did feel it, and by the pitying gods both of them were changed into birds. They mate and have their young ones. For seven placid days, in winter time,[1] Halcyone broods over her nest, which floats upon the sea. Then the way is safe to seamen. Aeolus guards the winds and keeps them from disturbing the deep. The sea is given up, for the time, to his grandchildren.

10. VERTUMNUS AND POMONA

The Hamadryads were Wood-nymphs. Pomona was of this class, and no one excelled her in love of the garden and the culture of fruit. She cared not for forests and rivers, but loved the cultivated country, and trees that bear delicious apples. Her right hand bore for its weapon not a javelin, but a pruning-knife. Armed with this, she busied herself at one time to repress the too luxuriant growths, and curtail the branches that straggled out of place; at another, to split the twig and insert therein a graft, making the branch adopt a nursling not its own. She took care, too, that her favourites should not suffer from drought, and led streams of water by them, that the thirsty roots might drink. This occupation was her pursuit, her passion; and she was free from that which Venus inspires. She was not without fear of the country people, and kept her orchard locked, and allowed not men to enter. The Fauns and Satyrs would have given all they possessed to win her, and so would old Sylvanus, who looks young for his years, and Pan, who wears a garland of pine leaves around his head. But Vertumnus loved her best of all; yet he sped no better than the rest. O how often, in the disguise of a reaper, did he bring her corn in a basket, and looked the very image of a reaper! With a hay band tied round him, one would think he had just come from turning over the grass. Sometimes he would have an ox-goad in his hand, and you would have said he had just unyoked his weary oxen. Now he bore a pruning-hook, and personated a vine-dresser; and again, with a ladder on his shoulder, he seemed as if he was going to gather apples.

[1] Hence, "the Halcyon days."

Sometimes he trudged along as a discharged soldier, and again he bore a fishing-rod, as if going to fish. In this way he gained admission to her again and again, and fed his passion with the sight of her.

One day he came in the guise of an old woman, her grey hair surmounted with a cap, and a staff in her hand. She entered the garden and admired the fruit. "It does you credit, my dear," she said, and kissed her, not exactly with an old woman's kiss. She sat down on a bank, and looked up at the branches laden with fruit which hung over her. Opposite was an elm entwined with a vine loaded with swelling grapes. She praised the tree and its associated vine, equally. "But," said she, "if the tree stood alone, and had no vine clinging to it, it would have nothing to attract or offer us but its useless leaves. And equally the vine, if it were not twined round the elm, would lie prostrate on the ground. Why will you not take a lesson from the tree and the vine, and consent to unite yourself with some one? I wish you would. Helen herself had not more numerous suitors, nor Penelope, the wife of shrewd Ulysses. Even while you spurn them, they court you,—rural deities and others of every kind that frequent these mountains. But if you are prudent and want to make a good alliance, and will let an old woman advise you,—who loves you better than you have any idea of,—dismiss all the rest and accept Vertumnus, on my recommendation. I know him as well as he knows himself. He is not a wandering deity, but belongs to these mountains. Nor is he like too many of the lovers nowadays, who love any one they happen to see; he loves you, and you only. Add to this, he is young and handsome, and has the art of assuming any shape he pleases, and can make himself just what you command him. Moreover, he loves the same things that you do, delights in gardening, and handles your apples with admiration. But *now* he cares nothing for fruits nor flowers, nor anything else, but only yourself. Take pity on him, and fancy him speaking now with my mouth. Remember that the gods punish cruelty, and that Venus hates a hard heart, and will visit such offences sooner or later. To prove this, let me tell you a story, which is well known in Cyprus to be a fact; and I hope it will have the effect to make you more merciful.

"Iphis was a young man of humble parentage, who saw

and loved Anaxarete, a noble lady of the ancient family of Teucer. He struggled long with his passion, but when he found he could not subdue it, he came a suppliant to her mansion. She mocked and laughed at him, adding cruel words to her ungentle treatment, and gave not the slightest gleam of hope.

"Iphis could not any longer endure the torments of hopeless love, and, standing before her doors, he spake these last words: 'Anaxarete, you have conquered, and shall no longer have to bear my importunities.' Thus he said, and, turning his pale face and weeping eyes towards her mansion, he fastened a rope to the gate-post, on which he had often hung garlands, and putting his head into the noose, he murmured, 'This garland at least will please you, cruel girl!' and falling hung suspended with his neck broken. As he fell he struck against the gate, and the sound was as the sound of a groan. The servants opened the door and found him dead, and with exclamations of pity raised him and carried him home to his mother, for his father was not living. The mournful funeral passed through the town, and the pale corpse was borne on a bier to the place of the funeral pile. By chance the home of Anaxarete was on the street where the procession passed, and the lamentations of the mourners met the ears of her whom the avenging deity had already marked for punishment.

"'Let us see this sad procession,' said she, and mounted to a turret, whence through an open window she looked upon the funeral. Scarce had her eyes rested upon the form of Iphis stretched on the bier, when they began to stiffen, and the warm blood in her body to become cold. Endeavouring to step back, she found she could not move her feet; trying to turn away her face, she tried in vain; and by degrees all her limbs became stony like her heart. Now think of these things, my dear, and lay aside your scorn and your delays, and accept a lover. So may neither the vernal frosts blight your young fruits, nor furious winds scatter your blossoms!"

When Vertumnus had spoken thus, he dropped the disguise of an old woman, and stood before her in his proper person, as a comely youth. It appeared to her like the sun bursting through a cloud. He would have renewed his entreaties, but there was no need; his arguments and the sight of his true form prevailed, and the Nymph no longer resisted, but owned a mutual flame.

11. CUPID AND PSYCHE

A certain king and queen had three daughters. The charms of the two elder were more than common, but the beauty of the youngest was so wonderful that the poverty of language is unable to express its due praise. The fame of her beauty was so great that strangers from neighbouring countries came in crowds to enjoy the sight, and looked on her with amazement, paying her that homage which is due only to Venus herself. In fact Venus found her altars deserted, while men turned their devotion to this young virgin. As she passed along, the people sang her praises, and strewed her way with chaplets and flowers.

This perversion of homage due only to the immortal powers to the exaltation of a mortal gave great offence to the real Venus. Shaking her ambrosial locks with indignation, she exclaimed, "Am I then to be eclipsed in my honours by a mortal girl?"

Thereupon she calls her winged son Cupid, mischievous enough in his own nature, and rouses and provokes him yet more by her complaints. She points out Psyche to him and says, "My dear son, punish that contumacious beauty; give thy mother a revenge as sweet as her injuries are great; infuse into the bosom of that haughty girl a passion for some low, mean, unworthy being, so that she may reap a mortification as great as her present exultation and triumph."

Cupid prepared to obey the commands of his mother. There are two fountains in Venus's garden, one of sweet waters, the other of bitter. Cupid filled two amber vases, one from each fountain, and suspending them from the top of his quiver, hastened to the chamber of Psyche, whom he found asleep. He shed a few drops from the bitter fountain over her lips, though the sight of her almost moved him to pity; then touched her side with the point of his arrow. At the touch she awoke, and opened eyes upon Cupid (himself invisible), which so startled him that in his confusion he wounded himself with his own arrow. Heedless of his wound, his whole thought now was to repair the mischief he had done, and he poured the balmy drops of joy over all her silken ringlets.

Psyche, henceforth frowned upon by Venus, derived no benefit from all her charms. True, all eyes were cast eagerly upon her, and every mouth spoke her praises; but neither king, royal youth, nor plebeian presented himself to demand her in marriage. Her two elder sisters of moderate charms had now long been married to two royal princes; but Psyche, in her lonely apartment, deplored her solitude, sick of that beauty which, while it procured abundance of flattery, had failed to awaken love.

Her parents, afraid that they had unwittingly incurred the anger of the gods, consulted the oracle of Apollo, and received this answer: "The virgin is destined for the bride of no mortal lover. Her future husband awaits her on the top of the mountain. He is a monster whom neither gods nor men can resist."

This dreadful decree of the oracle filled all the people with dismay, and her parents abandoned themselves to grief. But Psyche said, "Why, my dear parents, do you now lament me? You should rather have grieved when the people showered upon me undeserved honours, and with one voice called me a Venus. I now perceive that I am a victim to that name. I submit. Lead me to that rock to which my unhappy fate has destined me." Accordingly, all things being prepared, the royal maid took her place in the procession, which more resembled a funeral than a nuptial pomp, and with her parents, amid the lamentations of the people, ascended the mountain, on the summit of which they left her alone, and with sorrowful hearts returned home.

While Psyche stood on the ridge of the mountain, panting with fear and with eyes full of tears, the gentle Zephyr raised her from the earth and bore her with an easy motion into a flowery dale. By degrees her mind became composed, and she laid herself down on the grassy bank to sleep. When she awoke refreshed with sleep, she looked round and beheld near by a pleasant grove of tall and stately trees. She entered it, and in the midst discovered a fountain, sending forth clear and crystal waters, and fast by, a magnificent palace whose august front impressed the spectator that it was not the work of mortal hands, but the happy retreat of some god. Drawn by admiration and wonder, she approached the building and ventured to enter. Every object she met filled her with pleasure and amazement. Golden pillars supported the vaulted roof, and the walls were enriched with carvings and paintings representing beasts of the chase and rural scenes, adapted to delight the eye of the beholder. Proceeding onward, she perceived that besides the apartments of state there were others filled with all manner of treasures, and beautiful and precious productions of nature and art.

While her eyes were thus occupied, a voice addressed her, though she saw no one, uttering these words: "Sovereign lady, all that you see is yours. We whose voices you hear are your servants and shall obey all your commands with our utmost care and diligence. Retire, therefore, to your chamber and repose on your bed of down, and when you see fit repair to the bath. Supper awaits you in the adjoining alcove when it pleases you to take your seat there."

Psyche gave ear to the admonitions of her vocal attendants, and after repose and the refreshment of the bath, seated herself in the alcove, where a table immediately presented itself, without any visible aid from waiters or servants, and covered with the greatest delicacies of food and the most nectareous wines. Her ears too were feasted with music from invisible performers; of whom one sang, another played on the lute, and all closed in the wonderful harmony of a full chorus.

She had not yet seen her destined husband. He came only in the hours of darkness and fled before the dawn of morning, but his accents were full of love, and inspired a like passion in her. She often begged him to stay and let her behold him, but he would not consent. On the contrary he charged her to make no attempt to see him, for it was his pleasure, for the best of reasons, to keep concealed. "Why should you wish to behold me?" he said; "have you any doubt of my love? have you any wish ungratified? If you saw me, perhaps you would fear me, perhaps adore me, but all I ask of you is to love me. I would rather you would love me as an equal than adore me as a god."

This reasoning somewhat quieted Psyche for a time, and while the novelty lasted she felt quite happy. But at length the thought of her parents, left in ignorance of her fate, and of her sisters, precluded from sharing with her the delights of her situation, preyed on her mind and made her begin to feel her palace as but a splendid prison. When her husband came one night, she told him her distress, and at last drew from him an unwilling consent that her sisters should be brought to see her.

So, calling Zephyr, she acquainted him with her husband's commands, and he, promptly obedient, soon brought them across the mountain down to their sister's valley. They embraced her and she returned their caresses. "Come," said Psyche, "enter with me my house and refresh yourselves with whatever your sister has to offer." Then taking their hands she led them into her golden palace, and committed them to the care of her numerous train of attendant voices, to refresh them in her baths and at her table, and to show them all her treasures. The view of these celestial delights caused envy to enter their bosoms, at seeing their young sister possessed of such state and splendour, so much exceeding their own.

They asked her numberless questions, among others what sort of a person her husband was. Psyche replied that he was a beautiful youth, who generally spent the daytime in hunting upon the mountains. The sisters, not satisfied with this reply, soon made her confess that she had never seen him. Then they proceeded to fill her bosom with dark suspicions. "Call to mind," they said, "the Pythian oracle that declared you destined to marry a direful and tremendous monster. The inhabitants of this valley say that your husband is a terrible and monstrous serpent, who nourishes you for a while with dainties that he may by and by devour you. Take our advice. Provide yourself with a lamp and a sharp knife; put them in concealment that your husband may not discover them, and when he is sound asleep, slip out of bed, bring forth your lamp, and see for yourself whether what they say is true or not. If it is, hesitate not to cut off the monster's head, and thereby recover your liberty."

Psyche resisted these persuasions as well as she could, but

they did not fail to have their effect on her mind, and when her sisters were gone, their words and her own curiosity were too strong for her to resist. So she prepared her lamp and a sharp knife, and hid them out of sight of her husband. When he had fallen into his first sleep, she silently rose and uncovering her lamp beheld not a hideous monster, but the most beautiful and charming of the gods, with his golden ringlets wandering over his snowy neck and crimson cheek, with two dewy wings on his shoulders, whiter than snow, and with shining feathers like the tender blossoms of spring. As she leaned the lamp over to have a nearer view of his face a drop of burning oil fell on the shoulder of the god, startled with which he opened his eyes and fixed them full upon her; then, without saying one word, he spread his white wings and flew out of the window. Psyche, in vain endeavouring to follow him, fell from the window to the ground. Cupid, beholding her as she lay in the dust, stopped his flight for an instant and said, "O foolish Psyche, is it thus you repay my love? After having disobeyed my mother's commands and made you my wife, will you think me a monster and cut off my head? But go; return to your sisters, whose advice you seem to think preferable to mine. I inflict no other punishment on you than to leave you for ever. Love cannot dwell with suspicion." So saying, he fled away, leaving poor Psyche prostrate on the ground, filling the place with mournful lamentations.

When she had recovered some degree of composure she looked around her, but the palace and gardens had vanished, and she found herself in the open field not far from the city where her sisters dwelt. She repaired thither and told them the whole story of her misfortunes, at which, pretending to grieve, those spiteful creatures inwardly rejoiced. "For now," said they, "he will perhaps choose one of us." With this idea, without saying a word of her intentions, each of them rose early the next morning and ascended the mountain, and having reached the top, called upon Zephyr to receive her and bear her to his lord; then leaping up, and not being sustained by Zephyr, fell down the precipice and was dashed to pieces.

Psyche meanwhile wandered day and night, without food or repose, in search of her husband. Casting her eyes on a lofty mountain having on its brow a magnificent temple, she sighed and said to herself, "Perhaps my love, my lord, inhabits there," and directed her steps thither.

She had no sooner entered than she saw heaps of corn, some in loose ears and some in sheaves, with mingled ears of barley. Scattered about, lay sickles and rakes, and all the instruments of harvest, without order, as if thrown carelessly out of the weary reapers' hands in the sultry hours of the day.

This unseemly confusion the pious Psyche put an end to, by separating and sorting everything to its proper place and kind, believing that she ought to neglect none of the gods, but endeavour by her piety to engage them all in her behalf. The holy Ceres, whose temple it was, finding her so religiously employed, thus spoke to her: "O Psyche, truly worthy of our pity, though I cannot shield you from the frowns of Venus, yet I can teach you how best to allay her displeasure. Go, then, and voluntarily surrender yourself to your lady and sovereign, and try by modesty and submission to win her forgiveness, and perhaps her favour will restore you the husband you have lost."

Psyche obeyed the commands of Ceres and took her way to the temple of Venus, endeavouring to fortify her mind and ruminating on what she should say and how best propitiate the angry goddess, feeling that the issue was doubtful and perhaps fatal.

Venus received her with angry countenance. "Most undutiful and faithless of servants," said she, "do you at last remember that you really have a mistress? Or have you rather come to see your sick husband, yet laid up of the wound given him by his loving wife? You are so ill-favoured and disagreeable that the only way you can merit your lover must be by dint of industry and diligence. I will make trial of your housewifery." Then she ordered Psyche to be led to the storehouse of her temple, where was laid up a great quantity of wheat, barley, millet, vetches, beans, and lentils prepared for food for her pigeons, and said, "Take and separate all these grains, putting all of the same kind in a parcel by themselves, and see that you get it done before evening." Then Venus departed and left her to her task.

But Psyche, in a perfect consternation at the enormous work, sat stupid and silent, without moving a finger to the inextricable heap.

While she sat despairing, Cupid stirred up the little ant, a native of the fields, to take compassion on her. The leader of the ant-hill, followed by whole hosts of his six-legged subjects, approached the heap, and with the utmost diligence taking grain by grain, they separated the pile, sorting each kind to its parcel; and when it was all done, they vanished out of sight in a moment.

Venus at the approach of twilight returned from the banquet of the gods, breathing odours and crowned with roses. Seeing the task done, she exclaimed, "This is no work of yours, wicked one, but his, whom to your own and his misfortune you have enticed." So saying, she threw her a piece of black bread for her supper and went away.

Next morning Venus ordered Psyche to be called and said to her, "Behold yonder grove which stretches along the margin of the water. There you will find sheep feeding without a shepherd, with golden-shining fleeces on their backs. Go, fetch me a sample of that precious wool gathered from every one of their fleeces."

Psyche obediently went to the riverside, prepared to do her best to execute the command. But the river god inspired the reeds with harmonious murmurs, which seemed to say, "O maiden, severely tried, tempt not the dangerous flood, nor venture among the formidable rams on the other side, for as long as they are under the influence of the rising sun, they burn with a cruel rage to destroy mortals with their sharp horns or rude teeth. But when the noontide sun has driven the cattle to the shade, and the serene spirit of the flood has lulled them to rest, you may then cross in safety, and you will find the woolly gold sticking to the bushes and the trunks of the trees."

Thus the compassionate river god gave Psyche instructions how to accomplish her task, and by observing his directions she soon returned to Venus with her arms full of the golden fleece; but she received not the approbation of her implacable mistress, who said, "I know very well it is by none of your own doings that you have succeeded in this task, and I am not satisfied yet that you have any capacity to make yourself useful. But I have another task for you. Here, take this box and go your way to the infernal shades, and give this box to Proserpine and say, 'My mistress Venus desires you to send her a little of your beauty, for in tending her sick son she has lost some of her own.' Be not too long on your errand, for I must paint myself with it to appear at the circle of the gods and goddesses this evening."

Psyche was now satisfied that her destruction was at hand, being obliged to go with her own feet directly down to Erebus. Wherefore, to make no delay of what was not to be avoided, she goes to the top of a high tower to precipitate herself headlong, thus to descend the shortest way to the shades below. But a voice from the tower said to her, "Why, poor unlucky girl, dost thou design to put an end to thy days in so dreadful a manner? And what cowardice makes thee sink under this last danger who hast been so miraculously supported in all thy former?" Then the voice told her how by a certain cave she might reach the realms of Pluto, and how to avoid all the dangers of the road, to pass by Cerberus, the three-headed dog, and prevail on Charon, the ferryman, to take her across the black river and bring her back again. But the voice added, "When Proserpine has given you the box filled with her beauty, of all things this is chiefly to be observed by you, that you never once open or look into the box nor allow your curiosity to pry into the treasure of the beauty of the goddesses."

Psyche, encouraged by this advice, obeyed it in all things, and taking heed to her ways travelled safely to the kingdom of Pluto. She was admitted to the place of Proserpine, and without accepting the delicate seat or delicious banquet that was offered her, but contented with coarse bread for her food, she delivered her message from Venus. Presently the box was returned to her, shut and filled with the precious commodity. Then she returned the way she came, and glad was she to come out once more into the light of day.

But having got so far successfully through her dangerous task, a longing desire seized her to examine the contents of the box. "What," said she, "shall I, the carrier of this divine beauty, not take the least bit to put on my cheeks to appear to more advantage in the eyes of my beloved husband!" So she carefully opened the box, but found nothing there of any beauty at all, but an infernal and truly Stygian sleep, which being thus set free from its prison, took possession of her, and she fell down in the midst of the road, a sleepy corpse without sense or motion.

But Cupid, being now recovered from his wound, and not able longer to bear the absence of his beloved Psyche, slipping through the smallest crack of the window of his chamber which happened to be left open, flew to the spot where Psyche lay, and gathering up the sleep from her body closed it again in the box, and waked Psyche with a light touch of one of his arrows. "Again," said he, "hast thou almost perished by the same curiosity. But now perform exactly the task imposed on you by my mother, and I will take care of the rest."

Then Cupid, as swift as lightning penetrating the heights of heaven, presented himself before Jupiter with his supplication. Jupiter lent a favouring ear, and pleaded the cause of the lovers so earnestly with Venus that he won her consent. On this he sent Mercury to bring Psyche up to the heavenly assembly, and when she arrived, handing her a cup of ambrosia, he said, "Drink this, Psyche, and be immortal; nor shall Cupid ever break away from the knot in which he is tied, but these nuptials shall be perpetual."

Thus Psyche became at last united to Cupid, and in due time they had a daughter born to them whose name was Pleasure.

The fable of Cupid and Psyche is usually considered allegorical. The Greek name for a *butterfly* is Psyche, and the same word means the *soul*. There is no illustration of the immortality of the soul so striking and beautiful as the butterfly, bursting on brilliant wings from the tomb in which it has lain, after a dull, grovelling, caterpillar existence, to flutter in the blaze of day and feed on the most fragrant and delicate productions of the spring. Psyche, then, is the human soul, which is purified by sufferings and misfortunes, and is thus prepared for the enjoyment of true and pure happiness.

In works of art Psyche is represented as a maiden with the wings of a butterfly, along with Cupid, in the different situations described in the allegory.

The story of Cupid and Psyche first appears in the works of Apuleius, a writer of the second century of our era. It is therefore of much more recent date than most of the legends of the Age of Fable.

12. CADMUS — THE MYRMIDONS

Jupiter, under the disguise of a bull, had carried away
Europa, the daughter of Agenor, king of Phoenicia. Agenor commanded his son Cadmus to go in search of his sister, and not to return without her. Cadmus went and sought
long and far for his sister, but could not find her, and not
daring to return unsuccessful, consulted the oracle of Apollo
to know what country he should settle in. The oracle informed him that he should find a cow in the field, and
should follow her wherever she might wander, and where
she stopped, should build a city and call it Thebes. Cadmus
had hardly left the Castalian cave, from which the oracle
was delivered, when he saw a young cow slowly walking
before him. He followed her close, offering at the same
time his prayers to Phoebus. The cow went on till she passed
the shallow channel of Cephisus and came out into the plain
of Panope. There she stood still, raising her broad forehead
to the sky and filled the air with her lowings. Cadmus gave
thanks, and stooping down kissed the foreign soil, then lifting his eyes, greeted the surrounding mountains. Wishing to
offer a sacrifice to Jupiter, he sent his servants to seek pure
water for a libation. Near by there stood an ancient grove
which had never been profaned by the axe, in the midst of
which was a cave, thick covered with the growth of bushes,
its roof forming a low arch, from beneath which burst forth
a fountain of purest water. In the cave lurked a horrid serpent with a crested head and scales glittering like gold. His
eyes shone like fire, his body was swollen with venom, he
vibrated a triple tongue, and showed a triple row of teeth.
No sooner had the Tyrians dipped their pitchers in the
fountain, and the in-gushing waters made a sound, than the
glittering serpent raised his head out of the cave and uttered
a fearful hiss. The vessels fell from their hands, the blood
left their cheeks, they trembled in every limb. The serpent,
twisting his scaly body in a huge coil, raised his head so as
to overtop the tallest trees, and while the Tyrians from

terror could neither fight nor fly, slew some with his fangs, others in his folds, and others with his poisonous breath.

Cadmus, having waited for the return of his men till midday, went in search of them. His covering was a lion's hide, and besides his javelin he carried in his hand a lance, and in his breast a bold heart, a surer reliance than either. When he entered the wood, and saw the lifeless bodies of his men, and the monster with his bloody jaws, he exclaimed, "O faithful friends, I will avenge you, or share your death." So saying he lifted a huge stone and threw it with all his force at the serpent. Such a block would have shaken the wall of a fortress, but it made no impression on the monster. Cadmus next threw his javelin, which met with better success, for it penetrated the serpent's scales, and pierced through to his entrails. Fierce with pain, the monster turned back his head to view the wound, and attempted to draw out the weapon with his mouth, but broke it off, leaving the iron point rankling in his flesh. His neck swelled with rage, bloody foam covered his jaws, and the breath of his nostrils poisoned the air around. Now he twisted himself into a circle, then stretched himself out on the ground like the trunk of a fallen tree. As he moved onward, Cadmus retreated before him, holding his spear opposite to the monster's opened jaws. The serpent snapped at the weapon and attempted to bite its iron point. At last Cadmus, watching his chance, thrust the spear at a moment when the animal's head thrown back came against the trunk of a tree, and so succeeded in pinning him to its side. His weight bent the tree as he struggled in the agonies of death.

While Cadmus stood over his conquered foe, contemplating its vast size, a voice was heard (from whence he knew not, but he heard it distinctly) commanding him to take the dragon's teeth and sow them in the earth. He obeyed. He made a furrow in the ground, and planted the teeth, destined to produce a crop of men. Scarce had he done so when the clods began to move, and the points of spears to appear above the surface. Next helmets with their nodding plumes came up, and next the shoulders and breasts and limbs of men with weapons, and in time a harvest of armed warriors. Cadmus, alarmed, prepared to encounter a new enemy, but one of them said to him, "Meddle not with our civil war." With that he who had spoken smote one of his earth-born brothers with a sword, and he himself fell pierced with an arrow from another. The latter fell victim to a fourth, and in like manner the whole crowd dealt with each other till all fell, slain with mutual wounds, except five survivors. One of these cast away his weapons and said, "Brothers, let us live in peace!" These five joined with Cadmus in building his city, to which they gave the name of Thebes.

Cadmus obtained in marriage Harmonia, the daughter of Venus. The gods left Olympus to honour the occasion with their presence, and Vulcan presented the bride with a neck-lace of surpassing brilliancy, his own workmanship. But a fatality hung over the family of Cadmus in consequence of his killing the serpent sacred to Mars. Semele and Ino, his daughters, and Actaeon and Pentheus, his grandchildren, all perished unhappily, and Cadmus and Harmonia quitted Thebes, now grown odious to them, and emigrated to the country of the Enchelians, who received them with honour and made Cadmus their king. But the misfortunes of their children still weighed upon their minds; and one day Cadmus exclaimed, "If a serpent's life is so dear to the gods, I would I were myself a serpent." No sooner had he uttered the words than he began to change his form. Harmonia beheld it and prayed to the gods to let her share his fate. Both became serpents. They live in the woods, but mindful of their origin, they neither avoid the presence of man nor do they ever injure any one.

There is a tradition that Cadmus introduced into Greece the letters of the alphabet which were invented by the Phoenicians. This is alluded to by Byron, where, addressing the modern Greeks, he says:

"You have the letters Cadmus gave,
   Think you he meant them for a slave?"

The Myrmidons

The Myrmidons were the soldiers of Achilles, in the Trojan war. From them all zealous and unscrupulous followers of a political chief are called by that name, down to this day. But the origin of the Myrmidons would not give one the idea of a fierce and bloody race, but rather of a laborious and peaceful one.

Cephalus, king of Athens, arrived in the island of Aegina to seek assistance of his old friend and ally Aeacus, the king, in his war with Minos, king of Crete. Cephalus was most kindly received, and the desired assistance readily promised. "I have people enough," said Aeacus, "to protect myself and spare you such a force as you need." "I rejoice to see it," replied Cephalus, "and my wonder has been raised, I confess, to find such a host of youths as I see around me, all apparently of about the same age. Yet there are many individuals whom I previously knew, that I look for now in vain. What has become of them?" Aeacus groaned, and replied with a voice of sadness, "I have been intending to tell you, and will now do so, without more delay, that you may see how from the saddest beginning a happy result sometimes flows. Those whom you formerly knew are now dust and ashes! A plague sent by angry Juno devastated the land. She hated it because it bore the name of one of her husband's female favourites. While the disease appeared to spring from natural causes we resisted it as we best might, by natural remedies; but it soon appeared that the pestilence was too powerful for our efforts, and we yielded. At the beginning the sky seemed to settle down upon the earth, and thick clouds shut in the heated air. For four months together a deadly south wind prevailed. The disorder affected the wells and springs; thousands of snakes crept over the land and shed their poison in the fountains. The force of the disease was first spent on the lower animals—dogs, cattle, sheep, and birds. The luckless ploughman wondered to see his oxen fall in the midst of their work, and lie helpless in the unfinished furrow. The wool fell from the bleating sheep, and their bodies pined away. The horse, once foremost in the race, contested the palm no more, but groaned at his stall and died an inglorious death. The wild boar forgot his rage, the stag his swiftness, the bears no longer attacked the herds. Everything languished; dead bodies lay in the roads, the fields, and the woods; the air was poisoned by them. I tell you what is hardly credible, but neither dogs nor birds would touch them, nor starving wolves. Their decay spread the infection. Next the disease attacked the country people, and then the dwellers in the

city. At first the cheek was flushed, and the breath drawn
with difficulty. The tongue grew rough and swelled, and
the dry mouth stood open with its veins enlarged and gasped
for the air. Men could not bear the heat of their clothes
or their beds, but preferred to lie on the bare ground; and
the ground did not cool them, but, on the contrary, they
heated the spot where they lay. Nor could the physicians
help, for the disease attacked them also, and the contact
of the sick gave them infection, so that the most faithful were
the first victims. At last all hope of relief vanished, and men
learned to look upon death as the only deliverer from disease. At length all reverence for sacred things was lost.
Bodies were thrown out unburied, wood was wanting for
funeral piles, men fought with one another for the possession of them. Finally there were none left to mourn;
sons and husbands, old men and youths, perished alike unlamented.

"Standing before the altar I raised my eyes to heaven.
'O Jupiter,' I said, 'if thou art indeed my father, and art not
ashamed of thy offspring, give me back my people, or take
me also away!' At these words a clap of thunder was heard.
'I accept the omen,' I cried; 'O may it be a sign of a favourable disposition towards me!' By chance there grew by the
place where I stood an oak with wide-spreading branches,
sacred to Jupiter. I observed a troop of ants busy with their
labour, carrying minute grains in their mouths and following one another in a line up the trunk of the tree. Observing their numbers with admiration, I said, 'Give me, O father, citizens as numerous as these, and replenish my empty
city.' The tree shook and gave a rustling sound with its
branches, though no wind agitated them. I trembled in every
limb, yet I kissed the earth and the tree. I would not confess to myself that I hoped, yet I did hope. Night came on
and sleep took possession of my frame oppressed with cares.
The tree stood before me in my dreams, with its numerous
branches all covered with living, moving creatures. It
seemed to shake its limbs and throw down over the ground
a multitude of those industrious grain-gathering animals,
which appeared to gain in size, and grow larger and larger,
and by and by to stand erect, lay aside their superfluous
legs and their black colour, and finally to assume the human
form. Then I awoke, and my first impulse was to chide the

gods who had robbed me of a sweet vision and given me no reality in its place. Being still in the temple, my attention was caught by the sound of many voices without; a sound of late unusual to my ears. While I began to think I was yet dreaming, Telamon, my son, throwing open the temple gates, exclaimed: 'Father, approach, and behold things surpassing even your hopes!' I went forth; I saw a multitude of men such as I had seen in my dream, and they were passing in procession in the same manner. While I gazed with wonder and delight they approached, and kneeling hailed me as their king. I paid my vows to Jove, and proceeded to allot the vacant city to the new-born race, and to parcel out the fields among them. I called them Myrmidons, from the ant (myrmex) from which they sprang. You have seen these persons; their dispositions resemble those which they had in their former shape. They are a diligent and industrious race, eager to gain, and tenacious of their gains. Among them you may recruit your forces. They will follow you to the war, young in years and bold in heart."

This description of the plague is copied by Ovid from the account which Thucydides, the Greek historian, gives of the plague of Athens. The historian drew from life, and all the poets and writers of fiction since his day, when they have had occasion to describe a similar scene, have borrowed their details from him.

13. NISUS AND SCYLLA — ECHO AND NARCISSUS — CLYTIE — HERO AND LEANDER

Nisus and Scylla

Minos, king of Crete, made war upon Megara. Nisus was king of Megara, and Scylla was his daughter. The siege had now lasted six months and the city still held out, for it was decreed by fate that it should not be taken so long as a certain purple lock, which glittered among the hair of King

Nisus, remained on his head. There was a tower on the city walls, which overlooked the plain where Minos and his army were encamped. To this tower Scylla used to repair, and look abroad over the tents of the hostile army. The siege had lasted so long that she had learned to distinguish the persons of the leaders. Minos, in particular, excited her admiration. Arrayed in his helmet, and bearing his shield, she admired his graceful deportment; if he threw his javelin skill seemed combined with force in the discharge; if he drew his bow Apollo himself could not have done it more gracefully. But when he laid aside his helmet, and in his purple robes bestrode his white horse with its gay caparisons, and reined in its foaming mouth, the daughter of Nisus was hardly mistress of herself; she was almost frantic with admiration. She envied the weapon that he grasped, the reins that he held. She felt as if she could, if it were possible, go to him through the hostile ranks; she felt an impulse to cast herself down from the tower into the midst of his camp, or to open the gates to him, or do anything else, so only it might gratify Minos. As she sat in the tower, she talked thus with herself: "I know not whether to rejoice or grieve at this sad war. I grieve that Minos is our enemy; but I rejoice at any cause that brings him to my sight. Perhaps he would be willing to grant us peace, and receive me as a hostage. I would fly down, if I could, and alight in his camp, and tell him that we yield ourselves to his mercy. But then, to betray my father! No! rather would I never see Minos again. And yet no doubt it is sometimes the best thing for a city to be conquered, when the conqueror is clement and generous. Minos certainly has right on his side. I think we shall be conquered; and if that must be the end of it, why should not love unbar the gates to him, instead of leaving it to be done by war? Better spare delay and slaughter if we can. And O if any one should wound or kill Minos! No one surely would have the heart to do it; yet ignorantly, not knowing him, one might. I will, I will surrender myself to him, with my country as a dowry, and so put an end to the war. But how? The gates are guarded, and my father keeps the keys; he only stands in my way. O that it might please the gods to take him away! But why ask the gods to do it? Another woman, loving as I do, would remove with her own hands whatever stood in the way of her love. And can any other woman dare more than I? I would encounter fire and sword to gain my object; but here there is no need of fire and sword. I only need my father's purple lock. More precious than gold to me, that will give me all I wish."

While she thus reasoned night came on, and soon the whole palace was buried in sleep. She entered her father's bedchamber and cut off the fatal lock; then passed out of the city and entered the enemy's camp. She demanded to be led to the king, and thus addressed him: "I am Scylla, the daughter of Nisus. I surrender to you my country and my father's house. I ask no reward but yourself: for love of you I have done it. See here the purple lock! With this I give you my father and his kingdom." She held out her hand with the fatal spoil. Minos shrunk back and refused to touch it. "The gods destroy thee, infamous woman," he exclaimed; "disgrace of our time! May neither earth nor sea yield thee a resting-place! Surely, my Crete, where Jove himself was cradled, shall not be polluted with such a monster!" Thus he said, and gave orders that equitable terms should be allowed to the conquered city, and that the fleet should immediately sail from the island.

Scylla was frantic. "Ungrateful man," she exclaimed, "is it thus you leave me?—me who have given you victory,—who have sacrificed for you parent and country! I am guilty, I confess, and deserve to die, but not by your hand." As the ships left the shore, she leaped into the water, and seizing the rudder of the one which carried Minos, she was borne along an unwelcome companion of their course. A sea-eagle soaring aloft,—it was her father who had been changed into that form,—seeing her, pounced down upon her, and struck her with his beak and claws. In terror she let go the ship and would have fallen into the water, but some pitying deity changed her into a bird. The sea-eagle still cherishes the old animosity; and whenever he espies her in his lofty flight you may see him dart down upon her, with beak and claws, to take vengeance for the ancient crime.

Echo and Narcissus

Echo was a beautiful nymph, fond of the woods and hills, where she devoted herself to woodland sports. She was a favourite of Diana, and attended her in the chase. But Echo had one failing; she was fond of talking, and whether in chat or argument, would have the last word. One day Juno was seeking her husband, who, she had reason to fear, was amusing himself among the nymphs. Echo by her talk contrived to detain the goddess till the nymphs made their escape. When Juno discovered it, she passed sentence upon Echo in these words: "You shall forfeit the use of that tongue with which you have cheated me, except for that one purpose you are so fond of—*reply*. You shall still have the last word, but no power to speak first."

This nymph saw Narcissus, a beautiful youth, as he pursued the chase upon the mountains. She loved him and followed his footsteps. O how she longed to address him in the softest accents, and win him to converse! but it was not in her power. She waited with impatience for him to speak first, and had her answer ready. One day the youth, being separated from his companions, shouted aloud, "Who's here?" Echo replied, "Here." Narcissus looked around, but seeing no one, called out, "Come." Echo answered, "Come." As no one came, Narcissus called again, "Why do you shun me?" Echo asked the same question. "Let us join one another," said the youth. The maid answered with all her heart in the same words, and hastened to the spot, ready to throw her arms about his neck. He started back, exclaiming, "Hands off! I would rather die than you should have me!" "Have me," said she; but it was all in vain. He left her, and she went to hide her blushes in the recesses of the woods. From that time forth she lived in caves and among mountain cliffs. Her form faded with grief, till at last all her flesh shrank away. Her bones were changed into rocks and there was nothing left of her but her voice. With that she is still ready to reply to any one who calls her, and keeps up her old habit of having the last word.

Narcissus's cruelty in this case was not the only instance. He shunned all the rest of the nymphs, as he had done poor Echo. One day a maiden who had in vain endeavoured to attract him uttered a prayer that he might some time or other feel what it was to love and meet no return of affection. The avenging goddess heard and granted the prayer.

There was a clear fountain, with water like silver, to which the shepherds never drove their flocks, nor the mountain goats resorted, nor any of the beasts of the forests; nei-

ther was it defaced with fallen leaves or branches; but the
grass grew fresh around it, and the rocks sheltered it from
the sun. Hither came one day the youth, fatigued with hunting, heated and thirsty. He stooped down to drink, and saw
his own image in the water; he thought it was some beautiful
water-spirit living in the fountain. He stood gazing with admiration at those bright eyes, those locks curled like the
locks of Bacchus or Apollo, the rounded cheeks, the ivory
neck, the parted lips, and the glow of health and exercise
over all. He fell in love with himself. He brought his lips
near to take a kiss; he plunged his arms in to embrace the
beloved object. It fled at the touch, but returned again after
a moment and renewed the fascination. He could not tear
himself away; he lost all thought of food or rest, while he
hovered over the brink of the fountain gazing upon his own
image. He talked with the supposed spirit: "Why, beautiful
being, do you shun me? Surely my face is not one to repel
you. The nymphs love me, and you yourself look not indifferent upon me. When I stretch forth my arms you do the
same; and you smile upon me and answer my beckonings
with the like." His tears fell into the water and disturbed
the image. As he saw it depart, he exclaimed, "Stay, I entreat you! Let me at least gaze upon you, if I may not touch
you." With this, and much more of the same kind, he cherished the flame that consumed him, so that by degrees he
lost his colour, his vigour, and the beauty which formerly
had so charmed the nymph Echo. She kept near him, however, and when he exclaimed, "Alas! alas!" she answered
him with the same words. He pined away and died; and when
his shade passed the Stygian river, it leaned over the boat
to catch a look of itself in the waters. The nymphs mourned
for him, especially the water-nymphs; and when they smote
their breasts Echo smote hers also. They prepared a funeral
pile and would have burned the body, but it was nowhere to
be found; but in its place a flower, purple within, and surrounded with white leaves, which bears the name and pre-
serves the memory of Narcissus.

Clytie

Clytie was a water-nymph and in love with Apollo, who
made her no return. So she pined away, sitting all day long

upon the cold ground, with her unbound tresses streaming over her shoulders. Nine days she sat and tasted neither food nor drink, her own tears and the chilly dew her only food. She gazed on the sun when he rose, and as he passed through his daily course to his setting; she saw no other object, her face turned constantly on him. At last, they say, her limbs rooted in the ground, her face became a flower,[1] which turns on its stem so as always to face the sun throughout its daily course; for it retains to that extent the feeling of the nymph from whom it sprang. The sunflower is a favourite emblem of constancy.

Hero and Leander

Leander was a youth of Abydos, a town of the Asian side of the strait which separates Asia and Europe. On the opposite shore, in the town of Sestos, lived the maiden Hero, a priestess of Venus. Leander loved her, and used to swim the strait nightly to enjoy the company of his mistress, guided by a torch which she reared upon the tower for the purpose. But one night a tempest arose and the sea was rough; his strength failed, and he was drowned. The waves bore his body to the European shore, where Hero became aware of his death, and in her despair cast herself down from the tower into the sea and perished.

The story of Leander's swimming the Hellespont was looked upon as fabulous, and the feat considered impossible, till Lord Byron proved its possibility by performing it himself. In the "Bride of Abydos," he says,

"These limbs that buoyant wave hath borne."

The distance in the narrowest part is almost a mile, and there is a constant current setting out from the Sea of Marmora into the Archipelago. Since Byron's time the feat has been achieved by others; but it yet remains a test of strength and skill in the art of swimming sufficient to give a wide and lasting celebrity to any one who may dare to make the attempt and succeed in accomplishing it.

[1] The sunflower.

14. MINERVA — NIOBE

Minerva (Pallas Athena)

Minerva, the goddess of wisdom, was the daughter of Jupiter. She was said to have leaped forth from his brain, mature, and in complete armour. She presided over the useful and ornamental arts, both those of men—such as agriculture and navigation—and those of women,—spinning, weaving, and needlework. She was also a warlike divinity; but it was defensive war only that she patronized, and she had no sympathy with Mars's savage love of violence and bloodshed. Athens was her chosen seat, her own city, awarded to her as the prize of a contest with Neptune, who also aspired to it. The tale ran that in the reign of Cecrops, the first king of Athens, the two deities contended for the possession of the city. The gods decreed that it should be awarded to that one who produced the gift most useful to mortals. Neptune gave the horse; Minerva produced the olive. The gods gave judgment that the olive was the more useful of the two, and awarded the city to the goddess; and it was named after her, Athens, her name in Greek being Athena.

There was another contest, in which a mortal dared come in competition with Minerva. That mortal was Arachne, a maiden who had attained such skill in the arts of weaving and embroidery that the nymphs themselves would leave their groves and fountains to come and gaze upon her work. It was not only beautiful when it was done, but beautiful also in the doing. To watch her, as she took the wool in its rude state and formed it into rolls, or separated it with her fingers and carded it till it looked as light and soft as a cloud, or twirled the spindle with skilful touch, or wove the web, or, after it was woven, adorned it with her needle, one would have said that Minerva herself had taught her. But this she denied, and could not bear to be thought a pupil even of a goddess. "Let Minerva try her skill with mine," said she; "if beaten I will pay the penalty." Minerva heard

this and was displeased. She assumed the form of an old
woman and went and gave Arachne some friendly advice.
"I have had much experience," said she, "and I hope you
will not despise my counsel. Challenge your fellow-mortals
as you will, but do not compete with a goddess. On the contrary, I advise you to ask her forgiveness for what you have
said, and as she is merciful perhaps she will pardon you."
Arachne stopped her spinning and looked at the old dame
with anger in her countenance. "Keep your counsel," said
she, "for your daughters or handmaids; for my part I know
what I say, and I stand to it. I am not afraid of the goddess;
let her try her skill, if she dare venture." "She comes," said
Minerva; and dropping her disguise stood confessed. The
nymphs bent low in homage, and all the bystanders paid
reverence. Arachne alone was unterrified. She blushed, indeed; a sudden colour dyed her cheek, and then she grew
pale. But she stood to her resolve, and with a foolish con-
ceit of her own skill rushed on her fate. Minerva forbore
no longer nor interposed any further advice. They proceed
to the contest. Each takes her station and attaches the web
to the beam. Then the slender shuttle is passed in and out
among the threads. The reed with its fine teeth strikes up the
woof into its place and compacts the web. Both work with
speed; their skilful hands move rapidly, and the excitement
of the contest makes the labour light. Wool of Tyrian dye
is contrasted with that of other colours, shaded off into one
another so adroitly that the joining deceives the eye. Like
the bow, whose long arch tinges the heavens, formed by
sunbeams reflected from the shower,[1] in which, where the
colours meet they seem as one, but at a little distance from
the point of contact are wholly different.

Minerva wrought on her web the scene of her contest
with Neptune. Twelve of the heavenly powers are represented, Jupiter, with august gravity, sitting in the midst.
Neptune, the ruler of the sea, holds his trident, and appears
to have just smitten the earth, from which a horse has
leaped forth. Minerva depicted herself with helmed head,
her Aegis covering her breast. Such was the central circle;
and in the four corners were represented incidents illustrat-
ing the displeasure of the gods at such presumptuous mor-

[1] This correct description of the rainbow is literally translated from
Ovid.

tals as had dared to contend with them. These were meant as warnings to her rival to give up the contest before it was too late.

Arachne filled her web with subjects designedly chosen to exhibit the failings and errors of the gods. One scene represented Leda caressing the swan, under which form Jupiter had disguised himself; and another, Danaë, in the brazen tower in which her father had imprisoned her, but where the god effected his entrance in the form of a golden shower. Still another depicted Europa deceived by Jupiter under the disguise of a bull. Encouraged by the tameness of the animal Europa ventured to mount his back, whereupon Jupiter advanced into the sea and swam with her to Crete. You would have thought it was a real bull, so naturally was it wrought, and so natural the water in which it swam. She seemed to look with longing eyes back upon the shore she was leaving, and to call to her companions for help. She appeared to shudder with terror at the sight of the heaving waves, and to draw back her feet from the water.

Arachne filled her canvas with similar subjects, wonderfully well done, but strongly marking her presumption and impiety. Minerva could not forbear to admire, yet felt indignant at the insult. She struck the web with her shuttle and rent it in pieces; she then touched the forehead of Arachne and made her feel her guilt and shame. She could not endure it and went and hanged herself. Minerva pitied her as she saw her suspended by a rope. "Live," she said, "guilty woman! and that you may preserve the memory of this lesson, continue to hang, both you and your descendants, to all future times." She sprinkled her with the juices of aconite, and immediately her hair came off, and her nose and ears likewise. Her form shrank up, and her head grew smaller yet; her fingers cleaved to her side and served for legs. All the rest of her is body, out of which she spins her thread, often hanging suspended by it, in the same attitude as when Minerva touched her and transformed her into a spider.

Niobe

The fate of Arachne was noised abroad through all the country, and served as a warning to all presumptuous mortals not to compare themselves with the divinities. But one, and she a matron too, failed to learn the lesson of humility. It was Niobe, the queen of Thebes. She had indeed much to be proud of; but it was not her husband's fame, nor her own beauty, nor her great descent, nor the power of their kingdom that elated her. It was her children; and truly the happiest of mothers would Niobe have been if only she had not claimed to be so. It was on occasion of the annual celebration in honour of Latona and her offspring, Apollo and Diana,—when the people of Thebes were assembled, their brows crowned with laurel, bearing frankincense to the altars and paying their vows,—that Niobe appeared among the crowd. Her attire was splendid with gold and gems, and her aspect beautiful as the face of an angry woman can be. She stood and surveyed the people with haughty looks. "What folly," said she, "is this!—to prefer beings whom you never saw to those who stand before your eyes! Why should Latona be honoured with worship, and none be paid to me? My father was Tantalus, who was received as a guest at the table of the gods; my mother was a goddess. My husband built and rules this city, Thebes, and Phrygia is my paternal inheritance. Wherever I turn my eyes I survey the elements of my power; nor is my form and presence unworthy of a goddess. To all this let me add I have seven sons and seven daughters, and look for sons-in-law and daughters-in-law of pretensions worthy of my alliance. Have I not cause for pride? Will you prefer to me this Latona, the Titan's daughter, with her two children? I have seven times as many. Fortunate indeed am I, and fortunate I shall remain! Will any one deny this? My abundance is my security. I feel myself too strong for Fortune to subdue. She may take from me much; I shall still have much left. Were I to lose some of my children, I should hardly be left as poor as Latona with her two only. Away with you from these solemnities, —put off the laurel from your brows,—have done with this worship!" The people obeyed, and left the sacred services uncompleted.

The goddess was indignant. On the Cynthian mountain top where she dwelt she thus addressed her son and daughter: "My children, I who have been so proud of you both, and have been used to hold myself second to none of the goddesses except Juno alone, begin now to doubt whether

I am indeed a goddess. I shall be deprived of my worship altogether unless you protect me." She was proceeding in this strain, but Apollo interrupted her. "Say no more," said he; "speech only delays punishment." So said Diana also. Darting through the air, veiled in clouds, they alighted on the towers of the city. Spread out before the gates was a broad plain, where the youth of the city pursued their war-like sports. The sons of Niobe were there with the rest,— some mounted on spirited horses richly caparisoned, some driving gay chariots. Ismenos, the first-born, as he guided his foaming steeds, struck with an arrow from above, cried out, "Ah me!" dropped the reins, and fell lifeless. Another, hearing the sound of the bow,—like the boatman who sees the storm gathering and makes all sail for the port,—gave the reins to his horses and attempted to escape. The inevitable arrow overtook him, as he fled. Two others, younger boys, just from their tasks, had gone to the playground to have a game of wrestling. As they stood breast to breast, one arrow pierced them both. They uttered a cry together, together cast a parting look around them, and together breathed their last. Alphenor, an elder brother, seeing them fall, hastened to the spot to render assistance, and fell stricken in the act of brotherly duty. Only one was left, Ilioneus. He raised his arms to heaven to try whether prayer might not avail. "Spare me, ye gods!" he cried, addressing all, in his ignorance that all needed not his intercessions; and Apollo would have spared him, but the arrow had already left the string, and it was too late.

The terror of the people and grief of the attendants soon made Niobe acquainted with what had taken place. She could hardly think it possible; she was indignant that the gods had dared, and amazed that they had been able to do it. Her husband, Amphion, overwhelmed with the blow, destroyed himself. Alas! how different was this Niobe from her who had so lately driven away the people from the sacred rites, and held her stately course through the city, the envy of her friends, now the pity even of her foes! She knelt over the lifeless bodies, and kissed now one, now another of her dead sons. Raising her pallid arms to heaven, "Cruel Latona," said she, "feed full your rage with my anguish! Satiate your hard heart, while I follow to the grave my seven sons. Yet where is your triumph? Bereaved as I am, I am still richer than you, my conqueror." Scarce had she spoken, when the bow sounded and struck terror into all hearts except Niobe's alone. She was brave from excess of grief. The sisters stood in garments of mourning over the biers of their dead brothers. One fell, struck by an arrow, and died on the corpse she was bewailing. Another, attempting to console her mother, suddenly ceased to speak, and sank lifeless to the earth. A third tried to escape by flight, a fourth by concealment, another stood trembling, uncertain what course to take. Six were now dead, and only one remained, whom the mother held clasped in her arms, and covered as it were with her whole body. "Spare me one, and that the youngest! O spare me one of so many!" she cried; and while she spoke, that one fell dead. Desolate she sat, among sons, daughters, husband, all dead, and seemed torpid with grief. The breeze moved not her hair, no colour was on her cheek, her eyes glared fixed and immovable, there was no sign of life about her. Her very tongue cleaved to the roof of her mouth, and her veins ceased to convey the tide of life. Her neck bent not, her arms made no gesture, her foot no step. She was changed to stone, within and without. Yet tears continued to flow; and borne on a whirlwind to her native mountain, she still remains, a mass of rock, from which a trickling stream flows, the tribute of her never-ending grief.

15. THE GRAEAE AND GORGONS —
PERSEUS AND MEDUSA

The Graeae and Gorgons

The Graeae were three sisters who were gray-haired from their birth, whence their name. The Gorgons were monstrous females with huge teeth like those of swine, brazen claws, and snaky hair. None of these beings make much figure in mythology except Medusa, the Gorgon, whose story we shall next advert to. We mention them chiefly to introduce an ingenious theory of some modern writers, namely, that the Gorgons and Graeae were only personifications of the terrors of the sea, the former denoting the *strong* billows of the wide open main, and the latter the *white*-crested waves that dash against the rocks of the coast. Their names in Greek signify the above epithets.

Perseus and Medusa

Perseus was the son of Jupiter and Danaë. His grandfather Acrisius, alarmed by an oracle which had told him that his daughter's child would be the instrument of his death, caused the mother and child to be shut up in a chest and set adrift on the sea. The chest floated towards Seriphus, where it was found by a fisherman who conveyed the mother and infant to Polydectes, the king of the country, by whom they were treated with kindness. When Perseus was grown up Polydectes sent him to attempt the conquest of Medusa, a terrible monster who had laid waste the country. She was once a beautiful maiden whose hair was her chief glory, but as she dared to vie in beauty with Minerva, the goddess deprived her of her charms and changed her beautiful ringlets into hissing serpents. She became a cruel monster of so frightful an aspect that no living thing could behold her without being turned into stone. All around the cavern where she dwelt might be seen the stony figures of men and animals which had chanced to catch a glimpse of her and had been petrified with the sight. Perseus, favoured by Minerva and Mercury, the former of whom lent him her shield and the latter his winged shoes, approached Medusa while she slept and taking care not to look directly at her, but guided by her image reflected in the bright shield which he bore, he cut off her head and gave it to Minerva, who fixed it in the middle of her Aegis.

Perseus and Atlas

After the slaughter of Medusa, Perseus, bearing with him the head of the Gorgon, flew far and wide, over land and sea. As night came on, he reached the western limit of the earth, where the sun goes down. Here he would gladly have rested till morning. It was the realm of King Atlas, whose bulk surpassed that of all other men. He was rich in flocks and herds and had no neighbour or rival to dispute his state. But his chief pride was in his gardens, whose fruit was of gold, hanging from golden branches, half hid with golden leaves. Perseus said to him, "I come as a guest. If you honour illustrious descent, I claim Jupiter for my father; if mighty deeds, I plead the conquest of the Gorgon. I seek rest and food." But Atlas remembered that an ancient prophecy had warned him that a son of Jove should one day rob him of his golden apples. So he answered, "Begone! or neither your false claims of glory nor parentage shall protect you"; and he attempted to thrust him out. Perseus, finding the giant too strong for him, said, "Since you value my friendship so little, deign to accept a present"; and turning his face away, he held up the Gorgon's head. Atlas, with all his bulk, was changed into stone. His beard and hair became forests, his arms and shoulders cliffs, his head a summit, and his bones rocks. Each part increased in bulk till he became a mountain, and (such was the pleasure of the gods) heaven with all its stars rests upon his shoulders.

The Sea-monster

Perseus, continuing his flight, arrived at the country of the Aethiopians, of which Cepheus was king. Cassiopeia his queen, proud of her beauty, had dared to compare herself to the Sea-Nymphs, which roused their indignation to such a degree that they sent a prodigious sea-monster to ravage the coast. To appease the deities, Cepheus was directed by the oracle to expose his daughter Andromeda to be devoured by the monster. As Perseus looked down from his aerial height he beheld the virgin chained to a rock, and waiting the approach of the serpent. She was so pale and motionless that if it had not been for her flowing tears and her hair that moved in the breeze, he would have taken her for a marble statue. He was so startled at the sight that he almost forgot to wave his wings. As he hovered over her he said, "O virgin, undeserving of those chains, but rather of such as bind fond lovers together, tell me, I beseech you, your name, and the name of your country, and why you are thus bound." At first she was silent from modesty, and, if

she could, would have hid her face with her hands; but
when he repeated his questions, for fear she might be
thought guilty of some fault which she dared not tell, she
disclosed her name and that of her country, and her
mother's pride of beauty. Before she had done speaking, a
sound was heard off upon the water, and the sea-monster
appeared, with his head raised above the surface, cleaving
the waves with his broad breast. The virgin shrieked, the
father and mother who had now arrived at the scene,
wretched both, but the mother more justly so, stood by, not
able to afford protection, but only to pour forth lamentations and to embrace the victim. Then spoke Perseus:
"There will be time enough for tears; this hour is all we
have for rescue. My rank as the son of Jove and my renown
as the slayer of the Gorgon might make me acceptable as a
suitor; but I will try to win her by services rendered, if the
gods will only be propitious. If she be rescued by my valour,
I demand that she be my reward." The parents consent
(how could they hesitate?) and promise a royal dowry with
her.

And now the monster was within the range of a stone
thrown by a skilful slinger, when with a sudden bound the
youth soared into the air. As an eagle, when from his lofty
flight he sees a serpent basking in the sun, pounces upon
him and seizes him by the neck to prevent him from turning his head round and using his fangs, so the youth darted
down upon the back of the monster and plunged his sword
into its shoulder. Irritated by the wound, the monster raised
himself into the air, then plunged into the depth; then, like
a wild boar surrounded by a pack of barking dogs, turned
swiftly from side to side, while the youth eluded its attacks
by means of his wings. Wherever he can find a passage for
his sword between the scales he makes a wound, piercing
now the side, now the flank, as it slopes towards the tail.
The brute spouts from his nostrils water mixed with blood.
The wings of the hero are wet with it, and he dares no
longer trust to them. Alighting on a rock which rose above
the waves, and holding on by a projecting fragment, as the
monster floated near he gave him a death stroke. The people who had gathered on the shore shouted so that the hills
reëchoed with the sound. The parents, transported with joy,

embraced their future son-in-law, calling him their deliverer and the saviour of their house, and the virgin, both cause and reward of the contest, descended from the rock.

Cassiopeia was an Aethiopian, and consequently, in spite of her boasted beauty, black; at least so Milton seems to have thought, who alludes to this story in his "Penseroso," where he addresses Melancholy as the

> ". . . goddess, sage and holy,
> Whose saintly visage is too bright
> To hit the sense of human sight,
> And, therefore, to our weaker view,
> O'erlaid with black, staid Wisdom's hue.
> Black, but such as in esteem
> Prince Memnon's sister might beseem,
> Or that starred Aethiop queen that strove
> To set her beauty's praise above
> The sea-nymphs, and their powers offended."

Cassiopeia is called "the starred Aethiop queen" because after her death she was placed among the stars, forming the constellation of that name. Though she attained this honour, yet the Sea-Nymphs, her old enemies, prevailed so far as to cause her to be placed in that part of the heaven near the pole, where every night she is half the time held with her head downward, to give her a lesson of humility.

Memnon was an Aethiopian prince, of whom we shall tell in a future chapter.

The Wedding Feast

The joyful parents, with Perseus and Andromeda, repaired to the palace, where a banquet was spread for them, and all was joy and festivity. But suddenly a noise was heard of warlike clamour, and Phineus, the betrothed of the virgin, with a party of his adherents, burst in, demanding the maiden as his own. It was in vain that Cepheus remonstrated —"You should have claimed her when she lay bound to the rock, the monster's victim. The sentence of the gods dooming her to such a fate dissolved all engagements, as death itself would have done." Phineus made no reply, but hurled his javelin at Perseus, but it missed its mark and fell harmless. Perseus would have thrown his in turn, but the cowardly assailant ran and took shelter behind the altar. But his act was a signal for an onset by his band upon the guests of Cepheus. They defended themselves and a general conflict ensued, the old king retreating from the scene after fruitless expostulations, calling the gods to witness that he was guiltless of this outrage on the rights of hospitality.

Perseus and his friends maintained for some time the unequal contest; but the numbers of the assailants were too great for them, and destruction seemed inevitable, when a sudden thought struck Perseus,—"I will make my enemy defend me." Then with a loud voice he exclaimed, "If I have any friend here let him turn away his eyes!" and held aloft the Gorgon's head. "Seek not to frighten us with your jugglery," said Thescelus, and raised his javelin in the act to throw, and became stone in the very attitude. Ampyx was about to plunge his sword into the body of a prostrate foe, but his arm stiffened and he could neither thrust nor withdraw it. Another, in the midst of a vociferous challenge, stopped, his mouth open, but no sound issuing. One of Perseus's friends, Aconteus, caught sight of the Gorgon and stiffened like the rest. Astyages struck him with his sword, but instead of wounding, it recoiled with a ringing noise.

Phineus beheld this dreadful result of his unjust aggression, and felt confounded. He called aloud to his friends, but got no answer; he touched them and found them stone. Falling on his knees and stretching out his hands to Perseus, but turning his head away, he begged for mercy. "Take all," said he, "give me but my life." "Base coward," said Perseus, "thus much I will grant you; no weapon shall touch you; moreover, you shall be preserved in my house as a memorial of these events." So saying, he held the Gorgon's head to the side where Phineus was looking, and in the very form in which he knelt, with his hands outstretched and face averted, he became immovably, a mass of stone!

16. MONSTERS: GIANTS — SPHINX — PEGASUS AND CHIMAERA — CENTAURS — PYGMIES — GRIFFIN

Monsters, in the language of mythology, were beings of unnatural proportions or parts, usually regarded with terror, as possessing immense strength and ferocity, which they employed for the injury and annoyance of men. Some of them were supposed to combine the members of different animals; such were the Sphinx and Chimaera; and to these all the terrible qualities of wild beasts were attributed, together with human sagacity and faculties. Others, as the giants, differed from men chiefly in their size; and in this particular we must recognize a wide distinction among them. The human giants, if so they may be called, such as the Cyclops, Antaeus, Orion, and others, must be supposed not to be altogether disproportioned to human beings, for they mingled in love and strife with them. But the super-human giants, who warred with the gods, were of vastly larger dimensions. Tityus, we are told, when stretched on the plain, covered nine acres, and Enceladus required the whole of Mount Aetna to be laid upon him to keep him down.

We have already spoken of the war which the giants waged against the gods, and of its result. While this war lasted the giants proved a formidable enemy. Some of them, like Briareus, had a hundred arms; others, like Typhon, breathed out fire. At one time they put the gods to such fear that they fled into Egypt and hid themselves under various forms. Jupiter took the form of a ram, whence he was afterwards worshipped in Egypt as the god Ammon, with curved horns. Apollo became a crow, Bacchus a goat, Diana a cat, Juno a cow, Venus a fish, Mercury a bird. At another time the giants attempted to climb up into heaven, and for that purpose took up the mountain Ossa and piled it on Pelion.[1]

[1] See Proverbial Expressions, page 268.

They were at last subdued by thunderbolts, which Minerva invented, and taught Vulcan and his Cyclops to make for Jupiter.

The Sphinx

Laius, king of Thebes, was warned by an oracle that there was danger to his throne and life if his new-born son should be suffered to grow up. He therefore committed the child to the care of a herdsman with orders to destroy him; but the herdsman, moved with pity, yet not daring entirely to disobey, tied up the child by the feet and left him hanging to the branch of a tree. In this condition the infant was found by a peasant, who carried him to his master and mistress, by whom he was adopted and called Oedipus, or Swollen-foot.

Many years afterwards Laius being on his way to Delphi, accompanied only by one attendant, met in a narrow road a young man also driving in a chariot. On his refusal to leave the way at their command the attendant killed one of his horses, and the stranger, filled with rage, slew both Laius and his attendant. The young man was Oedipus, who thus unknowingly became the slayer of his own father.

Shortly after this event the city of Thebes was afflicted with a monster which infested the highroad. It was called the Sphinx. It had the body of a lion and the upper part of a woman. It lay crouched on the top of a rock, and arrested all travellers who came that way, proposing to them a riddle, with the condition that those who could solve it should pass safe, but those who failed should be killed. Not one had yet succeeded in solving it, and all had been slain. Oedipus was not daunted by these alarming accounts, but boldly advanced to the trial. The Sphinx asked him, "What animal is that which in the morning goes on four feet, at noon on two, and in the evening upon three?" Oedipus replied, "Man, who in childhood creeps on hands and knees, in manhood walks erect, and in old age with the aid of a staff." The Sphinx was so mortified at the solving of her riddle that she cast herself down from the rock and perished.

The gratitude of the people for their deliverance was so great that they made Oedipus their king, giving him in marriage their queen Jocasta. Oedipus, ignorant of his parentage, had already become the slayer of his father; in marrying the queen he became the husband of his mother. These horrors remained undiscovered, till at length Thebes was afflicted with famine and pestilence, and the oracle being consulted, the double crime of Oedipus came to light. Jocasta put an end to her own life, and Oedipus, seized with madness, tore out his eyes and wandered away from Thebes, dreaded and abandoned by all except his daughters, who faithfully adhered to him, till after a tedious period of miserable wandering he found the termination of his wretched life.

Pegasus and the Chimaera

When Perseus cut off Medusa's head, the blood sinking into the earth produced the winged horse Pegasus. Minerva caught and tamed him and presented him to the Muses. The fountain Hippocrene, on the Muses' mountain Helicon, was opened by a kick from his hoof.

The Chimaera was a fearful monster, breathing fire. The fore part of its body was a compound of the lion and the goat, and the hind part a dragon's. It made great havoc in Lycia, so that the king, Iobates, sought for some hero to destroy it. At that time there arrived at his court a gallant young warrior, whose name was Bellerophon. He brought letters from Proetus, the son-in-law of Iobates, recommending Bellerophon in the warmest terms as an unconquerable hero, but added at the close a request to his father-in-law to put him to death. The reason was that Proetus was jealous of him, suspecting that his wife Antea looked with too much admiration on the young warrior. From this instance of Bellerophon being unconsciously the bearer of his own death warrant, the expression "Bellerophontic letters" arose, to describe any species of communication which a person is made the bearer of, containing matter prejudicial to himself.

Iobates, on perusing the letters, was puzzled what to do, not willing to violate the claims of hospitality, yet wishing to oblige his son-in-law. A lucky thought occurred to him, to send Bellerophon to combat with the Chimaera. Bellerophon accepted the proposal, but before proceeding to the combat consulted the soothsayer Polyidus, who advised him to procure if possible the horse Pegasus for the conflict. For this purpose he directed him to pass the night in the temple of Minerva. He did so, and as he slept Minerva came to him and gave him a golden bridle. When he awoke the bridle remained in his hand. Minerva also showed him Pegasus drinking at the well of Pirene, and at sight of the bridle, the winged steed came willingly and suffered himself to be taken. Bellerophon mounted him, rose with him into the air, soon found the Chimaera, and gained an easy victory over the monster.

After the conquest of the Chimaera Bellerophon was exposed to further trials and labours by his unfriendly host, but by the aid of Pegasus he triumphed in them all, till at length Iobates, seeing that the hero was a special favourite of the gods, gave him his daughter in marriage and made him his successor on the throne. At last Bellerophon by his pride and presumption drew upon himself the anger of the gods; it is said he even attempted to fly up into heaven on his winged steed, but Jupiter sent a gadfly which stung Pegasus and made him throw his rider, who became lame and blind in consequence. After this Bellerophon wandered lonely through the Aleian field, avoiding the paths of men, and died miserably.

Shakespeare alludes to Pegasus in "Henry IV.," where Vernon describes Prince Henry:

> "I saw young Harry, with his beaver on,
>   His cuishes on his thighs, gallantly armed,
>   Rise from the ground like feathered Mercury,
>   And vaulted with such ease into his seat,
>   As if an angel dropped down from the clouds,
>   To turn and wind a fiery Pegasus,
>   And witch the world with noble horsemanship."

The Centaurs

These monsters were represented as men from the head to the loins, while the remainder of the body was that of a horse. The ancients were too fond of a horse to consider the union of his nature with man's as forming a very degraded compound, and accordingly the Centaur is the only one of the fancied monsters of antiquity to which any good traits

are assigned. The Centaurs were admitted to the companionship of man, and at the marriage of Pirithous with Hippo-
damia they were among the guests. At the feast Eurytion,
one of the Centaurs, becoming intoxicated with the wine, attempted to offer violence to the bride; the other Centaurs
followed his example, and a dreadful conflict arose in which
several of them were slain. This is the celebrated battle of
the Lapithae and Centaurs, a favourite subject with the
sculptors and poets of antiquity.

But not all the Centaurs were like the rude guests of
Pirithous. Chiron was instructed by Apollo and Diana, and
was renowned for his skill in hunting, medicine, music, and
the art of prophecy. The most distinguished heroes of Grecian story were his pupils. Among the rest the infant Aesculapius was intrusted to his charge by Apollo, his father.
When the sage returned to his home bearing the infant, his
daughter Ocyrhoe came forth to meet him, and at sight of
the child burst forth into a prophetic strain (for she was a
prophetess), foretelling the glory that he was to achieve.
Aesculapius when grown up became a renowned physician,
and even in one instance succeeded in restoring the dead to
life. Pluto resented this, and Jupiter, at his request, struck
the bold physician with lightning, and killed him, but after
his death received him into the number of the gods.

Chiron was the wisest and justest of all the Centaurs,
and at his death Jupiter placed him among the stars as the
constellation Saggitarius.

The Pygmies

The Pygmies were a nation of dwarfs, so called from a
Greek word which means the cubit or measure of about
thirteen inches, which was said to be the height of these
people. They lived near the sources of the Nile, or according to others, in India. Homer tells us that the cranes used
to migrate every winter to the Pygmies' country, and their
appearance was the signal of bloody warfare to the puny
inhabitants, who had to take up arms to defend their corn-
fields against the rapacious strangers. The Pygmies and
their enemies the Cranes form the subject of several works
of art.

Later writers tell of an army of Pygmies which finding

Hercules asleep, made preparations to attack him, as if they were about to attack a city. But the hero, awaking, laughed at the little warriors, wrapped some of them up in his lion's skin, and carried them to Eurystheus.

The Griffin, or Gryphon

The Griffin is a monster with the body of a lion, the head and wings of an eagle, and back covered with feathers. Like birds it builds its nest, and instead of an egg lays an agate therein. It has long claws and talons of such a size that the people of that country make them into drinking-cups. India was assigned as the native country of the Griffins. They found gold in the mountains and built their nests of it, for which reason their nests were very tempting to the hunters, and they were forced to keep vigilant guard over them. Their instinct led them to know where buried treasures lay, and they did their best to keep plunderers at a distance. The Arimaspians, among whom the Griffins flourished, were a one-eyed people of Scythia.

17. THE GOLDEN FLEECE — MEDEA

The Golden Fleece

In very ancient times there lived in Thessaly a king and queen named Athamas and Nephele. They had two children, a boy and a girl. After a time Athamas grew indifferent to his wife, put her away, and took another. Nephele suspected danger to her children from the influence of the step-mother, and took measures to send them out of her reach. Mercury assisted her, and gave her a ram with a *golden fleece*, on which she set the two children, trusting that the ram would convey them to a place of safety. The ram vaulted into the air with the children on his back, taking his course to the East, till when crossing the strait that divides Europe and Asia, the girl, whose name was Helle, fell from his back into the sea, which from her was called the Hellespont,—now the Dardanelles. The ram continued his career till he reached the kingdom of Colchis, on the eastern shore of the Black Sea, where he safely landed the boy Phryxus, who was hospitably received by Aeetes, king of the country. Phryxus sacrificed the ram to Jupiter, and gave the *Golden Fleece* to Aeetes, who placed it in a consecrated grove, under the care of a sleepless dragon.

There was another kingdom in Thessaly near to that of Athamas, and ruled over by a relative of his. The king Aeson, being tired of the cares of government, surrendered his crown to his brother Pelias on condition that he should hold it only during the minority of Jason, the son of Aeson. When Jason was grown up and came to demand the crown from his uncle Pelias pretended to be willing to yield it, but at the same time suggested to the young man the glorious adventure of going in quest of the Golden Fleece, which it was well known was in the kingdom of Colchis, and was, as Pelias pretended, the rightful property of their family. Jason was pleased with the thought and forthwith made preparations for the expedition. At that time the only species of navigation known to the Greeks consisted of small boats or canoes hollowed out from trunks of trees, so that when Jason employed Argus to build him a vessel capable of containing fifty men, it was considered a gigantic undertaking. It was accomplished, however, and the vessel named "Argo," from the name of the builder. Jason sent his invitation to all the adventurous young men of Greece, and soon found himself at the head of a band of bold youths, many of whom afterwards were renowned among the heroes and demigods of Greece. Hercules, Theseus, Orpheus, and Nestor were among them. They are called the Argonauts, from the name of their vessel.

The "Argo" with her crew of heroes left the shores of Thessaly and having touched at the Island of Lemnos, thence crossed to Mysia and thence to Thrace. Here they found the sage Phineus, and from him received instruction as to their future course. It seems the entrance of the Euxine Sea was impeded by two small rocky islands, which floated on the surface, and in their tossings and heavings occasionally came together, crushing and grinding to atoms any object that might be caught between them. They were called the Symplegades, or Clashing Islands. Phineus instructed the Argonauts how to pass this dangerous strait. When they reached the islands they let go a dove, which took her way between the rocks, and passed in safety, only losing some feathers of her tail. Jason and his men seized the favourable moment of the rebound, plied their oars with vigour, and passed safe through, though the islands closed behind them, and actually grazed their stern. They now rowed along the shore till they arrived at the eastern end of the sea, and landed at the kingdom of Colchis.

Jason made known his message to the Colchian king, Aeetes, who consented to give up the golden fleece if Jason would yoke to the plough two fire-breathing bulls with brazen feet, and sow the teeth of the dragon which Cadmus had slain, and from which it was well known that a crop of armed men would spring up, who would turn their weapons against their producer. Jason accepted the conditions, and a time was set for making the experiment. Previously, however, he found means to plead his cause to Medea, daughter of the king. He promised her marriage, and as they stood before the altar of Hecate, called the goddess to witness his oath. Medea yielded, and by her aid, for she was a potent sorceress, he was furnished with a charm, by which he could encounter safely the breath of the fire-breathing bulls and the weapons of the armed men.

At the time appointed, the people assembled at the grove of Mars, and the king assumed his royal seat, while the multitude covered the hill-sides. The brazen-footed bulls rushed in, breathing fire from their nostrils that burned up the herbage as they passed. The sound was like the roar of a furnace, and the smoke like that of water upon quick-lime. Jason advanced boldly to meet them. His friends, the chosen heroes of Greece, trembled to behold him. Regardless of the burning breath, he soothed their rage with his voice, patted their necks with fearless hand, and adroitly slipped over them the yoke, and compelled them to drag the plough. The Colchians were amazed; the Greeks shouted for joy. Jason next proceeded to sow the dragon's teeth and plough them in. And soon the crop of armed men sprang up, and, wonderful to relate! no sooner had they reached the surface than they began to brandish their weapons and rush upon Jason. The Greeks trembled for their hero, and even she who had provided him a way of safety and taught him how to use it, Medea herself, grew pale with fear. Jason for a time kept his assailants at bay with his sword and shield, till, finding their numbers overwhelming, he resorted to the charm which Medea had taught him, seized a stone and threw it in the midst of his foes. They immediately turned their arms against one another, and soon there was not one of the dragon's brood left alive. The Greeks embraced their hero, and Medea, if she dared, would have embraced him too.

It remained to lull to sleep the dragon that guarded the fleece, and this was done by scattering over him a few drops of a preparation which Medea had supplied. At the smell he relaxed his rage, stood for a moment motionless, then shut those great round eyes, that had never been known to shut before, and turned over on his side, fast asleep. Jason seized the fleece and with his friends and Medea accompanying, hastened to their vessel before Aeetes the king could arrest their departure, and made the best of their way back to Thessaly, where they arrived safe, and Jason delivered the fleece to Pelias, and dedicated the "Argo" to Neptune. What became of the fleece afterwards we do not know, but perhaps it was found after all, like many other golden prizes, not worth the trouble it had cost to procure it.

This is one of those mythological tales, says a late writer, in which there is reason to believe that a substratum of truth exists, though overlaid by a mass of fiction. It probably was the first important maritime expedition, and like the first attempts of the kind of all nations, as we know from history, was probably of a half-piratical character. If rich spoils were the result it was enough to give rise to the idea of the golden fleece.

Hercules left the expedition at Mysia, for Hylas, a youth beloved by him, having gone for water, was laid hold of and kept by the nymphs of the spring, who were fascinated by his beauty. Hercules went in quest of the lad, and while he was absent the "Argo" put to sea and left him.

Medea and Aeson

Amid the rejoicings for the recovery of the Golden Fleece, Jason felt that one thing was wanting, the presence of Aeson, his father, who was prevented by his age and infirmities from taking part in them. Jason said to Medea, "My spouse, would that your arts, whose power I have seen so mighty for my aid, could do me one further service, take some years from my life and add them to my father's." Medea replied, "Not at such a cost shall it be done, but if my art avails me, his life shall be lengthened without abridging yours." The next full moon she issued forth alone, while all creatures slept; not a breath stirred the foliage, and all was still. To the stars she addressed her incantations, and to the moon; to Hecate,[1] the goddess of the under-world, and to Tellus the goddess of the earth, by whose power plants potent for enchantment are produced. She invoked the gods of the woods and caverns, of mountains and valleys, of lakes and rivers, of winds and vapours. While she spoke the stars shone brighter, and presently a chariot descended through the air, drawn by flying serpents. She ascended it, and borne aloft made her way to distant regions, where potent plants grew which she knew how to select for her purpose. Nine nights she employed in her search, and during that time came not within the doors of her palace nor under any roof, and shunned all intercourse with mortals.

She next erected two altars, the one to Hecate, the other to Hebe, the goddess of youth, and sacrificed a black sheep, pouring libations of milk and wine. She implored Pluto and his stolen bride that they would not hasten to take the old man's life. Then she directed that Aeson should be led forth, and having thrown him into a deep sleep by a charm, had him laid on a bed of herbs, like one dead. Jason and all others were kept away from the place, that no profane eyes might look upon her mysteries. Then, with streaming hair, she thrice moved round the altars, dipped flaming twigs in the blood, and laid them thereon to burn. Meanwhile the cauldron with its contents was got ready. In it she put magic herbs, with seeds and flowers of acrid juice, stones from the distant east, and sand from the shore of all-surrounding

[1] Hecate was a mysterious divinity sometimes identified with Diana and sometimes with Proserpine. As Diana represents the moonlight splendour of night, so Hecate represents its darkness and terrors. She was the goddess of sorcery and witchcraft, and was believed to wander by night along the earth, seen only by the dogs, whose barking told her approach.

ocean; hoar frost, gathered by moonlight, a screech owl's head and wings, and the entrails of a wolf. She added fragments of the shells of tortoises, and the liver of stags—animals tenacious of life—and the head and beak of a crow, that outlives nine generations of men. These with many other things "without a name" she boiled together for her purposed work, stirring them up with a dry olive branch; and behold! the branch when taken out instantly became green, and before long was covered with leaves and a plentiful growth of young olives; and as the liquor boiled and bubbled, and sometimes ran over, the grass wherever the sprinklings fell shot forth with a verdure like that of spring.

Seeing that all was ready, Medea cut the throat of the old man and let out all his blood, and poured into his mouth and into his wound the juices of her cauldron. As soon as he had completely imbibed them, his hair and beard laid by their whiteness and assumed the blackness of youth; his paleness and emaciation were gone; his veins were full of blood, his limbs of vigour and robustness. Aeson is amazed at himself, and remembers that such as he now is, he was in his youthful days, forty years before.

Medea used her arts here for a good purpose, but not so in another instance, where she made them the instruments of revenge. Pelias, our readers will recollect, was the usurping uncle of Jason, and had kept him out of his kingdom. Yet he must have had some good qualities, for his daughters loved him, and when they saw what Medea had done for Aeson, they wished her to do the same for their father. Medea pretended to consent, and prepared her cauldron as before. At her request an old sheep was brought and plunged into the cauldron. Very soon a bleating was heard in the kettle, and when the cover was removed, a lamb jumped forth and ran frisking away into the meadow. The daughters of Pelias saw the experiment with delight, and appointed a time for their father to undergo the same operation. But Medea prepared her cauldron for him in a very different way. She put in only water and a few simple herbs. In the night she with the sisters entered the bed chamber of the old king, while he and his guards slept soundly under the influence of a spell cast upon them by Medea. The daughters stood by the bedside with their weapons drawn, but hesitated to strike, till Medea chid their irresolution.

Then turning away their faces, and giving random blows, they smote him with their weapons. He, starting from his sleep, cried out, "My daughters, what are you doing? Will you kill your father?" Their hearts failed them and their weapons fell from their hands, but Medea struck him a fatal blow, and prevented his saying more.

Then they placed him in the cauldron, and Medea hastened to depart in her serpent-drawn chariot before they discovered her treachery, or their vengeance would have been terrible. She escaped, however, but had little enjoyment of the fruits of her crime. Jason, for whom she had done so much, wishing to marry Creusa, princess of Corinth, put away Medea. She, enraged at his ingratitude, called on the gods for vengeance, sent a poisoned robe as a gift to the bride, and then killing her own children, and setting fire to the palace, mounted her serpent-drawn chariot and fled to Athens, where she married King Aegeus, the father of Theseus, and we shall meet her again when we come to the adventures of that hero.

There is another story of Medea almost too revolting for record even of a sorceress, a class of persons to whom both ancient and modern poets have been accustomed to attribute every degree of atrocity. In her flight from Colchis she had taken her young brother Absyrtus with her. Finding the pursuing vessels of Aeetes gaining upon the Argonauts, she caused the lad to be killed and his limbs to be strewn over the sea. Aeetes on reaching the place found these sorrowful fragments of his murdered son; but while he tarried to collect the scattered fragments and bestow upon them an honourable interment, the Argonauts escaped.

18. MELEAGER AND ATALANTA

One of the heroes of the Argonautic expedition was Meleager, son of Oeneus and Althea, king and queen of Calydon. Althea, when her son was born, beheld the three destinies, who as they spun their fatal thread, foretold that the life of the child should last no longer than a brand then burning upon the hearth. Althea seized and quenched the brand, and carefully preserved it for years, while Meleager grew to boyhood, youth and manhood. It chanced, then, that Oeneus, as he offered sacrifices to the gods, omitted to pay due honours to Diana; and she, indignant at the neglect, sent a wild boar of enormous size to lay waste the fields of Calydon. Its eyes shone with blood and fire, its bristles stood like threatening spears, its tusks were like those of Indian elephants. The growing corn was trampled, the vines and olive trees laid waste, the flocks and herds were driven in wild confusion by the slaughtering foe. All common aid seemed vain; but Meleager called on the heroes of Greece to join in a bold hunt for the ravenous monster. Theseus and his friend Pirithous, Jason, Peleus, afterwards the father of Achilles, Telamon the father of Ajax, Nestor, then a youth, but who in his age bore arms with Achilles and Ajax in the Trojan war—these and many more joined in the enterprise. With them came Atalanta, the daughter of Iasius, king of Arcadia. A buckle of polished gold confined her vest, an ivory quiver hung on her left shoulder, and her left hand bore the bow. Her face blent feminine beauty with the best graces of martial youth. Meleager saw and loved.

But now already they were near the monster's lair. They stretched strong nets from tree to tree; they uncoupled their dogs, they tried to find the footprints of their quarry in the grass. From the wood was a descent to marshy grounds. Here the boar, as he lay among the reeds, heard the shouts of his pursuers, and rushed forth against them. One and another is thrown down and slain. Jason throws his spear, with a prayer to Diana for success; and the favouring goddess allows the weapon to touch, but not to wound, removing the steel point of the spear in its flight. Nestor, assailed, seeks and finds safety in the branches of a tree. Telamon rushes on, but stumbling at a projecting root, falls prone. But an arrow from Atalanta at length for the first time tastes the monster's blood. It is a slight wound, but Meleager sees and joyfully proclaims it. Anceus, excited to envy by the praise given to a female, loudly proclaims his own valour, and defies alike the boar and the goddess who had sent it; but as he rushes on, the infuriated beast lays him low with a mortal wound. Theseus throws his lance, but it is turned aside by a projecting bough. The dart of Jason misses its object, and kills instead one of their own dogs. But Meleager, after one unsuccessful stroke, drives his spear into the monster's side, then rushes on and despatches him with repeated blows.

Then rose a shout from those around; they congratulated the conqueror, crowding to touch his hand. He, placing his foot upon the head of the slain boar, turned to Atalanta and bestowed on her the head and the rough hide which were the trophies of his success. But at this, envy excited the rest to strife. Plexippus and Toxeus, the brothers of Meleager's mother, beyond the rest opposed the gift, and snatched from the maiden the trophy she had received. Meleager, kindling with rage at the wrong done to himself, and still more at the insult offered to her whom he loved, forgot the claims of kindred, and plunged his sword into the offenders' hearts.

As Althea bore gifts of thankfulness to the temples for the victory of her son, the bodies of her murdered brothers met her sight. She shrieks, and beats her breast, and hastens to change the garments of rejoicing for those of mourning. But when the author of the deed is known, grief gives way to the stern desire of vengeance on her son. The fatal brand, which once she rescued from the flames, the brand which the destinies had linked with Meleager's life, she brings forth, and commands a fire to be prepared. Then four times she essays to place the brand upon the pile; four times draws back, shuddering at the thought of bringing destruction on her son. The feelings of the mother and the sister contend within her. Now she is pale at the thought of the proposed deed, now flushed again with anger at the act of her son. As a vessel, driven in one direction by the wind, and in the opposite by the tide, the mind of Althea hangs suspended in uncertainty. But now the sister prevails above the mother, and she begins as she holds the fatal wood: "Turn, ye Furies, goddesses of punishment! turn to behold the sacrifice I bring! Crime must atone for crime. Shall Oeneus rejoice in his victor son, while the house of Thestius is desolate? But, alas! to what deed am I borne along? Brothers, forgive a mother's weakness! my hand fails me. He deserves death, but not that I should destroy him. But shall he then live, and triumph, and reign over Calydon, while you, my brothers, wander unavenged among the shades? No! thou hast lived by my gift; die, now, for thine own crime. Return the life which twice I gave thee, first at thy birth, again when I snatched this brand from the flames. O that thou hadst then died! Alas! evil is the conquest; but, brothers, ye have conquered." And, turning away her face, she threw the fatal wood upon the burning pile.

It gave, or seemed to give, a deadly groan. Meleager, absent and unknowing of the cause, felt a sudden pang. He burns, and only by courageous pride conquers the pain which destroys him. He mourns only that he perishes by a bloodless and unhonoured death. With his last breath he calls upon his aged father, his brother, and his fond sisters, upon his beloved Atalanta, and upon his mother, the unknown cause of his fate. The flames increase, and with them the pain of the hero. Now both subside; now both are quenched. The brand is ashes, and the life of Meleager is breathed forth to the wandering winds.

Althea, when the deed was done, laid violent hands upon herself. The sisters of Meleager mourned their brother with uncontrollable grief; till Diana, pitying the sorrows of the house that once had aroused her anger, turned them into birds.

Atalanta

The innocent cause of so much sorrow was a maiden whose face you might truly say was boyish for a girl, yet too girlish for a boy. Her fortune had been told, and it was to this effect: "Atalanta, do not marry; marriage will be your ruin." Terrified by this oracle, she fled the society of men, and devoted herself to the sports of the chase. To all suitors (for she had many) she imposed a condition which was generally effectual in relieving her of their persecutions, —"I will be the prize of him who shall conquer me in the race; but death must be the penalty of all who try and fail." In spite of this hard condition some would try. Hippomenes was to be judge of the race. "Can it be possible that any will be so rash as to risk so much for a wife?" said he. But when he saw her lay aside her robe for the race, he changed his mind, and said, "Pardon me, youths, I knew not the prize you were competing for." As he surveyed them he wished them all to be beaten, and swelled with envy of any

one that seemed at all likely to win. While such were his
thoughts, the virgin darted forward. As she ran she looked
more beautiful than ever. The breezes seemed to give wings
to her feet; her hair flew over her shoulders, and the gay
fringe of her garment fluttered behind her. A ruddy hue
tinged the whiteness of her skin, such as a crimson curtain
casts on a marble wall. All her competitors were distanced,
and were put to death without mercy. Hippomenes, not
daunted by this result, fixing his eyes on the virgin, said,
"Why boast of beating those laggards? I offer myself for the
contest." Atalanta looked at him with a pitying countenance,
and hardly knew whether she would rather conquer him or
not. "What god can tempt one so young and handsome to
throw himself away? I pity him, not for his beauty (yet he is
beautiful), but for his youth. I wish he would give up the
race, or if he will be so mad, I hope he may outrun me."
While she hesitates, revolving these thoughts, the spectators
grow impatient for the race, and her father prompts her to
prepare. Then Hippomenes addressed a prayer to Venus:
"Help me, Venus, for you have led me on." Venus heard
and was propitious.

In the garden of her temple, in her own island of Cyprus,
is a tree with yellow leaves and yellow branches and golden
fruit. Hence she gathered three golden apples, and unseen
by any one else, gave them to Hippomenes, and told him
how to use them. The signal is given; each starts from the
goal and skims over the sand. So light their tread, you would
almost have thought they might run over the river surface
or over the waving grain without sinking. The cries of the
spectators cheered Hippomenes,—"Now, now, do your
best! haste, haste! you gain on her! relax not! one more
effort!" It was doubtful whether the youth or the maiden
heard these cries with the greater pleasure. But his breath
began to fail him, his throat was dry, the goal yet far off. At
that moment he threw down one of the golden apples. The
virgin was all amazement. She stopped to pick it up. Hippomenes shot ahead. Shouts burst forth from all sides. She re-
doubled her efforts, and soon overtook him. Again he threw
an apple. She stopped again, but again came up with him.
The goal was near; one chance only remained. "Now, goddess," said he, "prosper your gift!" and threw the last apple
off at one side. She looked at it, and hesitated; Venus im-

pelled her to turn aside for it. She did so, and was vanquished. The youth carried off his prize.

But the lovers were so full of their own happiness that they forgot to pay due honour to Venus; and the goddess was provoked at their ingratitude. She caused them to give offence to Cybele. That powerful goddess was not to be insulted with impunity. She took from them their human form and turned them into animals of characters resembling their own: of the huntress-heroine, triumphing in the blood of her lovers, she made a lioness, and of her lord and master a lion, and yoked them to her car, where they are still to be seen in all representations, in statuary or painting, of the goddess Cybele.

Cybele is the Latin name of the goddess called by the Greeks Rhea and Ops. She was the wife of Cronos and mother of Zeus. In works of art she exhibits the matronly air which distinguishes Juno and Ceres. Sometimes she is veiled, and seated on a throne with lions at her side, at other times riding in a chariot drawn by lions. She wears a mural crown, that is, a crown whose rim is carved in the form of towers and battlements. Her priests were called Corybantes.

19. HERCULES — HEBE AND GANYMEDE

Hercules

Hercules was the son of Jupiter and Alcmena. As Juno was always hostile to the offspring of her husband by mortal mothers, she declared war against Hercules from his birth. She sent two serpents to destroy him as he lay in his cradle, but the precocious infant strangled them with his own hands. He was, however, by the arts of Juno rendered subject to Eurystheus and compelled to perform all his commands. Eurystheus enjoined upon him a succession of desperate adventures, which are called the "Twelve Labours of Hercules." The first was the fight with the Nemean lion.

The valley of Nemea was infested by a terrible lion. Eurystheus ordered Hercules to bring him the skin of this monster. After using in vain his club and arrows against the lion, Hercules strangled the animal with his hands. He returned carrying the dead lion on his shoulders; but Eurystheus was so frightened at the sight of it and at this proof of the prodigious strength of the hero, that he ordered him to deliver the account of his exploits in future outside the town.

His next labour was the slaughter of the Hydra. This monster ravaged the country of Argos, and dwelt in a swamp near the well of Amymone. This well had been discovered by Amymone when the country was suffering from drought, and the story was that Neptune, who loved her, had permitted her to touch the rock with his trident, and a spring of three outlets burst forth. Here the Hydra took up his position, and Hercules was sent to destroy him. The Hydra had nine heads, of which the middle one was immortal. Hercules struck off its heads with his club, but in the place of the head knocked off, two new ones grew forth each time. At length with the assistance of his faithful servant Iolaus, he burned away the heads of the Hydra, and buried the ninth or immortal one under a huge rock.

Another labour was the cleaning of the Augean stables. Augeas, king of Elis, had a herd of three thousand oxen, whose stalls had not been cleansed for thirty years. Hercules brought the rivers Alpheus and Peneus through them, and cleansed them thoroughly in one day.

His next labour was of a more delicate kind. Admeta, the daughter of Eurystheus, longed to obtain the girdle of the queen of the Amazons, and Eurystheus ordered Hercules to go and get it. The Amazons were a nation of women. They were very warlike and held several flourishing cities. It was their custom to bring up only the female children; the boys were either sent away to the neighbouring nations or put to death. Hercules was accompanied by a number of volunteers, and after various adventures at last reached the country of the Amazons. Hippolyta, the queen, received him kindly, and consented to yield him her girdle, but Juno, taking the form of an Amazon, went and persuaded the rest that the strangers were carrying off their queen. They instantly armed and came in great numbers down to the ship.

Hercules, thinking that Hippolyta had acted treacherously, slew her, and taking her girdle made sail homewards.

Another task enjoined him was to bring to Eurystheus the oxen of Geryon, a monster with three bodies, who dwelt in the island of Erytheia (the red), so called because it lay at the west, under the rays of the setting sun. This description is thought to apply to Spain, of which Geryon was king. After traversing various countries, Hercules reached at length the frontiers of Libya and Europe, where he raised the two mountains of Calpe and Abyla, as monuments of his progress, or, according to another account, rent one mountain into two and left half on each side, forming the straits of Gibraltar, the two mountains being called the Pillars of Hercules. The oxen were guarded by the giant Eurytion and his two-headed dog, but Hercules killed the giant and his dog and brought away the oxen in safety to Eurystheus.

The most difficult labour of all was getting the golden apples of the Hesperides, for Hercules did not know where to find them. These were the apples which Juno had received at her wedding from the goddess of the Earth, and which she had intrusted to the keeping of the daughters of Hesperus, assisted by a watchful dragon. After various adventures Hercules arrived at Mount Atlas in Africa. Atlas was one of the Titans who had warred against the gods, and after they were subdued, Atlas was condemned to bear on his shoulders the weight of the heavens. He was the father of the Hesperides, and Hercules thought might, if any one could, find the apples and bring them to him. But how to send Atlas away from his post, or bear up the heavens while he was gone? Hercules took the burden on his own shoulders, and sent Atlas to seek the apples. He returned with them, and though somewhat reluctantly, took his burden upon his shoulders again, and let Hercules return with the apples to Eurystheus.

Milton, in his "Comus," makes the Hesperides the daughters of Hesperus and nieces of Atlas:

> ". . . amidst the gardens fair
>   Of Hesperus and his daughters three,
>   That sing about the golden tree."

The poets, led by the analogy of the lovely appearance of the western sky at sunset, viewed the west as a region of brightness and glory. Hence they placed in it the Isles of the Blest, the ruddy Isle Erytheia, on which the bright oxen of Geryon were pastured, and the Isle of the Hesperides. The apples are supposed by some to be the oranges of Spain, of which the Greeks had heard some obscure accounts.

A celebrated exploit of Hercules was his victory over Antaeus. Antaeus, the son of Terra, the Earth, was a mighty giant and wrestler, whose strength was invincible so long as he remained in contact with his mother Earth. He compelled all strangers who came to his country to wrestle with him, on condition that if conquered (as they all were) they should be put to death. Hercules encountered him, and finding it was of no avail to throw him, for he always rose with renewed strength from every fall, he lifted him up from the earth and strangled him in the air.

Cacus was a huge giant, who inhabited a cave on Mount Aventine, and plundered the surrounding country. When Hercules was driving home the oxen of Geryon, Cacus stole part of the cattle, while the hero slept. That their footprints might not serve to show where they had been driven, he dragged them backward by their tails to his cave; so their tracks all seemed to show that they had gone in the opposite direction. Hercules was deceived by this stratagem, and would have failed to find his oxen, if it had not happened that in driving the remainder of the herd past the cave where the stolen ones were concealed, those within began to low, and were thus discovered. Cacus was slain by Hercules.

The last exploit we shall record was bringing Cerberus from the lower world. Hercules descended into Hades, accompanied by Mercury and Minerva. He obtained permission from Pluto to carry Cerberus to the upper air, provided he could do it without the use of weapons; and in spite of the monster's struggling, he seized him, held him fast, and carried him to Eurystheus, and afterwards brought him back again. When he was in Hades he obtained the liberty of Theseus, his admirer and imitator, who had been detained a prisoner there for an unsuccessful attempt to carry off Proserpine.

Hercules in a fit of madness killed his friend Iphitus, and

was condemned for this offence to become the slave of Queen Omphale for three years. While in this service the hero's nature seemed changed. He lived effeminately, wearing at times the dress of a woman, and spinning wool with the hand-maidens of Omphale, while the queen wore his lion's skin. When this service was ended he married Dejanira and lived in peace with her three years. On one occasion as he was travelling with his wife, they came to a river, across which the Centaur Nessus carried travellers for a stated fee. Hercules himself forded the river, but gave Dejanira to Nessus to be carried across. Nessus attempted to run away with her, but Hercules heard her cries and shot an arrow into the heart of Nessus. The dying Centaur told Dejanira to take a portion of his blood and keep it, as it might be used as a charm to preserve the love of her husband.

Dejanira did so, and before long fancied she had occasion to use it. Hercules in one of his conquests had taken prisoner a fair maiden, named Iole, of whom he seemed more fond than Dejanira approved. When Hercules was about to offer sacrifices to the gods in honour of his victory, he sent to his wife for a white robe to use on the occasion. Dejanira, thinking it a good opportunity to try her love-spell, steeped the garment in the blood of Nessus. We are to suppose she took care to wash out all traces of it, but the magic power remained, and as soon as the garment became warm on the body of Hercules the poison penetrated into all his limbs and caused him the most intense agony. In his frenzy he seized Lichas, who had brought him the fatal robe, and hurled him into the sea. He wrenched off the garment, but it stuck to his flesh, and with it he tore away whole pieces of his body. In this state he embarked on board a ship and was conveyed home. Dejanira, on seeing what she had unwittingly done, hung herself. Hercules, prepared to die, ascended Mount Oeta, where he built a funeral pile of trees, gave his bow and arrows to Philoctetes, and laid himself down on the pile, his head resting on his club, and his lion's skin spread over him. With a countenance as serene as if he were taking his place at a festal board he commanded Philoctetes to apply the torch. The flames spread apace and soon invested the whole mass.

Milton thus alludes to the frenzy of Hercules:

"As when Alcides [1] from Oechalia crowned
With conquest, felt the envenomed robe, and tore,
Through pain, up by the roots Thessalian pines
And Lichas from the top of Oeta threw
Into the Euboic Sea."

The gods themselves felt troubled at seeing the champion
of the earth so brought to his end. But Jupiter with cheerful
countenance thus addressed them: "I am pleased to see
your concern, my princes, and am gratified to perceive that
I am the ruler of a loyal people, and that my son enjoys
your favour. For although your interest in him arises from
his noble deeds, yet it is not the less gratifying to me. But
now I say to you, Fear not. He who conquered all else is not
to be conquered by those flames which you see blazing on
Mount Oeta. Only his mother's share in him can perish;
what he derived from me is immortal. I shall take him, dead
to earth, to the heavenly shores, and I require of you all to
receive him kindly. If any of you feel grieved at his attain-
ing this honour, yet no one can deny that he has deserved
it." The gods all gave their assent; Juno only heard the closing words with some displeasure that she should be so particularly pointed at, yet not enough to make her regret the
determination of her husband. So when the flames had consumed the mother's share of Hercules, the diviner part, instead of being injured thereby, seemed to start forth with
new vigour, to assume a more lofty port and a more awful
dignity. Jupiter enveloped him in a cloud, and took him up
in a four-horse chariot to dwell among the stars. As he took
his place in heaven, Atlas felt the added weight.

Juno, now reconciled to him, gave him her daughter Hebe
in marriage.

Hebe and Ganymede

Hebe, the daughter of Juno, and goddess of youth, was
cup-bearer to the gods. The usual story is that she resigned
her office on becoming the wife of Hercules. But there is another statement. According to this, Hebe was dismissed from
her office in consequence of a fall which she met with one
day when in attendance on the gods. Her successor was

[1] Alcides, a name of Hercules.

Ganymede, a Trojan boy, whom Jupiter, in the disguise of an eagle, seized and carried off from the midst of his playfellows on Mount Ida, bore up to heaven, and installed in the vacant place.

20. THESEUS AND DAEDALUS — CASTOR AND POLLUX

Theseus

Theseus was the son of Aegeus, king of Athens, and of Aethra, daughter of the king of Troezen. He was brought up at Troezen, and when arrived at manhood was to proceed to Athens and present himself to his father. Aegeus on parting from Aethra, before the birth of his son, placed his sword and shoes under a large stone and directed her to send his son to him when he became strong enough to roll away the stone and take them from under it. When she thought the time had come, his mother led Theseus to the stone, and he removed it with ease and took the sword and shoes. As the roads were infested with robbers, his grandfather pressed him earnestly to take the shorter and safer way to his father's country—by sea; but the youth, feeling in himself the spirit and the soul of a hero, and eager to signalize himself like Hercules, with whose fame all Greece then rang, by destroying the evil-doers and monsters that oppressed the country, determined on the more perilous and adventurous journey by land.

His first day's journey brought him to Epidaurus, where dwelt a man named Periphetes, a son of Vulcan. This ferocious savage always went armed with a club of iron, and all travellers stood in terror of his violence. When he saw Theseus approach he assailed him, but speedily fell beneath the blows of the young hero, who took possession of his club and bore it ever afterwards as a memorial of his first victory.

Several similar contests with the petty tyrants and marauders of the country followed, in all of which Theseus was victorious. One of these evil-doers was called Procrustes, or the Stretcher. He had an iron bedstead, on which he used to tie all travellers who fell into his hands. If they were shorter than the bed, he stretched their limbs to make them fit it; if they were longer than the bed, he lopped off a portion. Theseus served him as he had served others.

Having overcome all the perils of the road, Theseus at length reached Athens, where new dangers awaited him. Medea, the sorceress, who had fled from Corinth after her separation from Jason, had become the wife of Aegeus, the father of Theseus. Knowing by her arts who he was, and fearing the loss of her influence with her husband if Theseus should be acknowledged as his son, she filled the mind of Aegeus with suspicions of the young stranger, and induced him to present him a cup of poison; but at the moment when Theseus stepped forward to take it, the sight of the sword which he wore discovered to his father who he was, and prevented the fatal draught. Medea, detected in her arts, fled once more from deserved punishment, and arrived in Asia, where the country afterwards called Media, received its name from her. Theseus was acknowledged by his father, and declared his successor.

The Athenians were at that time in deep affliction, on account of the tribute which they were forced to pay to Minos, king of Crete. This tribute consisted of seven youths and seven maidens, who were sent every year to be devoured by the Minotaur, a monster with a bull's body and a human head. It was exceedingly strong and fierce, and was kept in a labyrinth constructed by Daedalus, so artfully contrived that whoever was enclosed in it could by no means find his way out unassisted. Here the Minotaur roamed, and was fed with human victims.

Theseus resolved to deliver his countrymen from this calamity, or to die in the attempt. Accordingly, when the time of sending off the tribute came, and the youths and maidens were, according to custom, drawn by lot to be sent, he offered himself as one of the victims, in spite of the entreaties of his father. The ship departed under black sails, as usual, which Theseus promised his father to change for white, in case of his returning victorious. When they arrived in Crete, the youths and maidens were exhibited before

Minos; and Ariadne, the daughter of the king, being present, became deeply enamoured of Theseus, by whom her love was readily returned. She furnished him with a sword, with which to encounter the Minotaur, and with a clue of thread by which he might find his way out of the labyrinth. He was successful, slew the Minotaur, escaped from the labyrinth, and taking Ariadne as the companion of his way, with his rescued companions sailed for Athens. On their way they stopped at the island of Naxos, where Theseus abandoned Ariadne, leaving her asleep. His excuse for this ungrateful treatment of his benefactress was that Minerva appeared to him in a dream and commanded him to do so.

On approaching the coast of Attica, Theseus forgot the signal appointed by his father, and neglected to raise the white sails, and the old king, thinking his son had perished, put an end to his own life. Theseus thus became king of Athens.

One of the most celebrated of the adventures of Theseus is his expedition against the Amazons. He assailed them before they had recovered from the attack of Hercules, and carried off their queen Antiope. The Amazons in their turn invaded the country of Athens and penetrated into the city itself; and the final battle in which Theseus overcame them was fought in the very midst of the city. This battle was one of the favourite subjects of the ancient sculptors, and is commemorated in several works of art that are still extant.

The friendship between Theseus and Pirithous was of a most intimate nature, yet it originated in the midst of arms. Pirithous had made an irruption into the plain of Marathon, and carried off the herds of the king of Athens. Theseus went to repel the plunderers. The moment Pirithous beheld him, he was seized with admiration; he stretched out his hand as a token of peace, and cried, "Be judge thyself—what satisfaction dost thou require?" "Thy friendship," replied the Athenian, and they swore inviolable fidelity. Their deeds corresponded to their professions, and they ever continued true brothers in arms. Each of them aspired to espouse a daughter of Jupiter. Theseus fixed his choice on Helen, then but a child, afterwards so celebrated as the cause of the Trojan war, and with the aid of his friend he carried her off. Pirithous aspired to the wife of the monarch of Erebus; and Theseus, though aware of the danger, accompanied the ambitious lover in his descent to the underworld. But Pluto seized and set them on an enchanted rock at his palace gate, where they remained till Hercules arrived and liberated Theseus, leaving Pirithous to his fate.

After the death of Antiope, Theseus married Phaedra, daughter of Minos, king of Crete. Phaedra saw in Hippolytus, the son of Theseus, a youth endowed with all the graces and virtues of his father, and of an age corresponding to her own. She loved him, but he repulsed her advances, and her love was changed to hate. She used her influence over her infatuated husband to cause him to be jealous of his son, and he imprecated the vengeance of Neptune upon him. As Hippolytus was one day driving his chariot along the shore, a sea-monster raised himself above the waters, and frightened the horses so that they ran away and dashed the chariot to pieces. Hippolytus was killed, but by Diana's assistance Aesculapius restored him to life. Diana removed Hippolytus from the power of his deluded father and false stepmother, and placed him in Italy under the protection of the nymph Egeria.

Theseus at length lost the favour of his people, and retired to the court of Lycomedes, king of Scyros, who at first received him kindly, but afterwards treacherously slew him. In a later age the Athenian general Cimon discovered the place where his remains were laid, and caused them to be removed to Athens, where they were deposited in a temple called the Theseum, erected in honour of the hero.

The queen of the Amazons whom Theseus espoused is by some called Hippolyta. That is the name she bears in Shakespeare's "Midsummer Night's Dream,"—the subject of which is the festivities attending the nuptials of Theseus and Hippolyta.

Theseus is a semi-historical personage. It is recorded of him that he united the several tribes by whom the territory of Attica was then possessed into one state, of which Athens was the capital. In commemoration of this important event, he instituted the festival of Panathenaea, in honour of Minerva, the patron deity of Athens. This festival differed from the other Grecian games chiefly in two particulars. It was peculiar to the Athenians, and its chief feature was a solemn procession in which the Peplus, or sacred robe of Minerva, was carried to the Parthenon, and suspended before the statue of the goddess. The Peplus was covered with embroidery, worked by select virgins of the noblest families in Athens. The procession consisted of persons of all ages and both sexes. The old men carried olive branches in their hands, and the young men bore arms. The young women carried baskets on their heads, containing the sacred utensils, cakes, and all things necessary for the sacrifices. The procession formed the subject of the bas-reliefs which embellished the outside of the temple of the Parthenon. A considerable portion of these sculptures is now in the British Museum among those known as the "Elgin marbles."

Olympic and Other Games

It seems not inappropriate to mention here the other celebrated national games of the Greeks. The first and most distinguished were the Olympic, founded, it was said, by Jupiter himself. They were celebrated at Olympia in Elis. Vast numbers of spectators flocked to them from every part of Greece, and from Asia, Africa and Sicily. They were repeated every fifth year in midsummer, and continued five days. They gave rise to the custom of reckoning time and dating events by Olympiads. The first Olympiad is generally considered as corresponding with the year 776 B.C. The Pythian games were celebrated in the vicinity of Delphi, the Isthmian on the Corinthian Isthmus, the Nemean at Nemea, a city of Argolis.

The exercises in these games were of five sorts: running, leaping, wrestling, throwing the quoit, and hurling the javelin, or boxing. Besides these exercises of bodily strength and agility there were contests in music, poetry and eloquence. Thus these games furnished poets, musicians and authors the best opportunities to present their productions to the public, and the fame of the victors was diffused far and wide.

Daedalus

The labyrinth from which Theseus escaped by means of the clew of Ariadne was built by Daedalus, a most skilful artificer. It was an edifice with numberless winding passages and turnings opening into one another, and seeming to have neither beginning nor end, like the river Maeander, which returns on itself, and flows now onward, now backward, in its course to the sea. Daedalus built the labyrinth for King Minos, but afterwards lost the favour of the king, and was shut up in a tower. He contrived to make his escape from his prison, but could not leave the island by sea, as the king kept strict watch on all the vessels, and permitted none to sail without being carefully searched. "Minos may control the land and sea," said Daedalus, "but not the regions of the air. I will try that way." So he set to work to fabricate wings for himself and his young son Icarus. He wrought feathers together, beginning with the smallest and adding larger, so as to form an increasing surface. The larger ones he secured with thread and the smaller with wax, and gave the whole a gentle curvature like the wings of a bird. Icarus, the boy, stood and looked on, sometimes running to gather up the feathers which the wind had blown away, and then handling the wax and working it over with his fingers, by his play impeding his father in his labours. When at last the work was done, the artist, waving his wings, found himself buoyed upward, and hung suspended, poising himself on the beaten air. He next equipped his son in the same manner and taught him how to fly, as a bird tempts her young ones from the lofty nest into the air. When all was prepared for flight he said, "Icarus, my son, I charge you to keep at a moderate height, for if you fly too low the damp will clog your wings, and if too high the heat will melt them. Keep near me and you will be safe." While he gave him these instructions and fitted the wings to his shoulders, the face of the father was wet with tears, and his hands trembled. He kissed the boy, not knowing that it was for the last time. Then rising on his wings, he flew off, encouraging him to follow, and looked back from his own flight to see how his son managed his wings. As they flew the ploughman stopped his work to gaze, and the shepherd leaned on his staff and watched them, astonished at the sight, and thinking they were gods who could thus cleave the air.

They passed Samos and Delos on the left and Lebynthos on the right, when the boy, exulting in his career, began to leave the guidance of his companion and soar upward as if to reach heaven. The nearness of the blazing sun softened the wax which held the feathers together, and they came off.

He fluttered with his arms, but no feathers remained to hold the air. While his mouth uttered cries to his father it was submerged in the blue waters of the sea, which thenceforth was called by his name. His father cried, "Icarus, Icarus, where are you?" At last he saw the feathers floating on the water, and bitterly lamenting his own arts, he buried the body and called the land Icaria in memory of his child. Daedalus arrived safe in Sicily, where he built a temple to Apollo, and hung up his wings, an offering to the god.

Daedalus was so proud of his achievements that he could not bear the idea of a rival. His sister had placed her son Perdix under his charge to be taught the mechanical arts. He was an apt scholar and gave striking evidences of ingenuity. Walking on the sea-shore he picked up the spine of a fish. Imitating it, he took a piece of iron and notched it on the edge, and thus invented the *saw*. He put two pieces of iron together, connecting them at one end with a rivet, and sharpening the other ends, and made a pair of *compasses*. Daedalus was so envious of his nephew's performances that he took an opportunity, when they were together one day on the top of a high tower, to push him off. But Minerva, who favours ingenuity, saw him falling, and arrested his fate by changing him into a bird called after his name, the Partridge. This bird does not build his nest in the trees, nor take lofty flights, but nestles in the hedges, and mindful of his fall, avoids high places.

Castor and Pollux

Castor and Pollux were the offspring of Leda and the Swan, under which disguise Jupiter had concealed himself. Leda gave birth to an egg from which sprang the twins. Helen, so famous afterwards as the cause of the Trojan war, was their sister.

When Theseus and his friend Pirithous had carried off Helen from Sparta, the youthful heroes, Castor and Pollux, with their followers, hastened to her rescue. Theseus was absent from Attica and the brothers were successful in recovering their sister.

Castor was famous for taming and managing horses, and Pollux for skill in boxing. They were united by the warmest affection and inseparable in all their enterprises. They ac-

companied the Argonautic expedition. During the voyage a
storm arose, and Orpheus prayed to the Samothracian gods,
and played on his harp, whereupon the storm ceased and
stars appeared on the heads of the brothers. From this incident, Castor and Pollux came afterwards to be considered
the patron deities of seamen and voyagers, and the lambent
flames, which in certain states of the atmosphere play round
the sails and masts of vessels, were called by their names.

After the Argonautic expedition, we find Castor and Pollux engaged in a war with Idas and Lynceus. Castor was
slain, and Pollux, inconsolable for the loss of his brother,
besought Jupiter to be permitted to give his own life as a
ransom for him. Jupiter so far consented as to allow the two
brothers to enjoy the boon of life alternately, passing one
day under the earth and the next in the heavenly abodes.
According to another form of the story, Jupiter rewarded
the attachment of the brothers by placing them among the
stars as Gemini the Twins.

They received divine honours under the name of Dioscuri
(sons of Jove). They were believed to have appeared occasionally in later times, taking part with one side or the other,
in hard-fought fields, and were said on such occasions to be
mounted on magnificent white steeds. Thus in the early history of Rome they are said to have assisted the Romans at
the battle of Lake Regillus, and after the victory a temple
was erected in their honour on the spot where they appeared.

21. BACCHUS AND ARIADNE

Bacchus

Bacchus was the son of Jupiter and Semele. Juno, to gratify
her resentment against Semele, contrived a plan for her destruction. Assuming the form of Beroë, her aged nurse, she
insinuated doubts whether it was indeed Jove himself who
came as a lover. Heaving a sigh, she said, "I hope it will
turn out so, but I can't help being afraid. People are not al-

ways what they pretend to be. If he is indeed Jove, make
him give some proof of it. Ask him to come arrayed in all
his splendours, such as he wears in heaven. That will put the
matter beyond a doubt." Semele was persuaded to try the
experiment. She asks a favour, without naming what it is.
Jove gives his promise, and confirms it with the irrevocable
oath, attesting the river Styx, terrible to the gods themselves.
Then she made known her request. The god would have
stopped her as she spake, but she was too quick for him.
The words escaped, and he could neither unsay his promise
nor her request. In deep distress he left her and returned to
the upper regions. There he clothed himself in his splendours, not putting on all his terrors, as when he overthrew
the giants, but what is known among the gods as his lesser
panoply. Arrayed in this, he entered the chamber of Semele.
Her mortal frame could not endure the splendours of the
immortal radiance. She was consumed to ashes.

Jove took the infant Bacchus and gave him in charge to
the Nysaean nymphs, who nourished his infancy and childhood, and for their care were rewarded by Jupiter by being
placed, as the Hyades, among the stars. When Bacchus grew
up he discovered the culture of the vine and the mode of
extracting its precious juice; but Juno struck him with madness, and drove him forth a wanderer through various parts
of the earth. In Phrygia the goddess Rhea cured him and
taught him her religious rites, and he set out on a progress
through Asia, teaching the people the cultivation of the vine.
The most famous part of his wanderings is his expedition to
India, which is said to have lasted several years. Returning
in triumph, he undertook to introduce his worship into
Greece, but was opposed by some princes, who dreaded its
introduction on account of the disorder and madness it
brought with it.

As he approached his native city Thebes, Pentheus the
king, who had no respect for the new worship, forbade its
rites to be performed. But when it was known that Bacchus
was advancing, men and women, but chiefly the latter,
young and old, poured forth to meet him and to join his
triumphal march.

It was in vain Pentheus remonstrated, commanded and
threatened. "Go," said he to his attendants, "seize this vaga-

bond leader of the rout and bring him to me. I will soon make him confess his false claim of heavenly parentage and renounce his counterfeit worship." It was in vain his nearest friends and wisest counsellors remonstrated and begged him not to oppose the god. Their remonstrances only made him more violent.

But now the attendants returned whom he had despatched to seize Bacchus. They had been driven away by the Bacchanals, but had succeeded in taking one of them prisoner, whom, with his hands tied behind him, they brought before the king. Pentheus, beholding him with wrathful countenance, said, "Fellow! you shall speedily be put to death, that your fate may be a warning to others; but though I grudge the delay of your punishment, speak, tell us who you are, and what are these new rites you presume to celebrate."

The prisoner, unterrified, responded, "My name is Acetes; my country is Maeonia; my parents were poor people, who had no fields or flocks to leave me, but they left me their fishing rods and nets and their fisherman's trade. This I followed for some time, till growing weary of remaining in one place, I learned the pilot's art and how to guide my course by the stars. It happened as I was sailing for Delos we touched at the island of Dia and went ashore. Next morning I sent the men for fresh water, and myself mounted the hill to observe the wind; when my men returned bringing with them a prize, as they thought, a boy of delicate appearance, whom they had found asleep. They judged he was a noble youth, perhaps a king's son, and they might get a liberal ransom for him. I observed his dress, his walk, his face. There was something in them which I felt sure was more than mortal. I said to my men, 'What god there is concealed in that form I know not, but some one there certainly is. Pardon us, gentle deity, for the violence we have done you, and give success to our undertakings.' Dictys, one of my best hands for climbing the mast and coming down by the ropes, and Melanthus, my steersman, and Epopeus, the leader of the sailor's cry, one and all exclaimed, 'Spare your prayers for us.' So blind is the lust of gain! When they proceeded to put him on board I resisted them. 'This ship shall not be profaned by such impiety,' said I. 'I have a greater share in her than any of you.' But Lycabas, a turbulent fellow, seized me by the throat and attempted to throw me overboard, and I scarcely saved myself by clinging to the ropes. The rest approved the deed.

"Then Bacchus (for it was indeed he), as if shaking off his drowsiness, exclaimed, 'What are you doing with me? What is this fighting about? Who brought me here? Where are you going to carry me?' One of them replied, 'Fear nothing; tell us where you wish to go and we will take you there.' 'Naxos is my home,' said Bacchus; 'take me there and you shall be well rewarded.' They promised so to do, and told me to pilot the ship to Naxos. Naxos lay to the right, and I was trimming the sails to carry us there, when some by signs and others by whispers signified to me their will that I should sail in the opposite direction, and take the boy to Egypt to sell him for a slave. I was confounded and said, 'Let some one else pilot the ship'; withdrawing myself from any further agency in their wickedness. They cursed me, and one of them, exclaiming, 'Don't flatter yourself that we depend on you for our safety,' took my place as pilot, and bore away from Naxos.

"Then the god, pretending that he had just become aware of their treachery, looked out over the sea and said in a voice of weeping, 'Sailors, these are not the shores you promised to take me to; yonder island is not my home. What have I done that you should treat me so? It is small glory you will gain by cheating a poor boy.' I wept to hear him, but the crew laughed at both of us, and sped the vessel fast over the sea. All at once—strange as it may seem, it is true,—the vessel stopped, in the mid sea, as fast as if it was fixed on the ground. The men, astonished, pulled at their oars, and spread more sail, trying to make progress by the aid of both, but all in vain. Ivy twined round the oars and hindered their motion, and clung to the sails, with heavy clusters of berries. A vine, laden with grapes, ran up the mast, and along the sides of the vessel. The sound of flutes was heard and the odour of fragrant wine spread all around. The god himself had a chaplet of vine leaves, and bore in his hand a spear wreathed with ivy. Tigers crouched at his feet, and forms of lynxes and spotted panthers played around him. The men were seized with terror or madness; some leaped overboard; others preparing to do the same beheld their companions in the water undergoing a change, their bodies becoming flattened and ending in a crooked tail. One exclaimed, 'What miracle is this!' and as he spoke his mouth widened, his nostrils expanded, and scales covered all his body. Another, endeavouring to pull the oar, felt his hands shrink up and presently to be no longer hands but fins; another, trying to raise his arms to a rope, found he had no arms, and curving his mutilated body jumped into the sea. What had been his legs became the two ends of a crescent-shaped tail. The whole crew became dolphins and swam about the ship, now upon the surface, now under it, scattering the spray, and spouting the water from their broad nostrils. Of twenty men I alone was left. Trembling with fear, the god cheered me. "Fear not," said he; 'steer towards Naxos.' I obeyed, and when we arrived there, I kindled the altars and celebrated the sacred rites of Bacchus."

Pentheus here exclaimed, "We have wasted time enough on this silly story. Take him away and have him executed without delay." Acetes was led away by the attendants and shut up fast in prison; but while they were getting ready the instruments of execution the prison doors came open of their own accord and the chains fell from his limbs, and when they looked for him he was nowhere to be found.

Pentheus would take no warning, but instead of sending others, determined to go himself to the scene of the solemnities. The mountain Citheron was all alive with worshippers, and the cries of the Bacchanals resounded on every side. The noise roused the anger of Pentheus as the sound of a trumpet does the fire of a war-horse. He penetrated through the wood and reached an open space where the chief scene of the orgies met his eyes. At the same moment the women saw him; and first among them his own mother, Agave, blinded by the god, cried out, "See there the wild boar, the hugest monster that prowls in these woods! Come on, sisters! I will be the first to strike the wild boar." The whole band rushed upon him, and while he now confesses his crime and implores pardon, they press upon him and wound him. In vain he cries to his aunts to protect him from his mother. Autonoë seized one arm, Ino the other, and between them he was torn to pieces, while his mother shouted, "Victory! Victory! we have done it; the glory is ours!"

So the worship of Bacchus was established in Greece.

Ariadne

We have seen in the story of Theseus how Ariadne, the daughter of King Minos, after helping Theseus to escape from the labyrinth, was carried by him to the island of Naxos and was left there asleep, while the ungrateful Theseus pursued his way home without her. Ariadne, on waking and finding herself deserted, abandoned herself to grief. But Venus took pity on her, and consoled her with the promise that she should have an immortal lover, instead of the mortal one she had lost.

The island where Ariadne was left was the favourite island of Bacchus, the same that he wished the Tyrrhenian mariners to carry him to, when they so treacherously attempted to make prize of him. As Ariadne sat lamenting her fate, Bacchus found her, consoled her, and made her his wife. As a marriage present he gave her a golden crown, enriched with gems, and when she died, he took her crown and threw it up into the sky. As it mounted the gems grew brighter and were turned into stars, and preserving its form Ariadne's crown remains fixed in the heavens as a constellation, between the kneeling Hercules and the man who holds the serpent.

22. THE RURAL DEITIES — ERISICHTHON — RHOECUS — THE WATER DEITIES — THE CAMENAE — THE WINDS

The Rural Deities

Pan, the god of woods and fields, of flocks and shepherds, dwelt in grottos, wandered on the mountains and in valleys, and amused himself with the chase or in leading the dances of the nymphs. He was fond of music, and was, as we have seen, the inventor of the syrinx, or shepherd's pipe, which he himself played in a masterly manner. Pan, like other gods who dwelt in forests, was dreaded by those whose occupations caused them to pass through the woods by night, for the gloom and loneliness of such scenes dispose the mind to superstitious fears. Hence sudden fright without any visible cause was ascribed to Pan, and called a Panic terror.

As the name of the god signifies *all*, Pan came to be considered a symbol of the universe and personification of Nature; and later still to be regarded as a representative of all the gods and of heathenism itself.

Sylvanus and Faunus were Latin divinities, whose characteristics are so nearly the same as those of Pan that we may safely consider them as the same personage under different names.

The wood-nymphs, Pan's partners in the dance, were but one class of nymphs. There were besides them the Naiads, who presided over brooks and fountains, the Oreads, nymphs of mountains and grottos, and the Nereids, sea-nymphs. The three last named were immortal, but the wood-nymphs, called Dryads or Hamadryads, were believed to perish with the trees which had been their abode and with which they had come into existence. It was therefore an impious act wantonly to destroy a tree, and in some aggravated cases was severely punished, as in the instance of Erisichthon, which we are about to record.

Milton in his glowing description of the early creation, thus alludes to Pan as the personification of Nature:

". . . Universal Pan,
  Knit with the Graces and the Hours in dance,
  Led on the eternal spring."

It was a pleasing trait in the old Paganism that it loved to trace in every operation of nature the agency of deity. The imagination of the Greeks peopled all the regions of earth and sea with divinities, to whose agency it attributed those phenomena which our philosophy ascribes to the operation of the laws of nature. Sometimes in our poetical moods we feel disposed to regret the change, and to think that the heart has lost as much as the head has gained by the substitution. The poet Wordsworth thus strongly expresses this sentiment:

> "Great God, I'd rather be
> A Pagan, suckled in a creed outworn,
> So might I, standing on this pleasant lea,
> Have glimpses that would make me less forlorn;
> Have sight of Proteus rising from the sea,
> And hear old Triton blow his wreathed horn."

There is an early Christian tradition that when the heavenly host told the shepherds at Bethlehem of the birth of Christ, a deep groan, heard through all the isles of Greece, told that the great Pan was dead, and that all the royalty of Olympus was dethroned and the several deities were sent wandering in cold and darkness.

Erisichthon

Erisichthon was a profane person and a despiser of the gods. On one occasion he presumed to violate with the axe a grove sacred to Ceres. There stood in this grove a venerable oak, so large that it seemed a wood in itself, its ancient trunk towering aloft, whereon votive garlands were often hung and inscriptions carved expressing the gratitude of suppliants to the nymph of the tree. Often had the Dryads danced round it hand in hand. Its trunk measured fifteen cubits round, and it overtopped the other trees as they overtopped the shrubbery. But for all that, Erisichthon saw no reason why he should spare it and he ordered his servants to cut it down. When he saw them hesitate he snatched an axe from one, and thus impiously exclaimed: "I care not whether it be a tree beloved of the goddess or not; were it the goddess herself it should come down if it stood in my way." So saying, he lifted the axe and the oak seemed to shudder and utter a groan. When the first blow fell upon the trunk blood flowed from the wound. All the bystanders were horror-struck, and one of them ventured to remonstrate and hold back the fatal axe. Erisichthon, with a scornful look, said to him, "Receive the reward of your piety;"

and turned against him the weapon which he had held aside
from the tree, gashed his body with many wounds, and cut
off his head. Then from the midst of the oak came a voice,
"I who dwell in this tree am a nymph beloved of Ceres, and
dying by your hands forewarn you that punishment awaits
you." He desisted not from his crime, and at last the tree,
sundered by repeated blows and drawn by ropes, fell with a
crash and prostrated a great part of the grove in its fall.

The Dryads, in dismay at the loss of their companion and
at seeing the pride of the forest laid low, went in a body to
Ceres, all clad in garments of mourning, and invoked punishment upon Erisichthon. She nodded her assent, and as she
bowed her head the grain ripe for harvest in the laden fields
bowed also. She planned a punishment so dire that one
would pity him, if such a culprit as he could be pitied—to
deliver him over to Famine. As Ceres herself could not approach Famine, for the Fates have ordained that these two
goddesses shall never come together, she called an Oread
from her mountain and spoke to her in these words: "There
is a place in the farthest part of ice-clad Scythia, a sad and
sterile region without trees and without crops. Cold dwells
there, and Fear and Shuddering, and Famine. Go and tell
the last to take possession of the bowels of Erisichthon. Let
not abundance subdue her, nor the power of my gifts drive
her away. Be not alarmed at the distance" (for Famine
dwells very far from Ceres), "but take my chariot. The
dragons are fleet and obey the rein, and will take you
through the air in a short time." So she gave her the reins,
and she drove away and soon reached Scythia. On arriving
at Mount Caucasus she stopped the dragons and found
Famine in a stony field, pulling up with teeth and claws the
scanty herbage. Her hair was rough, her eyes sunk, her face
pale, her lips blanched, her jaws covered with dust, and her
skin drawn tight, so as to show all her bones. As the Oread
saw her afar off (for she did not dare to come near), she
delivered the commands of Ceres; and, though she stopped
as short a time as possible, and kept her distance as well as
she could, yet she began to feel hungry, and turned the
dragons' heads and drove back to Thessaly.

Famine obeyed the commands of Ceres and sped through
the air to the dwelling of Erisichthon, entered the bed-

chamber of the guilty man, and found him asleep. She enfolded him with her wings and breathed herself into him,
infusing her poison into his veins. Having discharged her
task, she hastened to leave the land of plenty and returned
to her accustomed haunts. Erisichthon still slept, and in
his dreams craved food, and moved his jaws as if eating.
When he awoke, his hunger was raging. Without a moment's delay he would have food set before him, of whatever kind earth, sea, or air produces; and complained of
hunger even while he ate. What would have sufficed for a
city or a nation, was not enough for him. The more he ate
the more he craved. His hunger was like the sea, which
receives all the rivers, yet is never filled; or like fire, that
burns all the fuel that is heaped upon it, yet is still vora-
cious for more.

His property rapidly diminished under the unceasing demands of his appetite, but his hunger continued unabated.
At length he had spent all and had only his daughter left,
a daughter worthy of a better parent. Her too he sold. She
scorned to be a slave of a purchaser and as she stood by
the seaside raised her hands in prayer to Neptune. He heard
her prayer, and though her new master was not far off and
had his eye upon her a moment before, Neptune changed
her form and made her assume that of a fisherman busy
at his occupation. Her master, looking for her and seeing
her in her altered form, addressed her and said, "Good
fisherman, whither went the maiden whom I saw just now,
with hair dishevelled and in humble garb, standing about
where you stand? Tell me truly; so may your luck be good
and not a fish nibble at your hook and get away." She perceived that her prayer was answered and rejoiced inwardly
at hearing herself inquired of about herself. She replied,
"Pardon me, stranger, but I have been so intent upon my
line that I have seen nothing else; but I wish I may never
catch another fish if I believe any woman or other person
except myself to have been hereabouts for some time." He
was deceived and went his way, thinking his slave had escaped. Then she resumed her own form. Her father was
well pleased to find her still with him, and the money too
that he got by the sale of her; so he sold her again. But she
was changed by the favour of Neptune as often as she was
sold, now into a horse, now a bird, now an ox, and now a

stag—got away from her purchasers and came home. By
this base method the starving father procured food; but
not enough for his wants, and at last hunger compelled
him to devour his limbs, and he strove to nourish his body
by eating his body, till death relieved him from the vengeance of Ceres.

Rhoecus

The Hamadryads could appreciate services as well as
punish injuries. The story of Rhoecus proves this. Rhoecus,
happening to see an oak just ready to fall, ordered his servants to prop it up. The nymph, who had been on the point
of perishing with the tree, came and expressed her gratitude
to him for having saved her life and bade him ask what
reward he would. Rhoecus boldly asked her love and the
nymph yielded to his desire. She at the same time charged
him to be constant and told him that a bee should be her
messenger and let him know when she would admit his society. One time the bee came to Rhoecus when he was
playing at draughts and he carelessly brushed it away. This
so incensed the nymph that she deprived him of sight.

The Water Deities

Oceanus and Tethys were the Titans who ruled over the
watery elements. When Jove and his brothers overthrew the
Titans and assumed their power, Neptune and Amphitrite
succeeded to the dominion of the waters in place of
Oceanus and Tethys.

Neptune (Poseidon)

Neptune was the chief of the water deities. The symbol
of his power was the trident, or spear with three points, with
which he used to shatter rocks, to call forth or subdue
storms, to shake the shores and the like. He created the
horse and was the patron of horse races. His own horses
had brazen hoofs and golden manes. They drew his chariot
over the sea, which became smooth before him, while the
monsters of the deep gambolled about his path.

Amphitrite

Amphitrite was the wife of Neptune. She was the daughter of Nereus and Doris, and the mother of Triton. Neptune, to pay his court to Amphitrite, came riding on a dolphin. Having won her he rewarded the dolphin by placing him among the stars.

Nereus and Doris

Nereus and Doris were the parents of the Nereids, the most celebrated of whom were Amphitrite, Thetis, the mother of Achilles, and Galatea, who was loved by the Cyclops Polyphemus. Nereus was distinguished for his knowledge and his love of truth and justice, whence he was termed an elder; the gift of prophecy was also assigned to him.

Triton and Proteus

Triton was the son of Neptune and Amphitrite, and the poets made him his father's trumpeter. Proteus was also a son of Neptune. He, like Nereus, is styled a sea-elder for his wisdom and knowledge of future events. His peculiar power was that of changing his shape at will.

Thetis

Thetis, the daughter of Nereus and Doris, was so beautiful that Jupiter himself sought her in marriage; but having learned from Prometheus the Titan that Thetis should bear a son who should be greater than his father, Jupiter desisted from his suit and decreed that Thetis should be the wife of a mortal. By the aid of Chiron the Centaur, Peleus succeeded in winning the goddess for his bride and their son was the renowned Achilles. In our chapter on the Trojan war it will appear that Thetis was a faithful mother to him, aiding him in all difficulties, and watching over his interests from the first to the last.

Leucothea and Palaemon

Ino, the daughter of Cadmus and wife of Athamas, flying from her frantic husband with her little son Melicertes in her arms, sprang from a cliff into the sea. The gods, out of compassion, made her a goddess of the sea, under the name of Leucothea, and him a god, under that of Palaemon. Both were held powerful to save from shipwreck and were invoked by sailors. Palaemon was usually represented riding on a dolphin. The Isthmian games were celebrated in his honour. He was called Portunus by the Romans, and believed to have jurisdiction of the ports and shores.

The Camenae

By this name the Latins designated the Muses, but included under it also some other deities, principally nymphs of fountains. Egeria was one of them, whose fountain and grotto are still shown. It was said that Numa, the second king of Rome, was favoured by this nymph with secret interviews, in which she taught him those lessons of wisdom and of law which he embodied in the institutions of his rising nation. After the death of Numa the nymph pined away and was changed into a fountain.

The Winds

When so many less active agencies were personified, it is not to be supposed that the winds failed to be so. They were Boreas or Aquilo, the north wind; Zephyrus or Favonius, the west; Notus or Auster, the south; and Eurus, the east. The first two have been chiefly celebrated by the poets, the former as the type of rudeness, the latter of gentleness. Boreas loved the nymph Orithyia, and tried to play the lover's part, but met with poor success. It was hard for him to breathe gently, and sighing was out of the question. Weary at last of fruitless endeavours, he acted out his true character, seized the maiden and carried her off. Their children were Zetes and Calais, winged warriors, who accompanied the Argonautic expedition, and did good service in an encounter with those monstrous birds the Harpies.

Zephyrus was the lover of Flora. Milton alludes to them in "Paradise Lost," where he describes Adam waking and contemplating Eve still asleep.

> ". . . He on his side
> Leaning half raised, with looks of cordial love,
> Hung over her enamoured, and beheld
> Beauty which, whether waking or asleep,
> Shot forth peculiar graces; then with voice,
> Mild as when Zephyrus on Flora breathes,
> Her hand soft touching, whispered thus: 'Awake!
> My fairest, my espoused, my latest found,
> Heaven's last, best gift, my ever-new delight.' "

23. ACHELOUS AND HERCULES — ADMETUS AND ALCESTIS — ANTIGONE — PENELOPE

Achelous and Hercules

The river god Achelous told the story of Erisichthon to Theseus and his companions, whom he was entertaining at his hospitable board, while they were delayed on their journey by the overflow of his waters. Having finished his story, he added, "But why should I tell of other persons' transformations when I myself am an instance of the possession of this power? Sometimes I become a serpent, and sometimes a bull, with horns on my head. Or I should say I once could do so; but now I have but one horn, having lost one." And here he groaned and was silent.

Theseus asked him the cause of his grief, and how he lost his horn. To which question the river-god replied as follows: "Who likes to tell of his defeats? Yet I will not hesitate to relate mine, comforting myself with the thought

of the greatness of my conqueror, for it was Hercules. Perhaps you have heard of the fame of Dejanira, the fairest of
maidens, whom a host of suitors strove to win. Hercules
and myself were of the number, and the rest yielded to us
two. He urged in his behalf his descent from Jove and his
labours by which he had exceeded the exactions of Juno,
his stepmother. I, on the other hand, said to the father of
the maiden, 'Behold me, the king of the waters that flow
through your land. I am no stranger from a foreign shore,
but belong to the country, a part of your realm. Let it not
stand in my way that royal Juno owes me no enmity nor
punishes me with heavy tasks. As for this man, who boasts
himself the son of Jove, it is either a false pretence, or dis-
graceful to him if true, for it cannot be true except by his
mother's shame.' As I said this Hercules scowled upon me,
and with difficulty restrained his rage. 'My hand will answer
better than my tongue,' said he. 'I yield to you the victory
in words, but trust my cause to the strife of deeds.' With
that he advanced towards me, and I was ashamed, after
what I had said, to yield. I threw off my green vesture and
presented myself for the struggle. He tried to throw me,
now attacking my head, now my body. My bulk was my
protection, and he assailed me in vain. For a time we
stopped, then returned to the conflict. We each kept our position, determined not to yield, foot to foot, I bending over
him, clenching his hand in mine, with my forehead almost
touching his. Thrice Hercules tried to throw me off, and
the fourth time he succeeded, brought me to the ground,
and himself upon my back. I tell you the truth, it was as if
a mountain had fallen on me. I struggled to get my arms
at liberty, panting and reeking with perspiration. He gave
me no chance to recover, but seized my throat. My knees
were on the earth and my mouth in the dust.

"Finding that I was no match for him in the warrior's
art, I resorted to others and glided away in the form of a
serpent. I curled my body in a coil and hissed at him with
my forked tongue. He smiled scornfully at this, and said,
'It was the labour of my infancy to conquer snakes.' So
saying he clasped my neck with his hands. I was almost
choked, and struggled to get my neck out of his grasp. Vanquished in this form, I tried what alone remained to me
and assumed the form of a bull. He grasped my neck with

his arm, and dragging my head down to the ground, overthrew me on the sand. Nor was this enough. His ruthless
hand rent my horn from my head. The Naiads took it, consecrated it, and filled it with fragrant flowers. Plenty adopted
my horn and made it her own, and called it 'Cornucopia.' "

The ancients were fond of finding a hidden meaning in
their mythological tales. They explain this fight of Achelous
with Hercules by saying Achelous was a river that in seasons of rain overflowed its banks. When the fable says that
Achelous loved Dejanira, and sought a union with her, the
meaning is that the river in its windings flowed through part
of Dejanira's kingdom. It was said to take the form of a
snake because of its winding, and of a bull because it made
a brawling or roaring in its course. When the river swelled,
it made itself another channel. Thus its head was horned.
Hercules prevented the return of these periodical overflows
by embankments and canals; and therefore he was said to
have vanquished the river-god and cut off his horn. Finally,
the lands formerly subject to overflow, but now redeemed,
became very fertile, and this is meant by the horn of plenty.

There is another account of the origin of the Cornucopia.
Jupiter at his birth was committed by his mother Rhea to
the care of the daughters of Melisseus, a Cretan king. They
fed the infant deity with the milk of the goat Amalthea.
Jupiter broke off one of the horns of the goat and gave it
to his nurses, and endowed it with the wonderful power of
becoming filled with whatever the possessor might wish.

The name of Amalthea is also given by some writers to
the mother of Bacchus.

Admetus and Alcestis

Aesculapius, the son of Apollo, was endowed by his
father with such skill in the healing art that he even restored the dead to life. At this Pluto took alarm, and prevailed on Jupiter to launch a thunderbolt at Aesculapius.
Apollo was indignant at the destruction of his son, and
wreaked his vengeance on the innocent workmen who had
made the thunderbolt. These were the Cyclopses, who have
their workshop under Mount Aetna, from which the smoke
and flames of their furnaces are constantly issuing. Apollo
shot his arrows at the Cyclopses, which so incensed Jupiter

that he condemned him as a punishment to become the
servant of a mortal for the space of one year. Accordingly
Apollo went into the service of Admetus, king of Thessaly,
and pastured his flocks for him on the verdant banks of the
river Amphrysos.

Admetus was a suitor, with others, for the hand of Alcestis, the daughter of Pelias, who promised her to him
who should come for her in a chariot drawn by lions and
boars. This task Admetus performed by the assistance of
his divine herdsman, and was made happy in the possession
of Alcestis. But Admetus fell ill, and being near to death,
Apollo prevailed on the Fates to spare him on condition
that some one would consent to die in his stead. Admetus,
in his joy at this reprieve, thought little of the ransom, and
perhaps remembering the declarations of attachment which
he had often heard from his courtiers and dependents fancied that it would be easy to find a substitute. But it was not
so. Brave warriors, who would willingly have perilled their
lives for their prince, shrunk from the thought of dying for
him on the bed of sickness; and old servants who had experienced his bounty and that of his house from their childhood up, were not willing to lay down the scanty remnant
of their days to show their gratitude. Men asked, "Why does
not one of his parents do it? They cannot in the course
of nature live much longer, and who can feel like them the
call to rescue the life they gave from an untimely end?"
But the parents, distressed though they were at the thought
of losing him, shrunk from the call. Then Alcestis, with a
generous self-devotion, proffered herself as the substitute.
Admetus, fond as he was of life, would not have submitted to receive it at such a cost; but there was no remedy.
The condition imposed by the Fates had been met, and the
decree was irrevocable. Alcestis sickened as Admetus revived, and she was rapidly sinking to the grave.

Just at this time Hercules arrived at the Palace of Admetus, and found all the inmates in great distress for the impending loss of the devoted wife and beloved mistress. Hercules, to whom no labour was too arduous, resolved to attempt her rescue. He went and lay in wait at the door of
the chamber of the dying queen, and when Death came for
his prey, he seized him and forced him to resign his victim.
Alcestis recovered, and was restored to her husband.

Milton alludes to the story of Alcestis in his Sonnet "on his deceased wife":

"Methought I saw my late espoused saint
  Brought to me like Alcestis from the grave,
  Whom Jove's great son to her glad husband gave,
Rescued from death by force, though pale and faint."

Antigone

Antigone was as bright an example of filial and sisterly fidelity as was Alcestis of connubial devotion. She was the daughter of Oedipus and Jocasta, who with all their descendants were the victims of an unrelenting fate, dooming them to destruction. Oedipus in his madness had torn out his eyes, and was driven forth from his kingdom Thebes, dreaded and abandoned by all men, as an object of divine vengeance. Antigone, his daughter, alone shared his wanderings and remained with him till he died, and then returned to Thebes.

Her brothers, Eteocles and Polynices, had agreed to share the kingdom between them, and reign alternately year by year. The first year fell to the lot of Eteocles, who, when his time expired, refused to surrender the kingdom to his brother. Polynices fled to Adrastus, king of Argos, who gave him his daughter in marriage, and aided him with an army to enforce his claim to the kingdom. This led to the celebrated expedition of the "Seven against Thebes," which furnished ample materials for the epic and tragic poets of Greece.

Amphiaraus, the brother-in-law of Adrastus, opposed the enterprise, for he was a soothsayer, and knew by his art that no one of the leaders except Adrastus would live to return. But Amphiaraus, on his marriage to Eriphyle, the king's sister, had agreed that whenever he and Adrastus should differ in opinion, the decision should be left to Eriphyle. Polynices, knowing this, gave Eriphyle the collar of Harmonia, and thereby gained her to his interest. This collar or necklace was a present which Vulcan had given to Harmonia on her marriage with Cadmus, and Polynices had taken it with him on his flight from Thebes. Eriphyle could not resist so tempting a bribe, and by her decision the war

was resolved on, and Amphiaraus went to his certain fate.
He bore his part bravely in the contest, but could not avert
his destiny. Pursued by the enemy, he fled along the river,
when a thunderbolt launched by Jupiter opened the ground,
and he, his chariot, and his charioteer were swallowed up.

It would not be in place here to detail all the acts of
heroism or atrocity which marked the contest; but we must
not omit to record the fidelity of Evadne as an offset to the
weakness of Eriphyle. Capaneus, the husband of Evadne, in
the ardour of the fight declared that he would force his way
into the city in spite of Jove himself. Placing a ladder
against the wall he mounted, but Jupiter, offended at his
impious language, struck him with a thunderbolt. When his
obsequies were celebrated, Evadne cast herself on his funeral pile and perished.

Early in the contest Eteocles consulted the soothsayer
Tiresias as to the issue. Tiresias in his youth had by chance
seen Minerva bathing. The goddess in her wrath deprived
him of his sight, but afterwards relenting gave him in com-
pensation the knowledge of future events. When consulted
by Eteocles, he declared that victory should fall to Thebes
if Menoeceus, the son of Creon, gave himself a voluntary
victim. The heroic youth, learning the response, threw away
his life in the first encounter.

The siege continued long, with various success. At length
both hosts agreed that the brothers should decide their quarrel by single combat. They fought and fell by each other's
hands. The armies then renewed the fight, and at last the
invaders were forced to yield, and fled, leaving their dead
unburied. Creon, the uncle of the fallen princes, now become king, caused Eteocles to be buried with distinguished
honour, but suffered the body of Polynices to lie where it
fell, forbidding every one on pain of death to give it burial.

Antigone, the sister of Polynices, heard with indignation
the revolting edict which consigned her brother's body to
the dogs and vultures, depriving it of those rites which were
considered essential to the repose of the dead. Unmoved
by the dissuading counsel of an affectionate but timid sister,
and unable to procure assistance, she determined to brave
the hazard, and to bury the body with her own hands. She
was detected in the act, and Creon gave orders that she
should be buried alive, as having deliberately set at naught

the solemn edict of the city. Her lover, Haemon, the son of Creon, unable to avert her fate, would not survive her, and fell by his own hand.

Antigone forms the subject of two fine tragedies of the Grecian poet Sophocles.

Penelope

Penelope is another of those mythic heroines whose beauties were rather those of character and conduct than of person. She was the daughter of Icarius, a Spartan prince. Ulysses, king of Ithaca, sought her in marriage, and won her, over all competitors. When the moment came for the bride to leave her father's house, Icarius, unable to bear the thoughts of parting with his daughter, tried to persuade her to remain with him, and not accompany her husband to Ithaca. Ulysses gave Penelope her choice, to stay or go with him. Penelope made no reply, but dropped her veil over her face. Icarius urged her no further, but when she was gone erected a statue to Modesty on the spot where they parted.

Ulysses and Penelope had not enjoyed their union more than a year when it was interrupted by the events which called Ulysses to the Trojan war. During his long absence, and when it was doubtful whether he still lived, and highly improbable that he would ever return, Penelope was importuned by numerous suitors, from whom there seemed no refuge but in choosing one of them for her husband. Penelope, however, employed every art to gain time, still hoping for Ulysses' return. One of her arts of delay was engaging in the preparation of a robe for the funeral canopy of Laertes, her husband's father. She pledged herself to make her choice among the suitors when the robe was finished. During the day she worked at the robe, but in the night she undid the work of the day. This is the famous Penelope's web, which is used as a proverbial expression for anything which is perpetually doing but never done. The rest of Penelope's history will be told when we give an account of her husband's adventures.

Orpheus and Eurydice

Orpheus was the son of Apollo and the Muse Calliope. He was presented by his father with a lyre and taught to play upon it, which he did to such perfection that nothing could withstand the charm of his music. Not only his fellow-mortals, but wild beasts were softened by his strains, and gathering round him laid by their fierceness, and stood entranced with his lay. Nay, the very trees and rocks were sensible to the charm. The former crowded round him and the latter relaxed somewhat of their hardness, softened by his notes.

Hymen had been called to bless with his presence the nuptials of Orpheus with Eurydice; but though he attended, he brought no happy omens with him. His very torch smoked and brought tears into their eyes. In coincidence with such prognostics, Eurydice, shortly after her marriage, while wandering with the nymphs, her companions, was seen by the shepherd Aristaeus, who was struck by her beauty and made advances to her. She fled, and in flying trod upon a snake in the grass, was bitten in the foot, and died. Orpheus sang his grief to all who breathed the upper air, both gods and men, and finding it all unavailing resolved to seek his wife in the regions of the dead. He descended by a cave situated on the side of the promontory of Taenarus and arrived at the Stygian realm. He passed through crowds of ghosts and presented himself before the throne of Pluto and Proserpine. Accompanying the words with the lyre, he sung, "O deities of the under-world, to whom all we who live must come, hear my words, for they are true. I come not to spy out the secrets of Tartarus, nor to try my strength against the three-headed dog with snaky hair who guards the entrance. I come to seek my wife, whose opening years the poisonous viper's fang has brought to an un-

timely end. Love has led me here, Love, a god all powerful
with us who dwell on the earth, and, if old traditions say
true, not less so here. I implore you by these abodes full
of terror, these realms of silence and uncreated things,
unite again the thread of Eurydice's life. We all are destined to you, and sooner or later must pass to your domain.
She too, when she shall have filled her term of life, will
rightly be yours. But till then grant her to me, I beseech
you. If you deny me, I cannot return alone; you shall triumph in the death of us both."

As he sang these tender strains, the very ghosts shed tears.
Tantalus, in spite of his thirst, stopped for a moment his
efforts for water, Ixion's wheel stood still, the vulture ceased
to tear the giant's liver, the daughters of Danaus rested
from their task of drawing water in a sieve, and Sisyphus
sat on his rock to listen. Then for the first time, it is said,
the cheeks of the Furies were wet with tears. Proserpine
could not resist, and Pluto himself gave way. Eurydice was
called. She came from among the new-arrived ghosts, limp-
ing with her wounded foot. Orpheus was permitted to take
her away with him on one condition, that he should not
turn around to look at her till they should have reached
the upper air. Under this condition they proceeded on their
way, he leading, she following, through passages dark and
steep, in total silence, till they had nearly reached the outlet
into the cheerful upper world, when Orpheus, in a moment
of forgetfulness, to assure himself that she was still following, cast a glance behind him, when instantly she was borne
away. Stretching out their arms to embrace each other,
they grasped only the air! Dying now a second time, she yet
cannot reproach her husband, for how can she blame his
impatience to behold her? "Farewell," she said, "a last farewell,"—and was hurried away, so fast that the sound hardly
reached his ears.

Orpheus endeavoured to follow her, and besought permission to return and try once more for her release; but the
stern ferryman repulsed him and refused passage. Seven
days he lingered about the brink, without food or sleep;
then bitterly accusing of cruelty the powers of Erebus, he
sang his complaints to the rocks and mountains, melting
the hearts of tigers and moving the oaks from their stations.
He held himself aloof from womankind, dwelling constantly

on the recollection of his sad mischance. The Thracian
maidens tried their best to captivate him, but he repulsed
their advances. They bore with him as long as they could;
but finding him insensible one day, excited by the rites of
Bacchus, one of them exclaimed, "See yonder our despiser!"
and threw at him her javelin. The weapon, as soon as it
came within the sound of his lyre, fell harmless at his feet.
So did also the stones that they threw at him. But the
women raised a scream and drowned the voice of the music,
and then the missiles reached him and soon were stained
with his blood. The maniacs tore him limb from limb, and
threw his head and his lyre into the river Hebrus, down
which they floated, murmuring sad music, to which the
shores responded a plaintive symphony. The Muses gathered up the fragments of his body and buried them at Li-
bethra, where the nightingale is said to sing over his grave
more sweetly than in any other part of Greece. His lyre
was placed by Jupiter among the stars. His shade passed a
second time to Tartarus, where he sought out his Eurydice
and embraced her with eager arms. They roam the happy
fields together now, sometimes he leading, sometimes she;
and Orpheus gazes as much as he will upon her, no longer in-
curring a penalty for a thoughtless glance.

Aristaeus, the Bee-Keeper

Man avails himself of the instincts of the inferior animals
for his own advantage. Hence sprang the art of keeping
bees. Honey must first have been known as a wild product,
the bees building their structures in hollow trees or holes
in the rocks, or any similar cavity that chance offered. Thus
occasionally the carcass of a dead animal would be occupied by the bees for that purpose. It was no doubt from
some such incident that the superstition arose that the bees
were engendered by the decaying flesh of the animal; and
Virgil, in the following story, shows how this supposed fact
may be turned to account for renewing the swarm when it
has been lost by disease or accident.

Aristaeus, who first taught the management of bees, was
the son of the water-nymph Cyrene. His bees had perished,
and he resorted for aid to his mother. He stood at the river-
side and thus addressed her: "O mother, the pride of my life

is taken from me! I have lost my precious bees. My care and skill have availed me nothing, and you, my mother, have not warded off from me the blow of misfortune." His mother heard these complaints as she sat in her palace at the bottom of the river, with her attendant nymphs around her. They were engaged in female occupations, spinning and weaving, while one told stories to amuse the rest. The sad voice of Aristaeus interrupting their occupation, one of them put her head above the water and seeing him, returned and gave information to his mother, who ordered that he should be brought into her presence. The river at her command opened itself and let him pass in, while it stood curled like a mountain on either side. He descended to the region where the fountains of the great rivers lie; he saw the enormous receptacles of waters and was almost deafened with the roar, while he surveyed them hurrying off in various directions to water the face of the earth. Arriving at his mother's apartment, he was hospitably received by Cyrene and her nymphs, who spread their table with the richest dainties. They first poured out libations to Neptune, then regaled themselves with the feast, and after that Cyrene thus addressed him: "There is an old prophet named Proteus, who dwells in the sea and is a favourite of Neptune, whose herd of sea-calves he pastures. We nymphs hold him in great respect, for he is a learned sage and knows all things, past, present, and to come. He can tell you, my son, the cause of the mortality among your bees and how you may remedy it. But he will not do it voluntarily, however you may entreat him. You must compel him by force. If you seize him and chain him, he will answer your questions in order to get released, for he cannot by all his arts get away if you hold fast the chains. I will carry you to his cave, where he comes at noon to take his midday repose. Then you may easily secure him. But when he finds himself captured, his resort is to a power he possesses of changing himself into various forms. He will become a wild boar or a fierce tiger, a scaly dragon or lion with yellow mane. Or he will make a noise like the crackling of flames or the rush of water, so as to tempt you to let go the chain, when he will make his escape. But you have only to keep him fast bound, and at last when he finds all his arts unavailing, he will return to his own figure and obey your commands." So saying she sprinkled her son with fragrant nectar, the beverage of the gods, and immediately an unusual vigour filled his frame, and courage his heart, while perfume breathed all around him.

The nymph led her son to the prophet's cave and concealed him among the recesses of the rocks, while she herself took her place behind the clouds. When noon came and the hour when men and herds retreat from the glaring sun to indulge in quiet slumber, Proteus issued from the water, followed by his herd of sea-calves which spread themselves along the shore. He sat on the rock and counted his herd; then stretched himself on the floor of the cave and went to sleep. Aristaeus hardly allowed him to get fairly asleep before he fixed the fetters on him and shouted aloud. Proteus, waking and finding himself captured, immediately resorted to his arts, becoming first a fire, then a flood, then a horrible wild beast, in rapid succession. But finding all would not do, he at last resumed his own form and addressed the youth in angry accents: "Who are you, bold youth, who thus invade my abode, and what do you want with me?" Aristaeus replied, "Proteus, you know already, for it is needless for any one to attempt to deceive you. And do you also cease your efforts to elude me. I am led hither by divine assistance, to know from you the cause of my misfortune and how to remedy it." At these words the prophet, fixing on him his grey eyes with a piercing look, thus spoke: "You receive the merited reward of your deeds, by which Eurydice met her death, for in flying from you she trod upon a serpent, of whose bite she died. To avenge her death, the nymphs, her companions, have sent this destruction to your bees. You have to appease their anger, and thus it must be done: Select four bulls, of perfect form and size, and four cows of equal beauty, build four altars to the nymphs, and sacrifice the animals, leaving their carcasses in the leafy grove. To Orpheus and Eurydice you shall pay such funeral honours as may allay their resentment. Returning after nine days, you will examine the bodies of the cattle slain and see what will befall." Aristaeus faithfully obeyed these directions. He sacrificed the cattle, he left their bodies in the grove, he offered funeral honours to the shades of Orpheus and Eurydice; then returning on the ninth day he examined the bodies of the animals, and,

wonderful to relate! a swarm of bees had taken possession
of one of the carcasses and were pursuing their labours
there as in a hive.

Amphion

Amphion was the son of Jupiter and Antiope, queen of
Thebes. With his twin brother Zethus, he was exposed at
birth on Mount Cithaeron, where they grew up among the
shepherds, not knowing their parentage. Mercury gave
Amphion a lyre and taught him to play upon it, and his
brother occupied himself in hunting and tending the flocks.
Meanwhile Antiope, their mother, who had been treated
with great cruelty by Lycus, the usurping king of Thebes,
and by Dirce, his wife, found means to inform her children of their rights and to summon them to her assistance.
With a band of their fellow-herdsmen they attacked and
slew Lycus, and tying Dirce by the hair of her head to a
bull, let him drag her till she was dead. Amphion, having
become king of Thebes, fortified the city with a wall. It is
said that when he played on his lyre the stones moved of
their own accord and took their places in the wall.

Linus

Linus was the instructor of Hercules in music, but having
one day reproved his pupil rather harshly, he roused the
anger of Hercules, who struck him with his lyre and killed
him.

Thamyris

An ancient Thracian bard, who in his presumption challenged the Muses to a trial of skill, and being overcome in
the contest, was deprived by them of his sight. Milton alludes to him with other blind bards, when speaking of his
own blindness, "Paradise Lost," Book III. 35.

Marsyas

Minerva invented the flute, and played upon it to the delight of all the celestial auditors; but the mischievous urchin

Cupid having dared to laugh at the queer face which the goddess made while playing, Minerva threw the instrument indignantly away, and it fell down to earth and was found by Marsyas. He blew upon it, and drew from it such ravishing sounds that he was tempted to challenge Apollo himself to a musical contest. The god of course triumphed, and punished Marsyas by flaying him alive.

Melampus

Melampus was the first mortal endowed with prophetic powers. Before his house there stood an oak tree containing a serpent's nest. The old serpents were killed by the servants, but Melampus took care of the young ones and fed them carefully. One day when he was asleep under the oak the serpents licked his ears with their tongues. On awaking he was astonished to find that he now understood the language of birds and creeping things. This knowledge enabled him to foretell future events, and he became a renowned soothsayer. At one time his enemies took him captive and kept him strictly imprisoned. Melampus in the silence of the night heard the woodworms in the timbers talking together, and found out by what they said that the timbers were nearly eaten through and the roof would soon fall in. He told his captors and demanded to be let out, warning them also. They took his warning, and thus escaped destruction, and rewarded Melampus and held him in high honour.

25. ARION — IBYCUS

Arion

Arion was a famous musician, and dwelt at the court of Periander, king of Corinth, with whom he was a great favourite. There was to be a musical contest in Sicily, and Arion longed to compete for the prize. He told his wish to Periander, who besought him like a brother to give up the thought. "Pray stay with me," he said, "and be contented. He who strives to win may lose." Arion answered, "A wandering life best suits the free heart of a poet. The talent which a god bestowed on me, I would fain make a source of pleasure to others. And if I win the prize, how will the enjoyment of it be increased by the consciousness of my widespread fame!" He went, won the prize, and embarked with his wealth in a Corinthian ship for home. On the second morning after setting sail, the wind breathed mild and fair. "O Periander," he exclaimed, "dismiss your fears! Soon shall you forget them in my embrace. With what lavish offerings will we display our gratitude to the gods, and how merry will we be at the festal board!" The wind and sea continued propitious. Not a cloud dimmed the firmament. He had not trusted too much to the ocean—but he had to man. He overheard the seamen exchanging hints with one another, and found they were plotting to possess themselves of his treasure. Presently they surrounded him loud and mutinous, and said, "Arion, you must die! If you would have a grave on shore, yield yourself to die on this spot; but if otherwise, cast yourself into the sea." "Will nothing satisfy you but my life?" said he. "Take my gold, and welcome, I willingly buy my life at that price." "No, no; we cannot spare you. Your life would be too dangerous to us. Where could we go to escape from Periander, if he should know that you had been robbed by us? Your gold would be of little use to us, if, on returning home, we could nevermore be free from fear." "Grant me, then," said he, "a last request, since nought will avail to save my life, that I may die, as I have lived, as becomes a bard. When I shall have sung my death song, and my harp-strings shall have ceased to vibrate, then I will bid farewell to life, and yield uncomplaining to my fate." This prayer, like the others, would have been unheeded,—they thought only of their booty,—but to hear so famous a musician, that moved their rude hearts. "Suffer me," he added, "to arrange my dress. Apollo will not favour me unless I be clad in my minstrel garb."

He clothed his well-proportioned limbs in gold and purple fair to see, his tunic fell around him in graceful folds, jewels adorned his arms, his brow was crowned with a golden wreath, and over his neck and shoulders flowed his hair

perfumed with odours. His left hand held the lyre, his right
the ivory wand with which he struck its chords. Like one
inspired, he seemed to drink the morning air and glitter
in the morning ray. The seamen gazed with admiration.
He strode forward to the vessel's side and looked down into
the deep blue sea. Addressing his lyre, he sang, "Companion of my voice, come with me to the realm of shades.
Though Cerberus may growl, we know the power of song
can tame his rage. Ye heroes of Elysium, who have passed
the darkling flood,—ye happy souls, soon shall I join your
band. Yet can ye relieve my grief? Alas, I leave my friend
behind me. Thou, who didst find thy Eurydice, and lose her
again as soon as found; when she had vanished like a dream,
how didst thou hate the cheerful light! I must away, but I
will not fear. The gods look down upon us. Ye who slay
me unoffending, when I am no more, your time of trembling shall come. Ye Nereids, receive your guest, who
throws himself upon your mercy!" So saying, he sprang
into the deep sea. The waves covered him, and the seamen
held on their way, fancying themselves safe from all danger of detection.

But the strains of his music had drawn round him the inhabitants of the deep to listen, and Dolphins followed the
ship as if chained by a spell. While he struggled in the
waves, a Dolphin offered him his back, and carried him
mounted thereon safe to shore. At the spot where he landed,
a monument of brass was afterwards erected upon the
rocky shore, to preserve the memory of the event.

When Arion and the Dolphin parted, each to his own
element, Arion thus poured forth his thanks: "Farewell,
thou faithful, friendly fish! Would that I could reward
thee; but thou canst not wend with me, nor I with thee.
Companionship we may not have. May Galatea, queen of
the deep, accord thee her favour, and thou, proud of the
burden, draw her chariot over the smooth mirror of the
deep."

Arion hastened from the shore, and soon saw before him
the towers of Corinth. He journeyed on, harp in hand,
singing as he went, full of love and happiness, forgetting his
losses, and mindful only of what remained, his friend and
his lyre. He entered the hospitable halls, and was soon

clasped in the embrace of Periander. "I come back to thee, my friend," he said. "The talent which a god bestowed has been the delight of thousands, but false knaves have stripped me of my well-earned treasure; yet I retain the consciousness of widespread fame." Then he told Periander all the wonderful events that had befallen him, who heard him with amazement. "Shall such wickedness triumph?" said he. "Then in vain is power lodged in my hands. That we may discover the criminals, you must remain here in concealment, and so they will approach without suspicion." When the ship arrived in the harbour, he summoned the mariners before him. "Have you heard anything of Arion?" he inquired. "I anxiously look for his return." They replied, "We left him well and prosperous in Tarentum." As they said these words, Arion stepped forth and faced them. His well-proportioned limbs were arrayed in gold and purple fair to see, his tunic fell around him in graceful folds, jewels adorned his arms, his brow was crowned with a golden wreath, and over his neck and shoulders flowed his hair perfumed with odours; his left hand held the lyre, his right the ivory wand with which he struck its chords. They fell prostrate at his feet, as if a lightning bolt had struck them. "We meant to murder him, and he has become a god. O Earth, open and receive us!" Then Periander spoke. "He lives, the master of the lay! Kind Heaven protects the poet's life. As for you, I invoke not the spirit of vengeance; Arion wishes not your blood. Ye slaves of avarice, begone! Seek some barbarous land, and never may aught beautiful delight your souls!"

Ibycus

In order to understand the story of Ibycus which follows it is necessary to remember, first, that the theatres of the ancients were immense fabrics capable of containing from ten to thirty thousand spectators, and as they were used only on festal occasions, and admission was free to all, they were usually filled. They were without roofs and open to the sky, and the performances were in the daytime. Secondly, the appalling representation of the Furies is not exaggerated in the story. It is recorded that Aeschylus, the tragic poet, having on one occasion represented the Furies in a chorus of fifty performers, the terror of the spectators was such that many fainted and were thrown into convulsions, and the magistrates forbade a like representation for the future.

Ibycus, the pious poet, was on his way to the chariot races and musical competitions held at the Isthmus of Corinth, which attracted all of Grecian lineage. Apollo had bestowed on him the gift of song, the honeyed lips of the poet, and he pursued his way with lightsome step, full of the god. Already the towers of Corinth crowning the height appeared in view, and he had entered with pious awe the sacred grove of Neptune. No living object was in sight, only a flock of cranes flew overhead taking the same course as himself in their migration to a southern clime. "Good luck to you, ye friendly squadrons," he exclaimed, "my companions from across the sea. I take your company for a good omen. We come from far and fly in search of hospitality. May both of us meet that kind reception which shields the stranger guest from harm!"

He paced briskly on, and soon was in the middle of the wood. There suddenly, at a narrow pass, two robbers stepped forth and barred his way. He must yield or fight. But his hand, accustomed to the lyre, and not to the strife of arms, sank powerless. He called for help on men and gods, but his cry reached no defender's ear. "Then here must I die," said he, "in a strange land, unlamented, cut off by the hand of outlaws, and see none to avenge my cause." Sore wounded, he sank to the earth, when hoarse screamed the cranes overhead. "Take up my cause, ye cranes," he said, "since no voice but yours answers to my cry." So saying he closed his eyes in death.

The body, despoiled and mangled, was found, and though disfigured with wounds, was recognized by the friend in Corinth who had expected him as a guest. "Is it thus I find you restored to me?" he exclaimed. "I who hoped to entwine your temples with the wreath of triumph in the strife of song!"

The guests assembled at the festival heard the tidings with dismay. All Greece felt the wound, every heart owned its loss. They crowded round the tribunal of the magistrates, and demanded vengeance on the murderers and expiation with their blood.

But what trace or mark shall point out the perpetrator from amidst the vast multitude attracted by the splendour of the feast? Did he fall by the hands of robbers or did some private enemy slay him? The all-discerning sun alone can tell, for no other eye beheld it. Yet not improbably the murderer even now walks in the midst of the throng, and enjoys the fruits of his crime, while vengeance seeks for him in vain. Perhaps in their own temple's enclosure he defies the gods, mingling freely in this throng of men that now presses into the amphitheatre.

For now crowded together, row on row, the multitude fills the seats till it seems as if the very fabric would give way. The murmur of voices sounds like the roar of the sea, while the circles widening in their ascent rise tier on tier, as if they would reach the sky.

And now the vast assemblage listens to the awful voice of the chorus personating the Furies, which in solemn guise advances with measured step, and moves around the circuit of the theatre. Can they be mortal women who compose that awful group, and can that vast concourse of silent forms be living beings?

The choristers, clad in black, bore in their fleshless hands torches blazing with a pitchy flame. Their cheeks were bloodless, and in place of hair writhing and swelling serpents curled around their brows. Forming a circle, these awful beings sang their hymns, rending the hearts of the guilty, and enchaining all their faculties. It rose and swelled, overpowering the sound of the instruments, stealing the judgment, palsying the heart, curdling the blood.

"Happy the man who keeps his heart pure from guilt and crime! Him we avengers touch not; he treads the path of life secure from us. But woe! woe! to him who has done the deed of secret murder. We, the fearful family of Night, fasten ourselves upon his whole being. Thinks he by flight to escape us? We fly still faster in pursuit, twine our snakes around his feet, and bring him to the ground. Unwearied we pursue; no pity checks our course; still on and on, to the end of life, we give him no peace nor rest." Thus the Eumenides sang, and moved in solemn cadence, while stillness like the stillness of death sat over the whole assembly as if in the presence of superhuman beings; and then in solemn march completing the circuit of the theatre, they passed out at the back of the stage.

Every heart fluttered between illusion and reality, and every breast panted with undefined terror, quailing before the awful power that watches secret crimes and winds unseen the skein of destiny. At that moment a cry burst forth from one of the uppermost benches—"Look! look! comrade, yonder are the cranes of Ibycus!" And suddenly there appeared sailing across the sky a dark object which a moment's inspection showed to be a flock of cranes flying directly over the theatre. "Of Ibycus! did he say?" The beloved name revived the sorrow in every breast. As wave follows wave over the face of the sea, so ran from mouth to mouth the words, "Of Ibycus! him whom we all lament, whom some murderer's hand laid low! What have the cranes to do with him?" And louder grew the swell of voices, while like a lightning's flash the thought sped through every heart, "Observe the power of the Eumenides! The pious poet shall be avenged! the murderer has informed against himself. Seize the man who uttered that cry and the other to whom he spoke!"

The culprit would gladly have recalled his words, but it was too late. The faces of the murderers, pale with terror, betrayed their guilt. The people took them before the judge, they confessed their crime, and suffered the punishment they deserved.

26. ENDYMION — ORION — AURORA AND TITHONUS — ACIS AND GALATEA

Endymion was a beautiful youth who fed his flock on Mount Latmos. One calm, clear night, Diana, the moon, looked down and saw him sleeping. The cold heart of the virgin goddess was warmed by his surpassing beauty, and she came down to him, kissed him, and watched over him while he slept.

Another story was that Jupiter bestowed on him the gift of perpetual youth united with perpetual sleep. Of one so gifted we can have but few adventures to record. Diana, it was said, took care that his fortunes should not suffer by his inactive life, for she made his flock increase, and guarded his sheep and lambs from the wild beasts.

Orion

Orion was the son of Neptune. He was a handsome giant and a mighty hunter. His father gave him the power of wading through the depths of the sea, or, as others say, of walking on its surface.

Orion loved Merope, the daughter of Oenopion, king of Chios, and sought her in marriage. He cleared the island of wild beasts, and brought the spoils of the chase as presents to his beloved; but as Oenopion constantly deferred his consent, Orion attempted to gain possession of the maiden by violence. Her father, incensed at this conduct, having made Orion drunk, deprived him of his sight and cast him out on the seashore. The blinded hero followed the sound of a Cyclops' hammer till he reached Lemnos, and came to the forge of Vulcan, who, taking pity on him, gave him Kedalion, one of his men, to be his guide to the abode of the sun. Placing Kedalion on his shoulders, Orion proceeded to the east, and there meeting the sun-god, was restored to sight by his beam.

After this he dwelt as a hunter with Diana, with whom he was a favourite, and it is even said she was about to marry him. Her brother was highly displeased and often chid her, but to no purpose. One day, observing Orion wading through the sea with his head just above the water, Apollo pointed it out to his sister and maintained that she could not hit that black thing on the sea. The archer-goddess discharged a shaft with fatal aim. The waves rolled the dead body of Orion to the land, and bewailing her fatal error with many tears, Diana placed him among the stars, where he appears as a giant, with a girdle, sword, lion's skin, and club. Sirius, his dog, follows him, and the Pleiads fly before him.

The Pleiads were daughters of Atlas, and nymphs of Diana's train. One day Orion saw them and became enam-

oured and pursued them. In their distress they prayed to
the gods to change their form, and Jupiter in pity turned
them into pigeons, and then made them a constellation in
the sky. Though their number was seven, only six stars are
visible, for Electra, one of them, it is said left her place
that she might not behold the ruin of Troy, for that city
was founded by her son Dardanus. The sight had such an
effect on her sisters that they have looked pale ever since.

Aurora and Tithonus

The goddess of the Dawn, like her sister the Moon, was
at times inspired with the love of mortals. Her greatest favourite was Tithonus, son of Laomedon, king of Troy. She
stole him away, and prevailed on Jupiter to grant him immortality; but, forgetting to have youth joined in the gift,
after some time she began to discern, to her great mortification, that he was growing old. When his hair was quite
white she left his society; but he still had the range of her
palace, lived on ambrosial food, and was clad in celestial
raiment. At length he lost the power of using his limbs, and
then she shut him up in his chamber, whence his feeble
voice might at times be heard. Finally she turned him into
a grasshopper.

Memnon was the son of Aurora and Tithonus. He was
king of the Aethiopians, and dwelt in the extreme east, on
the shore of Ocean. He came with his warriors to assist the
kindred of his father in the war of Troy. King Priam received him with great honours, and listened with admiration
to his narrative of the wonders of the ocean shore.

The very day after his arrival, Memnon, impatient of
repose, led his troops to the field. Antilochus, the brave son
of Nestor, fell by his hand, and the Greeks were put to
flight, when Achilles appeared and restored the battle. A
long and doubtful contest ensued between him and the son
of Aurora; at length victory declared for Achilles, Memnon
fell, and the Trojans fled in dismay.

Aurora, who from her station in the sky had viewed
with apprehension the danger of her son, when she saw him
fall, directed his brothers, the Winds, to convey his body
to the banks of the river Esepus in Paphlagonia. In the evening Aurora came, accompanied by the Hours and the

Pleiads, and wept and lamented over her son. Night, in sympathy with her grief, spread the heaven with clouds; all nature mourned for the offspring of the Dawn. The Aethiopians raised his tomb on the banks of the stream in the grove of the Nymphs, and Jupiter caused the sparks and cinders of his funeral pile to be turned into birds, which, dividing into two flocks, fought over the pile till they fell into the flames. Every year at the anniversary of his death they return and celebrate his obsequies in like manner. Aurora remains inconsolable for the loss of her son. Her tears still flow, and may be seen at early morning in the form of dew-drops on the grass.

Unlike most of the marvels of ancient mythology, there still exist some memorials of this. On the banks of the river Nile, in Egypt, are two colossal statues, one of which is said to be the statue of Memnon. Ancient writers record that when the first rays of the rising sun fall upon this statue a sound is heard to issue from it, which they compare to the snapping of a harp-string. There is some doubt about the identification of the existing statue with the one described by the ancients, and the mysterious sounds are still more doubtful. Yet there are not wanting some modern testimonies to their being still audible. It has been suggested that sounds produced by confined air making its escape from crevices or caverns in the rocks may have given some ground for the story.

Acis and Galatea

Scylla was a fair virgin of Sicily, a favourite of the Sea-Nymphs. She had many suitors, but repelled them all, and would go to the grotto of Galatea, and tell her how she was persecuted. One day the goddess, while Scylla dressed her hair, listened to the story, and then replied, "Yet, maiden, your persecutors are of the not ungentle race of men, whom, if you will, you can repel; but I, the daughter of Nereus, and protected by such a band of sisters, found no escape from the passion of the Cyclops but in the depths of the sea;" and tears stopped her utterance, which when the pitying maiden had wiped away with her delicate finger, and soothed the goddess, "Tell me, dearest," said she, "the

cause of your grief." Galatea then said, "Acis was the son
of Faunus, and a Naiad. His father and mother loved him
dearly, but their love was not equal to mine. For the beautiful youth attached himself to me alone, and he was just
sixteen years old, the down just beginning to darken his
cheeks. As much as I sought his society, so much did the
Cyclops seek mine; and if you ask me whether my love for
Acis or my hatred of Polyphemus was the stronger, I cannot tell you; they were in equal measure. O Venus, how
great is thy power! this fierce giant, the terror of the woods,
whom no hapless stranger escaped unharmed, who defied
even Jove himself, learned to feel what love was, and,
touched with a passion for me, forgot his flocks and his
well-stored caverns. Then for the first time he began to
take some care of his appearance, and to try to make himself agreeable; he harrowed those coarse locks of his with a
comb, and mowed his beard with a sickle, looked at his
harsh features in the water, and composed his countenance.
His love of slaughter, his fierceness and thirst of blood prevailed no more, and ships that touched at his island went
away in safety. He paced up and down the sea-shore, imprinting huge tracks with his heavy tread, and, when weary,
lay tranquilly in his cave.

"There is a cliff which projects into the sea, which washes
it on either side. Thither one day the huge Cyclops ascended, and sat down while his flocks spread themselves
around. Laying down his staff, which would have served for
a mast to hold a vessel's sail, and taking his instrument
compacted of numerous pipes, he made the hills and the
waters echo the music of his song. I lay hid under a rock by
the side of my beloved Acis, and listened to the distant strain.
It was full of extravagant praises of my beauty, mingled
with passionate reproaches of my coldness and cruelty.

"When he had finished he rose up, and, like a raging
bull that cannot stand still, wandered off into the woods.
Acis and I thought no more of him, till on a sudden he
came to a spot which gave him a view of us as we sat. 'I
see you,' he exclaimed, 'and I will make this the last of your
love-meetings.' His voice was a roar such as an angry Cyclops alone could utter. Aetna trembled at the sound. I,
overcome with terror, plunged into the water. Acis turned
and fled, crying, 'Save me, Galatea, save me, my parents!'

The Cyclops pursued him, and tearing a rock from the side
of the mountain hurled it at him. Though only a corner of it
touched him, it overwhelmed him.

"All that fate left in my power I did for Acis. I endowed
him with the honours of his grandfather, the river-god. The
purple blood flowed out from under the rock, but by degrees grew paler and looked like the stream of a river rendered turbid by rains, and in time it became clear. The
rock cleaved open, and the water, as it gushed from the
chasm, uttered a pleasing murmur."

Thus Acis was changed into a river, and the river retains
the name of Acis.

27. THE TROJAN WAR

Minerva was the goddess of wisdom, but on one occasion
she did a very foolish thing; she entered into competition
with Juno and Venus for the prize of beauty. It happened
thus: At the nuptials of Peleus and Thetis all the gods were
invited with the exception of Eris, or Discord. Enraged at
her exclusion, the goddess threw a golden apple among the
guests, with the inscription, "For the fairest." Thereupon
Juno, Venus, and Minerva each claimed the apple. Jupiter,
not willing to decide in so delicate a matter, sent the goddesses to Mount Ida, where the beautiful shepherd Paris
was tending his flocks, and to him was committed the decision. The goddesses accordingly appeared before him.
Juno promised him power and riches, Minerva glory and
renown in war, and Venus the fairest of women for his
wife, each attempting to bias his decision in her own favour.
Paris decided in favour of Venus and gave her the golden
apple, thus making the two other goddesses his enemies.
Under the protection of Venus, Paris sailed to Greece, and
was hospitably received by Menelaus, king of Sparta. Now
Helen, the wife of Menelaus, was the very woman whom
Venus had destined for Paris, the fairest of her sex. She
had been sought as a bride by numerous suitors, and before her decision was made known, they all, at the sugges-

tion of Ulysses, one of their number, took an oath that they would defend her from all injury and avenge her cause if necessary. She chose Menelaus, and was living with him happily when Paris became their guest. Paris, aided by Venus, persuaded her to elope with him, and carried her to Troy, whence arose the famous Trojan war, the theme of the greatest poems of antiquity, those of Homer and Virgil.

Menelaus called upon his brother chieftains of Greece to fulfil their pledge, and join him in his efforts to recover his wife. They generally came forward, but Ulysses, who had married Penelope, and was very happy in his wife and child, had no disposition to embark in such a troublesome affair. He therefore hung back and Palamedes was sent to urge him. When Palamedes arrived at Ithaca Ulysses pretended to be mad. He yoked an ass and an ox together to the plough and began to sow salt. Palamedes, to try him, placed the infant Telemachus before the plough, whereupon the father turned the plough aside, showing plainly that he was no madman, and after that could no longer refuse to fulfil his promise. Being now himself gained for the undertaking, he lent his aid to bring in other reluctant chiefs, especially Achilles. This hero was the son of that Thetis at whose marriage the apple of Discord had been thrown among the goddesses. Thetis was herself one of the immortals, a Sea-Nymph, and knowing that her son was fated to perish before Troy if he went on the expedition, she endeavoured to prevent his going. She sent him away to the court of King Lycomedes, and induced him to conceal himself in the disguise of a maiden among the daughters of the king. Ulysses, hearing he was there, went disguised as a merchant to the palace and offered for sale female ornaments, among which he had placed some arms. While the king's daughters were engrossed with the other contents of the merchant's pack, Achilles handled the weapons and thereby betrayed himself to the keen eye of Ulysses, who found no great difficulty in persuading him to disregard his mother's prudent counsels and join his countrymen in the war.

Priam was king of Troy, and Paris, the shepherd and seducer of Helen, was his son. Paris had been brought up in obscurity, because there were certain ominous forebodings

connected with him from his infancy that he would be the
ruin of the state. These forebodings seemed at length likely
to be realized, for the Grecian armament now in preparation was the greatest that had ever been fitted out. Agamemnon, king of Mycenae, and brother of the injured Menelaus,
was chosen commander-in-chief. Achilles was their most illustrious warrior. After him ranked Ajax, gigantic in size
and of great courage, but dull of intellect; Diomede, second
only to Achilles in all the qualities of a hero; Ulysses,
famous for his sagacity; and Nestor, the oldest of the Grecian chiefs, and one to whom they all looked up for counsel. But Troy was no feeble enemy. Priam, the king, was
now old, but he had been a wise prince and had strength-
ened his state by good government at home and numerous
alliances with his neighbours. But the principal stay and
support of his throne was his son Hector, one of the noblest
characters painted by heathen antiquity. He felt, from the
first, a presentiment of the fall of his country, but still per-
severed in his heroic resistance, yet by no means justified
the wrong which brought this danger upon her. He was
united in marriage with Andromache, and as a husband
and father his character was not less admirable than as a
warrior. The principal leaders on the side of the Trojans,
besides Hector, were Aeneas and Deiphobus, Glaucus and
Sarpedon.

After two years of preparation the Greek fleet and army
assembled in the port of Aulis in Boeotia. Here Agamemnon in hunting killed a stag which was sacred to Diana,
and the goddess in return visited the army with pestilence,
and produced a calm which prevented the ships from leaving the port. Calchas, the soothsayer, thereupon announced
that the wrath of the virgin goddess could only be appeased
by the sacrifice of a virgin on her altar, and that none other
but the daughter of the offender would be acceptable. Agamemnon, however reluctant, yielded his consent, and the
maiden Iphigenia was sent for under the pretence that she
was to be married to Achilles. When she was about to be
sacrificed the goddess relented and snatched her away, leaving a hind in her place, and Iphigenia, enveloped in a cloud,
was carried to Tauris, where Diana made her priestess of
her temple.

The wind now proving fair the fleet made sail and

brought the forces to the coast of Troy. The Trojans came
to oppose their landing, and at the first onset Protesilaus
fell by the hand of Hector. Protesilaus had left at home his
wife, Laodamia, who was most tenderly attached to him.
When the news of his death reached her she implored the
gods to be allowed to converse with him only three hours.
The request was granted. Mercury led Protesilaus back to
the upper world, and when he died a second time Laodamia
died with him. There was a story that the nymphs planted
elm trees round his grave which grew very well till they
were high enough to command a view of Troy, and then
withered away, while fresh branches sprang from the roots.

"The Iliad"

The war continued without decisive results for nine years.
Then an event occurred which seemed likely to be fatal to
the cause of the Greeks, and that was a quarrel between
Achilles and Agamemnon. It is at this point that the great
poem of Homer, "The Iliad," begins. The Greeks, though
unsuccessful against Troy, had taken the neighbouring and
allied cities, and in the division of the spoil a female captive, by name Chryseis, daughter of Chryses, priest of
Apollo, had fallen to the share of Agamemnon. Chryses
came bearing the sacred emblems of his office, and begged
the release of his daughter. Agamemnon refused. Thereupon Chryses implored Apollo to afflict the Greeks till they
should be forced to yield their prey. Apollo granted the
prayer of his priest, and sent pestilence into the Grecian
camp. Then a council was called to deliberate how to allay
the wrath of the gods and avert the plague. Achilles boldly
charged their misfortunes upon Agamemnon as caused by
his withholding Chryseis. Agamemnon, enraged, consented
to relinquish his captive, but demanded that Achilles should
yield to him in her stead Briseis, a maiden who had fallen
to Achilles' share in the division of the spoil. Achilles submitted, but forthwith declared that he would take no further part in the war. He withdrew his forces from the general camp and openly avowed his intention of returning
home to Greece.

The gods and goddesses interested themselves as much in
this famous war as the parties themselves. It was well

known to them that fate had decreed that Troy should fall,
at last, if her enemies should persevere and not voluntarily
abandon the enterprise. Yet there was room enough left for
chance to excite by turns the hopes and fears of the powers
above who took part with either side. Juno and Minerva,
in consequence of the slight put upon their charms by Paris,
were hostile to the Trojans; Venus for the opposite cause
favoured them. Venus enlisted her admirer Mars on the
same side, but Neptune favoured the Greeks. Apollo was
neutral, sometimes taking one side, sometimes the other,
and Jove himself, though he loved the good King Priam, yet
exercised a degree of impartiality; not, however, without
exceptions.

Thetis, the mother of Achilles, warmly resented the injury done to her son. She repaired immediately to Jove's
palace and besought him to make the Greeks repent of their
injustice to Achilles by granting success to the Trojan arms.
Jupiter consented, and in the battle which ensued the Trojans were completely successful. The Greeks were driven
from the field and took refuge in their ships.

Then Agamemnon called a council of his wisest and
bravest chiefs. Nestor advised that an embassy should be
sent to Achilles to persuade him to return to the field; that
Agamemnon should yield the maiden, the cause of the dispute, with ample gifts to atone for the wrong he had done.
Agamemnon consented, and Ulysses, Ajax and Phoenix
were sent to carry to Achilles the penitent message. They
performed that duty, but Achilles was deaf to their entreaties. He positively refused to return to the field, and persisted in his resolution to embark for Greece without delay.

The Greeks had constructed a rampart around their
ships, and now instead of besieging Troy they were in a
manner besieged themselves, within their rampart. The next
day after the unsuccessful embassy to Achilles, a battle was
fought, and the Trojans, favoured by Jove, were successful,
and succeeded in forcing a passage through the Grecian
rampart, and were about to set fire to the ships. Neptune,
seeing the Greeks so pressed, came to their rescue. He appeared in the form of Calchas the prophet, encouraged the
warriors with his shouts, and appealed to each individually till he raised their ardour to such a pitch that they
forced the Trojans to give way. Ajax performed prodigies

of valour, and at length encountered Hector. Ajax shouted defiance, to which Hector replied, and hurled his lance at the huge warrior. It was well aimed and struck Ajax, where the belts that bore his sword and shield crossed each other on the breast. The double guard prevented its penetrating and it fell harmless. Then Ajax, seizing a huge stone, one of those that served to prop the ships, hurled it at Hector. It struck him in the neck and stretched him on the plain. His followers instantly seized him and bore him off, stunned and wounded.

While Neptune was thus aiding the Greeks and driving back the Trojans, Jupiter saw nothing of what was going on, for his attention had been drawn from the field by the wiles of Juno. That goddess had arrayed herself in all her charms, and to crown all had borrowed of Venus her girdle, called "Cestus," which had the effect to heighten the wearer's charms to such a degree that they were quite irresistible. So prepared, Juno went to join her husband, who sat on Olympus watching the battle. When he beheld her she looked so charming that the fondness of his early love revived, and, forgetting the contending armies and all other affairs of state, he thought only of her and let the battle go as it would.

But this absorption did not continue long, and when, upon turning his eyes downward, he beheld Hector stretched on the plain almost lifeless from pain and bruises, he dismissed Juno in a rage, commanding her to send Iris and Apollo to him. When Iris came he sent her with a stern message to Neptune, ordering him instantly to quit the field. Apollo was despatched to heal Hector's bruises and to inspirit his heart. These orders were obeyed with such speed that, while the battle still raged, Hector returned to the field and Neptune betook himself to his own dominions.

An arrow from Paris's bow wounded Machaon, son of Aesculapius, who inherited his father's art of healing, and was therefore of great value to the Greeks as their surgeon, besides being one of their bravest warriors. Nestor took Machaon in his chariot and conveyed him from the field. As they passed the ships of Achilles, that hero, looking out over the field, saw the chariot of Nestor and recognized the old chief, but could not discern who the wounded chief was. So calling Patroclus, his companion and dearest friend, he sent him to Nestor's tent to inquire.

Patroclus, arriving at Nestor's tent, saw Machaon wounded, and having told the cause of his coming would have hastened away, but Nestor detained him, to tell him the extent of the Grecian calamities. He reminded him also how, at the time of departing for Troy, Achilles and himself had been charged by their respective fathers with different advice: Achilles to aspire to the highest pitch of glory, Patroclus, as the elder, to keep watch over his friend, and to guide his inexperience. "Now," said Nestor, "is the time for such influence. If the gods so please, thou mayest win him back to the common cause; but if not let him at least send his soldiers to the field, and come thou, Patroclus, clad in his armour, and perhaps the very sight of it may drive back the Trojans."

Patroclus was strongly moved with this address, and hastened back to Achilles, revolving in his mind all he had seen and heard. He told the prince the sad condition of affairs at the camp of their late associates: Diomede, Ulysses, Agamemnon, Machaon, all wounded, the rampart broken down, the enemy among the ships preparing to burn them, and thus to cut off all means of return to Greece. While they spoke the flames burst forth from one of the ships. Achilles, at the sight, relented so far as to grant Patroclus his request to lead the Myrmidons (for so were Achilles' soldiers called) to the field, and to lend him his armour, that he might thereby strike more terror into the minds of the Trojans. Without delay the soldiers were marshalled, Patroclus put on the radiant armour and mounted the chariot of Achilles, and led forth the men ardent for battle. But before he went, Achilles strictly charged him that he should be content with repelling the foe. "Seek not," said he, "to press the Trojans without me, lest thou add still more to the disgrace already mine." Then exhorting the troops to do their best he dismissed them full of ardour to the fight.

Patroclus and his Myrmidons at once plunged into the contest where it raged hottest; at the sight of which the joyful Grecians shouted and the ships re-echoed the acclaim. The Trojans, at the sight of the well-known armour, struck with terror, looked everywhere for refuge. First

those who had got possession of the ship and set it on fire
left and allowed the Grecians to retake it and extinguish
the flames. Then the rest of the Trojans fled in dismay.
Ajax, Menelaus, and the two sons of Nestor performed
prodigies of valour. Hector was forced to turn his horses'
heads and retire from the enclosure, leaving his men entangled in the fosse to escape as they could. Patroclus
drove them before him, slaying many, none daring to make
a stand against him.

At last Sarpedon, son of Jove, ventured to oppose himself in fight to Patroclus. Jupiter looked down upon him and
would have snatched him from the fate which awaited him,
but Juno hinted that if he did so it would induce all others
of the inhabitants of heaven to interpose in like manner
whenever any of their offspring were endangered; to which
reason Jove yielded. Sarpedon threw his spear, but missed
Patroclus, but Patroclus threw his with better success. It
pierced Sarpedon's breast and he fell, and, calling to his
friends to save his body from the foe, expired. Then a
furious contest arose for the possession of the corpse. The
Greeks succeeded and stripped Sarpedon of his armour;
but Jove would not allow the remains of his son to be dishonoured, and by his command Apollo snatched from the
midst of the combatants the body of Sarpedon and committed it to the care of the twin brothers Death and Sleep,
by whom it was transported to Lycia, the native land of
Sarpedon, where it received due funeral rites.

Thus far Patroclus had succeeded to his utmost wish in
repelling the Trojans and relieving his countrymen, but
now came a change of fortune. Hector, borne in his chariot,
confronted him. Patroclus threw a vast stone at Hector,
which missed its aim, but smote Cebriones, the charioteer,
and knocked him from the car. Hector leaped from the
chariot to rescue his friend, and Patroclus also descended
to complete his victory. Thus the two heroes met face to
face. At this decisive moment the poet, as if reluctant to
give Hector the glory, records that Phoebus took part
against Patroclus. He struck the helmet from his head and
the lance from his hand. At the same moment an obscure
Trojan wounded him in the back, and Hector, pressing forward, pierced him with his spear. He fell mortally wounded.

Then arose a tremendous conflict for the body of Patro-

clus, but his armour was at once taken possession of by
Hector, who retiring a short distance divested himself of
his own armour and put on that of Achilles, then returned
to the fight. Ajax and Menelaus defended the body, and
Hector and his bravest warriors struggled to capture it. The
battle raged with equal fortunes, when Jove enveloped the
whole face of heaven with a dark cloud. The lightning
flashed, the thunder roared, and Ajax, looking round for
some one whom he might despatch to Achilles to tell him
of the death of his friend, and of the imminent danger that
his remains would fall into the hands of the enemy, could
see no suitable messenger.

Jupiter dispersed the clouds. Then Ajax sent Antilochus
to Achilles with the intelligence of Patroclus's death, and
of the conflict raging for his remains. The Greeks at last
succeeded in bearing off the body to the ships, closely pursued by Hector and Aeneas and the rest of the Trojans.

Achilles heard the fate of his friend with such distress
that Antilochus feared for a while that he would destroy
himself. His groans reached the ears of his mother, Thetis,
far down in the deeps of ocean where she abode, and she
hastened to him to inquire the cause. She found him overwhelmed with self-reproach that he had indulged his resentment so far, and suffered his friend to fall a victim to
it. But his only consolation was the hope of revenge. He
would fly instantly in search of Hector. But his mother
reminded him that he was now without armour, and promised him, if he would but wait till the morrow, she would
procure for him a suit of armour from Vulcan more than
equal to that he had lost. He consented, and Thetis immediately repaired to Vulcan's palace. She found him busy
at his forge making tripods for his own use, so artfully constructed that they moved forward of their own accord when
wanted, and retired again when dismissed. On hearing the
request of Thetis, Vulcan immediately laid aside his work
and hastened to comply with her wishes. He fabricated a
splendid suit of armour for Achilles, first a shield adorned
with elaborate devices, then a helmet crested with gold,
then a corselet and greaves of impenetrable temper, all perfectly adapted to his form, and of consummate workmanship. It was all done in one night, and Thetis, receiving it,

descended with it to earth and laid it down at Achilles' feet at the dawn of day.

The first glow of pleasure that Achilles had felt since the death of Patroclus was at the sight of this splendid armour. And now, arrayed in it, he went forth into the camp, calling all the chiefs to council. When they were all assembled he addressed them. Renouncing his displeasure against Agamemnon and bitterly lamenting the miseries that had resulted from it, he called on them to proceed at once to the field. Agamemnon made a suitable reply, laying all the blame on Ate, the goddess of discord; and thereupon complete reconcilement took place between the heroes.

Then Achilles went forth to battle inspired with a rage and thirst for vengeance that made him irresistible. The bravest warriors fled before him or fell by his lance. Hector, cautioned by Apollo, kept aloof; but the god, assuming the form of one of Priam's sons, Lycaon, urged Aeneas to encounter the terrible warrior. Aeneas, though he felt himself unequal, did not decline the combat. He hurled his spear with all his force against the shield, the work of Vulcan. It was formed of five metal plates; two were of brass, two of tin, and one of gold. The spear pierced two thicknesses, but was stopped in the third. Achilles threw his with better success. It pierced through the shield of Aeneas, but glanced near his shoulder and made no wound. Then Aeneas seized a stone, such as two men of modern times could hardly lift, and was about to throw it, and Achilles, with sword drawn, was about to rush upon him, when Neptune, who looked out upon the contest, moved with pity for Aeneas, who he saw would surely fall a victim if not speedily rescued, spread a cloud between the combatants, and lifting Aeneas from the ground, bore him over the heads of warriors and steeds to the rear of the battle. Achilles, when the mist cleared away, looked round in vain for his adversary, and acknowledging the prodigy, turned his arms against other champions. But none dared stand before him, and Priam looking down from the city walls beheld his whole army in full flight towards the city. He gave command to open wide the gates to receive the fugitives, and to shut them as soon as the Trojans should have passed, lest the enemy should enter likewise. But Achilles was so close in pursuit that that would have been impossible if Apollo had not, in the form of Age-

nor, Priam's son, encountered Achilles for a while, then
turned to fly, and taken the way apart from the city. Achilles
pursued and had chased his supposed victim far from the
walls, when Apollo disclosed himself, and Achilles, perceiving how he had been deluded, gave up the chase.

But when the rest had escaped into the town Hector stood
without determined to await the combat. His old father
called to him from the walls and begged him to retire nor
tempt the encounter. His mother, Hecuba, also besought
him to the same effect, but all in vain. "How can I," said
he to himself, "by whose command the people went to this
day's contest, where so many have fallen, seek safety for
myself against a single foe? But what if I offer him to yield
up Helen and all her treasures and ample of our own beside? Ah, no! it is too late. He would not even hear me
through, but slay me while I spoke." While he thus rumi-
nated, Achilles approached, terrible as Mars, his armour
flashing lightning as he moved. At that sight Hector's heart
failed him and he fled. Achilles swiftly pursued. They ran,
still keeping near the walls, till they had thrice encircled the
city. As often as Hector approached the walls Achilles intercepted him and forced him to keep out in a wider circle.
But Apollo sustained Hector's strength and would not let
him sink in weariness. Then Pallas, assuming the form of
Deiphobus, Hector's bravest brother, appeared suddenly at
his side. Hector saw him with delight, and thus strength-
ened stopped his flight and turned to meet Achilles. Hector threw his spear, which struck the shield of Achilles and
bounded back. He turned to receive another from the hand
of Deiphobus, but Deiphobus was gone. Then Hector understood his doom and said, "Alas! it is plain this is my
hour to die! I thought Deiphobus at hand, but Pallas deceived me, and he is still in Troy. But I will not fall inglorious." So saying he drew his falchion from his side and
rushed at once to combat. Achilles, secure behind his shield,
waited the approach of Hector. When he came within reach
of his spear, Achilles choosing with his eye a vulnerable
part where the armour leaves the neck uncovered, aimed
his spear at that part and Hector fell, death-wounded, and
feebly said, "Spare my body! Let my parents ransom it,
and let me receive funeral rites from the sons and daughters of Troy." To which Achilles replied, "Dog, name not

ransom nor pity to me, on whom you have brought such dire distress. No! trust me, nought shall save thy carcass from the dogs. Though twenty ransoms and thy weight in gold were offered, I would refuse it all."

So saying he stripped the body of its armour, and fastening cords to the feet tied them behind his chariot, leaving the body to trail along the ground. Then mounting the chariot he lashed the steeds and so dragged the body to and fro before the city. What words can tell the grief of King Priam and Queen Hecuba at this sight! His people could scarce restrain the old king from rushing forth. He threw himself in the dust and besought them each by name to give him way. Hecuba's distress was not less violent. The citizens stood round them weeping. The sound of the mourning reached the ears of Andromache, the wife of Hector, as she sat among her maidens at work, and anticipating evil she went forth to the wall. When she saw the sight there presented, she would have thrown herself headlong from the wall, but fainted and fell into the arms of her maidens. Recovering, she bewailed her fate, picturing to herself her country ruined, herself a captive, and her son dependent for his bread on the charity of strangers.

When Achilles and the Greeks had taken their revenge on the killer of Patroclus they busied themselves in paying due funeral rites to their friend. A pile was erected, and the body burned with due solemnity; and then ensued games of strength and skill, chariot races, wrestling, boxing and archery. Then the chiefs sat down to the funeral banquet and after that retired to rest but Achilles neither partook of the feast nor of sleep. The recollection of his lost friend kept him awake, remembering their companionship in toil and dangers, in battle or on the perilous deep. Before the earliest dawn he left his tent, and joining to his chariot his swift steeds, he fastened Hector's body to be dragged behind. Twice he dragged him round the tomb of Patroclus, leaving him at length stretched in the dust. But Apollo would not permit the body to be torn or disfigured with all this abuse, but preserved it free from all taint or defilement.

While Achilles indulged his wrath in thus disgracing brave Hector, Jupiter in pity summoned Thetis to his presence. He told her to go to her son and prevail on him to restore the body of Hector to his friends. Then Jupiter sent

Iris to King Priam to encourage him to go to Achilles and beg the body of his son. Iris delivered her message, and Priam immediately prepared to obey. He opened his treasuries and took out rich garments and cloths, with ten talents in gold and two splendid tripods and a golden cup of matchless workmanship. Then he called to his sons and bade them draw forth his litter and place in it the various articles designed for a ransom to Achilles. When all was ready, the old king with a single companion as aged as himself, the herald Idaeus, drove forth from the gates, parting there with Hecuba, his queen, and all his friends, who lamented him as going to certain death.

But Jupiter, beholding with compassion the venerable king, sent Mercury to be his guide and protector. Mercury, assuming the form of a young warrior, presented himself to the aged couple, and while at the sight of him they hesitated whether to fly or yield, the god approached, and grasping Priam's hand offered to be their guide to Achilles' tent. Priam gladly accepted his offered service, and he, mounting the carriage, assumed the reins and soon conveyed them to the tent of Achilles. Mercury's wand put to sleep all the guards, and without hindrance he introduced Priam into the tent where Achilles sat, attended by two of his warriors. The old king threw himself at the feet of Achilles, and kissed those terrible hands which had destroyed so many of his sons. "Think, O Achilles," he said, "of thy own father, full of days like me, and trembling on the gloomy verge of life. Perhaps even now some neighbour chief oppresses him and there is none at hand to succour him in his distress. Yet doubtless knowing that Achilles lives he still rejoices, hoping that one day he shall see thy face again. But no comfort cheers me, whose bravest sons, so late the flower of Ilium, all have fallen. Yet one I had, one more than all the rest the strength of my age, whom, fighting for his country, thou hast slain. I come to redeem his body, bringing inestimable ransom with me. Achilles! reverence the gods! recollect thy father! for his sake show compassion to me!" These words moved Achilles, and he wept remembering by turns his absent father and his lost friend. Moved with pity of Priam's silver locks and beard, he raised him from the earth, and thus spake: "Priam, I know that thou hast reached this place conducted by some god, for without aid divine no mortal even in his prime of youth had dared the attempt. I grant thy request, moved thereto by the evident will of Jove." So saying he arose, and went forth with his two friends, and unloaded of its charge the litter, leaving two mantles and a robe for the covering of the body, which they placed on the litter, and spread the garments over it, that not unveiled it should be borne back to Troy. Then Achilles dismissed the old king with his attendants, having first pledged himself to allow a truce of twelve days for the funeral solemnities.

As the litter approached the city and was descried from the walls, the people poured forth to gaze once more on the face of their hero. Foremost of all, the mother and the wife of Hector came, and at the sight of the lifeless body renewed their lamentations. The people all wept with them, and to the going down of the sun there was no pause or abatement of their grief.

The next day preparations were made for the funeral solemnities. For nine days the people brought wood and built the pile, and on the tenth they placed the body on the summit and applied the torch; while all Troy thronging forth encompassed the pile. When it had completely burned, they quenched the cinders with wine, collected the bones and placed them in a golden urn, which they buried in the earth, and reared a pile of stones over the spot.

> "Such honours Ilium to her hero paid,
>   And peaceful slept the mighty Hector's shade."
> *Pope.*

28. THE FALL OF TROY — RETURN OF THE GREEKS — AGAMEMNON, ORESTES AND ELECTRA

The Fall of Troy

The story of the Iliad ends with the death of Hector, and it is from the Odyssey and later poems that we learn the fate of the other heroes. After the death of Hector, Troy did

not immediately fall, but receiving aid from new allies still
continued its resistance. One of these allies was Memnon,
the Aethiopian prince, whose story we have already told.
Another was Penthesilea, queen of the Amazons, who
came with a band of female warriors. All the authorities
attest their valour and the fearful effect of their war cry.
Penthesilea slew many of the bravest warriors, but was at
last slain by Achilles. But when the hero bent over his fallen
foe, and contemplated her beauty, youth and valour, he bitterly regretted his victory. Thersites, an insolent brawler
and demagogue, ridiculed his grief, and was in consequence slain by the hero.

Achilles by chance had seen Polyxena, daughter of King
Priam, perhaps on occasion of the truce which was allowed
the Trojans for the burial of Hector. He was captivated
with her charms, and to win her in marriage agreed to use
his influence with the Greeks to grant peace to Troy. While
in the temple of Apollo, negotiating the marriage, Paris discharged at him a poisoned arrow, which, guided by Apollo,
wounded Achilles in the heel, the only vulnerable part about
him. For Thetis his mother had dipped him when an infant
in the river Styx, which made every part of him invulnerable except the heel by which she held him.[1]

The body of Achilles so treacherously slain was rescued
by Ajax and Ulysses. Thetis directed the Greeks to bestow
her son's armour on the hero who of all the survivors should
be judged most deserving of it. Ajax and Ulysses were the
only claimants; a selected number of the other chiefs were
appointed to award the prize. It was awarded to Ulysses,
thus placing wisdom before valour, whereupon Ajax slew
himself. On the spot where his blood sank into the earth
a flower sprang up, called the hyacinth, bearing on its
leaves the first two letters of the name of Ajax, Ai, the
Greek for "woe." Thus Ajax is a claimant with the boy
Hyacinthus for the honour of giving birth to this flower.
There is a species of Larkspur which represents the hyacinth of the poets in preserving the memory of this event,
the Delphinium Ajacis—Ajax's Larkspur.

It was now discovered that Troy could not be taken but

---

[1] The story of the invulnerability of Achilles is not found in Homer, and
is inconsistent with his account. For how could Achilles require the aid of
celestial armour if he were invulnerable?

by the aid of the arrows of Hercules. They were in possession of Philoctetes, the friend who had been with Hercules at the last and lighted his funeral pyre. Philoctetes
had joined the Grecian expedition against Troy, but had
accidentally wounded his foot with one of the poisoned arrows, and the smell from his wound proved so offensive that
his companions carried him to the isle of Lemnos and left
him there. Diomed was now sent to induce him to rejoin
the army. He succeeded. Philoctetes was cured of his
wound by Machaon, and Paris was the first victim of the
fatal arrows. In his distress Paris bethought him of one
whom in his prosperity he had forgotten. This was the
nymph Oenone, whom he had married when a youth, and
had abandoned for the fatal beauty Helen. Oenone remembering the wrongs she had suffered, refused to heal the
wound, and Paris went back to Troy and died. Oenone
quickly repented, and hastened after him with remedies,
but came too late, and in her grief hung herself.

There was in Troy a celebrated statue of Minerva called
the Palladium. It was said to have fallen from heaven, and
the belief was that the city could not be taken so long as
this statue remained within it. Ulysses and Diomed entered
the city in disguise and succeeded in obtaining the Palladium, which they carried off to the Grecian camp.

But Troy still held out, and the Greeks began to despair
of ever subduing it by force, and by advice of Ulysses resolved to resort to stratagem. They pretended to be making
preparations to abandon the siege, and a portion of the
ships were withdrawn and lay hid behind a neighbouring
island. The Greeks then constructed an immense *wooden
horse*, which they gave out was intended as a propitiatory
offering to Minerva, but in fact was filled with armed men.
The remaining Greeks then betook themselves to their ships
and sailed away, as if for a final departure. The Trojans,
seeing the encampment broken up and the fleet gone, concluded the enemy to have abandoned the siege. The gates
were thrown open, and the whole population issued forth
rejoicing at the long-prohibited liberty of passing freely
over the scene of the late encampment. The great *horse*
was the chief object of curiosity. All wondered what it could
be for. Some recommended to take it into the city as a trophy; others felt afraid of it.

While they hesitate, Laocoön, the priest of Neptune, exclaims, "What madness, citizens, is this? Have you not learned enough of Grecian fraud to be on your guard against it? For my part, I fear the Greeks even when they offer gifts." [1] So saying he threw his lance at the horse's side. It struck, and a hollow sound reverberated like a groan. Then perhaps the people might have taken his advice and destroyed the fatal horse and all its contents; but just at that moment a group of people appeared, dragging forward one who seemed a prisoner and a Greek. Stupefied with terror, he was brought before the chiefs, who reassured him, promising that his life should be spared on condition of his returning true answers to the questions asked him. He informed them that he was a Greek, Sinon by name, and that in consequence of the malice of Ulysses he had been left behind by his countrymen at their departure. With regard to the wooden horse, he told them that it was a propitiatory offering to Minerva, and made so huge for the express purpose of preventing its being carried within the city; for Calchas the prophet had told them that if the Trojans took possesion of it they would assuredly triumph over the Greeks. This language turned the tide of the people's feelings and they began to think how they might best secure the monstrous horse and the favourable auguries connected with it, when suddenly a prodigy occurred which left no room to doubt. There appeared, advancing over the sea, two immense serpents. They came upon the land, and the crowd fled in all directions. The serpents advanced directly to the spot where Laocoön stood with his two sons. They first attacked the children, winding round their bodies and breathing their pestilential breath in their faces. The father, attempting to rescue them, is next seized and involved in the serpents' coils. He struggles to tear them away, but they overpower all his efforts and strangle him and the children in their poisonous folds. This event was regarded as a clear indication of the displeasure of the gods at Laocoön's irreverent treatment of the wooden horse, which they no longer hesitated to regard as a sacred object, and prepared to introduce with due solemnity into the city. This was done with songs and triumphal acclamations, and the day closed with festivity. In the night the armed men who were en-

---

[1] See Proverbial Expressions, page 268.

closed in the body of the horse, being let out by the traitor
Sinon, opened the gates of the city to their friends, who
had returned under cover of the night. The city was set on
fire; the people, overcome with feasting and sleep, put to
the sword, and Troy completely subdued.

One of the most celebrated groups of statuary in existence is that of Laocoön and his children in the embrace of
the serpents. The orginal is in the Vatican at Rome.

King Priam lived to see the downfall of his kingdom and
was slain at last on the fatal night when the Greeks took
the city. He had armed himself and was about to mingle
with the combatants, but was prevailed on by Hecuba, his
aged queen, to take refuge with herself and his daughters
as a suppliant at the altar of Jupiter. While there, his youngest son Polites, pursued by Pyrrhus, the son of Achilles,
rushed in wounded, and expired at the feet of his father;
whereupon Priam, overcome with indignation, hurled his
spear with feeble hand against Pyrrhus,[1] and was forthwith
slain by him.

Queen Hecuba and her daughter Cassandra were carried
captives to Greece. Cassandra had been loved by Apollo,
and he gave her the gift of prophecy; but afterwards offended with her, he rendered the gift unavailing by ordain-
ing that her predictions should never be believed. Polyxena,
another daughter, who had been loved by Achilles, was demanded by the ghost of that warrior, and was sacrificed by
the Greeks upon his tomb.

Menelaus and Helen

Our readers will be anxious to know the fate of Helen,
the fair but guilty occasion of so much slaughter. On the
fall of Troy Menelaus recovered possession of his wife, who
had not ceased to love him, though she had yielded to the
might of Venus and deserted him for another. After the
death of Paris she aided the Greeks secretly on several occasions, and in particular when Ulysses and Diomed entered
the city in disguise to carry off the Palladium. She saw and
recognized Ulysses, but kept the secret and even assisted
them in obtaining the image. Thus she became reconciled
to her husband, and they were among the first to leave the

[1] Pyrrhus's exclamation, "Not such aid nor such defenders does the time
require," has become proverbial. See Proverbial Expressions, page 268.

shores of Troy for their native land. But having incurred
the displeasure of the gods they were driven by storms from
shore to shore of the Mediterranean, visiting Cyprus, Phoenicia and Egypt. In Egypt they were kindly treated and
presented with rich gifts, of which Helen's share was a
golden spindle and a basket on wheels. The basket was to
hold the wool and spools for the queen's work.

Menelaus and Helen at length arrived in safety at Sparta,
resumed their royal dignity, and lived and reigned in splendour; and when Telemachus, the son of Ulysses, in search
of his father, arrived at Sparta, he found Menelaus and
Helen celebrating the marriage of their daughter Hermione
to Neoptolemus, son of Achilles.

Agamemnon, Orestes and Electra

Agamemnon, the general-in-chief of the Greeks, the
brother of Menelaus, and who had been drawn into the
quarrel to avenge his brother's wrongs, not his own, was
not so fortunate in the issue. During his absence his wife
Clytemnestra had been false to him, and when his return
was expected, she with her paramour, Aegisthus, laid a
plan for his destruction, and at the banquet given to celebrate his return, murdered him.

It was intended by the conspirators to slay his son Orestes
also, a lad not yet old enough to be an object of apprehension, but from whom, if he should be suffered to grow up,
there might be danger. Electra, the sister of Orestes, saved
her brother's life by sending him secretly away to his uncle
Strophius, King of Phocis. In the palace of Strophius
Orestes grew up with the king's son Pylades, and formed
with him that ardent friendship which has become proverbial. Electra frequently reminded her brother by messengers
of the duty of avenging his father's death, and when grown
up he consulted the oracle of Delphi, which confirmed
him in his design. He therefore repaired in disguise to
Argos, pretending to be a messenger from Strophius, who
had come to announce the death of Orestes, and brought
the ashes of the deceased in a funeral urn. After visiting
his father's tomb and sacrificing upon it, according to the
rites of the ancients, he made himself known to his sister
Electra, and soon after slew both Aegisthus and Clytemnestra.

This revolting act, the slaughter of a mother by her son, though alleviated by the guilt of the victim and the express command of the gods, did not fail to awaken in the breasts of the ancients the same abhorrence that it does in ours. The Eumenides, avenging deities, seized upon Orestes, and drove him frantic from land to land. Pylades accompanied him in his wanderings and watched over him. At length, in answer to a second appeal to the oracle, he was directed to go to Tauris in Scythia, and to bring thence a statue of Diana which was believed to have fallen from heaven. Accordingly Orestes and Pylades went to Tauris, where the barbarous people were accustomed to sacrifice to the goddess all strangers who fell into their hands. The two friends were seized and carried bound to the temple to be made victims. But the priestess of Diana was no other than Iphigenia, the sister of Orestes, who, our readers will remember, was snatched away by Diana at the moment when she was about to be sacrificed. Ascertaining from the prisoners who they were, Iphigenia disclosed herself to them, and the three made their escape with the statue of the goddess, and returned to Mycenae.

But Orestes was not yet relieved from the vengeance of the Erinyes. At length he took refuge with Minerva at Athens. The goddess afforded him protection, and appointed the court of Areopagus to decide his fate. The Erinyes brought forward their accusation, and Orestes made the command of the Delphic oracle his excuse. When the court voted and the voices were equally divided, Orestes was acquitted by the command of Minerva.

29. ADVENTURES OF ULYSSES —
THE LOTUS-EATERS — THE CYCLOPSES —
CIRCE — SIRENS — SCYLLA AND
CHARYBDIS — CALYPSO

Return of Ulysses

The romantic poem of the Odyssey is now to engage our attention. It narrates the wanderings of Ulysses (Odysseus in the Greek language) in his return from Troy to his own kingdom Ithaca.

From Troy the vessels first made land at Ismarus, city of the Ciconians, where, in a skirmish with the inhabitants, Ulysses lost six men from each ship. Sailing thence, they were overtaken by a storm which drove them for nine days along the sea till they reached the country of the Lotus-eaters. Here, after watering, Ulysses sent three of his men to discover who the inhabitants were. These men on coming among the Lotus-eaters were kindly entertained by them, and were given some of their own food, the lotus-plant, to eat. The effect of this food was such that those who partook of it lost all thoughts of home and wished to remain in that country. It was by main force that Ulysses dragged these men away, and he was even obliged to tie them under the benches of his ships.

They next arrived at the country of the Cyclopses. The Cyclopses were giants, who inhabited an island of which they were the only possessors. The name means "round eye," and these giants were so called because they had but one eye, and that placed in the middle of the forehead. They dwelt in caves and fed on the wild productions of the island and on what their flocks yielded, for they were shepherds. Ulysses left the main body of his ships at anchor, and with one vessel went to the Cyclopses' island to explore for supplies. He landed with his companions, carrying with them a jar of wine for a present, and coming to a large cave they entered it, and finding no one within examined its contents. They found it stored with the richest of the flock, quantities of cheese, pails and bowls of milk, lambs and kids in their pens, all in nice order. Presently arrived the master of the cave, Polyphemus, bearing an immense bundle of firewood, which he threw down before the cavern's mouth. He then drove into the cave the sheep and goats to be milked, and, entering, rolled to the cave's mouth an enormous rock, that twenty oxen could not draw. Next he sat down and milked his ewes, preparing a part for cheese, and setting the rest aside for his customary drink. Then, turning round his great eye, he discerned the strangers, and growled out to them, demanding who they were, and where from. Ulysses replied most humbly, stating that they were Greeks, from the great expedition that had lately won so much glory in the conquest of Troy; that they were now on their way home, and finished by imploring his hospitality in the name of the gods. Polyphemus deigned no answer, but reaching out his hand seized two of the Greeks, whom he hurled against the side of the cave, and dashed out their brains. He proceeded to devour them with great relish, and having made a hearty meal, stretched himself out on the floor to sleep. Ulysses was tempted to seize the opportunity and plunge his sword into him as he slept, but recollected that it would only expose them all to certain destruction, as the rock with which the giant had closed up the door was far beyond their power to remove, and they would therefore be in hopeless imprisonment. Next morning the giant seized two more of the Greeks, and despatched them in the same manner as their companions, feasting on their flesh till no fragment was left. He then moved away the rock from the door, drove out his flocks, and went out, carefully replacing the barrier after him. When he was gone Ulysses planned how he might take vengeance for his murdered friends, and effect his escape with his surviving companions. He made his men prepare a massive bar of wood cut by the Cyclops for a staff, which they found in the cave. They sharpened the end of it, and seasoned it in the fire, and hid it under the straw on the cavern floor. Then four of the boldest were selected, with whom Ulysses joined himself as a fifth. The Cyclops came home at evening, rolled away the stone and drove in his flock as usual. After milking them and making his arrangements as before, he seized

two more of Ulysses' companions and dashed their brains
out, and made his evening meal upon them as he had on
the others. After he had supped, Ulysses approaching him
handed him a bowl of wine, saying, "Cyclops, this is wine;
taste and drink after thy meal of men's flesh." He took and
drank it, and was hugely delighted with it, and called for
more. Ulysses supplied him once again, which pleased the
giant so much that he promised him as a favour that he
should be the last of the party devoured. He asked his
name, to which Ulysses replied, "My name is Noman."

After his supper the giant lay down to repose, and was
soon found asleep. Then Ulysses with his four select friends
thrust the end of the stake into the fire till it was all one
burning coal, then poising it exactly above the giant's only
eye, they buried it deeply into the socket, twirling it round
as a carpenter does his auger. The howling monster with
his outcry filled the cavern, and Ulysses with his aids nimbly
got out of his way and concealed themselves in the cave.
He, bellowing, called aloud on all the Cyclopses dwelling in
the caves around him, far and near. They on his cry flocked
round the den, and inquired what grievous hurt had caused
him to sound such an alarm and break their slumbers. He
replied, "O friends, I die, and Noman gives the blow."
They answered, "If no man hurts thee it is the stroke of
Jove, and thou must bear it." So saying, they left him
groaning.

Next morning the Cyclops rolled away the stone to let
his flock out to pasture, but planted himself in the door
of the cave to feel of all as they went out, that Ulysses and
his men should not escape with them. But Ulysses had
made his men harness the rams of the flock three abreast,
with osiers which they found on the floor of the cave. To
the middle ram of the three one of the Greeks suspended
himself, so protected by the exterior rams on either side.
As they passed, the giant felt of the animals' backs and
sides, but never thought of their bellies; so the men all
passed safe, Ulysses himself being on the last one that
passed. When they had got a few paces from the cavern,
Ulysses and his friends released themselves from their rams,
and drove a good part of the flock down to the shore to
their boat. They put them aboard with all haste, then
pushed off from the shore, and when at a safe distance

Ulysses shouted out, "Cyclops, the gods have well requited thee for thy atrocious deeds. Know it is Ulysses to whom thou owest thy shameful loss of sight." The Cyclops, hearing this, seized a rock that projected from the side of the mountain, and rending it from its bed he lifted it high in the air, then exerting all his force, hurled it in the direction of the voice. Down came the mass, just clearing the vessel's stern. The ocean, at the plunge of the huge rock, heaved the ship towards the land, so that it barely escaped being swamped by the waves. When they had with the utmost difficulty pulled off shore, Ulysses was about to hail the giant again, but his friends besought him not to do so. He could not forbear, however, letting the giant know that they had escaped his missile, but waited till they had reached a safer distance than before. The giant answered them with curses, but Ulysses and his friends plied their oars vigorously; and soon regained their companions.

Ulysses next arrived at the island of Aeolus. To this monarch Jupiter had intrusted the government of the winds, to send them forth or retain them at his will. He treated Ulysses hospitably, and at his departure gave him, tied up in a leathern bag with a silver string, such winds as might be hurtful and dangerous, commanding fair winds to blow the barks towards their country. Nine days they sped before the wind, and all that time Ulysses had stood at the helm, without sleep. At last quite exhausted he lay down to sleep. While he slept, the crew conferred together about the mysterious bag, and concluded it must contain treasures given by the hospitable King Aeolus to their commander. Tempted to secure some portion for themselves, they loosed the string, when immediately the winds rushed forth. The ships were driven far from their course, and back again to the island they had just left. Aeolus was so indignant at their folly that he refused to assist them further, and they were obliged to labour over their course once more by means of their oars.

The Laestrygonians

Their next adventure was with the barbarous tribe of Laestrygonians. The vessels all pushed into the harbour, tempted by the secure appearance of the cove, completely land-locked; only Ulysses moored his vessel without. As

soon as the Laestrygonians found the ships completely in
their power they attacked them, heaving huge stones which
broke and overturned them, and with their spears despatched the seamen as they struggled in the water. All
the vessels with their crews were destroyed, except Ulysses'
own ship, which had remained outside, and finding no safety
but in flight, he exhorted his men to ply their oars vigorously, and they escaped.

With grief for their slain companions mixed with joy at
their own escape, they pursued their way till they arrived at
the Aeaean isle, where Circe dwelt, the daughter of the
sun. Landing here, Ulysses climbed a hill, and gazing round
saw no signs of habitation except in one spot at the centre
of the island, where he perceived a palace embowered with
trees. He sent forward one-half of his crew, under the command of Eurylochus, to see what prospect of hospitality they
might find. As they approached the palace, they found themselves surrounded by lions, tigers, and wolves, not fierce,
but tamed by Circe's art, for she was a powerful magician.
All these animals had once been men, but had been changed
by Circe's enchantments into the forms of beasts. The
sounds of soft music were heard from within, and a sweet
female voice singing. Eurylochus called aloud and the goddess came forth and invited them in; they all gladly entered
except Eurylochus, who suspected danger. The goddess
conducted her guests to a seat, and had them served with
wine and other delicacies. When they had feasted heartily,
she touched them one by one with her wand, and they became immediately changed into *swine*, in "head, body, voice,
and bristles," yet with their intellects as before. She shut
them in her sties and supplied them with acorns and such
other things as swine love.

Eurylochus hurried back to the ship and told the tale.
Ulysses thereupon determined to go himself, and try if by
any means he might deliver his companions. As he strode
onward alone, he met a youth who addressed him familiarly, appearing to be acquainted with his adventures. He
announced himself as Mercury, and informed Ulysses of
the arts of Circe, and of the danger of approaching her. As
Ulysses was not to be dissuaded from his attempt, Mercury
provided him with a sprig of the plant Moly, of wonderful
power to resist sorceries, and instructed him how to act.

Ulysses proceeded, and reaching the palace was courteously received by Circe, who entertained him as she had done his companions, and after he had eaten and drank, touched him with her wand, saying, "Hence, seek the sty and wallow with thy friends." But he, instead of obeying, drew his sword and rushed upon her with fury in his countenance. She fell on her knees and begged for mercy. He dictated a solemn oath that she would release his companions and practise no further harm against him or them; and she repeated it, at the same time promising to dismiss them all in safety after hospitably entertaining them. She was as good as her word. The men were restored to their shapes, the rest of the crew summoned from the shore, and the whole magnificently entertained day after day, till Ulysses seemed to have forgotten his native land, and to have reconciled himself to an inglorious life of ease and pleasure.

At length his companions recalled him to nobler sentiments, and he received their admonition gratefully. Circe aided their departure, and instructed them how to pass safely by the coast of the Sirens. The Sirens were sea-nymphs who had the power of charming by their song all who heard them, so that the unhappy mariners were irresistibly impelled to cast themselves into the sea to their destruction. Circe directed Ulysses to fill the ears of his seamen with wax, so that they should not hear the strain; and to cause himself to be bound to the mast, and his people to be strictly enjoined, whatever he might say or do, by no means to release him till they should have passed the Sirens' island. Ulysses obeyed these directions. He filled the ears of his people with wax, and suffered them to bind him with cords firmly to the mast. As they approached the Sirens' island, the sea was calm, and over the waters came the notes of music so ravishing and attractive that Ulysses struggled to get loose, and by cries and signs to his people begged to be released; but they, obedient to his previous orders, sprang forward and bound him still faster. They held on their course, and the music grew fainter till it ceased to be heard, when with joy Ulysses gave his companions the signal to unseal their ears, and they relieved him from his bonds.

Scylla and Charybdis

Ulysses had been warned by Circe of the two monsters Scylla and Charybdis. We have already met with Scylla in the story of Glaucus, and remember that she was once a beautiful maiden and was changed into a snaky monster by Circe. She dwelt in a cave high up on the cliff, from whence she was accustomed to thrust forth her long necks (for she had six heads), and in each of her mouths seize one of the crew of every vessel passing within reach. The other terror, Charybdis, was a gulf, nearly on a level with the water. Thrice each day the water rushed into a frightful chasm, and thrice was disgorged. Any vessel coming near the whirlpool when the tide was rushing in must inevitably be ingulfed; not Neptune himself could save it.

On approaching the haunt of the dread monsters, Ulysses kept strict watch to discover them. The roar of the waters as Charybdis ingulfed them, gave warning at a distance, but Scylla could nowhere be discerned. While Ulysses and his men watched with anxious eyes the dreadful whirlpool, they were not equally on their guard from the attack of Scylla, and the monster, darting forth her snaky heads, caught six of his men, and bore them away, shrieking, to her den. It was the saddest sight Ulysses had yet seen; to behold his friends thus sacrificed and hear their cries, unable to afford them any assistance.

Circe had warned him of another danger. After passing Scylla and Charybdis the next land he would make was Thrinakia, an island whereon were pastured the cattle of Hyperion, the Sun, tended by his daughters Lampetia and Phaëthusa. These flocks must not be violated, whatever the wants of the voyagers might be. If this injunction were transgressed destruction was sure to fall on the offenders.

Ulysses would willingly have passed the island of the Sun without stopping, but his companions so urgently pleaded for the rest and refreshment that would be derived from anchoring and passing the night on shore, that Ulysses yielded. He bound them, however, with an oath that they would not touch one of the animals of the sacred flocks and herds, but content themselves with what provision they yet had left of the supply which Circe had put on board.

So long as this supply lasted the people kept their oath, but
contrary winds detained them at the island for a month,
and after consuming all their stock of provisions, they were
forced to rely upon the birds and fishes they could catch.
Famine pressed them, and at length one day, in the absence of Ulysses, they slew some of the cattle, vainly attempting to make amends for the deed by offering from
them a portion to the offended powers. Ulysses, on his return to the shore, was horror-struck at perceiving what they
had done, and the more so on account of the portentous
signs which followed. The skins crept on the ground, and
the joints of meat lowed on the spits while roasting.

The wind becoming fair they sailed from the island. They
had not gone far when the weather changed, and a storm
of thunder and lightning ensued. A stroke of lightning shattered their mast, which in its fall killed the pilot. At last the
vessel itself came to pieces. The keel and mast floating side
by side, Ulysses formed of them a raft, to which he clung,
and, the wind changing, the waves bore him to Calypso's
island. All the rest of the crew perished.

Scylla and Charybdis have become proverbial, to denote
opposite dangers which beset one's course.[1]

Calypso

Calypso was a sea-nymph, which name denotes a numerous class of female divinities of lower rank, yet sharing
many of the attributes of the gods. Calypso received Ulysses
hospitably, entertained him magnificently, became enamoured of him, and wished to retain him for ever, conferring
on him immortality. But he persisted in his resolution to
return to his country and his wife and son. Calypso at last
received the command of Jove to dismiss him. Mercury
brought the message to her.

Calypso with much reluctance proceeded to obey the
commands of Jupiter. She supplied Ulysses with the means
of constructing a raft, provisioned it well for him, and gave
him a favouring gale. He sped on his course prosperously
for many days, till at length, when in sight of land, a storm
arose that broke his mast, and threatened to rend the raft

[1] See Proverbial Expressions, page 268

asunder. In this crisis he was seen by a compassionate sea-nymph, who in the form of a cormorant alighted on the raft, and presented him a girdle, directing him to bind it beneath his breast, and if he should be compelled to trust himself to the waves, it would buoy him up and enable him by swimming to reach the land.

Fénelon, in his romance of "Telemachus," has given us the adventures of the son of Ulysses in search of his father. Among other places at which he arrived, following on his father's footsteps, was Calypso's isle, and, as in the former case, the goddess tried every art to keep him with her, and offered to share her immortality with him. But Minerva, who in the shape of Mentor accompanied him and governed all his movements, made him repel her allurements, and when no other means of escape could be found, the two friends leaped from a cliff into the sea, and swam to a vessel which lay becalmed off shore.

30. THE PHAEACIANS — FATE OF THE SUITORS

The Phaeacians

Ulysses clung to the raft while any of its timbers kept together, and when it no longer yielded him support, binding the girdle around him, he swam. Minerva smoothed the billows before him and sent him a wind that rolled the waves towards the shore. The surf beat high on the rocks and seemed to forbid approach; but at length finding calm water at the mouth of a gentle stream, he landed, spent with toil, breathless and speechless and almost dead. After some time, reviving, he kissed the soil, rejoicing, yet at a loss what course to take. At a short distance he perceived a wood to which he turned his steps. There, finding a covert sheltered by intermingling branches alike from the sun and the rain, he collected a pile of leaves and formed a bed, on which he stretched himself, and heaping the leaves over him, fell asleep.

The land where he was thrown was Scheria, the country of the Phaeacians. These people dwelt originally near the Cyclopses; but being oppressed by that savage race, they migrated to the isle of Scheria, under the conduct of Nausithoüs, their king. They were, the poet tells us, a people akin to the gods, who appeared manifestly and feasted among them when they offered sacrifices and did not conceal themselves from solitary wayfarers when they met them. They had abundance of wealth and lived in the enjoyment of it undisturbed by the alarms of war, for as they dwelt remote from gain-seeking men, no enemy ever approached their shores, and they did not even require to make use of bows and quivers. Their chief employment was navigation. Their ships, which went with the velocity of birds, were endued with intelligence; they knew every port and needed no pilot. Alcinoüs, the son of Nausithoüs, was now their king, a wise and just sovereign, beloved by his people.

Now it happened that the very night on which Ulysses was cast ashore on the Phaeacian island, and while he lay sleeping on his bed of leaves, Nausicaa, the daughter of the king, had a dream sent by Minerva, reminding her that her wedding-day was not far distant, and that it would be but a prudent preparation for that event to have a general washing of the clothes of the family. This was no slight affair, for the fountains were at some distance, and the garments must be carried thither. On awaking, the princess hastened to her parents to tell them what was on her mind; not alluding to her wedding-day, but finding other reasons equally good. Her father readily assented and ordered the grooms to furnish forth a wagon for the purpose. The clothes were put therein, and the queen mother placed in the wagon, likewise, an abundant supply of food and wine. The princess took her seat and plied the lash, her attendant virgins following her on foot. Arrived at the river side, they turned out the mules to graze, and unlading the carriage, bore the garments down to the water, and working with cheerfulness and alacrity soon despatched their labour. Then having spread the garments on the shore to dry, and having themselves bathed, they sat down to enjoy their meal; after which they rose and

amused themselves with a game of ball, the princess singing
to them while they played. But when they had refolded the
apparel and were about to resume their way to the town,
Minerva caused the ball thrown by the princess to fall into
the water, whereat they all screamed and Ulysses awaked
at the sound.

Now we must picture to ourselves Ulysses, a shipwrecked
mariner, but a few hours escaped from the waves, and utterly destitute of clothing, awaking and discovering that only
a few bushes were interposed between him and a group of
young maidens whom, by their deportment and attire, he
discovered to be not mere peasant girls, but of a higher
class. Sadly needing help, how could he yet venture, naked
as he was, to discover himself and make his wants known?
It certainly was a case worthy of the interposition of his
patron goddess Minerva, who never failed him at a crisis.
Breaking off a leafy branch from a tree, he held it before
him and stepped out from the thicket. The virgins at sight
of him fled in all directions, Nausicaa alone excepted, for
her Minerva aided and endowed with courage and discern-
ment. Ulysses, standing respectfully aloof, told his sad case,
and besought the fair object (whether queen or goddess he
professed he knew not) for food and clothing. The princess
replied courteously, promising present relief and her father's hospitality when he should become acquainted with
the facts. She called back her scattered maidens, chiding
their alarm, and reminding them that the Phaeacians had
no enemies to fear. This man, she told them, was an unhappy wanderer, whom it was a duty to cherish, for the poor
and stranger are from Jove. She bade them bring food and
clothing, for some of her brothers' garments were among
the contents of the wagon. When this was done, and Ulysses,
retiring to a sheltered place, had washed his body free from
the sea-foam, clothed and refreshed himself with food,
Pallas dilated his form and diffused grace over his ample
chest and manly brows.

The princess, seeing him, was filled with admiration, and
scrupled not to say to her damsels that she wished the gods
would send her such a husband. To Ulysses she recommended that he should repair to the city, following herself
and train so far as the way lay through the fields; but when
they should approach the city she desired that he would no

longer be seen in her company, for she feared the remarks
which rude and vulgar people might make on seeing her return accompanied by such a gallant stranger. To avoid
which she directed him to stop at a grove adjoining the city,
in which were a farm and garden belonging to the king.
After allowing time for the princess and her companions to
reach the city, he was then to pursue his way thither, and
would be easily guided by any he might meet to the royal
abode.

Ulysses obeyed the directions and in due time proceeded
to the city, on approaching which he met a young woman
bearing a pitcher forth for water. It was Minerva, who had
assumed that form. Ulysses accosted her and desired to be
directed to the palace of Alcinoüs the king. The maiden replied respectfully, offering to be his guide; for the palace,
she informed him, stood near her father's dwelling. Under
the guidance of the goddess, and by her power enveloped in
a cloud which shielded him from observation, Ulysses
passed among the busy crowd, and with wonder observed
their harbour, their ships, their forum (the resort of heroes),
and their battlements, till they came to the palace, where the
goddess, having first given him some information of the
country, king, and people he was about to meet, left him.
Ulysses, before entering the courtyard of the palace, stood
and surveyed the scene. Its splendour astonished him.
Brazen walls stretched from the entrance to the interior
house, of which the doors were gold, the doorposts silver,
the lintels silver ornamented with gold. On either side were
figures of mastiffs wrought in gold and silver, standing in
rows as if to guard the approach. Along the walls were seats
spread through all their length with mantles of finest texture,
the work of Phaeacian maidens. On these seats the princes
sat and feasted, while golden statues of graceful youths held
in their hands lighted torches which shed radiance over the
scene. Full fifty female menials served in household offices,
some employed to grind the corn, others to wind off the
purple wool or ply the loom. For the Phaeacian women as
far exceeded all other women in household arts as the mariners of that country did the rest of mankind in the management of ships. Without the court a spacious garden lay, four
acres in extent. In it grew many a lofty tree, pomegranate,
pear, apple, fig, and olive. Neither winter's cold nor sum-

mer's drought arrested their growth, but they flourished in constant succession, some budding while others were maturing. The vineyard was equally prolific. In one quarter you might see the vines, some in blossom, some loaded with ripe grapes, and in another observe the vintagers treading the wine press. On the garden's borders flowers of all hues bloomed all the year round, arranged with neatest art. In the midst two fountains poured forth their waters, one flowing by artificial channels over all the garden, the other conducted through the courtyard of the palace, whence every citizen might draw his supplies.

Ulysses stood gazing in admiration, unobserved himself, for the cloud which Minerva spread around him still shielded him. At length, having sufficiently observed the scene, he advanced with rapid step into the hall where the chiefs and senators were assembled, pouring libation to Mercury, whose worship followed the evening meal. Just then Minerva dissolved the cloud and disclosed him to the assembled chiefs. Advancing to the place where the queen sat, he knelt at her feet and implored her favour and assistance to enable him to return to his native country. Then withdrawing, he seated himself in the manner of suppliants, at the hearth side.

For a time none spoke. At last an aged statesman, addressing the king, said, "It is not fit that a stranger who asks our hospitality should be kept waiting in suppliant guise, none welcoming him. Let him therefore be led to a seat among us and supplied with food and wine." At these words the king rising gave his hand to Ulysses and led him to a seat, displacing thence his own son to make room for the stranger. Food and wine were set before him and he ate and refreshed himself.

The king then dismissed his guests, notifying them that the next day he would call them to council to consider what had best be done for the stranger.

When the guests had departed and Ulysses was left alone with the king and queen, the queen asked him who he was and whence he came, and (recognizing the clothes which he wore as those which her maidens and herself had made) from whom he received those garments. He told them of his residence in Calypso's isle and his departure thence; of the wreck of his raft, his escape by swimming, and of the relief afforded by the princess. The parents heard approvingly, and the king promised to furnish a ship in which his guest might return to his own land.

The next day the assembled chiefs confirmed the promise of the king. A bark was prepared and a crew of stout rowers selected, and all betook themselves to the palace, where a bounteous repast was provided. After the feast the king proposed that the young men should show their guest their proficiency in manly sports, and all went forth to the arena for games of running, wrestling, and other exercises. After all had done their best, Ulysses being challenged to show what he could do, at first declined, but being taunted by one of the youths, seized a quoit of weight far heavier than any of the Phaeacians had thrown, and sent it farther than the utmost throw of theirs. All were astonished, and viewed their guest with greatly increased respect.

After the games they returned to the hall, and the herald led in Demodocus, the blind bard,

> ". . . Dear to the Muse,
>   Who yet appointed him both good and ill,
>   Took from him sight, but gave him strains divine."

He took for his theme the "Wooden Horse," by means of which the Greeks found entrance into Troy. Apollo inspired him, and he sang so feelingly the terrors and the exploits of that eventful time that all were delighted, but Ulysses was moved to tears. Observing which, Alcinoüs, when the song was done, demanded of him why at the mention of Troy his sorrows awaked. Had he lost there a father, or brother, or any dear friend? Ulysses replied by announcing himself by his true name, and at their request, recounted the adventures which had befallen him since his departure from Troy. This narrative raised the sympathy and admiration of the Phaeacians for their guest to the highest pitch. The king proposed that all the chiefs should present him with a gift, himself setting the example. They obeyed, and vied with one another in loading the illustrious stranger with costly gifts.

The next day Ulysses set sail in the Phaeacian vessel, and in a short time arrived safe at Ithaca, his own island. When the vessel touched the strand he was asleep. The mariners, without waking him, carried him on shore, and landed with him the chest containing his presents, and then sailed away.

Neptune was so displeased at the conduct of the Phaeacians in thus rescuing Ulysses from his hands that on the return of the vessel to port he transformed it into a rock, right opposite the mouth of the harbour.

Fate of the Suitors

Ulysses had now been away from Ithaca for twenty years, and when he awoke he did not recognize his native land. Minerva appeared to him in the form of a young shepherd, informed him where he was, and told him the state of things at his palace. More than a hundred nobles of Ithaca and of the neighbouring islands had been for years suing for the hand of Penelope, his wife, imagining him dead, and lording it over his palace and people, as if they were owners of both. That he might be able to take vengeance upon them, it was important that he should not be recognized. Minerva accordingly metamorphosed him into an unsightly beggar, and as such he was kindly received by Eumaeus, the swineherd, a faithful servant of his house.

Telemachus, his son, was absent in quest of his father. He had gone to the courts of the other kings, who had returned from the Trojan expedition. While on the search, he received counsel from Minerva to return home. He arrived and sought Eumaeus to learn something of the state of affairs at the palace before presenting himself among the suitors. Finding a stranger with Eumaeus, he treated him courteously, though in the garb of a beggar, and promised him assistance. Eumaeus was sent to the palace to inform Penelope privately of her son's arrival, for caution was necessary with regard to the suitors, who, as Telemachus had learned, were plotting to intercept and kill him. When Eumaeus was gone, Minerva presented herself to Ulysses, and directed him to make himself known to his son. At the same time she touched him, removed at once from him the appearance of age and penury, and gave him the aspect of vigorous manhood that belonged to him. Telemachus viewed him with astonishment, and at first thought he must be more than mortal. But Ulysses announced himself as his father,

and accounted for the change of appearance by explaining
that it was Minerva's doing.

> ". . . Then threw Telemachus
> His arms around his father's neck and wept.
> Desire intense of lamentation seized
> On both; soft murmurs uttering, each indulged
> His grief."

The father and son took counsel together how they should
get the better of the suitors and punish them for their out-
rages. It was arranged that Telemachus should proceed to
the palace and mingle with the suitors as formerly; that
Ulysses should also go as a beggar, a character which in the
rude old times had different privileges from what we con-
cede to it now. As traveller and storyteller, the beggar was
admitted in the halls of chieftains, and often treated like a
guest; though sometimes, also, no doubt, with contumely.
Ulysses charged his son not to betray, by any display of
unusual interest in him, that he knew him to be other than
he seemed, and even if he saw him insulted, or beaten, not
to interpose otherwise than he might do for any stranger. At
the palace they found the usual scene of feasting and riot
going on. The suitors pretended to receive Telemachus with
joy at his return, though secretly mortified at the failure of
their plots to take his life. The old beggar was permitted to
enter, and provided with a portion from the table. A touching incident occurred as Ulysses entered the courtyard of
the palace. An old dog lay in the yard almost dead with age,
and seeing a stranger enter, raised his head, with ears erect.
It was Argus, Ulysses' own dog, that he had in other days
often led to the chase.

> ". . . Soon as he perceived
> Long-lost Ulysses nigh, down fell his ears
> Clapped close, and with his tail glad sign he gave
> Of gratulation, impotent to rise,
> And to approach his master as of old.
> Ulysses, noting him, wiped off a tear
> Unmarked.
> . . . Then his destiny released

Old Argus, soon as he had lived to see
Ulysses in the twentieth year restored."

As Ulysses sat eating his portion in the hall, the suitors
began to exhibit their insolence to him. When he mildly
remonstrated, one of them raised a stool and with it gave
him a blow. Telemachus had hard work to restrain his indignation at seeing his father so treated in his own hall, but
remembering his father's injunctions, said no more than
what became him as master of the house, though young,
and protector of his guests.

Penelope had protracted her decision in favour of either
of her suitors so long that there seemed to be no further
pretence for delay. The continued absence of her husband
seemed to prove that his return was no longer to be expected. Meanwhile her son had grown up, and was able to
manage his own affairs. She therefore consented to submit
the question of her choice to a trial of skill among the
suitors. The test selected was shooting with the bow. Twelve
rings were arranged in a line, and he whose arrow was sent
through the whole twelve was to have the queen for his
prize. A bow that one of his brother heroes had given to
Ulysses in former times was brought from the armoury, and
with its quiver full of arrows was laid in the hall. Telemachus had taken care that all other weapons should be
removed, under pretence that in the heat of competition there
was danger, in some rash moment, of putting them to an
improper use.

All things being prepared for the trial, the first thing to
be done was to bend the bow in order to attach the string.
Telemachus endeavoured to do it, but found all his efforts
fruitless; and modestly confessing that he had attempted a
task beyond his strength, he yielded the bow to another. *He*
tried it with no better success, and, amidst the laughter and
jeers of his companions, gave it up. Another tried it and
another; they rubbed the bow with tallow, but all to no
purpose; it would not bend. Then spoke Ulysses, humbly
suggesting that he should be permitted to try; for, said he,
"beggar as I am, I was once a soldier, and there is still some
strength in these old limbs of mine." The suitors hooted with
derision, and commanded to turn him out of the hall for his
insolence. But Telemachus spoke up for him, and, merely

to gratify the old man, bade him to try. Ulysses took the bow, and handled it with the hand of a master. With ease he adjusted the cord to its notch, then fitting an arrow to the bow he drew the string and sped the arrow unerring through the rings.

Without allowing them time to express their astonishment, he said, "Now for another mark!" and aimed direct at the most insolent one of the suitors. The arrow pierced through his throat and he fell dead. Telemachus, Eumaeus, and another faithful follower, well armed, now sprang to the side of Ulysses. The suitors, in amazement, looked round for arms, but found none, neither was there any way of escape, for Eumaeus had secured the door. Ulysses left them not long in uncertainty; he announced himself as the long-lost chief, whose house they had invaded, whose substance they had squandered, whose wife and son they had persecuted for ten long years; and told them he meant to have ample vengeance. All were slain, and Ulysses was left master of his palace and possessor of his kingdom and his wife.

31. ADVENTURES OF AENEAS —
THE HARPIES — DIDO — PALINURUS

Adventures of Aeneas

We have followed one of the Grecian heroes, Ulysses, in his wanderings on his return home from Troy, and now we propose to share the fortunes of the remnant of the *conquered* people, under their chief Aeneas, in their search for a new home, after the ruin of their native city. On that fatal night when the wooden horse disgorged its contents of armed men, and the capture and conflagration of the city were the result, Aeneas made his escape from the scene of destruction, with his father, and his wife, and young son. The father, Anchises, was too old to walk with the speed required, and Aeneas took him upon his shoulders.[1] Thus

[1] See Proverbial Expressions, page 268.

burdened, leading his son and followed by his wife, he made the best of his way out of the burning city; but, in the confusion, his wife was swept away and lost.

On arriving at the place of rendezvous, numerous fugitives, of both sexes, were found, who put themselves under the guidance of Aeneas. Some months were spent in preparation, and at length they embarked. They first landed on the neighbouring shores of Thrace, and were preparing to build a city, but Aeneas was deterred by a prodigy. Preparing to offer sacrifice, he tore some twigs from one of the bushes. To his dismay the wounded part dropped blood. When he repeated the act a voice from the ground cried out to him, "Spare me, Aeneas; I am your kinsman, Polydore, here murdered with many arrows, from which a bush has grown, nourished with my blood." These words recalled to the recollection of Aeneas that Polydore was a young prince of Troy, whom his father had sent with ample treasures to the neighbouring land of Thrace, to be there brought up, at a distance from the horrors of war. The king to whom he was sent had murdered him and seized his treasures. Aeneas and his companions, considering the land accursed by the stain of such a crime, hastened away.

They next landed on the island of Delos, which was once a floating island, till Jupiter fastened it by adamantine chains to the bottom of the sea. Apollo and Diana were born there, and the island was sacred to Apollo. Here Aeneas consulted the oracle of Apollo, and received an answer, ambiguous as usual,—"Seek your ancient mother; there the race of Aeneas shall dwell, and reduce all other nations to their sway." The Trojans heard with joy and immediately began to ask one another, "Where is the spot intended by the oracle?" Anchises remembered that there was a tradition that their forefathers came from Crete and thither they resolved to steer. They arrived at Crete and began to build their city, but sickness broke out among them, and the fields that they had planted failed to yield a crop. In this gloomy aspect of affairs Aeneas was warned in a dream to leave the country and seek a western land, called Hesperia, whence Dardanus, the true founder of the Trojan race, had originally migrated. To Hesperia, now called Italy, therefore, they directed their future course, and not till after many adventures and the lapse of time sufficient to carry a modern navigator several times round the world, did they arrive there.

Their first landing was at the island of the Harpies. These were disgusting birds with the heads of maidens, with long claws and faces pale with hunger. They were sent by the gods to torment a certain Phineus, whom Jupiter had deprived of his sight, in punishment of his cruelty; and whenever a meal was placed before him the Harpies darted down from the air and carried it off. They were driven away from Phineus by the heroes of the Argonautic expedition, and took refuge in the island where Aeneas now found them.

When they entered the port the Trojans saw herds of cattle roaming over the plain. They slew as many as they wished and prepared for a feast. But no sooner had they seated themselves at the table than a horrible clamour was heard in the air, and a flock of these odious Harpies came rushing down upon them, seizing in their talons the meat from the dishes and flying away with it. Aeneas and his companions drew their swords and dealt vigorous blows among the monsters, but to no purpose, for they were so nimble it was almost impossible to hit them, and their feathers were like armour impenetrable to steel. One of them, perched on a neighbouring cliff, screamed out, "Is it thus, Trojans, you treat us innocent birds, first slaughter our cattle and then make war on ourselves?" She then predicted dire sufferings to them in their future course, and having vented her wrath flew away. The Trojans made haste to leave the country, and next found themselves coasting along the shore of Epirus. Here they landed, and to their astonishment learned that certain Trojan exiles, who had been carried there as prisoners, had become rulers of the country. Andromache, the widow of Hector, became the wife of one of the victorious Grecian chiefs, to whom she bore a son. Her husband dying, she was left regent of the country, as guardian of her son, and had married a fellow-captive, Helenus, of the royal race of Troy. Helenus and Andromache treated the exiles with the utmost hospitality, and dismissed them loaded with gifts.

From hence Aeneas coasted along the shore of Sicily and passed the country of the Cyclopses. Here they were hailed from the shore by a miserable object, whom by his garments, tattered as they were, they perceived to be a Greek. He told

them he was one of Ulysses' companions, left behind by that
chief in his hurried departure. He related the story of
Ulysses' adventure with Polyphemus, and besought them to
take him off with them as he had no means of sustaining his
existence where he was but wild berries and roots, and lived
in constant fear of the Cyclopses. While he spoke Polyphemus made his appearance; "a terrible monster, shapeless,
vast, whose only eye had been put out." [1] He walked with
cautious steps, feeling his way with a staff, down to the seaside, to wash his eye-socket in the waves. When he reached
the water, he waded out towards them, and his immense
height enabled him to advance far into the sea, so that the
Trojans, in terror, took to their oars to get out of his way.
Hearing the oars, Polyphemus shouted after them, so that
the shores resounded, and at the noise the other Cyclopses
came forth from their caves and woods and lined the shore,
like a row of lofty pine trees. The Trojans plied their oars
and soon left them out of sight.

Aeneas had been cautioned by Helenus to avoid the strait
guarded by the monsters Scylla and Charybdis. There Ulysses, the reader will remember, had lost six of his men, seized
by Scylla while the navigators were wholly intent upon
avoiding Charybdis. Aeneas, following the advice of Helenus, shunned the dangerous pass and coasted along the
island of Sicily.

Juno, seeing the Trojans speeding their way prosperously
towards their destined shore, felt her old grudge against
them revive, for she could not forget the slight that Paris had
put upon her, in awarding the prize of beauty to another.
"In heavenly minds can such resentments dwell!" [1] Accordingly she hastened to Aeolus, the ruler of the winds,—the
same who supplied Ulysses with favouring gales, giving him
the contrary ones tied up in a bag. Aeolus obeyed the goddess and sent forth his sons, Boreas, Typhon, and the other
winds, to toss the ocean. A terrible storm ensued and the
Trojan ships were driven out of their course towards the
coast of Africa. They were in imminent danger of being
wrecked, and were separated, so that Aeneas thought that
all were lost except his own.

At this crisis, Neptune, hearing the storm raging, and
knowing that he had given no orders for one, raised his head

[1] See Proverbial Expressions, page 269.

above the waves, and saw the fleet of Aeneas driving before the gale. Knowing the hostility of Juno, he was at no loss to account for it, but his anger was not the less at this interference in his province. He called the winds and dismissed them with a severe reprimand. He then soothed the waves, and brushed away the clouds from before the face of the sun. Some of the ships which had got on the rocks he prised off with his own trident, while Triton and a sea-nymph, putting their shoulders under others, set them afloat again. The Trojans, when the sea became calm, sought the nearest shore, which was the coast of Carthage, where Aeneas was so happy as to find that one by one the ships all arrived safe, though badly shaken.

Dido

Carthage, where the exiles had now arrived, was a spot on the coast of Africa opposite Sicily, where at that time a Tyrian colony under Dido, their queen, were laying the foundations of a state destined in later ages to be the rival of Rome itself. Dido was the daughter of Belus, king of Tyre, and sister of Pygmalion, who succeeded his father on the throne. Her husband was Sichaeus, a man of immense wealth, but Pygmalion, who coveted his treasures, caused him to be put to death. Dido, with a numerous body of friends and followers, both men and women, succeeded in effecting their escape from Tyre, in several vessels, carrying with them the treasures of Sichaeus. On arriving at the spot which they selected as the seat of their future home, they asked of the natives only so much land as they could enclose with a bull's hide. When this was readily granted, she caused the hide to be cut into strips, and with them enclosed a spot on which she built a citadel, and called it Byrsa (a hide). Around this fort the city of Carthage rose, and soon became a powerful and flourishing place.

Such was the state of affairs when Aeneas with his Trojans arrived there. Dido received the illustrious exiles with friendliness and hospitality. "Not unacquainted with distress," she said, "I have learned to succour the unfortunate." [1] The queen's hospitality displayed itself in festivities at which games of strength and skill were exhibited. The

[1] See Proverbial Expressions, page 269.

strangers contended for the palm with her own subjects, on equal terms, the queen declaring that whether the victor were "Trojan or Tyrian should make no difference to her." [1] At the feast which followed the games, Aeneas gave at her request a recital of the closing events of the Trojan history and his own adventures after the fall of the city. Dido was charmed with his discourse and filled with admiration of his exploits. She conceived an ardent passion for him, and he for his part seemed well content to accept the fortunate chance which appeared to offer him at once a happy termination of his wanderings, a home, a kingdom, and a bride. Months rolled away in the enjoyment of pleasant intercourse, and it seemed as if Italy and the empire destined to be founded on its shores were alike forgotten. Seeing which, Jupiter despatched Mercury with a message to Aeneas recalling him to a sense of his high destiny, and commanding him to resume his voyage.

Aeneas parted from Dido, though she tried every allurement and persuasion to detain him. The blow to her affection and her pride was too much for her to endure, and when she found that he was gone, she mounted a funeral pile which she had caused to be erected, and having stabbed herself was consumed with the pile. The flames rising over the city were seen by the departing Trojans, and, though the cause was unknown, gave to Aeneas some intimation of the fatal event.

The following epigram is from the Latin:

"Unhappy, Dido, was thy fate
In first and second married state!
One husband caused thy flight by dying,
Thy death the other caused by flying."

Palinurus

After touching at the island of Sicily, where Acestes, a prince of Trojan lineage, bore sway, who gave them a hospitable reception, the Trojans re-embarked, and held on their course for Italy. Venus now interceded with Neptune to allow her son at last to attain the wished-for goal and find an end of his perils on the deep. Neptune consented, stipu-

[1] See Proverbial Expressions, page 269.

lating only for one life as a ransom for the rest. The victim
was Palinurus, the pilot. As he sat watching the stars, with
his hand on the helm, Somnus sent by Neptune approached
in the guise of Phorbas and said: "Palinurus, the breeze is
fair, the water smooth, and the ship sails steadily on her
course. Lie down awhile and take needful rest. I will stand
at the helm in your place." Palinurus replied, "Tell me not
of smooth seas or favouring winds,—me who have seen so
much of their treachery. Shall I trust Aeneas to the chances
of the weather and the winds?" And he continued to grasp
the helm and to keep his eyes fixed on the stars. But Somnus
waved over him a branch moistened with Lethaean dew, and
his eyes closed in spite of all his efforts. Then Somnus
pushed him overboard and he fell: but keeping his hold
upon the helm, it came away with him. Neptune was mindful of his promise and kept the ship on her track without
helm or pilot, till Aeneas discovered his loss, and, sorrow-
ing deeply for his faithful steersman, took charge of the ship
himself.

The ships at last reached the shores of Italy, and joyfully
did the adventurers leap to land. While his people were employed in making their encampment Aeneas sought the
abode of the Sibyl. It was a cave connected with a temple
and grove, sacred to Apollo and Diana. While Aeneas contemplated the scene, the Sibyl accosted him. She seemed to
know his errand, and under the influence of the deity of the
place, burst forth in a prophetic strain, giving dark intima-
tions of labours and perils through which he was destined to
make his way to final success. She closed with the encouraging words which have become proverbial: "Yield not to
disasters, but press onward the more bravely." [1] Aeneas replied that he had prepared himself for whatever might
await him. He had but one request to make. Having been
directed in a dream to seek the abode of the dead in order
to confer with his father, Anchises, to receive from him a
revelation of his future fortunes and those of his race, he
asked her assistance to enable him to accomplish the task.
The Sibyl replied, "The descent to Avernus is easy: the gate
of Pluto stands open night and day; but to retrace one's
steps and return to the upper air, that is the toil, that the

[1] See Proverbial Expressions, page 269.

difficulty." [1] She instructed him to seek in the forest a tree on which grew a golden branch. This branch was to be plucked off and borne as a gift to Proserpine, and if fate was propitious it would yield to the hand and quit its parent trunk, but otherwise no force could rend it away. If torn away, another would succeed.[1]

Aeneas followed the directions of the Sibyl. His mother, Venus, sent two of her doves to fly before him and show him the way, and by their assistance he found the tree, plucked the branch, and hastened back with it to the Sibyl.

32. THE INFERNAL REGIONS —
THE SIBYL

The Infernal Regions

As at the commencement of our series we have given the pagan account of the creation of the world, so as we approach its conclusion we present a view of the regions of the dead, depicted by one of their most enlightened poets, who drew his doctrines from their most esteemed philosophers. The region where Virgil locates the entrance to this abode is perhaps the most strikingly adapted to excite ideas of the terrific and preternatural of any on the face of the earth. It is the volcanic region near Vesuvius, where the whole country is cleft with chasms, from which sulphurous flames arise, while the ground is shaken with pent-up vapours, and mysterious sounds issue from the bowels of the earth. The lake Avernus is supposed to fill the crater of an extinct volcano. It is circular, half a mile wide, and very deep, surrounded by high banks, which in Virgil's time were covered with a gloomy forest. Mephitic vapours rise from its waters, so that no life is found on its banks, and no birds fly over it. Here, according to the poet, was the cave which afforded access to the infernal regions, and here Aeneas offered sacrifices to the infernal deities, Proserpine, Hecate, and the

[1] See Proverbial Expressions, page 269.

Furies. Then a roaring was heard in the earth, the woods on the hill-tops were shaken, and the howling of dogs announced the approach of the deities. "Now," said the Sibyl, "summon up your courage, for you will need it." She descended into the cave, and Aeneas followed. Before the threshold of hell they passed through a group of beings who are enumerated as Griefs and avenging Cares, pale Diseases and melancholy Age, Fear and Hunger that tempt to crime, Toil, Poverty, and Death,—forms horrible to view. The Furies spread the couches there, and Discord, whose hair was of vipers tied up with a bloody fillet. Here also were the monsters, Briareus, with his hundred arms, Hydras hissing, and Chimaeras breathing fire. Aeneas shuddered at the sight, drew his sword and would have struck, but the Sibyl restrained him. They then came to the black river Cocytus, where they found the ferryman, Charon, old and squalid, but strong and vigorous, who was receiving passengers of all kinds into his boat, magnanimous heroes, boys and unmarried girls, as numerous as the leaves that fall at autumn, or the flocks that fly southward at the approach of winter. They stood pressing for a passage and longing to touch the opposite shore. But the stern ferryman took in only such as he chose, driving the rest back. Aeneas, wondering at the sight, asked the Sibyl, "Why this discrimination?" She answered, "Those who are taken on board the bark are the souls of those who have received due burial rites; the host of others who have remained unburied are not permitted to pass the flood but wander a hundred years, and flit to and fro about the shore, till at last they are taken over." Aeneas grieved at recollecting some of his own companions who had perished in the storm. At that moment he beheld Palinurus, his pilot, who fell overboard and was drowned. He addressed him and asked him the cause of his misfortune. Palinurus replied that the rudder was carried away, and he, clinging to it, was swept away with it. He besought Aeneas most urgently to extend to him his hand and take him in company to the opposite shore. But the Sibyl rebuked him for the wish thus to transgress the laws of Pluto; but consoled him by informing him that the people of the shore where his body had been wafted by the waves should be stirred up by prodigies to give it due burial, and that the promontory should bear the name of Cape Palinurus, which it does to this day. Leaving Palinurus consoled by these words, they approached the boat. Charon, fixing his eyes sternly upon the advancing warrior, demanded by what right he, living and armed, approached that shore. To which the Sibyl replied that they would commit no violence, that Aeneas's only object was to see his father, and finally exhibited the golden branch, at sight of which Charon's wrath relaxed, and he made haste to turn his bark to the shore, and receive them on board. The boat, adapted only to the light freight of bodiless spirits, groaned under the weight of the hero. They were soon conveyed to the opposite shore. There they were encountered by the three-headed dog, Cerberus, with his necks bristling with snakes. He barked with all his three throats till the Sibyl threw him a medicated cake which he eagerly devoured, and then stretched himself out in his den and fell asleep. Aeneas and the Sibyl sprang to land. The first sound that struck their ears was the wailing of young children, who had died on the threshold of life, and near to these were they who had perished under false charges. Minos presides over them as judge, and examines the deeds of each. The next class was of those who had died by their own hand, hating life and seeking refuge in death. O how willingly would they now endure poverty, labour, and any other infliction, if they might but return to life! Next were situated the regions of sadness, divided off into retired paths, leading through groves of myrtle. Here roamed those who had fallen victims to unrequited love, not freed from pain even by death itself. Among these, Aeneas thought he descried the form of Dido, with a wound still recent. In the dim light he was for a moment uncertain, but approaching, perceived it was indeed herself. Tears fell from his eyes, and he addressed her in the accents of love. "Unhappy Dido! was then the rumour true that you had perished? and was I, alas! the cause? I call the gods to witness that my departure from you was reluctant, and in obedience to the commands of Jove; nor could I believe that my absence would cost you so dear. Stop, I beseech you, and refuse me not a last farewell." She stood for a moment with averted countenance, and eyes fixed on the ground, and then silently passed on, as insensible to his pleadings as a rock. Aeneas followed for some distance; then, with a heavy heart, rejoined his companion and resumed his route.

They next entered the fields where roam the heroes who have fallen in battle. Here they saw many shades of Grecian and Trojan warriors. The Trojans thronged around him, and could not be satisfied with the sight. They asked the cause of his coming, and plied him with innumerable questions. But the Greeks, at the sight of his armour glittering through the murky atmosphere, recognized the hero, and filled with terror turned their backs and fled, as they used to do on the plains of Troy.

Aeneas would have lingered long with his Trojan friends, but the Sibyl hurried him away. They next came to a place where the road divided, the one leading to Elysium, the other to the regions of the condemned. Aeneas beheld on one side the walls of a mighty city, around which Phlegethon rolled its fiery waters. Before him was the gate of adamant that neither gods nor men can break through. An iron tower stood by the gate, on which Tisiphone, the avenging Fury, kept guard. From the city were heard groans, and the sound of the scourge, the creaking of iron, and the clanking of chains. Aeneas, horror-struck, inquired of his guide what crimes were those whose punishments produced the sounds he heard? The Sibyl answered, "Here is the judgment hall of Rhadamanthus, who brings to light crimes done in life, which the perpetrator vainly thought impenetrably hid. Tisiphone applies her whip of scorpions, and delivers the offender over to her sister Furies." At this moment with horrid clang the brazen gates unfolded, and Aeneas saw within a Hydra with fifty heads guarding the entrance. The Sibyl told him that the gulf of Tartarus descended deep, so that its recesses were as far beneath their feet as heaven was high above their heads. In the bottom of this pit, the Titan race, who warred against the gods, lie prostrate; Salmoneus, also, who presumed to vie with Jupiter, and built a bridge of brass over which he drove his chariot that the sound might resemble thunder, launching flaming brands at his people in imitation of lightning, till Jupiter struck him with a real thunderbolt, and taught him the difference between mortal weapons and divine. Here, also, is Tityus, the giant, whose form is so immense that as he lies he stretches over nine acres, while a vulture preys upon his liver, which as fast as it is devoured grows again, so that his punishment will have no end.

Aeneas saw groups seated at tables loaded with dainties, while near by stood a Fury who snatched away the viands from their lips as fast as they prepared to taste them. Others beheld suspended over their heads huge rocks, threatening to fall, keeping them in a state of constant alarm. These were they who had hated their brothers, or struck their parents, or defrauded the friends who trusted them, or who, having grown rich, kept their money to themselves, and gave no share to others; the last being the most numerous class. Here also were those who had violated the marriage vow, or fought in a bad cause, or failed in fidelity to their employers. Here was one who had sold his country for gold, another who perverted the laws, making them say one thing to-day and another to-morrow.

Ixion was there, fastened to the circumference of a wheel ceaselessly revolving; and Sisyphus, whose task was to roll a huge stone up to a hill-top, but when the steep was well-nigh gained, the rock, repulsed by some sudden force, rushed again headlong down to the plain. Again he toiled at it, while the sweat bathed all his weary limbs, but all to no effect. There was Tantalus, who stood in a pool, his chin level with the water, yet he was parched with thirst, and found nothing to assuage it; for when he bowed his hoary head, eager to quaff, the water fled away, leaving the ground at his feet all dry. Tall trees laden with fruit stooped their heads to him, pears, pomegranates, apples, and luscious figs; but when with a sudden grasp he tried to seized them winds whirled them high above his reach.

The Sibyl now warned Aeneas it was time to turn from these melancholy regions and seek the city of the blessed. They passed through a middle tract of darkness, and came upon the Elysian fields, the groves where the happy reside. They breathed a freer air, and saw all objects clothed in a purple light. The region has a sun and stars of its own. The inhabitants were enjoying themselves in various ways, some in sports on the grassy turf, in games of strength or skill, others dancing or singing. Orpheus struck the chords of his lyre, and called forth ravishing sounds. Here Aeneas saw the founders of the Trojan state, magnanimous heroes who lived in happier times. He gazed with admiration on the war chariots and glittering arms now reposing in disuse. Spears stood fixed in the ground, and the horses, unharnessed, roamed over the plain. The same pride in splendid armour and generous steeds which the old heroes felt in life, accompanied them here. He saw another group feasting and listening to the strains of music. They were in a laurel grove, whence the great river Po has its origin, and flows out among men. Here dwelt those who fell by wounds received in their country's cause, holy priests also, and poets who have uttered thoughts worthy of Apollo, and others who have contributed to cheer and adorn life by their discoveries in the useful arts, and have made their memory blessed by rendering service to mankind. They wore snow-white fillets about their brows. The Sibyl addressed a group of these, and inquired where Anchises was to be found. They were directed where to seek him, and soon found him in a verdant valley, where he was contemplating the ranks of his posterity, their destinies and worthy deeds to be achieved in coming times. When he recognized Aeneas approaching, he stretched out both hands to him, while tears flowed freely. "Have you come at last," said he, "long expected, and do I behold you after such perils past? O my son, how have I trembled for you as I have watched your career!" To which Aeneas replied, "O father! your image was always before me to guide and guard me." Then he endeavoured to enfold his father in his embrace, but his arms enclosed only an unsubstantial image.

Aeneas perceived before him a spacious valley, with trees gently waving to the wind, a tranquil landscape, through which the river Lethe flowed. Along the banks of the stream wandered a countless multitude, numerous as insects in the summer air. Aeneas, with surprise, inquired who were these. Anchises answered, "They are souls to which bodies are to be given in due time. Meanwhile they dwell on Lethe's bank, and drink oblivion of their former lives." "O father!" said Aeneas, "is it possible that any can be so in love with life as to wish to leave these tranquil seats for the upper world?" Anchises replied by explaining the plan of creation. The Creator, he told him, originally made the material of which souls are composed of the four elements, fire, air, earth, and water, all which when united took the form of the most excellent part, fire, and became *flame*. This material was scattered like seed among the heavenly bodies, the sun, moon, and stars. Of this seed the inferior gods created man and all other animals, mingling it with various proportions of earth, by which its purity was alloyed and reduced. Thus, the more earth predominates in the composition the less pure is the individual; and we see men and women with their full-grown bodies have not the purity of childhood. So in proportion to the time which the union of body and soul has lasted is the impurity contracted by the spiritual part. This impurity must be purged away after death, which is done by ventilating the souls in the current of winds, or merging them in water, or burning out their impurities by fire. Some few, of whom Anchises intimates that he is one, are admitted at once to Elysium, there to remain. But the rest, after the impurities of earth are purged away, are sent back to life endowed with new bodies, having had the remembrance of their former lives effectually washed away by the waters of Lethe. Some, however, there still are, so thoroughly corrupted, that they are not fit to be intrusted with human bodies, and these are made into brute animals, lions, tigers, cats, dogs, monkeys, etc. This is what the ancients called Metempsychosis, or the transmigration of souls; a doctrine which is still held by the natives of India, who scruple to destroy the life even of the most insignificant animal, not knowing but it may be one of their relations in an altered form.

Anchises, having explained so much, proceeded to point out to Aeneas individuals of his race, who were hereafter to be born, and to relate to him the exploits they should perform in the world. After this he reverted to the present, and told his son of the events that remained to him to be accomplished before the complete establishment of himself and his followers in Italy. Wars were to be waged, battles fought, a bride to be won, and in the result a Trojan state founded, from which should arise the Roman power, to be in time the sovereign of the world.

Aeneas and the Sibyl then took leave of Anchises, and returned by some short cut, which the poet does not explain, to the upper world.

Elysium

Virgil, we have seen, places his Elysium under the earth, and assigns it for a residence to the spirits of the blessed.

But in Homer Elysium forms no part of the realms of the dead. He places it on the west of the earth, near Ocean, and describes it as a happy land, where there is neither snow, nor cold, nor rain, and always fanned by the delightful breezes of Zephyrus. Hither favoured heroes pass without dying and live happy under the rule of Rhadamanthus. The Elysium of Hesiod and Pindar is in the Isles of the Blessed, or Fortunate Islands, in the Western Ocean. From these sprang the legend of the happy island Atlantis. This blissful region may have been wholly imaginary, but possibly may have sprung from the reports of some storm-driven mariners who had caught a glimpse of the coast of America.

The Sibyl

As Aeneas and the Sibyl pursued their way back to earth, he said to her, "Whether thou be a goddess or a mortal beloved of the gods, by me thou shalt always be held in reverence. When I reach the upper air I will cause a temple to be built to thy honour, and will myself bring offerings." "I am no goddess," said the Sibyl; "I have no claim to sacrifice or offering. I am mortal; yet if I could have accepted the love of Apollo I might have been immortal. He promised me the fulfilment of my wish, if I would consent to be his. I took a handful of sand, and holding it forth, said, 'Grant me to see as many birthdays as there are sand grains in my hand.' Unluckily I forgot to ask for enduring youth. This also he would have granted, could I have accepted his love, but offended at my refusal, he allowed me to grow old. My youth and youthful strength fled long ago. I have lived seven hundred years, and to equal the number of the sand grains I have still to see three hundred springs and three hundred harvests. My body shrinks up as years increase, and in time, I shall be lost to sight, but my voice will remain, and future ages will respect my sayings."

These concluding words of the Sibyl alluded to her prophetic power. In her cave she was accustomed to inscribe on leaves gathered from the trees the names and fates of individuals. The leaves thus inscribed were arranged in order within the cave, and might be consulted by her votaries. But if perchance at the opening of the door the wind rushed in and dispersed the leaves the Sibyl gave no aid in restoring them again, and the oracle was irreparably lost.

The following legend of the Sibyl is fixed at a later date. In the reign of one of the Tarquins there appeared before the king a woman who offered him nine books for sale. The king refused to purchase them, whereupon the woman went away and burned three of the books, and returning offered the remaining books for the same price she had asked for the nine. The king again rejected them; but when the woman, after burning three books more, returned and asked for the three remaining the same price which she had before asked for the nine, his curiosity was excited, and he purchased the books. They were found to contain the destinies of the Roman state. They were kept in the temple of Jupiter Capitolinus, preserved in a stone chest, and allowed to be inspected only by special officers appointed for that duty, who, on great occasions, consulted them and interpreted their oracles to the people.

There were various Sibyls; but the Cumaean Sibyl, of whom Ovid and Virgil write, is the most celebrated of them. Ovid's story of her life protracted to one thousand years may be intended to represent the various Sibyls as being only reappearances of one and the same individual.

33. AENEAS IN ITALY — CAMILLA — EVANDER — NISUS AND EURYALUS — MEZENTIUS — TURNUS

Aeneas, having parted from the Sibyl and rejoined his fleet, coasted along the shores of Italy and cast anchor in the mouth of the Tiber. The poet, having brought his hero to this spot, the destined termination of his wanderings, invokes his Muse to tell him the situation of things at that eventful moment. Latinus, third in descent from Saturn, ruled the country. He was now old and had no male descendant, but had one charming daughter, Lavinia, who was sought in marriage by many neighbouring chiefs, one of whom, Turnus, king of the Rutulians, was favoured by the wishes of her parents. But Latinus had been warned in a dream by his father Faunus, that the destined husband of Lavinia should come from a foreign land. From that union should spring a race destined to subdue the world.

Our readers will remember that in the conflict with the Harpies one of those half-human birds had threatened the Trojans with dire sufferings. In particular she predicted that before their wanderings ceased they should be pressed by hunger to devour their tables. This portent now came true; for as they took their scanty meal, seated on the grass, the men placed their hard biscuit on their laps, and put thereon whatever their gleanings in the woods supplied. Having despatched the latter they finished by eating the crusts. Seeing which, the boy Iulus said playfully, "See, we are eating our tables." Aeneas caught the words and accepted the omen. "All hail, promised land!" he exclaimed, "this is our home, this our country." He then took measures to find out who were the present inhabitants of the land, and who their rulers. A hundred chosen men were sent to the village of Latinus, bearing presents and a request for friendship and alliance. They went and were favourably received. Latinus immediately concluded that the Trojan hero was no other than the promised son-in-law announced by the oracle. He cheerfully granted his alliance and sent back the messengers mounted on steeds from his stables, and loaded with gifts and friendly messages.

Juno, seeing things go thus prosperously for the Trojans, felt her old animosity revive, summoned Alecto from Erebus, and sent her to stir up discord. The Fury first took possession of the queen, Amata, and roused her to oppose in every way the new alliance. Alecto then speeded to the city of Turnus, and assuming the form of an old priestess, informed him of the arrival of the foreigners and of the attempts of their prince to rob him of his bride. Next she turned her attention to the camp of the Trojans. There she saw the boy Iulus and his companions amusing themselves with hunting. She sharpened the scent of the dogs, and led them to rouse up from the thicket a tame stag, the favourite of Silvia, the daughter of Tyrrheus, the king's herdsman. A javelin from the hand of Iulus wounded the animal, and he had only strength left to run homewards, and died at his mistress's feet. Her cries and tears roused her brothers and the herdsmen, and they, seizing whatever weapons came to hand, furiously assaulted the hunting party. These were protected by their friends, and the herdsmen were finally driven back with the loss of two of their number.

These things were enough to rouse the storm of war, and the queen, Turnus, and the peasants all urged the old king to drive the strangers from the country. He resisted as long as he could, but, finding his opposition unavailing, finally gave way and retreated to his retirement.

Opening the Gates of Janus

It was the custom of the country, when war was to be undertaken, for the chief magistrate, clad in his robes of office, with solemn pomp to open the gates of the temple of Janus, which were kept shut as long as peace endured. His people now urged the old king to perform that solemn office, but he refused to do so. While they contested, Juno herself, descending from the skies, smote the doors with irresistible force, and burst them open. Immediately the whole country was in a flame. The people rushed from every side breathing nothing but war.

Turnus was recognized by all as leader; others joined as allies, chief of whom was Mezentius, a brave and able soldier, but of detestable cruelty. He had been the chief of one of the neighbouring cities, but his people drove him out. With him was joined his son Lausus, a generous youth, worthy of a better sire.

Camilla

Camilla, the favourite of Diana, a huntress and warrior, after the fashion of the Amazons, came with her band of mounted followers, including a select number of her own sex, and ranged herself on the side of Turnus. This maiden had never accustomed her fingers to the distaff or the loom, but had learned to endure the toils of war, and in speed to outstrip the wind. It seemed as if she might run over the standing corn without crushing it, or over the surface of the water without dipping her feet. Camilla's history had been singular from the beginning. Her father, Metabus, driven from his city by civil discord, carried with him in his flight his infant daughter. As he fled through the woods, his enemies in hot pursuit, he reached the bank of the river Amazenus, which, swelled by rain, seemed to debar a passage. He paused for a moment, then decided what to do. He tied the infant to his lance with wrappers of bark, and poising the weapon in his upraised hand, thus addressed Diana: "Goddess of the woods! I consecrate this maid to you"; then hurled the weapon with its burden to the opposite bank. The spear flew across the roaring water. His pursuers were already upon him, but he plunged into the river and swam across, and found the spear, with the infant safe on the other side. Thenceforth he lived among the shepherds and brought up his daughter in woodland arts. While a child she was taught to use the bow and throw the javelin. With her sling she could bring down the crane or the wild swan. Her dress was a tiger's skin. Many mothers sought her for a daughter-in-law, but she continued faithful to Diana and repelled the thought of marriage.

Evander

Such were the formidable allies that ranged themselves against Aeneas. It was night and he lay stretched in sleep on the bank of the river under the open heavens. The god of the stream, Father Tiber, seemed to raise his head above the willows and to say, "O goddess-born, destined possessor of the Latin realms, this is the promised land, here is to be your home, here shall terminate the hostility of the heavenly powers, if only you faithfully persevere. There are friends not far distant. Prepare your boats and row up my stream; I will lead you to Evander, the Arcadian chief. He has long been at strife with Turnus and the Rutulians, and is prepared to become an ally of yours. Rise! offer your vows to Juno, and deprecate her anger. When you have achieved your victory then think of me." Aeneas woke and paid immediate obedience to the friendly vision. He sacrificed to Juno, and invoked the god of the river and all his tributary fountains to lend their aid. Then for the first time a vessel filled with armed warriors floated on the stream of the

Tiber. The river smoothed its waves, and bade its current flow gently, while, impelled by the vigorous strokes of the rowers, the vessels shot rapidly up the stream.

About the middle of the day they came in sight of the scattered buildings of the infant town, where in after times the proud city of Rome grew, whose glory reached the skies. By chance the old king, Evander, was that day celebrating annual solemnities in honour of Hercules and all the gods. Pallas, his son, and all the chiefs of the little commonwealth stood by. When they saw the tall ship gliding onward near the wood, they were alarmed at the sight, and rose from the tables. But Pallas forbade the solemnities to be interrupted, and seizing a weapon, stepped forward to the river's bank. He called aloud, demanding who they were, and what their object. Aeneas, holding forth an olive-branch, replied, "We are Trojans, friends to you, and enemies to the Rutulians. We seek Evander, and offer to join our arms with yours." Pallas, in amaze at the sound of so great a name, invited them to land, and when Aeneas touched the shore he seized his hand, and held it long in friendly grasp. Proceeding through the wood, they joined the king and his party and were most favourably received.

Infant Rome

When the solemnities were ended all moved towards the city. The king, bending with age, walked between his son and Aeneas, taking the arm of one or the other of them, and with much variety of pleasing talk shortening the way. Evander said, "These extensive groves were once inhabited by fauns and nymphs, and a rude race of men who sprang from the trees themselves, and had neither laws nor social culture. They knew not how to yoke the cattle nor raise a harvest, nor provide from present abundance for future want; but browsed like beasts upon the leafy boughs, or fed voraciously on their hunted prey. Such were they when Saturn, expelled from Olympus by his sons, came among them and drew together the fierce savages, formed them into society and gave them laws. Such peace and plenty ensued that men ever since have called his reign the golden age; but by degrees far other times succeeded, and the thirst of gold and the thirst of blood prevailed. The land was a prey to successive tyrants, till fortune and resistless destiny brought me hither, an exile from my native land, Arcadia."

Having thus said, he showed him the Tarpeian rock, and the rude spot then overgrown with bushes where in after times the Capitol rose in all its magnificence. He next pointed to some dismantled walls, and said, "Here stood Janiculum, built by Janus, and there Saturnia, the town of Saturn." Such discourse brought them to the cottage of poor Evander, whence they saw the lowing herds roaming over the plain where now the proud and stately Forum stands. They entered, and a couch was spread for Aeneas.

Next morning, awakened by the dawn and the shrill song of birds beneath the eaves of his low mansion, old Evander rose. Clad in a tunic, and a panther's skin thrown over his shoulders, with sandals on his feet and his good sword girded to his side, he went forth to seek his guest. Two mastiffs followed him, his whole retinue and body guard. He found the hero attended by his faithful Achates, and, Pallas soon joining them, the old king spoke thus:

"Illustrious Trojan, it is but little we can do in so great a cause. Our state is feeble, hemmed in on one side by the river, on the other by the Rutulians. But I propose to ally you with a people numerous and rich, to whom fate has brought you at the propitious moment. The Etruscans hold the country beyond the river. Mezentius was their king, a monster of cruelty, who invented unheard-of torments to gratify his vengeance. He would fasten the dead to the living, hand to hand and face to face, and leave the wretched victims to die in that dreadful embrace. At length the people cast him out, him and his house. They burned his palace and slew his friends. He escaped and took refuge with Turnus, who protects him with arms. The Etruscans demand that he shall be given up to deserved punishment, and would ere now have attempted to enforce their demand; but the priests restrain them, telling them that it is the will of heaven that no native of the land shall guide them to victory, and that their destined leader must come from across the sea. They have offered the crown to me, but I am too old to undertake such great affairs, and my son is native-born, which precludes him from the choice. You, equally by birth and time of life, and fame in arms, pointed out by the gods, have but to appear to be hailed at once as their leader. With you I will join Pallas, my son, my only hope and comfort. Under you he shall learn the art of war, and strive to emulate your great exploits."

Then the king ordered horses to be furnished for the Trojan chiefs, and Aeneas, with a chosen band of followers and Pallas accompanying, mounted and took the way to the Etruscan city,[1] having sent back the rest of his party in the ships. Aeneas and his band safely arrived at the Etruscan camp and were received with open arms by Tarchon and his countrymen.

Nisus and Euryalus

In the meanwhile Turnus had collected his bands and made all necessary preparations for the war. Juno sent Iris to him with a message inciting him to take advantage of the absence of Aeneas and surprise the Trojan camp. Accordingly the attempt was made, but the Trojans were found on their guard, and having received strict orders from Aeneas not to fight in his absence, they lay still in their intrenchments, and resisted all the efforts of the Rutulians to draw them into the field. Night coming on, the army of Turnus, in high spirits at their fancied superiority, feasted and enjoyed themselves, and finally stretched themselves on the field and slept secure.

In the camp of the Trojans things were far otherwise. There all was watchfulness and anxiety and impatience for Aeneas's return. Nisus stood guard at the entrance of the camp, and Euryalus, a youth distinguished above all in the army for graces of person and fine qualities, was with him. These two were friends and brothers in arms. Nisus said to his friend, "Do you perceive what confidence and carelessness the enemy display? Their lights are few and dim, and the men seem all oppressed with wine or sleep. You know how anxiously our chiefs wish to send to Aeneas, and to get intelligence from him. Now, I am strongly moved to make my way through the enemy's camp and to go in search of our chief. If I succeed, the glory of the deed will be reward

[1] The poet here inserts a famous line which is thought to imitate in its sound the galloping of horses. It may be thus translated: "Then struck the hoofs of the steeds on the ground with a four-footed trampling."— See Proverbial Expressions, page 270.

enough for me, and if they judge the service deserves anything more, let them pay it to you."

Euryalus, all on fire with the love of adventure, replied,
"Would you, then, Nisus, refuse to share your enterprise
with me? And shall I let you go into such danger alone?
Not so my brave father brought me up, nor so have I
planned for myself when I joined the standard of Aeneas,
and resolved to hold my life cheap in comparison with honour." Nisus replied, "I doubt it not, my friend; but you
know the uncertain event of such an undertaking, and whatever may happen to me, I wish you to be safe. You are
younger than I and have more of life in prospect. Nor can I
be the cause of such grief to your mother, who has chosen
to be here in the camp with you rather than stay and live in
peace with the other matrons in Acestes' city." Euryalus replied, "Say no more. In vain you seek arguments to dis-
suade me. I am fixed in the resolution to go with you. Let
us lose no time." They called the guard, and committing the
watch to them, sought the general's tent. They found the
chief officers in consultation, deliberating how they should
send notice to Aeneas of their situation. The offer of the
two friends was gladly accepted, themselves loaded with
praises and promised the most liberal rewards in case of success. Iulus especially addressed Euryalus, assuring him of
his lasting friendship. Euryalus replied, "I have but one
boon to ask. My aged mother is with me in the camp. For
me she left the Trojan soil, and would not stay behind with
the other matrons at the city of Acestes. I go now without
taking leave of her. I could not bear her tears nor set at
nought her entreaties. But do thou, I beseech you, comfort
her in her distress. Promise me that and I shall go more
boldly into whatever dangers may present themselves."
Iulus and the other chiefs were moved to tears, and promised to do all his request. "Your mother shall be mine," said
Iulus, "and all that I have promised to you shall be made
good to her, if you do not return to receive it."

The two friends left the camp and plunged at once into
the midst of the enemy. They found no watch, no sentinels
posted, but, all about, the sleeping soldiers strewn on the
grass and among the wagons. The laws of war at that early
day did not forbid a brave man to slay a sleeping foe, and
the two Trojans slew, as they passed such of the enemy as

they could without exciting alarm. In one tent Euryalus made prize of a helmet brilliant with gold and plumes. They had passed through the enemy's ranks without being discovered, but now suddenly appeared a troop directly in front of them, which, under Volscens, their leader, were approaching the camp. The glittering helmet of Euryalus caught their attention, and Volscens hailed the two, and demanded who and whence they were. They made no answer, but plunged into the wood. The horsemen scattered in all directions to intercept their flight. Nisus had eluded pursuit and was out of danger, but Euryalus being missing he turned back to seek him. He again entered the wood and soon came within sound of voices. Looking through the thicket he saw the whole band surrounding Euryalus with noisy questions. What should he do? how extricate the youth, or would it be better to die with him?

Raising his eyes to the moon, which now shone clear, he said, "Goddess! favour my effort!" and aiming his javelin at one of the leaders of the troop, struck him in the back and stretched him on the plain with a death-blow. In the midst of their amazement another weapon flew and another of the party fell dead. Volscens, the leader, ignorant whence the darts came, rushed sword in hand upon Euryalus. "You shall pay the penalty of both," he said, and would have plunged the sword into his bosom, when Nisus, who from his concealment saw the peril of his friend, rushed forward exclaiming, " 'Twas I, 'twas I; turn your swords against me, Rutulians, I did it; he only followed me as a friend." While he spoke the sword fell, and pierced the comely bosom of Euryalus. His head fell on his shoulder, like a flower cut down by the plough. Nisus rushed upon Volscens and plunged his sword into his body, and was himself slain on the instant by numberless blows.

Mezentius

Aeneas, with his Etrurian allies, arrived on the scene of action in time to rescue his beleaguered camp; and now the two armies being nearly equal in strength, the war began in good earnest. We cannot find space for all the details, but must simply record the fate of the principal characters whom we have introduced to our readers. The tyrant Mezentius, finding himself engaged against his revolting subjects, raged like a wild beast. He slew all who dared to withstand him, and put the multitude to flight wherever he appeared. At last he encountered Aeneas, and the armies stood still to see the issue. Mezentius threw his spear, which striking Aeneas's shield glanced off and hit Anthor. He was a Grecian by birth, who had left Argos, his native city, and followed Evander into Italy. The poet says of him with simple pathos which has made the words proverbial, "He fell, unhappy, by a wound intended for another, looked up to the skies, and dying remembered sweet Argos." [1] Aeneas now in turn hurled his lance. It pierced the shield of Mezentius, and wounded him in the thigh. Lausus, his son, could not bear the sight, but rushed forward and interposed himself, while the followers pressed round Mezentius and bore him away. Aeneas held his sword suspended over Lausus and delayed to strike, but the furious youth pressed on and he was compelled to deal the fatal blow. Lausus fell, and Aeneas bent over him in pity. "Hapless youth," he said, "what can I do for you worthy of your praise? Keep those arms in which you glory, and fear not but that your body shall be restored to your friends, and have due funeral honours." So saying, he called the timid followers and delivered the body into their hands.

Mezentius meanwhile had been borne to the river-side, and washed his wound. Soon the news reached him of Lausus's death, and rage and despair supplied the place of strength. He mounted his horse and dashed into the thickest of the fight, seeking Aeneas. Having found him, he rode round him in a circle, throwing one javelin after another, while Aeneas stood fenced with his shield, turning every way to meet them. At last, after Mezentius had three times made the circuit, Aeneas threw his lance directly at the horse's head. It pierced his temples and he fell, while a shout from both armies rent the skies. Mezentius asked no mercy, but only that his body might be spared the insults of his revolted subjects, and be buried in the same grave with his son. He received the fatal stroke not unprepared, and poured out his life and his blood together.

[1] See Proverbial Expressions, page 270.

Pallas, Camilla, Turnus

While these things were doing in one part of the field, in another Turnus encountered the youthful Pallas. The contest between champions so unequally matched could not be doubtful. Pallas bore himself bravely, but fell by the lance of Turnus. The victor almost relented when he saw the brave youth lying dead at his feet, and spared to use the privilege of a conqueror in despoiling him of his arms. The belt only, adorned with studs and carvings of gold, he took and clasped round his own body. The rest he remitted to the friends of the slain.

After the battle there was a cessation of arms for some days to allow both armies to bury their dead. In this interval Aeneas challenged Turnus to decide the contest by single combat, but Turnus evaded the challenge. Another battle ensued, in which Camilla, the virgin warrior, was chiefly conspicuous. Her deeds of valor surpassed those of the bravest warriors, and many Trojans and Etruscans fell pierced with her darts or struck down by her battle-axe. At last an Etruscan named Aruns, who had watched her long, seeking for some advantage, observed her pursuing a flying enemy whose splendid armour offered a tempting prize. Intent on the chase she observed not her danger, and the javelin of Aruns struck her and inflicted a fatal wound. She fell and breathed her last in the arms of her attendant maidens. But Diana, who beheld her fate, suffered not her slaughter to be unavenged. Aruns, as he stole away, glad but frightened, was struck by a secret arrow, launched by one of the nymphs of Diana's train, and died ignobly and unknown.

At length the final conflict took place between Aeneas and Turnus. Turnus had avoided the contest as long as he could, but at last, impelled by the ill success of his arms and by the murmurs of his followers, he braced himself to the conflict. It could not be doubtful. On the side of Aeneas were the expressed decree of destiny, the aid of his goddess-mother at every emergency, and impenetrable armour fabricated by Vulcan, at her request, for her son. Turnus, on the other hand, was deserted by his celestial allies, Juno having been expressly forbidden by Jupiter to assist him any longer. Turnus threw his lance, but it recoiled harmless from the shield of Aeneas. The Trojan hero then threw his, which penetrated the shield of Turnus, and pierced his thigh. Then Turnus's fortitude forsook him and he begged for mercy; and Aeneas would have given him life, but at the instant his eye fell on the belt of Pallas, which Turnus had taken from the slaughtered youth. Instantly his rage revived, and exclaiming, "Pallas immolates thee with this blow," he thrust him through with his sword.

Here the poem of the "Aeneid" closes, and we are left to infer that Aeneas, having triumphed over his foes, obtained Lavinia for his bride. Tradition adds that he founded his city, and called it after her name, Lavinium. His son Iulus founded Alba Longa, which was the birthplace of Romulus and Remus and the cradle of Rome itself.

34. ORACLES — POETS OF MYTHOLOGY

Oracles

Oracle was the name used to denote the place where answers were supposed to be given by any of the divinities to those who consulted them respecting the future. The word was also used to signify the response which was given.

The most ancient Grecian oracle was that of Jupiter at Dodona. According to one account, it was established in the following manner: Two black doves took their flight from Thebes in Egypt. One flew to Dodona in Epirus, and alighting in a grove of oaks, it proclaimed in human language to the inhabitants of the district that they must establish there an oracle of Jupiter. The other dove flew to the temple of Jupiter Ammon in the Libyan Oasis, and delivered a similar command there. Another account is, that they were not doves, but priestesses, who were carried off from Thebes in Egypt by the Phoenicians, and set up oracles at the Oasis and Dodona. The responses of the oracle were given from the trees, by the branches rustling in the wind, the sounds being interpreted by the priests.

But the most celebrated of the Grecian oracles was that

of Apollo at Delphi, a city built on the slopes of Parnassus in Phocis.

It had been observed at a very early period that the goats feeding on Parnassus were thrown into convulsions when they approached a certain long deep cleft in the side of the mountain. This was owing to a peculiar vapour arising out of the cavern, and one of the goatherds was induced to try its effects upon himself. Inhaling the intoxicating air, he was affected in the same manner as the cattle had been, and the inhabitants of the surrounding country, unable to explain the circumstance, imputed the convulsive ravings to which he gave utterance while under the power of the exhalations to a divine inspiration. The fact was speedily circulated widely, and a temple was erected on the spot. The prophetic influence was at first variously attributed to the goddess Earth, to Neptune, Themis, and others, but it was at length assigned to Apollo, and to him alone. A priestess was appointed whose office it was to inhale the hallowed air, and who was named the Pythia. She was prepared for this duty by previous ablution at the fountain of Castalia, and being crowned with laurel was seated upon a tripod similarly adorned, which was placed over the chasm whence the divine afflatus proceeded. Her inspired words while thus situated were interpreted by the priests.

Oracle of Aesculapius

There were numerous oracles of Aesculapius, but the most celebrated one was at Epidaurus. Here the sick sought responses and the recovery of their health by sleeping in the temple. It has been inferred from the accounts that have come down to us that the treatment of the sick resembled what is now called Animal Magnetism or Mesmerism.

Serpents were sacred to Aesculapius, probably because of a superstition that those animals have a faculty of renewing their youth by a change of skin.

The worship of Aesculapius was introduced into Rome in a time of great sickness, and an embassy sent to the temple of Epidaurus to entreat the aid of the god. Aesculapius was propitious and on the return of the ship accompanied it in the form of a serpent. Arriving in the river Tiber, the serpent glided from the vessel and took possession of an island in the river, and a temple was there erected to his honour.

The Poets of Mythology

Homer, from whose poems of the "Iliad" and "Odyssey" we have taken the chief part of our chapters of the Trojan war and the return of the Grecians, is almost as mythical a personage as the heroes he celebrates. The traditionary story is that he was a wandering minstrel, blind and old, who travelled from place to place singing his lays to the music of his harp, in the courts of princes or the cottages of peasants, and dependent upon the voluntary offerings of his hearers for support. Byron calls him "The blind old man of Scio's rocky isle," and a well-known epigram, alluding to the uncertainty of the fact of his birthplace, says:

> "Seven wealthy towns contend for Homer dead,
>   Through which the living Homer begged his bread."

These seven were Smyrna, Scio, Rhodes, Colophon, Salamis, Argos, and Athens.

Modern scholars have doubted whether the Homeric poems are the work of any single mind. This arises from the difficulty of believing that poems of such length could have been committed to writing at so early an age as that usually assigned to these, an age earlier than the date of any remaining inscriptions or coins, and when no materials capable of containing such long productions were yet introduced into use. On the other hand it is asked how poems of such length could have been handed down from age to age by means of the memory alone. This is answered by the statement that there was a professional body of men, called Rhapsodists, who recited the poems of others, and whose business it was to commit to memory and rehearse for pay the national and patriotic legends.

The prevailing opinion of the learned, at this time, seems to be that the framework and much of the structure of the poems belongs to Homer, but that there are numerous interpolations and additions by other hands.

The date assigned to Homer, on the authority of Herodotus, is 850 B.C.

Virgil

Virgil, called also by his surname, Maro, from whose poem of the "Aeneid" we have taken the story of Aeneas, was one of the great poets who made the reign of the Roman emperor Augustus so celebrated, under the name of the Augustan age. Virgil was born in Mantua in the year 70 B.C. His great poem is ranked next to those of Homer, in the highest class of poetical composition, the Epic. Virgil is far inferior to Homer in originality and invention, but superior to him in correctness and elegance.

Ovid,

often alluded to in poetry by his other name of Naso, was born in the year 43 B.C. He was educated for public life and held some offices of considerable dignity, but poetry was his delight, and he early resolved to devote himself to it. He accordingly sought the society of the contemporary poets, and was acquainted with Horace and saw Virgil, though the latter died when Ovid was yet too young and undistinguished to have formed his acquaintance. Ovid spent an easy life at Rome in the enjoyment of a competent income. He was intimate with the family of Augustus, the emperor, and it is supposed that some serious offence given to some member of that family was the cause of an event which reversed the poet's happy circumstances and clouded all the latter portion of his life. At the age of fifty he was banished from Rome, and ordered to betake himself to Tomi, on the borders of the Black Sea. Here, among the barbarous people and in a severe climate, the poet, who had been accustomed to all the pleasures of a luxurious capital and the society of his most distinguished contemporaries, spent the last ten years of his life, worn out with grief and anxiety. His only consolation in exile was to address his wife and absent friends, and his letters were all poetical. Though these poems (the "Tristia" and "Letters from Pontus") have no other topic than the poet's sorrows, his exquisite taste and fruitful invention have redeemed them from the charge of being tedious, and they are read with pleasure and even with sympathy.

The two great words of Ovid are his "Metamorphoses" and his "Fasti." They are both mythological poems, and from the former we have taken most of our stories of Grecian and Roman mythology. A late writer thus characterizes these poems:

"The rich mythology of Greece furnished Ovid, as it may still furnish the poet, the painter, and the sculptor, with materials for his art. With exquisite taste, simplicity, and pathos he has narrated the fabulous traditions of early ages, and given to them that appearance of reality which only a master-hand could impart. His pictures of nature are striking and true; he selects with care that which is appropriate; he rejects the superfluous; and when he has completed his work, it is neither defective nor redundant. The 'Metamorphoses' are read with pleasure by youth, and are re-read in more advanced age with still greater delight. The poet ventured to predict that his poem would survive him, and be read wherever the Roman name was known."

The prediction above alluded to is contained in the closing lines of the "Metamorphoses," of which we give a literal translation below:

"And now I close my work, which not the ire
  Of Jove, nor tooth of time, nor sword, nor fire
  Shall bring to nought. Come when it will that day
  Which o'er the body, not the mind, has sway,
  And snatch the remnant of my life away,
  My better part above the stars shall soar,
  And my renown endure for evermore.
  Where'er the Roman arms and arts shall spread,
  There by the people shall my book be read;
  And, if aught true in poet's visions be,
  My name and fame have immortality."

35. MODERN MONSTERS —
THE PHOENIX — BASILISK — UNICORN

Modern Monsters

There is a set of imaginary beings which seem to have been
the successors of the "Gorgons, Hydras, and Chimeras dire"
of the old superstitions, and, having no connection with the
false gods of Paganism, to have continued to enjoy an
existence in the popular belief after Paganism was super-
seded by Christianity. They are mentioned perhaps by the
classical writers, but their chief popularity and currency
seem to have been in more modern times. We seek our accounts of them not so much in the poetry of the ancients as
in the old natural history books and narrations of travellers.

The Phoenix

Ovid tells the story of the Phoenix as follows: "Most beings spring from other individuals; but there is a certain
kind which reproduces itself. The Assyrians call it the
Phoenix. It does not live on fruit or flowers, but on frankincense and odoriferous gums. When it has lived five hundred
years, it builds itself a nest in the branches of an oak, or on
the top of a palm tree. In this it collects cinnamon, and
spikenard, and myrrh, and of these materials builds a pile
on which it deposits itself, and dying, breathes out its last
breath amidst odours. From the body of the parent bird, a
young Phoenix issues forth, destined to live as long a life as
its predecessor. When this has grown up and gained sufficient strength, it lifts its nest from the tree (its own cradle
and its parent's sepulchre), and carries it to the city of
Heliopolis in Egypt, and deposits it in the temple of the
Sun."

Such is the account given by a poet. Now let us see that
of a philosophic historian. Tacitus says, "in the consulship

of Paulus Fabius (A.D. 34) the miraculous bird known to
the world by the name of the Phoenix, after disappearing
for a series of ages, revisited Egypt. It was attended in its
flight by a group of various birds, all attracted by the novelty, and gazing with wonder at so beautiful an appearance." He then gives an account of the bird, not varying
materially from the preceding, but adding some details.
"The first care of the young bird as soon as fledged, and able
to trust to his wings, is to perform the obsequies of his father. But this duty is not undertaken rashly. He collects a
quantity of myrrh, and to try his strength makes frequent
excursions with a load on his back. When he has gained
sufficient confidence in his own vigour, he takes up the body
of his father and flies with it to the altar of the Sun, where
he leaves it to be consumed in flames of fragrance." Other
writers add a few particulars. The myrrh is compacted in
the form of an egg, in which the dead Phoenix is enclosed.
From the mouldering flesh of the dead bird a worm springs,
and this worm, when grown large, is transformed into a
bird. Herodotus *describes* the bird, though he says, "I have
not seen it myself, except in a picture. Part of his plumage
is gold-coloured, and part crimson; and he is for the most
part very much like an eagle in outline and bulk."

The first writer who disclaimed a belief in the existence
of the Phoenix was Sir Thomas Browne, in his "Vulgar Errors," published in 1646. He was replied to a few years
later by Alexander Ross, who says, in answer to the objec-
tion of the Phoenix so seldom making his appearance, "His
instinct teaches him to keep out of the way of the tyrant of
the creation, *man,* for if he were to be got at, some wealthy
glutton would surely devour him, though there were no
more in the world."

The Cockatrice, or Basilisk

This animal was called the king of the serpents. In con-
firmation of his royalty, he was said to be endowed with a
crest, or comb upon the head, constituting a crown. He was
supposed to be produced from the egg of a cock hatched
under toads or serpents. There were several species of this
animal. One species burned up whatever they approached;
a second were a kind of wandering Medusa's heads, and

their look caused an instant horror which was immediately followed by death. In Shakespeare's play of "Richard the Third," Lady Anne, in answer to Richard's compliment on her eyes, says, "Would they were basilisk's, to strike thee dead!"

The basilisks were called kings of serpents because all other serpents and snakes, behaving like good subjects, and wisely not wishing to be burned up or struck dead, fled the moment they heard the distant hiss of their king, although they might be in full feed upon the most delicious prey, leaving the sole enjoyment of the banquet to the royal monster.

The Roman naturalist Pliny thus describes him. "He does not impel his body, like other serpents, by a multiplied flexion, but advances lofty and upright. He kills the shrubs, not only by contact, but by breathing on them, and splits the rocks, such power of evil is there in him." It was formerly believed that if killed by a spear from on horseback the power of the poison conducted through the weapon killed not only the rider, but the horse also. To this Lucan alludes in these lines:

"What though the Moor the basilisk hath slain,
    And pinned him lifeless to the sandy plain,
Up through the spear the subtle venom flies,
    The hand imbibes it, and the victor dies."

Such a prodigy was not likely to be passed over in the legends of the saints. Accordingly we find it recorded that a certain holy man, going to a fountain in the desert, suddenly beheld a basilisk. He immediately raised his eyes to heaven, and with a pious appeal to the Deity laid the monster dead at his feet.

These wonderful powers of the basilisk are attested by a host of learned persons, such as Galen, Avicenna, Scaliger, and others. Occasionally one would demur to some part of the tale while he admitted the rest. Jonston, a learned physician, sagely remarks, "I would scarcely believe that it kills with its look, for who could have seen it and lived to tell the story?" The worthy sage was not aware that those who went to hunt the basilisk of this sort took with them a mirror, which reflected back the deadly glare upon its author, and by a kind of poetical justice slew the basilisk with his own weapon.

But what was to attack this terrible and unapproachable monster? There is an old saying that "everything has its enemy"—and the cockatrice quailed before the weasel. The basilisk might look daggers, the weasel cared not, but advanced boldly to the conflict. When bitten, the weasel retired for a moment to eat some rue, which was the only plant the basilisks could not wither, returned with renewed strength and soundness to the charge, and never left the enemy till he was stretched dead on the plain. The monster, too, as if conscious of the irregular way in which he came into the world, was supposed to have a great antipathy to a cock; and well he might, for as soon as he heard the cock crow he expired.

The basilisk was of some use after death. Thus we read that its carcass was suspended in the temple of Apollo, and in private houses, as a sovereign remedy against spiders, and that it was also hung up in the temple of Diana, for which reason no swallow ever dared enter the sacred place.

The reader will, we apprehend, by this time have had enough of absurdities, but still we can imagine his anxiety to know what a cockatrice was like. The following is from Aldrovandus, a celebrated naturalist of the sixteenth century, whose work on natural history, in thirteen folio volumes, contains with much that is valuable a large proportion of fables and inutilities. In particular he is so ample on the subject of the cock and the bull that from his practice, all rambling, gossiping tales of doubtful credibility are called *cock and bull stories*.

The Unicorn

Pliny, the Roman naturalist, out of whose account of the unicorn most of the modern unicorns have been described and figured, records it as "a very ferocious beast, similar in the rest of its body to a horse, with the head of a deer, the feet of an elephant, the tail of a boar, a deep, bellowing voice, and a single black horn, two cubits in length, standing out in the middle of its forehead." He adds that "it cannot be taken alive"; and some such excuse may have been necessary in those days for not producing the living animal upon the arena of the amphitheatre.

The unicorn seems to have been a sad puzzle to the hunters, who hardly knew how to come at so valuable a piece of game. Some described the horn as movable at the will of the animal, a kind of small sword, in short, with which no hunter who was not exceedingly cunning in fence could have a chance. Others maintained that all the animal's strength lay in its horn, and that when hard pressed in pursuit, it would throw itself from the pinnacle of the highest rocks horn foremost, so as to pitch upon it, and then quietly march off not a whit the worse for its fall.

But it seems they found out how to circumvent the poor unicorn at last. They discovered that it was a great lover of purity and innocence, so they took the field with a young virgin, who was placed in the unsuspecting admirer's way. When the unicorn spied her, he approached with all reverence, crouched beside her, and laying his head in her lap, fell asleep. The treacherous virgin then gave a signal, and the hunters made in and captured the simple beast.

36. NORTHERN MYTHOLOGY — VALHALLA — THE VALKYRIOR

Northern Mythology

The stories which have engaged our attention thus far relate to the mythology of southern regions. But there is another branch of ancient superstitions which ought not to be entirely overlooked, especially as it belongs to the nations from which we, through our English ancestors, derive our origin. It is that of the northern nations, called Scandinavians, who inhabited the countries now known as Sweden, Denmark, Norway, and Iceland. These mythological records are contained in two collections called the Eddas, of which the oldest is in poetry and dates back to the year 1056, the more modern or prose Edda being of the date of 1640.

According to the Eddas there was once no heaven above

nor earth beneath, but only a bottomless deep, and a world of mist in which flowed a fountain. Twelve rivers issued from this fountain, and when they had flowed far from their source, they froze into ice, and one layer accumulating over another, the great deep was filled up.

Southward from the world of mist was the world of light. From this flowed a warm wind upon the ice and melted it. The vapours rose in the air and formed clouds, from which sprang Ymir, the Frost giant and his progeny, and the cow Audhumbla, whose milk afforded nourishment and food to the giant. The cow got nourishment by licking the hoar frost and salt from the ice. While she was one day licking the salt stones there appeared at first the hair of a man, on the second day the whole head, and on the third the entire form endowed with beauty, agility, and power. This new being was a god, from whom and his wife, a daughter of the giant race, sprang the three brothers Odin, Vili, and Ve. They slew the giant Ymir, and out of his body formed the earth, of his blood the seas, of his bones the mountains, of his hair the trees, of his skull the heavens, and of his brain clouds, charged with hail and snow. Of Ymir's eyebrows the gods formed Midgard (mid earth), destined to become the abode of man.

Odin then regulated the periods of day and night and the seasons by placing in the heavens the sun and moon, and appointing to them their respective courses. As soon as the sun began to shed its rays upon the earth, it caused the vegetable world to bud and sprout. Shortly after the gods had created the world they walked by the side of the sea, pleased with their new work, but found that it was still incomplete, for it was without human beings. They therefore took an ash tree and made a man out of it, and they made a woman out of an alder, and called the man Aske and the woman Embla. Odin then gave them life and soul, Vili reason and motion, and Ve bestowed upon them the senses, expressive features, and speech. Midgard was then given them as their residence, and they became the progenitors of the human race.

The mighty ash tree Ygdrasill was supposed to support the whole universe. It sprang from the body of Ymir, and had three immense roots, extending one into Asgard (the dwelling of the gods), the other into Jotunheim (the abode of the giants), and the third to Niffleheim (the regions of darkness and cold). By the side of each of these roots is a spring, from which it is watered. The root that extends into Asgard is carefully tended by the three Norns, goddesses, who are regarded as the dispensers of fate. They are Urdur (the past), Verdandi (the present), Skuld (the future). The spring at the Jotunheim side is Ymir's well, in which wisdom and wit lie hidden, but that of Niffleheim feeds the adder Nidhogge (darkness), which perpetually gnaws at the root. Four harts run across the branches of the tree and bite the buds; they represent the four winds. Under the tree lies Ymir, and when he tries to shake off its weight the earth quakes.

Asgard is the name of the abode of the gods, access to which is only gained by crossing the bridge Bifrost (the rainbow). Asgard consists of golden and silver palaces, the dwellings of the gods, but the most beautiful of these is Valhalla, the residence of Odin. When seated on his throne he overlooks all heaven and earth. Upon his shoulders are the ravens Hugin and Munin, who fly every day over the whole world, and on their return report to him all they have seen and heard. At his feet lie his two wolves, Geri and Freki, to whom Odin gives all the meat that is set before him, for he himself stands in no need of food. Mead is for him both food and drink. He invented the Runic characters, and it is the business of the Norns to engrave the runes of fate upon a metal shield. From Odin's name, spelt Woden, as it sometimes is, came Wednesday, the name of the fourth day of the week.

Odin is frequently called Alfdaur (All-father), but this name is sometimes used in a way that shows that the Scandinavians had an idea of a deity superior to Odin, uncreated and eternal.

Of the Joys of Valhalla

Valhalla is the great hall of Odin, wherein he feasts with his chosen heroes, all those who have fallen bravely in battle, for all who die a peaceful death are excluded. The flesh of the boar Schrimnir is served up to them, and is abundant for all. For although this boar is cooked every morning, he becomes whole again every night. For drink the heroes are supplied abundantly with mead from the she-goat Heidrum. When the heroes are not feasting they amuse themselves with fighting. Every day they ride out into the court or field and fight until they cut each other in pieces. This is their pastime; but when meal time comes they recover from their wounds and return to feast in Valhalla.

The Valkyrior

The Valkyrior are warlike virgins, mounted upon horses and armed with helmets and spears. Odin, who is desirous to collect a great many heroes in Valhalla, to be able to meet the giants in a day when the final contest must come, sends down to every battlefield to make choice of those who shall be slain. The Valkyrior are his messengers, and their name means "Choosers of the slain." When they ride forth on their errand, their armour sheds a strange flickering light, which flashes up over the northern skies, making what men call the "Aurora Borealis," or "Northern Lights."

Of Thor and the Other Gods

Thor, the thunderer, Odin's eldest son, is the strongest of gods and men, and possesses three very precious things. The first is a hammer, which both the Frost and the Mountain giants know to their cost, when they see it hurled against them in the air, for it has split many a skull of their fathers and kindred. When thrown, it returns to his hand of its own accord. The second rare thing he possesses is called the belt of strength. When he girds it about him his divine might is doubled. The third, also very precious, is his iron gloves, which he puts on whenever he would use his mallet efficiently. From Thor's name is derived our word Thursday.

Frey is one of the most celebrated of the gods. He presides over rain and sunshine and all the fruits of the earth. His sister Freya is the most propitious of the goddesses. She loves music, spring, and flowers, and is particularly fond of the Elves (fairies). She is very fond of love ditties, and all lovers would do well to invoke her.

Bragi is the god of poetry, and his song records the deeds

of warriors. His wife, Iduna, keeps in a box the apples which the gods, when they feel old age approaching, have only to taste of to become young again.

Heimdall is the watchman of the gods, and is therefore placed on the borders of heaven to prevent the giants from forcing their way over the bridge Bifrost (the rainbow). He requires less sleep than a bird, and sees by night as well as by day a hundred miles around him. So acute is his ear that no sound escapes him, for he can even hear the grass grow and the wool on a sheep's back.

Of Loki and His Progeny

There is another deity who is described as the calumniator of the gods and the contriver of all fraud and mischief. His name is Loki. He is handsome and well made, but of a very fickle mood and most evil disposition. He is of the giant race, but forced himself into the company of the gods, and seems to take pleasure in bringing them into difficulties, and in extricating them out of the danger by his cunning, wit and skill. Loki has three children. The first is the wolf Fenris, the second the Midgard serpent, the third Hela (Death). The gods were not ignorant that these monsters were growing up, and that they would one day bring much evil upon gods and men. So Odin deemed it advisable to send one to bring them to him. When they came he threw the serpent into that deep ocean by which the earth is surrounded. But the monster had grown to such an enormous size that holding his tail in his mouth he encircles the whole earth. Hela he cast into Niffleheim, and gave her power over nine worlds or regions, into which she distributes those who are sent to her; that is, all who die of sickness or old age. Her hall is called Elvidner. Hunger is her table, Starvation her knife, Delay her man, Slowness her maid, Precipice her threshold, Care her bed, and Burning Anguish forms the hangings of the apartments. She may easily be recognized, for her body is half flesh colour and half blue, and she has a dreadfully stern and forbidding countenance.

The wolf Fenris gave the gods a great deal of trouble before they succeeded in chaining him. He broke the strongest fetters as if they were made of cobwebs. Finally the gods sent a messenger to the mountain spirits, who made for them the chain called Gleipnir. It is fashioned of six things, viz., the noise made by the footfall of a cat, the beards of women, the roots of stones, the breath of fishes, the nerves (sensibilities) of bears, and the spittle of birds. When finished it was as smooth and soft as a silken string. But when the gods asked the wolf to suffer himself to be bound with this apparently slight ribbon, he suspected their design, fearing that it was made by enchantment. He therefore only consented to be bound with it upon condition that one of the gods put his hand in his (Fenris's) mouth as a pledge that the band was to be removed again. Tyr (the god of battles) alone had courage enough to do this. But when the wolf found that he could not break his fetters, and that the gods would not release him, he bit off Tyr's hand, and he has ever since remained one-handed.

How Thor Paid the Mountain Giant His Wages

Once on a time, when the gods were constructing their abodes and had already finished Midgard and Valhalla, a certain artificer came and offered to build them a residence so well fortified that they should be perfectly safe from the incursions of the Frost giants and the giants of the mountains. But he demanded for his reward the goddess Freya, together with the sun and moon. The gods yielded to his terms, provided he would finish the whole work himself without any one's assistance, and all within the space of one winter. But if anything remained unfinished on the first day of summer he should forfeit the recompense agreed on. On being told these terms the artificer stipulated that he should be allowed the use of his horse Svadilfari, and this by the advice of Loki was granted to him. He accordingly set to work on the first day of winter, and during the night let his horse draw stone for the building. The enormous size of the stones struck the gods with astonishment, and they saw clearly that the horse did one-half more of the toilsome work than his master. Their bargain, however, had been concluded, and confirmed by solemn oaths, for without these precautions a giant would not have thought himself safe among the gods, especially when Thor should return from an expedition he had then undertaken against the evil demons.

As the winter drew to a close, the building was far advanced, and the bulwarks were sufficiently high and massive to render the place impregnable. In short, when it wanted but three days to summer, the only part that remained to be finished was the gateway. Then sat the gods on their seats of justice and entered into consultation, inquiring of one another who among them could have advised to give Freya away, or to plunge the heavens in darkness by permitting the giant to carry away the sun and the moon.

They all agreed that no one but Loki, the author of so many evil deeds, could have given such bad counsel, and that he should be put to a cruel death if he did not contrive some way to prevent the artificer from completing his task and obtaining the stipulated recompense. They proceeded to lay hands on Loki, who in his fright promised upon oath that, let it cost him what it would, he would so manage matters that the man should lose his reward. That very night when the man went with Svadilfari for building stone, a mare suddenly ran out of a forest and began to neigh. The horse thereat broke loose and ran after the mare into the forest, which obliged the man also to run after his horse, and thus between one and another the whole night was lost, so that at dawn the work had not made the usual progress. The man, seeing that he must fail of completing his task, resumed his own gigantic stature, and the gods now clearly perceived that it was in reality a mountain giant who had come amongst them. Feeling no longer bound by their oaths, they called on Thor, who immediately ran to their assistance, and lifting up his mallet, paid the workman his wages, not with the sun and moon, and not even by sending him back to Jotunheim, for with the first blow he shattered the giant's skull to pieces and hurled him headlong into Niffleheim.

The Recovery of the Hammer

Once upon a time it happened that Thor's hammer fell into the possession of the giant Thrym, who buried it eight fathoms deep under the rocks of Jotunheim. Thor sent Loki to negotiate with Thrym, but he could only prevail so far as to get the giant's promise to restore the weapon if Freya would consent to be his bride. Loki returned and reported the result of his mission, but the goddess of love was quite horrified at the idea of bestowing her charms on the king of the Frost giants. In this emergency Loki persuaded Thor to dress himself in Freya's clothes and accompany him to Jotunheim. Thrym received his veiled bride with due courtesy, but was greatly surprised at seeing her eat for her supper eight salmons and a full grown ox, besides other delicacies, washing the whole down with three tuns of mead. Loki, however, assured him that she had not tasted anything for eight long nights, so great was her desire to see her lover, the renowned ruler of Jotunheim. Thrym had at length the curiosity to peep under his bride's veil, but started back in affright and demanded why Freya's eyeballs glistened with fire. Loki repeated the same excuse and the giant was satisfied. He ordered the hammer to be brought in and laid on the maiden's lap. Thereupon Thor threw off his disguise, grasped his redoubted weapon, and slaughtered Thrym and all his followers.

Frey also possessed a wonderful weapon, a sword which would of itself spread a field with carnage whenever the owner desired it. Frey parted with this sword, but was less fortunate than Thor and never recovered it. It happened in this way: Frey once mounted Odin's throne, from whence one can see over the whole universe, and looking round saw far off in the giant's kingdom a beautiful maid, at the sight of whom he was struck with sudden sadness, insomuch that from that moment he could neither sleep, nor drink, nor speak. At last Skirnir, his messenger, drew his secret from him, and undertook to get him the maiden for his bride, if he would give him his sword as a reward. Frey consented and gave him the sword, and Skirnir set off on his journey and obtained the maiden's promise that within the nine nights she would come to a certain place and there wed Frey. Skirnir having reported the success of his errand, Frey exclaimed:

> "Long is one night,
>   Long are two nights,
>   But how shall I hold out three?
>   Shorter hath seemed

A month to me oft
Than of this longing time the half."

So Frey obtained Gerda, the most beautiful of all women, for his wife, but he lost his sword.

37. THOR'S VISIT TO JOTUNHEIM

Thor's Visit to Jotunheim, the Giant's Country

One day the god Thor, with his servant Thialfi, and accompanied by Loki, set out on a journey to the giant's country. Thialfi was of all men the swiftest afoot. He bore Thor's wallet, containing their provisions. When night came on they found themselves in an immense forest, and searched on all sides for a place where they might pass the night, and at last came to a very large hall, with an entrance that took the whole breadth of the building. Here they lay down to sleep, but towards midnight were alarmed by an earthquake which shook the whole edifice. Thor, rising up, called on his companions to seek with him a place of safety. On the right they found an adjoining chamber, into which the others entered, but Thor remained at the doorway with his mallet in his hand, prepared to defend himself, whatever might happen. A terrible groaning was heard during the night, and at dawn of day Thor went out and found lying near him a huge giant, who slept and snored in the way that had alarmed them so. It is said that for once Thor was afraid to use his mallet, and as the giant soon waked up, Thor contented himself with simply asking his name.

"My name is Skrymir," said the giant, "but I need not ask thy name, for I know that thou art the god Thor. But what has become of my glove?" Thor then perceived that what they had taken overnight for a hall was the giant's glove, and the chamber where his two companions had sought refuge was the thumb. Skrymir then proposed that they should travel in company, and Thor consenting, they sat down to eat their breakfast, and when they had done, Skrymir packed all the provisions into one wallet, threw it over his shoulder, and strode on before them, taking such tremendous strides that they were hard put to it to keep up with him. So they travelled the whole day, and at dusk Skrymir chose a place for them to pass the night in under a large oak tree. Skrymir then told them he would lie down to sleep. "But take ye the wallet," he added, "and prepare your supper."

Skrymir soon fell asleep and began to snore strongly; but when Thor tried to open the wallet, he found the giant had tied it up so tight he could not untie a single knot. At last Thor became wroth, and grasping his mallet with both hands he struck a furious blow on the giant's head. Skrymir, awakening, merely asked whether a leaf had not fallen on his head, and whether they had supped and were ready to go to sleep. Thor answered that they were just going to sleep, and so saying went and laid himself down under another tree. But sleep came not that night to Thor, and when Skrymir snored again so loud that the forest re-echoed with the noise, he arose, and grasping his mallet launched it with such force at the giant's skull that it made a deep dint in it. Skrymir, awakening, cried out, "What's the matter? Are there any birds perched on this tree? I felt some moss from the branches fall on my head. How fares it with thee, Thor?" But Thor went away hastily, saying that he had just then awoke, and that as it was only midnight, there was still time for sleep. He, however, resolved that if he had an opportunity of striking a third blow, it should settle all matters between them. A little before daybreak he perceived that Skrymir was again fast asleep, and again grasping his mallet, he dashed it with such violence that it forced its way into the giant's skull up to the handle. But Skrymir sat up, and stroking his cheek said, "An acorn fell on my head. What! Art thou awake, Thor? Methinks it is time for us to get up and dress ourselves; but you have not now a long way before you to the city called Utgard. I have heard you whispering to one another that I am not a man of small dimensions; but if you come to Utgard you will see there many men much taller than I. Wherefore I advise you, when you come there, not to make too much of yourselves, for the followers of Utgard-Loki will not brook the boasting of such little fellows as you are. You must take the road that leads eastward, mine lies northward, so we must part here."

Hereupon he threw his wallet over his shoulders and turned away from them into the forest, and Thor had no wish to stop him or to ask for any more of his company.

Thor and his companions proceeded on their way, and towards noon descried a city standing in the middle of a plain. It was so lofty that they were obliged to bend their necks quite back on their shoulders in order to see to the top of it. On arriving they entered the city, and seeing a large palace before them with the door wide open, they went in, and found a number of men of prodigious stature, sitting on benches in the hall. Going further, they came before the king, Utgard-Loki, whom they saluted with great respect. The king, regarding them with a scornful smile, said, "If I do not mistake me, that stripling yonder must be the god Thor." Then addressing himself to Thor, he said, "Perhaps thou mayest be more than thou appearest to be. What are the feats that thou and thy fellows deem yourselves skilled in, for no one is permitted to remain here who does not, in some feat or other, excel all other men?"

"The feat that I know," said Loki, "is to eat quicker than any one else, and in this I am ready to give a proof against any one here who may choose to compete with me."

"That will indeed be a feat," said Utgard-Loki, "if thou performest what thou promisest, and it shall be tried forthwith."

He then ordered one of his men who was sitting at the farther end of the bench, and whose name was Logi, to come forward and try his skill with Loki. A trough filled with meat having been set on the hall floor, Loki placed himself at one end, and Logi at the other, and each of them began to eat as fast as he could, until they met in the middle of the trough. But it was found that Loki had only eaten the flesh, while his adversary had devoured both flesh and bone, and the trough to boot. All the company therefore adjudged that Loki was vanquished.

Utgard-Loki then asked what feat the young man who accompanied Thor could perform. Thialfi answered that he would run a race with any one who might be matched against him. The king observed that skill in running was something to boast of, but if the youth would win the match he must display great agility. He then arose and went with all who were present to a plain where there was good ground for running on, and calling a young man named Hugi, bade him run a match with Thialfi. In the first course Hugi so much outstripped his competitor that he turned back and met him not far from the starting place. Then they ran a second and a third time, but Thialfi met with no better success.

Utgard-Loki then asked Thor in what feats he would choose to give proofs of that prowess for which he was so famous. Thor answered that he would try a drinking match with any one. Utgard-Loki bade his cupbearer bring the large horn which his followers were obliged to empty when they had trespassed in any way against the law of the feast. The cupbearer having presented it to Thor, Utgard-Loki said, "Whoever is a good drinker will empty that horn at a single draught, though most men make two of it, but the most puny drinker can do it in three."

Thor looked at the horn, which seemed of no extraordinary size though somewhat long; however, as he was very thirsty, he set it to his lips, and without drawing breath, pulled as long and as deeply as he could, that he might not be obliged to make a second draught of it; but when he set the horn down and looked in, he could scarcely perceive that the liquor was diminished.

After taking breath, Thor went to it again with all his might, but when he took the horn from his mouth, it seemed to him that he had drunk rather less than before, although the horn could now be carried without spilling.

"How now, Thor?" said Utgard-Loki; "thou must not spare thyself; if thou meanest to drain the horn at the third draught thou must pull deeply; and I must needs say that thou wilt not be called so mighty a man here as thou art at home if thou showest no greater prowess in other feats than methinks will be shown in this."

Thor, full of wrath, again set the horn to his lips, and did his best to empty it; but on looking in found the liquor was only a little lower, so he resolved to make no further attempt, but gave back the horn to the cupbearer.

"I now see plainly," said Utgard-Loki, "that thou art not quite so stout as we thought thee: but wilt thou try any other feat, though methinks thou art not likely to bear any prize away with thee hence."

"What new trial hast thou to propose?" said Thor.

"We have a very trifling game here," answered Utgard-Loki, "in which we exercise none but children. It consists in merely lifting my cat from the ground; nor should I have dared to mention such a feat to the great Thor if I had not already observed that thou art by no means what we took thee for."

As he finished speaking, a large grey cat sprang on the hall floor. Thor put his hand under the cat's belly and did his utmost to raise him from the floor, but the cat, bending his back, had, notwithstanding all Thor's efforts, only one of his feet lifted up, seeing which Thor made no further attempt.

"This trial has turned out," said Utgard-Loki, "just as I imagined it would. The cat is large, but Thor is little in comparison to our men."

"Little as ye call me," answered Thor, "let me see who among you will come hither now I am in wrath and wrestle with me."

"I see no one here," said Utgard-Loki, looking at the men sitting on the benches, "who would not think it beneath him to wrestle with thee; let somebody, however, call hither that old crone, my nurse Elli, and let Thor wrestle with her if he will. She has thrown to the ground many a man not less strong than this Thor is."

A toothless old woman then entered the hall, and was told by Utgard-Loki to take hold of Thor. The tale is shortly told. The more Thor tightened his hold on the crone the firmer she stood. At length after a very violent struggle Thor began to lose his footing, and was finally brought down upon one knee. Utgard-Loki then told them to desist, adding that Thor had now no occasion to ask any one else in the hall to wrestle with him, and it was also getting late; so he showed Thor and his companions to their seats, and they passed the night there in good cheer.

The next morning, at break of day, Thor and his companions dressed themselves and prepared for their departure. Utgard-Loki ordered a table to be set for them, on which there was no lack of victuals or drink. After the repast Utgard-Loki led them to the gate of the city, and on parting asked Thor how he thought his journey had turned out, and whether he had met with any men stronger than himself. Thor told him that he could not deny but that he had brought great shame on himself. "And what grieves me most," he added, "is that ye will call me a person of little worth."

"Nay," said Utgard-Loki, "it behooves me to tell thee the truth, now thou art out of the city, which so long as I live and have my way thou shalt never enter again. And, by my troth, had I known beforehand that thou hadst so much strength in thee, and wouldst have brought me so near to a great mishap, I would not have suffered thee to enter this time. Know then that I have all along deceived thee by my illusions; first in the forest, where I tied up the wallet with iron wire so that thou couldst not untie it. After this thou gavest me three blows with thy mallet; the first, though the least, would have ended my days had it fallen on me, but I slipped aside and thy blows fell on the mountain, where thou wilt find three glens, one of them remarkably deep. These are the dints made by thy mallet. I have made use of similar illusions in the contests you have had with my followers. In the first, Loki, like hunger itself, devoured all that was set before him, but Logi was in reality nothing else than Fire, and therefore consumed not only the meat, but the trough which held it. Hugi, with whom Thialfi contended in running, was Thought, and it was impossible for Thialfi to keep pace with that. When thou in thy turn didst attempt to empty the horn, thou didst perform, by my troth, a deed so marvellous that had I not seen it myself I should never have believed it. For one end of that horn reached the sea, which thou wast not aware of, but when thou comest to the shore thou wilt perceive how much the sea has sunk by thy draughts. Thou didst perform a feat no less wonderful by lifting up the cat, and to tell thee the truth, when we saw that one of his paws was off the floor, we were all of us terror-stricken, for what thou tookest for a cat was in reality the Midgard serpent that encompasseth the earth, and he was so stretched by thee that he was barely long enough to enclose it between his head and tail. Thy wrestling with Elli was also a most astonishing feat, for there was never yet a man, nor ever will be, whom Old Age, for such in fact was Elli, will not sooner or later lay low. But now, as we are going to part, let me tell thee that it will be better for both of us if thou never come near me again, for shouldst thou do so, I shall again defend myself by other illusions, so that thou wilt only lose thy labour and get no fame from the contest with me."

On hearing these words Thor in a rage laid hold of his mallet and would have launched it at him, but Utgard-Loki had disappeared, and when Thor would have returned to the city to destroy it, he found nothing around him but a verdant plain.

38. THE DEATH OF BALDUR — THE ELVES — RUNIC LETTERS — SKALDS — ICELAND

The Death of Baldur

Baldur the Good, having been tormented with terrible dreams indicating that his life was in peril, told them to the assembled gods, who resolved to conjure all things to avert from him the threatened danger. Then Frigga, the wife of Odin, exacted an oath from fire and water, from iron and all other metals, from stones, trees, diseases, beasts, birds, poisons, and creeping things, that none of them would do any harm to Baldur. Odin, not satisfied with all this, and feeling alarmed for the fate of his son, determined to consult the prophetess Angerbode, a giantess, mother of Fenris, Hela, and the Midgard serpent. She was dead, and Odin was forced to seek her in Hela's dominions.

But the other gods, feeling that what Frigga had done was quite sufficient, amused themselves with using Baldur as a mark, some hurling darts at him, some stones, while others hewed at him with their swords and battle-axes; for do what they would, none of them could harm him. And this became a favourite pastime with them and was regarded as an honour shown to Baldur. But when Loki beheld the scene he was sorely vexed that Baldur was not hurt. Assuming, therefore, the shape of a woman, he went to Fensalir, the mansion of Frigga. That goddess, when she saw the pretended woman, inquired of her if she knew what the gods were doing at their meetings. She replied that they were throwing darts and stones at Baldur, without being able to hurt him. "Ay," said Frigga, "neither stones, nor sticks, nor anything else can hurt Baldur, for I have exacted an oath from all of them." "What," exclaimed the woman, "have all things sworn to spare Baldur?" "All things," replied Frigga, "except one little shrub that grows on the eastern side of Valhalla, and is called Mistletoe, and which I thought too young and feeble to crave an oath from."

As soon as Loki heard this he went away, and resuming his natural shape, cut off the mistletoe, and repaired to the place where the gods were assembled. There he found Hodur standing apart, without partaking of the sports, on account of his blindness, and going up to him, said, "Why dost thou not also throw something at Baldur?"

"Because I am blind," answered Hodur, "and see not where Baldur is, and have, moreover, nothing to throw."

"Come, then," said Loki, "do like the rest, and show honour to Baldur by throwing this twig at him, and I will direct thy arm towards the place where he stands."

Hodur then took the mistletoe, and under the guidance of Loki, darted it at Baldur, who, pierced through and through, fell down lifeless. Surely never was there witnessed, either among gods or men, a more atrocious deed than this. When Baldur fell, the gods were struck speechless with horror, and then they looked at each other and all were of one mind to lay hands on him who had done the deed, but they were obliged to delay their vengeance out of respect for the sacred place where they were assembled. They gave vent to their grief by loud lamentations. When the gods came to themselves, Frigga asked who among them wished to gain all her love and good will. "For this," said she, "shall he have who will ride to Hel and offer Hela a ransom if she will let Baldur return to Asgard." Whereupon Hermod, surnamed the Nimble, the son of Odin, offered to undertake the journey. Odin's horse, Sleipnir, which has eight legs and can outrun the wind, was then led forth, on which Hermod mounted and galloped away on his mission. For the space of nine days and as many nights he rode through deep glens so dark that he could not discern anything, until he arrived at the river Gyoll, which he passed over on a bridge covered with glittering gold. The maiden who kept the bridge asked him his name and lineage, telling him that the day before five bands of dead persons had ridden over the bridge, and did not shake it as much as he alone. "But," she added, "thou hast not death's hue on thee; why then ridest thou here on the way to Hel?"

"I ride to Hel," answered Hermod, "to seek Baldur. Hast thou perchance seen him pass this way?"

She replied, "Baldur hath ridden over Gyoll's bridge, and yonder lieth the way he took to the abodes of death."

Hermod pursued his journey until he came to the barred gates of Hel. Here he alighted, girthed his saddle tighter, and remounting clapped both spurs to his horse, who cleared the gate by a tremendous leap without touching it. Hermod then rode on to the palace, where he found his brother Baldur occupying the most distinguished seat in the hall, and passed the night in his company. The next morning he besought Hela to let Baldur ride home with him, assuring her that nothing but lamentations were to be heard among the gods. Hela answered that it should now be tried whether Baldur was so beloved as he was said to be. "If, therefore," she added, "all things in the world, both living and lifeless, weep for him, then shall he return to life; but if any one thing speak against him or refuse to weep, he shall be kept in Hel."

Hermod then rode back to Asgard and gave an account of all he had heard and witnessed.

The gods upon this despatched messengers throughout the world to beg everything to weep in order that Baldur might be delivered from Hel. All things very willingly complied with this request, both men and every other living being, as well as earths, and stones, and trees, and metals, just as we have all seen these things weep when they are brought from a cold place into a hot one. As the messengers were returning, they found an old hag named Thaukt sitting in a cavern, and begged her to weep Baldur out of Hel. But she answered:

> "Thaukt will wail
> With dry tears
> Baldur's bale-fire.
> Let Hela keep her own."

It was strongly suspected that this hag was no other than Loki himself, who never ceased to work evil among gods and men. So Baldur was prevented from coming back to Asgard.

The Funeral of Baldur

The gods took up the dead body and bore it to the sea-shore where stood Baldur's ship "Hringham," which passed for the largest in the world. Baldur's dead body was put on the funeral pile, on board the ship, and his wife Nanna was so struck with grief at the sight that she broke her heart, and her body was burned on the same pile with her husband's. There was a vast concourse of various kinds of people at Baldur's obsequies. First came Odin accompanied by Frigga, the Valkyrior, and his ravens; then Frey in his car drawn by Gullinbursti, the boar; Heimdall rode his horse Gulltopp, and Freya drove in her chariot drawn by cats. There were also a great many Frost giants and giants of the mountain present. Baldur's horse was led to the pile fully caparisoned and consumed in the same flames with his master.

But Loki did not escape his deserved punishment. When he saw how angry the gods were, he fled to the mountain, and there built himself a hut with four doors, so that he could see every approaching danger. He invented a net to catch the fishes, such as fishermen have used since his time. But Odin found out his hiding-place and the gods assembled to take him. He, seeing this, changed himself into a salmon, and lay hid among the stones of the brook. But the gods took his net and dragged the brook, and Loki, finding he must be caught, tried to leap over the net; but Thor caught him by the tail and compressed it, so that salmons ever since have had that part remarkably fine and thin. They bound him with chains and suspended a serpent over his head, whose venom falls upon his face drop by drop. His wife Siguna sits by his side and catches the drops as they fall, in a cup; but when she carries it away to empty it, the venom falls upon Loki, which makes him howl with horror, and twist his body about so violently that the whole earth shakes, and this produces what men call earthquakes.

The Elves

The Edda mentions another class of beings, inferior to the gods, but still possessed of great power; these were called Elves. The white spirits, or Elves of Light, were exceedingly fair, more brilliant than the sun, and clad in garments of a delicate and transparent texture. They loved the light, were kindly disposed to mankind, and generally appeared as fair and lovely children. Their country was called Alfheim, and was the domain of Freyr, the god of the sun, in whose light they were always sporting.

The black or Night Elves were a different kind of creatures. Ugly, long-nosed dwarfs, of a dirty brown colour, they appeared only at night, for they avoided the sun as their most deadly enemy, because whenever his beams fell upon any of them they changed them immediately into stones. Their language was the echo of solitudes, and their dwelling-places subterranean caves and clefts. They were supposed to have come into existence as maggots produced by the decaying flesh of Ymir's body, and were afterwards endowed by the gods with a human form and great understanding. They were particularly distinguished for a knowledge of the mysterious powers of nature, and for the runes which they carved and explained. They were the most skilful artificers of all created beings, and worked in metals and in wood. Among their most noted works were Thor's hammer, and the ship "Skidbladnir," which they gave to Freyr, and which was so large that it could contain all the deities with their war and household implements, but so skilfully was it wrought that when folded together it could be put into a side pocket.

Ragnarok, the Twilight of the Gods

It was a firm belief of the northern nations that a time would come when all the visible creation, the gods of Valhalla and Niffleheim, the inhabitants of Jotunheim, Alfheim, and Midgard, together with their habitations, would be destroyed. The fearful day of destruction will not, however, be without its forerunners. First will come a triple winter, during which snow will fall from the four corners of the heavens, the frost be very severe, the wind piercing, the weather tempestuous, and the sun impart no gladness. Three such winters will pass away without being tempered by a single summer. Three other similar winters will then follow, during which war and discord will spread over the universe. The earth itself will be frightened and begin to tremble, the sea leave its basin, the heavens tear asunder, and men perish in great numbers, and the eagles of the air feast upon their still quivering bodies. The wolf Fenris will now break his bands, the Midgard serpent rise out of her bed in the sea, and Loki, released from his bonds, will join the enemies of the gods. Amidst the general devastation the sons of Muspelheim will rush forth under their leader Surtur, before and behind whom are flames and burning fire. Onward they ride over Bifrost, the rainbow bridge, which breaks under the horses' hoofs. But they, disregarding its fall, direct their course to the battlefield called Vigrid. Thither also repair the wolf Fenris, the Midgard serpent, Loki with all the followers of Hela, and the Frost giants.

Heimdall now stands up and sounds the Giallar horn to assemble the gods and heroes for the contest. The gods advance, led on by Odin, who engages the wolf Fenris, but falls a victim to the monster, who is, however, slain by Vidar, Odin's son. Thor gains great renown by killing the Midgard serpent, but recoils and falls dead, suffocated with the venom which the dying monster vomits over him. Loki and Heimdall meet and fight till they are both slain. The gods and their enemies having fallen in battle, Surtur, who has killed Freyr, darts fire and flames over the world, and the whole universe is burned up. The sun becomes dim, the earth sinks into the ocean, the stars fall from heaven, and time is no more.

After this Alfadur (the Almighty) will cause a new heaven and a new earth to arise out of the sea. The new earth filled with abundant supplies will spontaneously produce its fruits without labour or care. Wickedness and misery will no more be known, but the gods and men will live happily together.

Runic Letters

One cannot travel far in Denmark, Norway, or Sweden without meeting with great stones of different forms, engraven with characters called Runic, which appear at first sight very different from all we know. The letters consist almost invariably of straight lines, in the shape of little sticks either singly or put together. Such sticks were in early times used by the northern nations for the purpose of ascertaining future events. The sticks were shaken up, and from the figures that they formed a kind of divination was derived.

The Runic characters were of various kinds. They were chiefly used for magical purposes. The noxious, or, as they called them, the *bitter* runes, were employed to bring various evils on their enemies; the favourable averted misfortune. Some were medicinal, others employed to win love, etc. In later times they were frequently used for inscriptions, of which more than a thousand have been found. The language is a dialect of the Gothic, called Norse, still in use in Iceland. The inscriptions may therefore be read with certainty, but hitherto very few have been found which throw the least light on history. They are mostly epitaphs on tombstones.

The Skalds

The Skalds were the bards and poets of the nation, a very important class of men in all communities in an early stage of civilization. They are the depositaries of whatever historic lore there is, and it is their office to mingle something of intellectual gratification with the rude feasts of the warriors, by rehearsing, with such accomplishments of poetry and music as their skill can afford, the exploits of their heroes, living or dead. The compositions of the Skalds were called Sagas, many of which have come down to us, and contain valuable materials of history, and a faithful picture of the state of society at the time to which they relate.

Iceland

The Eddas and Sagas have come to us from Iceland. The following extract from Carlyle's lectures on "Heroes and Hero Worship" gives an animated account of the region where the strange stories we have been reading had their origin. Let the reader contrast it for a moment with Greece, the parent of classical mythology:

"In that strange island, Iceland,—burst up, the geologists say, by fire from the bottom of the sea, a wild land of barrenness and lava, swallowed many months of every year in black tempests, yet with a wild, gleaming beauty in summer time, towering up there stern and grim in the North Ocean, with its snow yokuls [mountains], roaring geysers [boiling springs], sulphur pools, and horrid volcanic chasms, like the waste, chaotic battlefield of Frost and Fire,—where, of all places, we least looked for literature or written memorials,—the record of these things was written down. On the seaboard of this wild land is a rim of grassy country, where cattle can subsist, and men by means of them and of what the sea yields; and it seems they were poetic men these, men who had deep thoughts in them and uttered musically their thoughts. Much would be lost had Iceland not been burst up from the sea, not been discovered by the Northmen!"

39. THE DRUIDS

The Druids were the priests or ministers of religion among the ancient Celtic nations in Gaul, Britain, and Germany. Our information respecting them is borrowed from notices in the Greek and Roman writers, compared with the remains of Welsh and Gaelic poetry still extant.

The Druids combined the functions of the priest, the magistrate, the scholar, and the physician. They stood to the people of the Celtic tribes in a relation closely analogous to that in which the Brahmans of India, the Magi of Persia, and the priests of the Egyptians stood to the people respectively by whom they were revered.

The Druids taught the existence of one god, to whom they gave a name "Be' al," which Celtic antiquaries tell us means "the life of everything," or "the source of all beings," and which seems to have affinity with the Phoenician Baal. What renders this affinity more striking is that the Druids as well as the Phoenicians identified this, their supreme deity, with the *Sun*. Fire was regarded as a symbol of the divinity. The Latin writers assert that the Druids also worshipped numerous inferior gods.

They used no images to represent the object of their worship, nor did they meet in temples or buildings of any kind for the performance of their sacred rites. A circle of stones (each stone generally of vast size), enclosing an area of from twenty feet to thirty yards in diameter, constituted their sacred place. The most celebrated of these now remaining is Stonehenge, on Salisbury Plain, England.

These sacred circles were generally situated near some stream, or under the shadow of a grove or widespreading oak. In the centre of the circle stood the Cromlech or altar, which was a large stone, placed in the manner of a table upon other stones set up on end. The Druids had also their high places, which were large stones or piles of stones on the summits of hills. These were called Cairns, and were used in the worship of the deity under the symbol of the sun.

That the Druids offered sacrifices to their deity there can be no doubt. But there is some uncertainty as to what they offered, and of the ceremonies connected with their religious services we know almost nothing. The classical (Roman) writers affirm that they offered on great occasions human sacrifices; as for success in war or for relief from dangerous diseases. Caesar has given a detailed account of the manner in which this was done. "They have images of immense size, the limbs of which are framed with twisted twigs and filled with living persons. These being set on fire, those within are encompassed by the flames." Many attempts have been made by Celtic writers to shake the testimony of the Roman historians to this fact, but without success.

The Druids observed two festivals in each year. The former took place in the beginning of May, and was called Beltane or "fire of God." On this occasion a large fire was kindled on some elevated spot, in honour of the sun, whose returning beneficence they thus welcomed after the gloom and desolation of winter. Of this custom a trace remains in the name given to Whitsunday in parts of Scotland to this day. Sir Walter Scott uses the word in the "Boat Song" in the "Lady of the Lake":

"Ours is no sapling, chance sown by the fountain,
Blooming at Beltane in winter to fade;" etc.

The other great festival of the Druids was called "Samh'
in," or "fire of peace," and was held on Hallow-eve (first of
November), which still retains this designation in the Highlands of Scotland. On this occasion the Druids assembled
in solemn conclave, in the most central part of the district,
to discharge the judicial functions of their order. All questions, whether public or private, all crimes against person
or property, were at this time brought before them for ad-
judication. With these judicial acts were combined certain
superstitious usages, especially the kindling of the sacred
fire, from which all the fires in the district, which had been
beforehand scrupulously extinguished, might be relighted.
This usage of kindling fires on Hallow-eve lingered in the
British islands long after the establishment of Christianity.

Besides these two great annual festivals, the Druids were
in the habit of observing the full moon, and especially the
sixth day of the moon. On the latter they sought the Mistletoe, which grew on their favourite oaks, and to which, as
well as to the oak itself, they ascribed a peculiar virtue and
sacredness. The discovery of it was an occasion of rejoicing
and solemn worship. "They call it," says Pliny, "by a word
in their language, which means 'heal-all,' and having made
solemn preparation for feasting and sacrifice under the tree,
they drive thither two milk-white bulls, whose horns are
then for the first time bound. The priest then, robed in
white, ascends the tree, and cuts off the mistletoe with a
golden sickle. It is caught in a white mantle, after which they
proceed to slay the victims, at the same time praying that
God would render his gift prosperous to those to whom he
had given it." They drink the water in which it has been
infused, and think it a remedy for all diseases. The mistletoe is a parasitic plant, and is not always nor often found
on the oak, so that when it is found it is the more precious.

The Druids were the teachers of morality as well as of
religion. Of their ethical teaching a valuable specimen is
preserved in the Triads of the Welsh Bards, and from this
we may gather that their views of moral rectitude were on
the whole just, and that they held and inculcated many very

noble and valuable principles of conduct. They were also the men of science and learning of their age and people. Whether they were acquainted with letters or not has been disputed, though the probability is strong that they were, to some extent. But it is certain that they committed nothing of their doctrine, their history, or their poetry to writing. Their teaching was oral, and their literature (if such a word may be used in such a case) was preserved solely by tradition. But the Roman writers admit that "they paid much attention to the order and laws of nature, and investigated and taught to the youth under their charge many things concerning the stars and their motions, the size of the world and the lands, and concerning the might and power of the immortal gods."

Their history consisted in traditional tales, in which the heroic deeds of their forefathers were celebrated. These were apparently in verse, and thus constituted part of the poetry as well as the history of the Druids. In the poems of Ossian we have, if not the actual productions of Druidical times, what may be considered faithful representations of the songs of the Bards.

The Bards were an essential part of the Druidical hierarchy. One author, Pennant, says, "The Bards were supposed to be endowed with powers equal to inspiration. They were the oral historians of all past transactions, public and private. They were also accomplished genealogists," etc.

Pennant gives a minute account of the Eisteddfods or sessions of the Bards and minstrels, which were held in Wales for many centuries, long after the Druidical priesthood in its other departments became extinct. At these meetings none but Bards of merit were suffered to rehearse their pieces, and minstrels of skill to perform. Judges were appointed to decide on their respective abilities, and suitable degrees were conferred. In the earlier period the judges were appointed by the Welsh princes, and after the conquest of Wales, by commission from the kings of England. Yet the tradition is that Edward I, in revenge for the influence of the Bards in animating the resistance of the people to his sway, persecuted them with great cruelty.

The Druidical system was at its height at the time of the Roman invasion under Julius Caesar. Against the Druids, as their chief enemies, these conquerors of the world directed their unsparing fury. The Druids, harassed at all points on the mainland, retreated to Anglesey and Iona, where for a season they found shelter and continued their now dishonoured rites.

The Druids retained their predominance in Iona and over the adjacent islands and mainland until they were supplanted and their superstitions overturned by the arrival of St. Columba, the apostle of the Highlands, by whom the inhabitants of that district were first led to profess Christianity.

40. BEOWULF

Although the manuscript which contains the epic of Beowulf was written about 1000 A.D., the poem itself was known and had been elaborated upon for centuries by minstrels who recited the heroic exploits of the son of Ecgtheow and nephew of Hygelac, King of the Geats, whose kingdom was what is now Southern Sweden.

In his boyhood Beowulf gave evidence of the great feats of strength and courage which in manhood made him the deliverer of Hrothgar, King of Denmark, from the monster, Grendel, and later in his own kingdom from the fiery dragon which dealt Beowulf a mortal blow.

Beowulf's first renown followed his conquest of many sea-monsters while he swam for seven days and nights before he came to the country of the Finns. Helping to defend the land of the Hetware, he killed many of the enemy and again showed his prowess as a swimmer by bringing to his ship the armor of thirty of his slain pursuers. Offered the crown of his native land, Beowulf, just entering manhood, refused it in favor of Heardred, the young son of the queen. Instead, he acted as guardian and counsellor until the boy-king grew old enough to rule alone.

For twelve years, Hrothgar, King of Denmark, suffered while his kingdom was being ravaged by a devouring monster, named Grendel. This Grendel bore a charmed life against all weapons forged by man. He lived in the wastelands and nightly prowled out to visit the hall of Hrothgar, carrying off and slaughtering many of the guests.

Beowulf, hearing from mariners of Grendel's murderous visits, sailed from Geatland with fourteen stalwart companions to render Hrothgar the help of his great strength. Landing on the Danish coast, Beowulf was challenged as a spy. He persuaded the coast-guards to let him pass, and he was received and feasted by King Hrothgar. When the king and his court retired for the night, Beowulf and his companions were left alone in the hall. All but Beowulf fell asleep. Grendel entered. With a stroke he killed one of Beowulf's sleeping men, but Beowulf, unarmed, wrestled with the monster and by dint of his great strength managed to tear Grendel's arm out at the shoulder. Grendel, mortally wounded, retreated, leaving a bloody trail from the hall to his lair.

All fear of another attack by Grendel allayed, the Danes returned to the hall, and Beowulf and his companions were sheltered elsewhere. Grendel's mother came to avenge the fatal injury to her monster son and carried off a Danish nobleman and Grendel's torn-off paw. Following the blood trail, Beowulf went forth to despatch the mother. Armed with his sword, Hrunting, he came to the water's edge. He plunged in and swam to a chamber under the sea. There he fought with Grendel's mother, killing her with an old sword he found in the sea cavern. Nearby was Grendel's body. Beowulf cut off its head and brought it back as a trophy to King Hrothgar. Great was the rejoicing in the hall and greater was Beowulf's welcome when he returned to Geatland, where he was given great estates and many high honors.

Shortly afterward, Heardred, the boy-king, was killed in the war with the Swedes. Beowulf succeeded him to the throne.

For fifty years Beowulf ruled his people in peace and serenity. Then suddenly a dragon, furious at having his treasure stolen from his hoard in a burial mound, began to ravage Beowulf's kingdom. Like Grendel, this monster left its den at night on its errand of murder and pillage.

Beowulf, now an aged monarch, resolved to do battle, unaided, with the dragon. He approached the entrance to its den, whence boiling steam issued forth. Undaunted, Beowulf strode forward shouting his defiance. The dragon came out, sputtering flames from its mouth. The monster rushed upon Beowulf with all its fury and almost crushed him in its first charge. So fearful grew the struggle that all but one of Beowulf's men deserted and fled for their lives. Wiglaf remained to help his aged monarch. Another rush of the dragon shattered Beowulf's sword and the monster's fangs sunk into Beowulf's neck. Wiglaf, rushing into the struggle, helped the dying Beowulf to kill the dragon.

Before his death, Beowulf named Wiglaf his successor to the throne of Geatland and ordered that his own ashes be placed in a memorial shrine at the top of a high cliff commanding the sea. Beowulf's body was burned on a vast funeral pyre, while twelve Geats rode around the mound singing their sorrow and their praise for the good and great man, Beowulf.

PROVERBIAL EXPRESSIONS

No. 1. Page 43

Medio tutissimus ibis.—Ovid.
You will go most safely in the middle.

No. 2. Page 45

Hic situs est Phaëton, currus auriga paterni,
Quem si non tenuit, magnis tamen excidit ausis.—Ovid.
Here lies Phaëton, the driver of his father's chariot, which
if he failed to manage, yet he fell in a great undertaking.

No. 3. Page 102

Imponere Pelio Ossam.—Virgil.
To pile Ossa upon Pelion.

No. 4. Page 184

Timeo Danaos et dona ferentes.—Virgil.
I fear the Greeks even when they offer gifts.

No. 5. Page 185

Non tali auxilio nec defensoribus istis
Tempus eget.—Virgil.
Not such aid nor such defenders does the time require.

No. 6. Page 195

Incidit in Scyllam, cupiens vitare Charybdim.
He runs on Scylla, wishing to avoid Charybdis.

No. 7. Page 205

Sequitur patrem, non passibus aequis.—Virgil.
He follows his father with unequal steps.

No. 8. Page 208

Monstrum horrendum, informe, ingens, cui lumen ademptum.—VIRGIL.
A horrible monster, misshapen, vast, whose only eye had been put out.

No. 9. Page 208

Tantaene animis coelestibus irae?—VIRGIL.
In heavenly minds can such resentments dwell?

No. 10. Page 209

Haud ignara mali, miseris succurrere disco.—VIRGIL.
Not unacquainted with distress, I have learned to succour the unfortunate.

No. 11. Page 210

Tros, Tyriusve mihi nullo discrimine agetur.—VIRGIL.
Whether Trojan or Tyrian shall make no difference to me.

No. 12. Page 211

Tu ne cede malis, sed contra audentior ito.—VIRGIL.
Yield thou not to adversity, but press on the more bravely.

No. 13. Page 212

Facilis descensus Averni;
Noctes atque dies patet atri janua Ditis;
Sed revocare gradum, superasque evadere ad auras,
Hoc opus, hic labor est.—VIRGIL.
The descent to Avernus is easy; the gate of Pluto stands open night and day; but to retrace one's steps and return to the upper air, that is the toil, that the difficulty.

No. 14. Page 212

Uno avulso non deficit alter.—VIRGIL.
When one is torn away another succeeds.

No. 15. Page 226

Quadrupedante putrem sonitu quatit ungula campum.
—VIRGIL.

Then struck the hoofs of the steeds on the ground with a four-footed trampling.

No. 16. Page 229

Sternitur infelix alieno vulnere, coelumque
Adspicit et moriens dulces reminiseitur Argos.—VIRGIL.

He falls, unhappy, by a wound intended for another; looks up to the skies, and dying remembers sweet Argos.

The Age of Chivalry
or
Legends of
King Arthur

Throngs of knights and barons bold,
In weeds of peace high triumphs hold,
With store of ladies, whose bright eyes
Rain influence and judge the prize.

MILTON

PREFACE

In the present volume the attempt has been made to treat in a form adapted to the modern taste the stories of the second "age of fable," the age which witnessed the dawn of the several states of Modern Europe.

It is believed that this presentation of a literature which held unrivalled sway over the imaginations of our ancestors, for many centuries, will not be without benefit to the reader, in addition to the amusement it may afford. The tales, though not to be trusted for their facts, are worthy of all credit as pictures of manners; and it is beginning to be held that the manners and modes of thinking of an age are a more important part of its history than the conflicts of its peoples, generally leading to no result. Besides this, the literature of romance is a treasure-house of poetical material, to which modern poets frequently resort.

These legends are so connected with each other, so consistently adapted to a group of characters strongly individualized in Arthur, Launcelot, and their compeers, and so lighted up by the fires of imagination and invention, that they seem as well adapted to the poet's purpose as the legends of the Greek and Roman mythology. And if every well-educated young person is expected to know the story of the Golden Fleece, why is the quest of the Sangreal less worthy of his acquaintance? Or if an allusion to the shield of Achilles ought not to pass unapprehended, why should one to Excalibar, the famous sword of Arthur:—

> "Of Arthur, who, to upper light restored,
> With that terrific sword,
> Which yet he brandishes for future war,
> Shall lift his country's fame above the polar star?" [1]

It is an additional recommendation of our subject, that it tends to cherish in our minds the idea of the source from which we sprung.

BOSTON, 1858   THOMAS BULFINCH

1. INTRODUCTION

On the decline of the Roman power, about five centuries after Christ, the countries of Northern Europe were left almost destitute of a national government. Numerous chiefs, more or less powerful, held local sway, as far as each could enforce his dominion, and occasionally those chiefs would unite for a common object; but, in ordinary times, they were much more likely to be found in hostility to one another. In such a state of things, the rights of the humbler classes of society were at the mercy of every assailant; and it is plain that, without some check upon the lawless power of the chiefs, society must have relapsed into barbarism. Such checks were found, first, in the rivalry of the chiefs themselves, whose mutual jealousy made them restraints upon one another; secondly, in the influence of the Church,

[1] Wordsworth.

which, by every motive, pure or selfish, was pledged to interpose for the protection of the weak; and lastly, in the generosity and sense of right which, however crushed under the weight of passion and selfishness, dwell naturally in the heart of man. From this last source sprang Chivalry, which framed an ideal of the heroic character, combining invincible strength and valor, justice, modesty, loyalty to superiors, courtesy to equals, compassion to weakness, and devotedness to the Church; an ideal which, if never met with in real life, was acknowledged by all as the highest model for emulation.

The word Chivalry is derived from the French *cheval*, a horse. The word *knight*, which originally meant boy or servant, was particularly applied to a young man after he was admitted to the privilege of bearing arms. This privilege was conferred on youths of family and fortune only, for the mass of the people were not furnished with arms. The knight then was a mounted warrior, a man of rank, or in the service and maintenance of some man of rank, generally possessing some independent means of support, but often relying mainly on the gratitude of those whom he served for the supply of his wants, and often, no doubt, resorting to the means which power confers on its possessor.

In time of war the knight was, with his followers, in the camp of his sovereign, or commanding in the field, or holding some castle for him. In time of peace he was often in attendance at his sovereign's court, gracing with his presence the banquets and tournaments with which princes cheered their leisure. Or he was traversing the country in quest of adventure, professedly bent on redressing wrongs and enforcing rights, sometimes in fulfilment of some vow of religion or of love. These wandering knights were called knights-errant; they were welcome guests in the castles of the nobility, for their presence enlivened the dulness of those secluded abodes, and they were received with honor at the abbeys, which often owed the best part of their revenues to the patronage of the knights; but if no castle or abbey or hermitage were at hand, their hardy habits made it not intolerable to them to lie down, supperless, at the foot of some wayside cross, and pass the night.

It is evident that the justice administered by such an instrumentality must have been of the rudest description. The force whose legitimate purpose was to redress wrongs, might easily be perverted to inflict them. Accordingly, we find in the romances, which, however fabulous in facts, are true as pictures of manners, that a knightly castle was often a terror to the surrounding country; that its dungeons were full of oppressed knights and ladies, waiting for some champion to appear to set them free, or to be ransomed with money; that hosts of idle retainers were ever at hand to enforce their lord's behests, regardless of law and justice; and that the rights of the unarmed multitude were of no account. This contrariety of fact and theory in regard to chivalry will account for the opposite impressions which exist in men's minds respecting it. While it has been the theme of the most fervid eulogium on the one part, it has been as eagerly denounced on the other.

The Training of a Knight

The preparatory education of candidates for knighthood was long and arduous. At seven years of age the noble children were usually removed from their father's house to the court or castle of their future patron, and placed under the care of a governor, who taught them the first articles of religion, and respect and reverence for their lords and superiors, and initiated them in the ceremonies of a court. They were called *pages, valets* or *varlets,* and their office was to carve, to wait at table, and to perform other menial services, which were not then considered humiliating. In their leisure hours they learned to dance and play on the harp, were instructed in the mysteries of *woods* and *rivers,* that is, in hunting, falconry, and fishing, and in wrestling, tilting with spears, and performing other military exercises on horseback. At fourteen the page became an esquire, and began a course of severer and more laborious exercises. To vault on a horse in heavy armor; to run, to scale walls, and spring over ditches, under the same encumbrance; to wrestle, to wield the battle-axe for a length of time, without raising the visor or taking breath; to perform with grace all the evolutions of horsemanship,—were necessary preliminaries to the reception of knighthood, which was usually conferred at twenty-one years of age, when the young man's education was supposed to be completed. In the meantime, the esquires were no less assiduously engaged in acquiring all those refinements of civility which formed what was in that age called *courtesy*. The same castle in which they received their education was usually thronged with young persons of the other sex, and the page was encouraged, at a very early age, to select some lady of the court as the mistress of his heart, to whom he was taught to refer all his sentiments, words, and actions. The service of his mistress was the glory and occupation of a knight, and her smiles, bestowed at once by affection and gratitude, were held out as the recompense of his well-directed valor. Religion united its influence with those of loyalty and love, and the order of knighthood, endowed with all the sanctity and religious awe that attended the priesthood, became an object of ambition to the greatest sovereigns.

The ceremonies of initiation were peculiarly solemn. After undergoing a severe fast, and spending whole nights in prayer, the candidate confessed, and received the sacrament. He then clothed himself in snow-white garments, and repaired to the church, or the hall, where the ceremony was to take place, bearing a knightly sword suspended from his neck, which the officiating priest took and blessed, and then returned to him. The candidate then, with folded arms, knelt before the presiding knight, who, after some questions about his motives and purposes in requesting admission, administered to him the oaths, and granted his request. Some of the knights present, sometimes even ladies and damsels, handed to him in succession the spurs, the coat of mail, the hauberk, the armlet and gauntlet, and lastly he girded on the sword. He then knelt again before the president, who, rising from his seat, gave him the "accolade," which consisted of three strokes, with the flat of a sword, on the shoulder or neck of the candidate, accompanied by the words: "In the name of God, of St. Michael, and St. George, I make thee a knight; be valiant, courteous, and loyal!" Then he received his helmet, his shield, and spear; and thus the investiture ended.

Freemen, Villains, Serfs, and Clerks

The other classes of which society was composed were, first, *freemen*, owners of small portions of land, independent, though they sometimes voluntarily became the vassals of their more opulent neighbors, whose power was necessary for their protection. The other two classes, which were much the most numerous, were either serfs or villains, both of which were slaves.

The *serfs* were in the lowest state of slavery. All the fruits of their labor belonged to the master whose land they tilled, and by whom they were fed and clothed.

The *villains* were less degraded. Their situation seems to have resembled that of the Russian peasants at this day. Like the serfs, they were attached to the soil, and were transferred with it by purchase; but they paid only a fixed rent to the landlord, and had a right to dispose of any surplus that might arise from their industry.

The term *clerk* was of very extensive import. It comprehended, originally, such persons only as belonged to the clergy, or clerical order, among whom, however, might be found a multitude of married persons, artisans or others. But in process of time a much wider rule was established; every one that could read being accounted a *clerk*, or *clericus*, and allowed the "benefit of clergy," that is, exemption from capital and some other forms of punishment, in case of crime.

Tournaments

The splendid pageant of a tournament between knights, its gaudy accessories and trappings, and its chivalrous regulations, originated in France. Tournaments were repeatedly condemned by the Church, probably on account of the quarrels they led to, and the often fatal results. The "joust," or "just," was different from the tournament. In these, knights fought with their lances, and their object was to unhorse their antagonists; while the tournaments were intended for a display of skill and address in evolutions, and with various weapons, and greater courtesy was observed in the regulations. By these it was forbidden to wound the horse, or to use the point of the sword, or to strike a knight after he had raised his visor, or unlaced his helmet. The ladies encouraged their knights in these exercises; they bestowed prizes, and the conqueror's feats were the theme of

romance and song. The stands overlooking the ground, of
course, were varied in the shapes of towers, terraces, gal-
leries, and pensile gardens, magnificently decorated with
tapestry, pavilions, and banners. Every combatant proclaimed the name of the lady whose *servant d'amour* he
was. He was wont to look up to the stand, and strengthen
his courage by the sight of the bright eyes that were rain-
ing their influence on him from above. The knights also
carried *favors,* consisting of scarfs, veils, sleeves, bracelets,
clasps,—in short, some piece of female habiliment,—attached to their helmets, shields, or armor. If, during the
combat, any of these appendages were dropped or lost, the
fair donor would at times send her knight new ones, especially if pleased with his exertions.

Mail Armor

Mail armor, of which the hauberk is a species, and which
derived its name from *maille,* a French word for mesh, was
of two kinds, *plate* or *scale* mail, and *chain* mail. It was
originally used for the protection of the body only, reaching no lower than the knees. It was shaped like a carter's
frock, and bound round the waist by a girdle. Gloves and
hose of mail were afterwards added, and a hood, which,
when necessary, was drawn over the head, leaving the face
alone uncovered. To protect the skin from the impression of
the iron network of the chain mail, a quilted lining was employed, which, however, was insufficient, and the bath was
used to efface the marks of the armor.

The hauberk was a complete covering of double chain
mail. Some hauberks opened before, like a modern coat;
others were closed like a shirt.

The chain mail of which they were composed was formed
by a number of iron links, each link having others inserted
into it, the whole exhibiting a kind of network, of which
(in some instances at least) the meshes were circular, with
each link separately riveted.

The hauberk was proof against the most violent blow of
a sword; but the point of a lance might pass through the
meshes, or drive the iron into the flesh. To guard against
this, a thick and well-stuffed doublet was worn underneath,

under which was commonly added an iron breastplate. Hence the expression "to pierce both plate and mail," so common in the earlier poets.

Mail armor continued in general use till about the year 1300, when it was gradually supplanted by plate armor, or suits consisting of pieces or plates of solid iron, adapted to the different parts of the body.

Shields were generally made of wood, covered with leather, or some similar substance. To secure them, in some sort, from being cut through by the sword, they were surrounded with a hoop of metal.

Helmets

The helmet was composed of two parts: the *headpiece*, which was strenthened within by several circles of iron; and the *visor*, which, as the name implies, was a sort of grating to see through, so contrived as, by sliding in a groove, or turning on a pivot, to be raised or lowered at pleasure. Some helmets had a further improvement called a *bever*, from the Italian *bevere*, to drink. The *ventayle*, or "air-passage," is another name for this.

To secure the helmet from the possibility of falling, or of being struck off, it was tied by several laces to the meshes of the hauberk; consequently, when a knight was overthrown, it was necessary to undo these laces before he could be put to death; though this was sometimes effected by lifting up the skirt of the hauberk, and stabbing him in the belly. The instrument of death was a small dagger, worn on the right side.

Romances

In ages when there were no books, when noblemen and princes themselves could not read, history or tradition was monopolized by the story-tellers. They inherited, generation after generation, the wondrous tales of their predecessors, which they retailed to the public with such additions of their own as their acquired information supplied them with. Anachronisms became of course very common, and errors of geography, of locality, of manners, equally so.

Spurious genealogies were invented, in which Arthur and his knights, and Charlemagne and his paladins, were made to derive their descent from Aeneas, Hector, or some other of the Trojan heroes.

With regard to the derivation of the word *Romance*, we trace it to the fact that the dialects which were formed in Western Europe, from the admixture of Latin with the native languages, took the name of *Langue Romaine*. The French language was divided into two dialects. The river Loire was their common boundary. In the provinces to the south of that river the affirmative, *yes*, was expressed by the word *oc*; in the north it was called *oil (oui)*; and hence Dante has named the southern language *langue d'oc*, and the northern *langue d'oil*. The latter, which was carried into England by the Normans, and is the origin of the present French, may be called the French Romane; and the former the Provençal, or Provencial Romane, because it was spoken by the people of Provence and Languedoc, southern provinces of France.

At a time when chivalry excited universal admiration, and when all the efforts of that chivalry were directed against the enemies of religion, it was natural that literature should receive the same impulse, and that history and fable should be ransacked to furnish examples of courage and piety that might excite increased emulation. Arthur and Charlemagne were the two heroes selected for this purpose. Arthur's pretensions were that he was a brave, though not always a successful warrior; he had withstood with great resolution the arms of the infidels, that is to say, of the Saxons, and his memory was held in the highest estimation by his countrymen, the Britons, who carried with them into Wales, and into the kindred country of Armorica, or Brittany, the memory of his exploits, which their national vanity insensibly exaggerated, till the little prince of the Silures (South Wales) was magnified into the conqueror of England, of Gaul, and of the greater part of Europe. His genealogy was gradually carried up to an imaginary Brutus, and to the period of the Trojan war, and a sort of chronicle was composed in the Welsh, or Armorican language, which, under the pompous title of the History of the Kings of Britain, was translated into Latin by Geoffrey of Monmouth, about the year 1150.

The Welsh critics consider the material of the work to have been an older history, written by St. Talian, Bishop of St. Asaph, in the seventh century.

As to Charlemagne, though his real merits were sufficient to secure his immortality, it was impossible that his *holy wars* against the Saracens should not become a favorite topic for fiction. Accordingly, the fabulous history of these wars was written, probably towards the close of the eleventh century, by a monk, who, thinking it would add dignity to his work to embellish it with a contemporary name, boldly ascribed it to Turpin, who was Archbishop of Rheims about the year 773.

These fabulous chronicles were for a while imprisoned in languages of local only or of professional access. Both Turpin and Geoffrey might indeed be read by ecclesiastics, the sole Latin scholars of those times, and Geoffrey's British original would contribute to the gratification of Welshmen; but neither could become extensively popular till translated into some language of general and familiar use. The Anglo-Saxon was at that time used only by a conquered and enslaved nation; the Spanish and Italian languages were not yet formed; the Norman French alone was spoken and understood by the nobility in the greater part of Europe, and therefore was a proper vehicle for the new mode of composition.

That language was fashionable in England before the Conquest, and became, after that event, the only language used at the court of London. As the various conquests of the Normans, and the enthusiastic valor of that extraordinary people, had familiarized the minds of men with the most marvellous events, their poets eagerly seized the fabulous legends of Arthur and Charlemagne, translated them into the language of the day, and soon produced a variety of imitations. The adventures attributed to these monarchs, and to their distinguished warriors, together with those of many other traditionary or imaginary heroes, composed by degrees that formidable body of marvellous histories which, from the dialect in which the most ancient of them were written, were called Romances.

Metrical Romances

The earliest form in which romances appear is that of a rude kind of verse. In this form it is supposed they were sung or recited at the feasts of princes and knights in their baronial halls.

It was not till toward the end of the thirteenth century that the *prose* romances began to appear. These works generally began with disowning and discrediting the sources from which in reality they drew their sole information. As every romance was supposed to be a real history, the compilers of those in prose would have forfeited all credit if they had announced themselves as mere copyists of the minstrels. On the contrary, they usually state that, as the popular poems upon the matter in question contain many "lesings," they had been induced to translate the real and true history of such or such a knight from the original Latin or Greek, or from the ancient British or Armorican authorities, which authorities existed only in their own assertion.

A specimen of the style of the prose romance may be found in the following extract from one of the most celebrated and latest of them, the Morte d'Arthur of Sir Thomas Mallory, of the date of 1485. From this work much of the contents of this volume has been drawn, with as close an adherence to the original style as was thought consistent with our plan of adapting our narrative to the taste of modern readers.

"It is notoyrly knowen thorugh the vnyuersal world that there been IX worthy and the best that ever were. That is to wete thre paynyms, thre Jewes, and thre crysten men. As for the paynyms, they were tofore the Incarnacyon of Cryst whiche were named, the fyrst Hector of Troye; the second Alysaunder the grete, and the thyrd Julyus Cezar, Emperour of Rome, of whome thystoreys ben well kno and had. And as for the thre Jewes whyche also were tofore thyncarnacyon of our Lord, of whome the fyrst was Duc Josue, whyche brought the chyldren of Israhel into the londe of beheste; the second Dauyd, kyng of Jherusalem, and the thyrd Judas Machabeus; of these thre the bybble rehearceth al theyr noble hystoryes and actes. And sythe the sayd Incarnacyon haue ben the noble crysten men stalled and admytted thorugh the vnyuersal word to the nombre of the IX beste and worthy, of whome was fyrst the noble Arthur, whose noble actes I purpose to wryte in this present book here folowyng. The second was Charlemayn, or Charles the grete, of whome thystorye is had in many places both in frensshe and englysshe, and the thyrd and last was Godefray of boloyn."

2. THE MYTHICAL HISTORY
OF ENGLAND

According to the earliest accounts, Albion, a giant, and son of Neptune, a contemporary of Hercules, ruled over the island, to which he gave his name. Presuming to oppose the progress of Hercules in his western march, he was slain by him.

Another story is that Histion, the son of Japhet, the son of Noah, had four sons,—Francus, Romanus, Alemannus, and Britto, from whom descended the French, Roman, German, and British people.

Rejecting these and other like stories, Milton gives more regard to the story of Brutus, the Trojan, which, he says, is supported by "descents of ancestry long continued, laws and exploits not plainly seeming to be borrowed or devised, which on the common belief have wrought no small impression; defended by many, denied utterly by few." The principal authority is Geoffrey of Monmouth, whose history, written in the twelfth century, purports to be a translation of a history of Britain, brought over from the opposite shore of France, which, under the name of Brittany, was chiefly peopled by natives of Britain, who from time to time emigrated thither, driven from their own country by the inroads of the Picts and Scots. According to this authority, Brutus was the son of Silvius, and he of Ascanius, the son of Aeneas, whose flight from Troy and settlement in Italy will be found narrated in "The Age of Fable."

Brutus, at the age of fifteen, attending his father to the

chase, unfortunately killed him with an arrow. Banished
therefor by his kindred, he sought refuge in that part of
Greece where Helenus, with a band of Trojan exiles, had become established. But Helenus was now dead, and the descendants of the Trojans were oppressed by Pandrasus, the
king of the country. Brutus, being kindly received among
them, so throve in virtue and in arms as to win the regard of
all the eminent of the land above all others of his age. In consequence of this the Trojans not only began to hope, but
secretly to persuade him to lead them the way to liberty.
To encourage them they had the promise of help from
Assaracus, a noble Greek youth, whose mother was a Trojan. He had suffered wrong at the hands of the king, and for
that reason the more willingly cast in his lot with the Trojan
exiles.

Choosing a fit opportunity, Brutus with his countrymen
withdrew to the woods and hills, as the safest place from
which to expostulate, and sent this message to Pandrasus:
"That the Trojans, holding it unworthy of their ancestors
to serve in a foreign land, had retreated to the woods, choosing rather a savage life than a slavish one. If that displeased
him, then, with his leave, they would depart to some other
country." Pandrasus, not expecting so bold a message from
the sons of captives, went in pursuit of them, with such
forces as he could gather, and met them on the banks of
the Achelous, where Brutus got the advantage, and took the
king captive. The result was, that the terms demanded by
the Trojans were granted; the king gave his daughter Imo-
gen in marriage to Brutus, and furnished shipping, money,
and fit provision for them all to depart from the land.

The marriage being solemnized, and shipping from all
parts got together, the Trojans, in a fleet of no less than
three hundred and twenty sail, betook themselves to the
sea. On the third day they arrived at a certain island, which
they found destitute of inhabitants, though there were appearances of former habitation, and among the ruins a
temple of Diana. Brutus, here performing sacrifice at the
shrine of the goddess, invoked an oracle for his guidance.

To whom Diana, in a vision, thus answered:—

"Brutus! far to the west, in the ocean wide,
    Beyond the realm of Gaul, a land there lies,

Seagirt it lies, where giants dwelt of old;
Now, void, it fits thy people: thither bend
Thy course; there shalt thou find a lasting seat;
There to thy sons another Troy shall rise,
And kings be born of thee, whose dreaded might
Shall save the world, and conquer nations bold."

Brutus, guided now, as he thought, by Divine direction, sped his course towards the west, and, arriving at a place on the Tyrrhene sea, found there the descendants of certain Trojans who with Antenor came into Italy, of whom Corineus was the chief. These joined company, and the ships pursued their way till they arrived at the mouth of the river Loire, in France, where the expedition landed, with a view to a settlement, but were so rudely assaulted by the inhabitants that they put to sea again, and arrived at a part of the coast of Britain now called Devonshire, where Brutus felt convinced that he had found the promised end of his voyage, landed his colony, and took possession.

The island, not yet Britain, but Albion, was in a manner desert and inhospitable, occupied only by a remnant of the giant race whose excessive force and tyranny had destroyed the others. The Trojans encountered these and extirpated them, Corineus in particular signalizing himself by his exploits against them; from whom Cornwall takes its name, for that region fell to his lot, and there the hugest giants dwelt, lurking in rocks and caves, till Corineus rid the land of them.

Brutus built his capital city, and called it Trojanova (New Troy), changed in time to Trinovantum, now London;[1] and, having governed the isle twenty-four years, died, leaving three sons, Locrine, Albanact, and Camber. Locrine had the middle part, Camber the west, called Cambria from him, and Albanact Albania, now Scotland. Locrine was married to Guendolen, the daughter of Corineus; but, having seen a fair maid named Estrildis, who had been brought captive from Germany, he became enamored of her, and had by her a daughter, whose name was Sabra. This matter was kept secret while Corineus lived; but after his death,

---

[1] "For noble Britons sprong from Trojans bold,
    And Troynovant was built of old Troy's ashes cold."
                              SPENSER, Book III, Canto IX. 38.

Locrine divorced Guendolen, and made Estrildis his queen.
Guendolen, all in rage, departed to Cornwall, where Madan,
her son, lived, who had been brought up by Corineus, his
grandfather. Gathering an army of her father's friends and
subjects, she gave battle to her husband's forces, and Locrine was slain. Guendolen caused her rival, Estrildis, with
her daughter Sabra, to be thrown into the river, from which
cause the river thenceforth bore the maiden's name, which
by length of time is now changed into Sabrina or Severn.
Milton alludes to this in his address to the river—and in

> "Severn swift, guilty of maiden's death";—

his "Comus" tells the story with a slight variation, thus:—

"There is a gentle nymph not far from hence,
  That with moist curb sways the smooth Severn stream;
  Sabrina is her name, a virgin pure:
Whilom she was the daughter of Locrine,
  That had the sceptre from his father, Brute.
  She, guiltless damsel, flying the mad pursuit
Of her enragéd step-dame, Guendolen,
Commended her fair innocence to the flood,
That stayed her flight with his cross-flowing course.
The water-nymphs that in the bottom played
Held up their pearléd wrists and took her in,
Bearing her straight to aged Nereus' hall,
Who, piteous of her woes, reared her lank head,
And gave her to his daughters to imbathe
In nectared lavers strewed with asphodel,
And through the porch and inlet of each sense
Dropped in ambrosial oils till she revived,
And underwent a quick, immortal change,
Made goddess of the river," etc.

If our readers ask when all this took place, we must answer, in the first place, that mythology is not careful of
dates; and next that, as Brutus was the great-grandson of
Aeneas, it must have been not far from a century subse-
quent to the Trojan war, or about 1100 years before the
invasion of the island by Julius Caesar. This long interval
is filled with the names of princes whose chief occupation

was in warring with one another. Some few, whose names remain connected with places, or embalmed in literature, we will mention.

Bladud

Bladud built the city of Bath, and dedicated the medicinal waters to Minerva. He was a man of great invention, and practised the arts of magic, till, having made him wings to fly, he fell down upon the temple of Apollo, in Trinovant, and so died, after twenty years' reign.

Leir

Leir, who next reigned, built Leicester, and called it after his name. He had no male issue, but only three daughters. When grown old, he determined to divide his kingdom among his daughters, and bestow them in marriage. But first, to try which of them loved him best, he determined to ask them solemnly in order, and judge of the warmth of their affection by their answers. Goneril, the eldest, knowing well her father's weakness, made answer that she loved him, "above her soul." "Since thou so honorest my declining age," said the old man, "to thee and to thy husband I give the third part of my realm." Such good success for a few words soon uttered was ample instruction to Regan, the second daughter, what to say. She therefore, to the same question replied, that "she loved him more than all the world beside"; and so received an equal reward with her sister. But Cordeilla, the youngest, and hitherto the best beloved, too honest to profess in words more than she felt in her heart, was not moved from the solid purpose of a sincere and virtuous answer, and replied: "Father, my love towards you is as my duty bids. They who pretend beyond this flatter." When the old man, sorry to hear this, and wishing her to recall these words, persisted in asking, she still restrained her expressions so as to say rather less than more than the truth. Then Leir, all in a passion, burst forth: "Since thou hast not reverenced thy aged father like thy sisters, think not to have any part in my kingdom or what else I have";—and without delay, giving in marriage his other daughters, Goneril to the Duke of Albany, and

Regan to the Duke of Cornwall, he divides his kingdom between them. Cordeilla, portionless, married the prince of France, who shortly after succeeded his father upon the throne.

King Leir went to reside with his eldest daughter, attended only by a hundred knights. But in a short time his attendants, being complained of as too numerous and disorderly, are reduced to thirty. Resenting that affront, the old king betakes him to his second daughter; but she, instead of soothing his wounded pride, takes part with her sister, and refuses to admit a retinue of more than five. Then back he returns to the other, who now will not receive him with more than one attendant. Then the remembrance of Cordeilla comes to his thoughts, and he takes his journey into France to seek her, with little hope of kind consideration from one whom he had so injured, but to pay her the last recompense he can render,—confession of his injustice. When Cordeilla is informed of his approach, and of his sad condition, she pours forth true filial tears. And, not willing that her own or others' eyes should see him in that forlorn condition, she sends one of her trusted servants to meet him, and convey him privately to some comfortable abode, and to furnish him with such state as befitted his dignity. After which Cordeilla, with the king her husband, went in state to meet him, and, after an honorable reception, the king permitted his wife Cordeilla to go with an army and set her father again upon his throne. They prospered, subdued the wicked sisters and their consorts, and Leir obtained the crown and held it three years. Cordeilla succeeded him, and reigned five years; but the sons of her sisters, after that, rebelled against her, and she lost both her crown and life.

Shakespeare has chosen this story as the subject of his tragedy of King Lear, varying its details in some respects. The madness of Lear, and the ill success of Cordeilla's attempt to reinstate her father, are the principal variations, and those in the names will also be noticed. Our narrative is drawn from Milton's History; and thus the reader will perceive that the story of Leir has had the distinguished honor of being told by the two acknowledged chiefs of British literature.

Ferrex and Porrex

Ferrex and Porrex were brothers, who held the kingdom after Leir. They quarrelled about the supremacy, and Porrex expelled his brother, who, obtaining aid from Suard, king of the Franks, returned and made war upon Porrex. Ferrex was slain in battle, and his forces dispersed. When their mother came to hear of her son's death, who was her favorite, she fell into a great rage, and conceived a mortal hatred against the survivor. She took, therefore, her opportunity when he was asleep, fell upon him, and, with the assistance of her women, tore him in pieces. This horrid story would not be worth relating, were it not for the fact that it has furnished the plot for the first tragedy which was written in the English language. It was entitled Gorboduc, but in the second edition Ferrex and Porrex, and was the production of Thomas Sackville, afterwards Earl of Dorset, and Thomas Norton, a barrister. Its date was 1561.

Dunwallo Molmutius

This is the next name of note. Molmutius established the Molmutine laws, which bestowed the privilege of sanctuary on temples, cities, and the roads leading to them, and gave the same protection to ploughs, extending a religious sanction to the labors of the field. Shakespeare alludes to him in Cymbeline, Act III, Sc. I.:—

"Molmutius made our laws;
Who was the first of Britain which did put
His brows within a golden crown, and called
Himself a king."

Brennus and Belinus,

the sons of Molmutius, succeeded him. They quarrelled, and Brennus was driven out of the island, and took refuge in Gaul, where he met with such favor from the king of the Allobroges, that he gave him his daughter in marriage, and made him his partner on the throne. Brennus is the name which the Roman historians give to the famous leader of the Gauls who took Rome in the time of Camillus. Geoffrey of Monmouth claims the glory of the conquest for the British prince, after he had become king of the Allobroges.

Elidure

After Belinus and Brennus there reigned several kings of little note, and then came Elidure. Arthgallo, his brother, being king, gave great offence to his powerful nobles, who rose against him, deposed him, and advanced Elidure to the throne. Arthgallo fled, and endeavored to find assistance in the neighboring kingdoms to reinstate him, but found none. Elidure reigned prosperously and wisely. After five years' possession of the kingdom, one day, when hunting, he met in the forest his brother, Arthgallo, who had been deposed. After long wandering, unable longer to bear the poverty to which he was reduced, he had returned to Britain, with only ten followers, designing to repair to those who had formerly been his friends. Elidure, at the sight of his brother in distress, forgetting all animosities, ran to him, and embraced him. He took Arthgallo home with him, and concealed him in the palace. After this he feigned himself sick, and, calling his nobles about him, induced them, partly by persuasion, partly by force, to consent to his abdicating the kingdom, and reinstating his brother on the throne. The agreement being ratified, Elidure took the crown from his own head, and put it on his brother's head. Arthgallo after this reigned ten years, well and wisely, exercising strict justice towards all men.

He died, and left the kingdom to his sons, who reigned with various fortunes, but were not long-lived, and left no offspring, so that Elidure was again advanced to the throne, and finished the course of his life in just and virtuous actions, receiving the name of *the pious,* from the love and admiration of his subjects.

Lud

After Elidure the Chronicle names many kings, but none of special note, till we come to Lud, who greatly enlarged Trinovant, his capital, and surrounded it with a wall. He changed its name, bestowing upon it his own, so that thenceforth it was called Lud's town, afterwards London. Lud was buried by the gate of the city called after him Ludgate. He had two sons, but they were not old enough at the time of their father's death to sustain the cares of government, and therefore their uncle Caswallaun, or Cassibellaunus, succeeded to the kingdom. He was a brave and magnificent prince, so that his fame reached to distant countries.

Cassibellaunus

About this time it happened (as is found in the Roman histories) that Julius Caesar, having subdued Gaul, came to the shore opposite Britain. And having resolved to add this island also to his conquest, he prepared ships and transported his army across the sea, to the mouth of the river Thames. Here he was met by Cassibellaun, with all his forces, and a battle ensued, in which Nennius, the brother of Cassibellaun, engaged in single combat with Caesar. After several furious blows given and received, the sword of Caesar stuck so fast in the shield of Nennius, that it could not be pulled out, and, the combatants being separated by the intervention of the troops, Nennius remained possessed of this trophy. At last, after the greater part of the day was spent, the Britons poured in so fast that Caesar was forced to retire to his camp and fleet. And finding it useless to continue the war any longer at that time, he returned to Gaul.

Shakespeare alludes to Cassibellaunus, in Cymbeline:—

> "The famed Cassibelan, who was once at point
> (O giglot fortune!) to master Caesar's sword,
> Made Lud's town with rejoicing fires bright,
> And Britons strut with courage."

Kymbelinus, or Cymbeline

Caesar, on a second invasion of the island, was more fortunate, and compelled the Britons to pay tribute. Cymbeline, the nephew of the king, was delivered to the Romans as a hostage for the faithful fulfilment of the treaty, and, being carried to Rome by Caesar, he was there brought up in the Roman arts and accomplishments. Being afterwards restored to his country, and placed on the throne,

he was attached to the Romans, and continued through all
his reign at peace with them. His sons, Guiderius and Arviragus, who make their appearance in Shakespeare's play of
Cymbeline, succeeded their father, and, refusing to pay
tribute to the Romans, brought on another invasion. Guiderius was slain but Arviragus afterward made terms with
the Romans, and reigned prosperously many years.

Armorica

The next event of note is the conquest and colonization
of Armorica, by Maximus, a Roman general, and Conan,
lord of Miniadoc or Denbigh-land, in Wales. The name of
the country was changed to Brittany, or Lesser Britain; and
so completely was it possessed by the British colonists,
that the language became assimilated to that spoken in
Wales, and it is said that to this day the peasantry of the
two countries can understand each other when speaking
their native language.

The Romans eventually succeeded in establishing themselves in the island, and after the lapse of several generations they became blended with the natives so that no distinction existed between the two races. When at length the
Roman armies were withdrawn from Britain, their departure was a matter of regret to the inhabitants, as it left them
without protection against the barbarous tribes, Scots,
Picts, and Norwegians, who harassed the country inces-
santly. This was the state of things when the era of King
Arthur began.

3. ARTHUR

We shall begin our history of King Arthur by giving those
particulars of his life which appear to rest on historical evidence; and then proceed to record those legends concerning
him which form the earliest portion of British literature.

Arthur was a prince of the tribe of Britons called Silures,
whose country was South Wales,—the son of Uther, named
Pendragon, a title given to an elective sovereign, paramount

over the many kings of Britain. He appears to have commenced his martial career about the year 500, and was raised to the Pendragonship about ten years later. He is said to have gained twelve victories over the Saxons. The most important of them was that of Badon, by some supposed to be Bath, by others Berkshire. This was the last of his battles with the Saxons, and checked their progress so effectually that Arthur experienced no more annoyance from them, and reigned in peace, until the revolt of his nephew Modred, twenty years later, which led to the fatal battle of Camlan, in Cornwall, in 542. Modred was slain, and Arthur, mortally wounded was conveyed by sea to Glastonbury, where he died, and was buried. Tradition preserved the memory of the place of his interment within the abbey, as we are told by Giraldus Cambrensis, who was present when the grave was opened by command of Henry II. in 1150, and saw the bones and sword of the monarch, and a leaden cross let into his tombstone, with the inscription in rude Roman letters, "Here lies buried the famous King Arthur, in the island Avolonia." A popular traditional belief was long entertained among the Britons that Arthur was not dead, but had been carried off to be healed of his wounds in Fairy-land, and that he would reappear to avenge his countrymen, and reinstate them in the sovereignty of Britain.

It must not be concealed, that the very existence of Arthur has been denied by some. Milton says of him: "As to Arthur, more renowned in songs and romances than in true stories, who he was, and whether ever any such reigned in Britain, hath been doubted heretofore, and may again, with good reason." Modern critics, however, admit that there was a prince of this name, and find proof of it in the frequent mention of him in the writings of the Welsh bards. But the Arthur of romance, according to Mr. Owen, a Welsh scholar and antiquarian, is a mythological person. "Arthur," he says, "is the Great Bear, as the name literally implies (Arctos, Arcturus), and perhaps this constellation, being so near the pole, and visibly describing a circle in a small space, is the origin of the famous Round Table." Let us now turn to the history of King Arthur, as recorded by the romantic chroniclers.

Constans, king of Britain, had three sons, Moines, Ambrosius, otherwise called Uther, and Pendragon. Moines, soon after his accession to the crown, was vanquished by the Saxons, in consequence of the treachery of his seneschal, Vortigern, and growing unpopular, through misfortune, he was killed by his subjects, and the traitor Vortigern chosen in his place.

Vortigern was soon after defeated in a great battle by Uther and Pendragon, the surviving brothers of Moines, and Pendragon ascended the throne.

This prince had great confidence in the wisdom of Merlin, and made him his chief adviser. About this time a dreadful war arose between the Saxons and Britons. Merlin obliged the royal brothers to swear fidelity to each other, but predicted that one of them must fall in the first battle. The Saxons were routed, and Pendragon, being slain, was succeeded by Uther, who now assumed, in addition to his own name, the appellation of Pendragon.

Merlin still continued a favorite counsellor. At the request of Uther, he transported by magic art enormous stones from Ireland, to form the sepulchre of Pendragon. These stones constitute the monument now called Stonehenge, on Salisbury Plain.

Merlin next proceeded to Carlisle to prepare the Round Table, at which he seated an assemblage of the great nobles of the country. The companions admitted to this high order were bound by oath to assist each other at the hazard of their own lives, to attempt singly the most perilous adventures, to lead, when necessary, a life of monastic solitude, to fly to arms at the first summons, and never to retire from battle till they had defeated the enemy, unless night intervened and separated the combatants.

Soon after this institution, the king invited all his barons to the celebration of a great festival, which he proposed holding annually at Carlisle.

As the knights had obtained the sovereign's permission to bring their ladies along with them, the beautiful Igerne accompanied her husband, Gerlois, Duke of Tintadiel, to one of these anniversaries. The king became deeply enamored of the Duchess, and disclosed his passion; but Igerne repelled his advances, and revealed his solicitations to her husband. On hearing this, the Duke instantly removed from court with Igerne, and without taking leave of Uther. The

king complained to his council of this want of duty, and
they decided that the Duke should be summoned to court,
and, if refractory, should be treated as a rebel. As he refused to obey the citation, the king carried war into the
estates of his vassal, and besieged him in the strong castle
of Tintadiel. Merlin transformed the king into the likeness
of Gerlois, and enabled him to have many stolen interviews with Igerne. At length the Duke was killed in battle,
and the king espoused Igerne.

From this union sprang Arthur, who succeeded his father, Uther, upon the throne.

Arthur Chosen King

Arthur, though only fifteen years old at his father's death,
was elected king, at a general meeting of the nobles. It was
not done without opposition, for there were many ambitious
competitors; but Bishop Brice, a person of great sanctity,
on Christmas eve addressed the assembly, and represented
that it would well become them, at that solemn season, to put
up their prayers for some token which should manifest the
intentions of Providence respecting their future sovereign.
This was done, and with such success, that the service was
scarcely ended, when a miraculous stone was discovered,
before the church door, and in the stone was firmly fixed a
sword, with the following words engraven on its hilt:—

> "I am hight Escalibore,
> Unto a king fair tresore."

Bishop Brice, after exhorting the assembly to offer up
their thanksgivings for this signal miracle, proposed a law,
that whoever should be able to draw out the sword from
the stone, should be acknowledged as sovereign of the
Britons; and his proposal was decreed by general acclama-
tion. The tributary kings of Uther, and the most famous
knights, successively put their strength to the proof, but
the miraculous sword resisted all their efforts. It stood
till Candlemas; it stood till Easter, and till Pentecost, when
the best knights in the kingdom usually assembled for the
annual tournament. Arthur, who was at that time serving
in the capacity of squire to his foster-brother, Sir Kay, at-

tended his master to the lists. Sir Kay fought with great
valor and success, but had the misfortune to break his
sword, and sent Arthur to his mother for a new one. Arthur hastened home, but did not find the lady; but having
observed near the church a sword sticking in a stone, he
galloped to the place, drew out the sword with great ease,
and delivered it to his master. Sir Kay would willingly have
assumed to himself the distinction conferred by the possession of the sword; but when, to confirm the doubters, the
sword was replaced in the stone, he was utterly unable to
withdraw it, and it would yield a second time to no hand
but Arthur's. Thus decisively pointed out by Heaven as their
king, Arthur was by general consent proclaimed as such,
and an early day appointed for his solemn coronation.

Immediately after his election to the crown, Arthur found
himself opposed by eleven kings and one duke, who with
a vast army were actually encamped in the forest of Rock-
ingham. By Merlin's advice Arthur sent an embassy to Brittany to solicit aid of King Ban and King Bohort, two of the
best knights in the world. They accepted the call, and with
a powerful army crossed the sea, landing at Portsmouth,
where they were received with great rejoicing. The rebel
kings were still superior in numbers; but Merlin by a powerful enchantment, caused all their tents to fall down at
once, and in the confusion Arthur with his allies fell upon
them and totally routed them.

After defeating the rebels, Arthur took the field against
the Saxons. As they were too strong for him unaided, he
sent an embassy to Armorica, beseeching the assistance of
Hoel, who soon after brought over an army to his aid. The
two kings joined their forces, and sought the enemy, whom
they met, and both sides prepared for a decisive engage-
ment. "Arthur himself," as Geoffrey of Monmouth relates,
"dressed in a breastplate worthy of so great a king, places
on his head a golden helmet engraved with the semblance
of a dragon. Over his shoulders he throws his shield called
Priwen, on which a picture of the Holy Virgin constantly
recalled her to his memory. Girt with Caliburn, a most excellent sword, and fabricated in the isle of Avalon, he graces
his right hand with the lance named Ron. This was a long
and broad spear, well contrived for slaughter." After a severe conflict, Arthur, calling on the name of the Virgin,

rushes into the midst of his enemies, and destroys multi-
tudes of them with the formidable Caliburn, and puts the
rest to flight. Hoel, being detained by sickness, took no part
in this battle.

This is called the victory of Mount Badon, and, however
disguised by fable, it is regarded by historians as a real
event.

Merlin

> "—The most famous man of all those times,
> Merlin, who knew the range of all their arts,
> Had built the King his havens, ships and halls,
> Was also Bard, and knew the starry heavens;
> The people called him wizard."—TENNYSON

Now Merlin, of whom we have already heard somewhat
and shall hear more, was the son of no mortal father, but
of an Incubus, one of a class of beings not absolutely
wicked, but far from good, who inhabit the regions of the
air. Merlin's mother was a virtuous young woman, who, on
the birth of her son, intrusted him to a priest, who hurried
him to the baptismal fount, and so saved him from sharing
the lot of his father, though he retained many marks of his
unearthly origin.

At this time Vortigern reigned in Britain. He was a
usurper, who had caused the death of his sovereign, Moines,
and driven the two brothers of the late king, whose names
were Uther and Pendragon, into banishment. Vortigern,
who lived in constant fear of the return of the rightful heirs
of the kingdom, began to erect a strong tower for defence.
The edifice, when brought by the workmen to a certain
height, three times fell to the ground, without any appar-
ent cause. The king consulted his astrologers on this wonderful event, and learned from them that it would be necessary to bathe the cornerstone of the foundation with the
blood of a child born without a mortal father.

In search of such an infant, Vortigern sent his messengers all over the kingdom, and they by accident discovered
Merlin, whose lineage seemed to point him out as the individual wanted. They took him to the king; but Merlin,
young as he was, explained to the king the absurdity of at-

tempting to rescue the fabric by such means, for he told
him the true cause of the instability of the tower was its being placed over the den of two immense dragons, whose
combats shook the earth above them. The king ordered his
workmen to dig beneath the tower, and when they had done
so they discovered two enormous serpents, the one white as
milk, the other red as fire. The multitude looked on with
amazement, till the serpents, slowly rising from their den,
and expanding their enormous folds, began the combat,
when every one fled in terror, except Merlin, who stood by
clapping his hands and cheering on the conflict. The red
dragon was slain, and the white one, gliding through a cleft
in the rock, disappeared.

These animals typified, as Merlin afterwards explained,
the invasion of Uther and Pendragon, the rightful princes,
who soon after landed with a great army. Vortigern was defeated, and afterwards burned alive in the castle he had
taken such pains to construct. On the death of Vortigern,
Pendragon ascended the throne. Merlin became his chief
adviser, and often assisted the king by his magical arts.
Among other endowments, he had the power to transform
himself into any shape he pleased. At one time he appeared
as a dwarf, at others as a damsel, a page, or even a grey-
hound or a stag. This faculty he often employed for the
service of the king, and sometimes also for the diversion
of the court and the sovereign.

Merlin continued to be a favorite counsellor through
the reigns of Pendragon, Uther, and Arthur, and at last
disappeared from view, and was no more found among
men, through the treachery of his mistress, Viviane, the
Fairy, which happened in this wise.

Merlin, having become enamored of the fair Viviane, the
Lady of the Lake, was weak enough to impart to her various important secrets of his art, being impelled by a fatal
destiny, of which he was at the same time fully aware. The
lady, however, was not content with her devotion, unbounded as it seems to have been, but "cast about," the Romance tells us, how she might "detain him for evermore,"
and one day addressed him in these terms: "Sir, I would
that we should make a fair place and a suitable, so contrived by art and by cunning that it might never be undone,
and that you and I should be there in joy and solace." "My

lady," said Merlin, "I will do all this." "Sir," said she, "I
would not have you do it, but you shall teach me, and I
will do it, and then it will be more to my mind." "I grant
you this," said Merlin. Then he began to devise, and the
damsel put it all in writing. And when he had devised the
whole, then had the damsel full great joy, and showed him
greater semblance of love than she had ever before made,
and they sojourned together a long while. At length it fell
out that, as they were going one day in hand through the
forest of Brécéliande, they found a bush of white-thorn,
which was laden with flowers; and they seated themselves,
under the shade of this white-thorn, upon the grass, and
Merlin laid his head upon the damsel's lap, and fell asleep.
Then the damsel rose, and made a ring with her wimple
round the bush, and round Merlin, and began her enchantments, such as he himself had taught her; and nine times
she made the ring, and nine times she made the enchantment, and then she went and sat down by him, and placed
his head again upon her lap. And when he awoke, and
looked round him, it seemed to him that he was enclosed
in the strongest tower in the world, and laid upon a fair
bed. Then said he to the dame: "My lady, you have deceived
me, unless you abide with me, for no one hath power to
unmake this tower but you alone." She then promised that
she would be often there, and in this she held her covenant
with him. And Merlin never went out of that tower where
his Mistress Viviane had enclosed him; but she entered and
went out again when she listed.

After this event Merlin was never more known to hold
converse with any mortal but Viviane, except on one occasion. Arthur, having for some time missed him from his
court, sent several of his knights in search of him, and
among the number Sir Gawain, who met with a very un-
pleasant adventure while engaged in this quest. Happening
to pass a damsel on his road, and neglecting to salute her,
she revenged herself for his incivility by transforming him
into a hideous dwarf. He was bewailing aloud his evil fortune as he went through the forest of Brécéliande, when
suddenly he heard the voice of one groaning on his right
hand; and, looking that way, he could see nothing save a
kind of smoke, which seemed like air, and through which
he could not pass. Merlin then addressed him from out the

smoke, and told him by what misadventure he was imprisoned there. "Ah, sir!" he added, "you will never see me more, and that grieves me, but I cannot remedy it; I shall never more speak to you, nor to any other person, save only my mistress. But do thou hasten to King Arthur, and charge him from me to undertake, without delay, the quest of the Sacred Graal. The knight is already born, and has received knighthood at his hands, who is destined to accomplish this quest." And after this he comforted Gawain under his transformation, assuring him that he should speedily be disenchanted; and he predicted to him that he should find the king at Carduel, in Wales, on his return, and that all the other knights who had been on like quest would arrive there the same day as himself. And all this came to pass as Merlin had said.

Guenever

"Leodogran, the King of Cameliard,
    Had one fair daughter, and none other child,
    And she was fairest of all flesh on earth,
    Guenevere, and in her his one delight."
                                    TENNYSON

Merlin had planned for Arthur a marriage with the daughter of King Laodegan [1] of Carmalide. By his advice Arthur paid a visit to the court of that sovereign, attended only by Merlin and by thirty-nine knights whom the magician had selected for that service. On their arrival they found Laodegan and his peers sitting in council, endeavoring, but with small prospect of success, to devise means for resisting the impending attack of Ryence, King of Ireland, who, with fifteen tributary kings and an almost innumerable army, had nearly surrounded the city. Merlin, who acted as leader of the band of British knights, announced them as strangers, who came to offer the king their services in his wars; but under the express condition that they should be at liberty to conceal their names and quality until they should think proper to divulge them. These terms were

[1] The spelling of these proper names is very often only a matter of taste. I think, however, *Leodogran* and *Guenevere* are less common than *Laodegan* and *Guenever*.

thought very strange, but were thankfully accepted, and the strangers, after taking the usual oath to the king, retired to the lodging which Merlin had prepared for them.

A few days after this, the enemy, regardless of a truce into which they had entered with King Laodegan, suddenly issued from their camp and made an attempt to surprise the city. Cleodalis, the king's general, assembled the royal forces with all possible despatch. Arthur and his companions also flew to arms, and Merlin appeared at their head, bearing a standard on which was emblazoned a terrific dragon. Merlin advanced to the gate, and commanded the porter to open it, which the porter refused to do, without the king's order. Merlin thereupon took up the gate, with all its appurtenances of locks, bars, and bolts, and directed his troop to pass through, after which he replaced it in perfect order. He then set spurs to his horse, and dashed, at the head of the little troop, into a body of two thousand Pagans. The disparity of numbers being so enormous, Merlin cast a spell upon the enemy, so as to prevent their seeing the small number of their assailants; notwithstanding which the British knights were hard pressed. But the people of the city, who saw from the walls this unequal contest, were ashamed of leaving the small body of strangers to their fate, so they opened the gate and sallied forth. The numbers were now more nearly equal, and Merlin revoked his spell, so that the two armies encountered on fair terms. Where Arthur, Ban, Bohort, and the rest fought, the king's army had the advantage; but in another part of the field the king himself was surrounded and carried off by the enemy. This sad sight was seen by Guenever, the fair daughter of the king, who stood on the city wall and looked at the battle. She was in dreadful distress, tore her hair, and swooned away.

But Merlin, aware of what passed in every part of the field, suddenly collected his knights, led them out of the battle, intercepted the passage of the party who were carrying away the king, charged them with irresistible impetuosity, cut in pieces or dispersed the whole escort, and rescued the king. In the fight Arthur encountered Caulang, a giant fifteen feet high, and the fair Guenever, who already began to feel a strong interest in the handsome young stranger, trembled for the issue of the contest. But Arthur, dealing a dreadful blow on the shoulder of the monster, cut through his neck so that his head hung over on one side, and in this condition his horse carried him about the field, to the great horror and dismay of the Pagans. Guenever could not refrain from expressing aloud her wish that the gentle knight, who dealt with giants so dexterously, were destined to become her husband, and the wish was echoed by her attendants. The enemy soon turned their backs, and fled with precipitation, closely pursued by Laodegan and his allies.

After the battle Arthur was disarmed and conducted to the bath by the Princess Guenever, while his friends were attended by the other ladies of the court. After the bath the knights were conducted to a magnificent entertainment, at which they were diligently served by the same fair attendants. Laodegan, more and more anxious to know the name and quality of his generous deliverers, and occasionally forming a secret wish that the chief of his guests might be captivated by the charms of his daughter, appeared silent and pensive, and was scarcely roused from his reverie by the banter of his courtiers. Arthur, having had an opportunity of explaining to Guenever his great esteem for her merit, was in the joy of his heart, and was still further delighted by hearing from Merlin the late exploits of Gawain at London, by means of which his immediate return to his dominions was rendered unnecessary, and he was left at liberty to protract his stay at the court of Laodegan. Every day contributed to increase the admiration of the whole court for the gallant strangers, and the passion of Guenever for their chief; and when at last Merlin announced to the king that the object of the visit of the party was to procure a bride for their leader, Laodegan at once presented Guenever to Arthur, telling him that, whatever might be his rank, his merit was sufficient to entitle him to the possession of the heiress of Carmalide. Arthur accepted the lady with the utmost gratitude, and Merlin then proceeded to satisfy the king of the rank of his son-in-law; upon which Laodegan, with all his barons, hastened to do homage to their lawful sovereign, the successor of Uther Pendragon. The fair Guenever was then solemnly betrothed to Arthur, and a magnificent festival was proclaimed, which lasted seven days. At the end of that time, the enemy appearing again with renewed force, it became necessary to resume military operations.[1]

We must now relate what took place at or near London while Arthur was absent from his capital. At this very time a band of young heroes were on their way to Arthur's court, for the purpose of receiving knighthood from him. They were Gawain and his three brothers, nephews of Arthur, sons of King Lot, and Galachin, another nephew, son of King Nanters. King Lot had been one of the rebel chiefs whom Arthur had defeated, but he now hoped by means of the young men to be reconciled to his brother-in-law. He equipped his sons and his nephew with the utmost magnificence, giving them a splendid retinue of young men, sons of earls and barons, all mounted on the best horses, with complete suits of choice armor. They numbered in all seven hundred, but only nine had yet received the order of knighthood; the rest were candidates for that honor, and anxious to earn it by an early encounter with the enemy. Gawain, the leader, was a knight of wonderful strength; but what was most remarkable about him was that his strength was greater at certain hours of the day than at others. From nine o'clock till noon his strength was doubled, and so it was from three to even-song; for the rest of the time it was less remarkable, though at all times surpassing that of ordinary men.

After a march of three days they arrived in the vicinity of London, where they expected to find Arthur and his court; and very unexpectedly fell in with a large convoy belonging to the enemy, consisting of numerous carts and wagons, all loaded with provisions, and escorted by three thousand men, who had been collecting spoil from all the country round. A single charge from Gawain's impetuous cavalry was sufficient to disperse the escort and to recover the convoy, which was instantly despatched to London. But before long a body of seven thousand fresh soldiers advanced to the attack of the five princes and their little army. Gawain, singling out a chief named Choas, of gigantic size, began the battle by splitting him from the crown of the

[1] Guenever, the name of Arthur's queen, also written Genievre and Geneura, is familiar to all who are conversant with chivalric lore. It is to her adventures, and those of her true knight, Sir Launcelot, that Dante alludes in the beautiful episode of Francesca da Rimini.

head to the breast. Galachin encountered King Sanagran, who was also very huge, and cut off his head. Agrivain and Gahariet also performed prodigies of valor. Thus they kept the great army of assailants at bay, though hard pressed, till of a sudden they perceived a strong body of the citizens advancing from London, where the convoy which had been recovered by Gawain had arrived, and informed the mayor and citizens of the danger of their deliverer. The arrival of the Londoners soon decided the contest. The enemy fled in all directions, and Gawain and his friends, escorted by the grateful citizens, entered London, and were received with acclamations.

After the great victory of Mount Badon, by which the Saxons were for the time effectually put down, Arthur turned his arms against the Scots and Picts, whom he routed at Lake Lomond, and compelled to sue for mercy. He then went to York to keep his Christmas, and employed himself in restoring the Christian churches which the Pagans had rifled and overthrown. The following summer he conquered Ireland, and then made a voyage with his fleet to Iceland, which he also subdued. The kings of Gothland and of the Orkneys came voluntarily and made their submission, promising to pay tribute. Then he returned to Britain, where, having established the kingdom, he dwelt twelve years in peace.

During this time he invited over to him all persons whatsoever that were famous for valor in foreign nations, and augmented the number of his domestics, and introduced such politeness into his court as people of the remotest countries thought worthy of their imitation. So that there was not a nobleman who thought himself of any consideration unless his clothes and arms were made in the same fashion as those of Arthur's knights.

Finding himself so powerful at home, Arthur began to form designs for extending his power abroad. So, having prepared his fleet, he first attempted Norway, that he might procure the crown of it for Lot, his sister's husband. Arthur landed in Norway, fought a great battle with the king of that country, defeated him, and pursued the victory till he had reduced the whole country under his dominion, and established Lot upon the throne. Then Arthur made a voyage to Gaul and laid siege to the city of Paris. Gaul was at that time a Roman province, and governed by Flollo, the Tribune. When the siege of Paris had continued a month, and the people began to suffer from famine, Flollo challenged Arthur to single combat, proposing to decide the conquest in that way. Arthur gladly accepted the challenge, and slew his adversary in the contest, upon which the citizens surrendered the city to him. After the victory Arthur divided his army into two parts, one of which he committed to the conduct of Hoel, whom he ordered to march into Aquitaine, while he with the other part should endeavor to subdue the other provinces. At the end of nine years, in which time all the parts of Gaul were entirely reduced, Arthur returned to Paris, where he kept his court, and calling an assembly of the clergy and people, established peace and the just administration of the laws in that kingdom. Then he bestowed Normandy upon Bedver, his butler, and the province of Andegavia upon Kay, his steward,[1] and several others upon his great men that attended him. And, having settled the peace of the cities and countries, he returned back in the beginning of spring to Britain.

Upon the approach of the feast of Pentecost, Arthur, the better to demonstrate his joy after such triumphant successes, and for the more solemn observation of that festival, and reconciling the minds of the princes that were now subject to him, resolved during that season to hold a magnificent court, to place the crown upon his head, and to invite all the kings and dukes under his subjection to the solemnity. And he pitched upon Caerleon, the City of Legions, as the proper place for his purpose. For, besides its great wealth above the other cities,[2] its situation upon the river Usk, near the Severn sea, was most pleasant and fit for so great a solemnity. For on one side it was washed by that noble river, so that the kings and princes from the coun-

---

[1] This name, in the French romances, is spelled Queux, which means *head cook*. This would seem to imply that it was a title, and not a name; yet the personage who bore it is never mentioned by any other. He is the chief, if not the only, comic character among the heroes of Arthur's court. He is the Seneschal or Steward, his duties also embracing those of chief of the cooks. In the romances his general character is a compound of valor and buffoonery, always ready to fight, and generally getting the worst of the battle. He is also sarcastic and abusive in his remarks, by which he often gets into trouble. Yet Arthur seems to have an attachment to him, and often takes his advice, which is generally wrong.

ARTHUR 305

tries beyond the seas might have the convenience of sailing up to it. On the other side the beauty of the meadows and groves, and magnificence of the royal palaces, with lofty gilded roofs that adorned it, made it even rival the grandeur of Rome. It was also famous for two churches, whereof one was adorned with a choir of virgins, who devoted themselves wholly to the service of God, and the other maintained a convent of priests. Besides, there was a college of two hundred philosophers, who, being learned in astronomy and the other arts, were diligent in observing the courses of the stars, and gave Arthur true predictions of the events that would happen. In this place, therefore, which afforded such delights, were preparations made for the ensuing festival.

When all were assembled, upon the day of the solemnity, the archbishops were conducted to the palace in order to place the crown upon the king's head. Then Dubricius, inasmuch as the court was held in his diocese, made himself ready to celebrate the office. As soon as the king was invested with his royal habiliments, he was conducted in great pomp to the metropolitan church, having four kings, viz., of Albania, Cornwall, Demetia, and Venedotia, bearing four golden swords before him. On another part was the queen, dressed out in her richest ornaments, conducted by the archbishops and bishops to the Church of Virgins; the four queens, also, of the kings last mentioned, bearing before her four white doves, according to ancient custom.

---

² Several cities are allotted to King Arthur by the romance-writers. The principal are Caerleon, Camelot, and Carlisle.

Caerleon derives its name from its having been the station of one of the legions during the dominion of the Romans. It is called by Latin writers Urbs Legionum, the City of Legions,—the former word being rendered into Welsh by *Caer*, meaning city, and the latter contracted into *lleon*. The river Usk retains its name in modern geography, and there is a town or city of Caerleon upon it, though the city of Cardiff is thought to be the scene of Arthur's court. Chester also bears the Welsh name of Caerleon; for Chester, derived from *castra*, Latin for *camp*, is the designation of military headquarters.

Camelot is thought to be Winchester.

Shalott is Guildford.

Hamo's Port is Southampton.

Carlisle is the city still retaining that name, near the Scottish border. But this name is also sometimes applied to other places, which were, like itself, military stations.

When the whole procession was ended, so transporting was the harmony of the musical instruments and voices, whereof there was a vast variety in both churches, that the knights who attended were in doubt which to prefer; and therefore crowded from one to the other by turns, and were far from being tired of the solemnity, though the whole day had been spent in it. At last, when divine service was over at both churches, the king and queen put off their crowns, and, putting on their lighter ornaments, went to the banquet. When they had all taken their seats according to precedence, Kay the sewer, in rich robes of ermine, with a thousand young noblemen all in like manner clothed in rich attire, served up the dishes. From another part Bedver the butler was followed by the same number of attendants, who waited with all kinds of cups and drinking-vessels. And there was food and drink in abundance, and everything was of the best kind, and served in the best manner. For at that time Britain had arrived at such a pitch of grandeur that in riches, luxury, and politeness it far surpassed all other kingdoms.

Then the king established all his knights, and to them that were not rich he gave lands, and charged them all never to do outrage nor murder, and always to flee treason; also, by no means to be cruel, but to give mercy unto him that asked mercy, upon pain of forfeiture of their worship and lordship; and always to do ladies, damosels, and gentlewomen service, upon pain of death. Also that no man take battle in a wrongful quarrel, for no law, nor for any world's goods. Unto this were all the knights sworn of the Table Round, both old and young. And at every year were they sworn at the high feast of Pentecost.

King Arthur Gets a Sword from the Lady of the Lake

One day King Arthur rode forth, and on a sudden he was ware of three churls chasing Merlin to have slain him. And the king rode unto them and bade them, "Flee, churls!" Then were they afraid when they saw a knight, and fled. "O Merlin," said Arthur, "here hadst thou been slain, for all thy crafts, had I not been by." "Nay," said Merlin, "not so, for I could save myself if I would; but thou art more near thy death than I am." So, as they went thus talking,

King Arthur perceived where sat a knight on horseback, as if to guard the pass. "Sir knight," said Arthur, "for what cause abidest thou here?" Then the knight said, "There may no knight ride this way unless he joust with me, for such is the custom of the pass." "I will amend that custom," said the king. Then they ran together, and they met so hard that their spears were shivered. Then they drew their swords and fought a strong battle, with many great strokes. But at length the sword of the knight smote King Arthur's sword in two pieces. Then said the knight unto Arthur, "Thou art in my power, whether to save thee or slay thee, and unless thou yield thee as overcome and recreant thou shalt die." "As for death," said King Arthur, "welcome be it when it cometh; but to yield me unto thee as recreant I will not." Then he leapt upon the knight, and took him by the middle and threw him down; but the knight was a passing strong man, and anon he brought Arthur under him, and would have razed off his helm to slay him. Then said Merlin, "Knight, hold thy hand, for this knight is a man of more worship than thou art aware of." "Why, who is he?" said the knight. "It is King Arthur." Then would he have slain him for dread of his wrath, and lifted up his sword to slay him; and therewith Merlin cast an enchantment on the knight, so that he fell to the earth in a great sleep. Then Merlin took up King Arthur and set him on his horse. "Alas!" said Arthur, "what hast thou done, Merlin? hast thou slain this good knight by thy crafts?" "Care ye not," said Merlin; "he is wholer than ye be. He is only asleep, and will wake in three hours."

Right so the king and he departed, and went unto an hermit that was a good man and a great leech. So the hermit searched all his wounds and gave him good salves; so the king was there three days, and then were his wounds well amended that he might ride and go, and so departed. And as they rode Arthur said, "I have no sword." "No force," said Merlin; "hereby is a sword that shall be yours." So they rode till they came to a lake, the which was a fair water and broad, and in the midst of the lake Arthur was ware of an arm clothed in white samite, that held a fair sword in that hand. "So," said Merlin, "yonder is that sword that I spake of." With that they saw a damsel going upon the lake. "What damsel is that?" said Arthur. "That is the Lady of the Lake," said Merlin; "and within that lake is a rock, and therein is as fair a place as any on earth, and richly beseen, and this damsel will come to you anon, and then speak ye fair to her and she will give thee that sword." Anon withal came the damsel unto Arthur and saluted him, and he her again. "Damsel," said Arthur, "what sword is that that yonder the arm holdeth above the waves? I would it were mine, for I have no sword." "Sir Arthur king," said the damsel, "that sword is mine, and if ye will give me a gift when I ask it you ye shall have it." "By my faith," said Arthur, "I will give ye what gift ye shall ask." "Well," said the damsel, "go you into yonder barge and row yourself to the sword, and take it and the scabbard with you, and I will ask my gift when I see my time." So Arthur and Merlin alighted, and tied their horses to two trees, and so they went into the ship, and when they came to the sword that the hand held, Arthur took it by the handles, and took it with him. And the arm and the hand went under the water.

Then they returned unto the land and rode forth. And Sir Arthur looked on the sword and liked it right well.

So they rode unto Caerleon, whereof his knights were passing glad. And when they heard of his adventures they marvelled that he would jeopard his person so alone. But all men of worship said it was a fine thing to be under such a chieftain as would put his person in adventure as other poor knights did.

4. SIR GAWAIN

Sir Gawain was nephew to King Arthur, by his sister Morgana, married to Lot, king of Orkney, who was by Arthur made king of Norway. Sir Gawain was one of the most famous knights of the Round Table, and is characterized by the romancers as the *sage* and *courteous* Gawain. To this Chaucer alludes in his "Squiere's Tale," in which the strange knight "saluteth" all the court—

"With so high reverence and observance,
As well in speeche as in countenance,

That Gawain, with his olde curtesie,
Though he were come agen out of faërie,
Ne coude him not amenden with a word."

Gawain's brothers were Agravain, Gaharet, and Gareth.

Sir Gawain's Marriage

Once upon a time King Arthur held his court in merry
Carlisle, when a damsel came before him and craved a
boon. It was for vengeance upon a caitiff knight, who had
made her lover captive and despoiled her of her lands.
King Arthur commanded to bring him his sword, Excalibar,
and to saddle his steed, and rode forth without delay to
right the lady's wrong. Ere long he reached the castle of
the grim baron, and challenged him to the conflict. But
the castle stood on magic ground, and the spell was such
that no knight could tread thereon but straight his courage
fell and his strength decayed. King Arthur felt the charm,
and before a blow was struck his sturdy limbs lost their
strength, and his head grew faint. He was fain to yield himself prisoner to the churlish knight, who refused to release
him except upon condition that he should return at the end
of a year, and bring a true answer to the question, "What
thing is it which women most desire?" or in default thereof
surrender himself and his lands. King Arthur accepted the
terms, and gave his oath to return at the time appointed.
During the year the king rode east, and he rode west, and
inquired of all whom he met what thing it is which all
women most desire. Some told him riches; some pomp and
state; some mirth; some flattery; and some a gallant knight.
But in the diversity of answers he could find no sure de-
pendence. The year was well nigh spent when, one day, as
he rode thoughtfully through a forest, he saw sitting beneath
a tree a lady of such hideous aspect that he turned away
his eyes, and when she greeted him in seemly sort made
no answer. "What wight art thou," the lady said, "that will
not speak to me? It may chance that I may resolve thy
doubts, though I be not fair of aspect." "If thou wilt do so,"
said King Arthur, "choose what reward thou wilt, thou grim
lady, and it shall be given thee." "Swear me this upon thy
faith," she said, and Arthur swore it. Then the lady told

him the secret, and demanded her reward, which was that the king should find some fair and courtly knight to be her husband.

King Arthur hastened to the grim baron's castle and told him one by one all the answers which he had received from his various advisers, except the last, and not one was admitted as the true one. "Now yield thee, Arthur," the giant said, "for thou hast not paid thy ransom, and thou and thy lands are forfeited to me." Then King Arthur said:—

> "Yet hold thy hand, thou proud baron,
>   I pray thee hold thy hand.
> And give me leave to speak once more,
>   In rescue of my land.
> This morn, as I came over a moor,
>   I saw a lady set,
> Between an oak and a green holly,
>   All clad in red scarlet.
> She says *all women would have their will,*
>   This is their chief desire;
> Now yield, as thou art a baron true,
>   That I have paid my hire."

"It was my sister that told thee this," the churlish baron exclaimed. "Vengeance light on her! I will some time or other do her as ill a turn."

King Arthur rode homeward, but not light of heart; for he remembered the promise he was under to the loathly lady to give her one of his young and gallant knights for a husband. He told his grief to Sir Gawain, his nephew, and he replied, "Be not sad, my lord, for I will marry the loathly lady." King Arthur replied:—

> "Now nay, now nay, good Sir Gawaine,
>   My sister's son ye be;
> The loathly lady's all too grim,
>   And all too foule for thee."

But Gawain persisted, and the king at last, with sorrow of heart, consented that Gawain should be his ransom. So, one day, the king and his knights rode to the forest, met the loathly lady, and brought her to the court. Sir Gawain stood the scoffs and jeers of his companions as he best might, and the marriage was solemnized, but not with the usual festivities. Chaucer tells us:—

> "There was no joye, ne feste at alle;
> There n'as but hevinesse and mochel sorwe,
> For prively he wed her on the morwe,
> And all day after hid him as an owle,
> So wo was him his wife loked so foule!" [1]

When night came, and they were alone together, Sir Gawain could not conceal his aversion; and the lady asked him why he sighed so heavily, and turned away his face. He candidly confessed it was on account of three things, her age, her ugliness, and her low degree. The lady, not at all offended, replied with excellent arguments to all his objections. She showed him that with age is discretion, with ugliness security from rivals, and that all true gentility depends, not upon the accident of birth, but upon the character of the individual.

Sir Gawain made no reply; but, turning his eyes on his bride, what was his amazement to perceive that she wore no longer the unseemly aspect that had so distressed him. She then told him that the form she had worn was not her true form, but a disguise imposed upon her by a wicked enchanter, and that she was condemned to wear it until two things should happen; one, that she should obtain some young and gallant knight to be her husband. This having been done, one half of the charm was removed. She was now at liberty to wear her true form for half the time, and she bade him choose whether he would have her fair by day and ugly by night, or the reverse. Sir Gawain would fain have had her look her best by night, when he alone should see her, and show her repulsive visage, if at all, to others. But she reminded him how much more pleasant it would be to her to wear her best looks in the throng of knights and ladies by day. Sir Gawain yielded, and gave up his will to hers. This alone was wanting to dissolve the charm. The lovely lady now with joy assured him that she

[1] N'as is not was, contracted; in modern phrase, there was not. Mochel sorwe is much sorrow: morwe is morrow.

should change no more; but as she now was so would she remain by night as well as by day.

> "Sweet blushes stayned her rud-red cheek,
>   Her eyen were black as sloe,
> The ripening cherrye swelled her lippe,
>   And all her neck was snow.
> Sir Gawain kist that ladye faire
>   Lying upon the sheete,
> And swore, as he was a true knight,
>   The spice was never so swete."

The dissolution of the charm which had held the lady also released her brother, the "grim baron," for he too had been implicated in it. He ceased to be a churlish oppressor, and became a gallant and generous knight as any at Arthur's court.

5. LAUNCELOT OF THE LAKE

King Ban, of Brittany, the faithful ally of Arthur, was attacked by his enemy Claudas, and, after a long war, saw himself reduced to the possession of a single fortress, where he was besieged by his enemy. In this extremity he determined to solicit the assistance of Arthur, and escaped in a dark night, with his wife Helen and his infant son Launcelot, leaving his castle in the hands of his seneschal, who immediately surrendered the place to Claudas. The flames of his burning citadel reached the eyes of the unfortunate monarch during his flight, and he expired with grief. The wretched Helen, leaving her child on the brink of a lake, flew to receive the last sighs of her husband, and on returning perceived the little Launcelot in the arms of a nymph, who, on the approach of the queen, threw herself into the lake with the child. This nymph was Viviane, mistress of the enchanter Merlin, better known by the name of the Lady of the Lake. Launcelot received his appellation from having been educated at the court of this enchantress, whose palace was situated in the midst, not of a real, but, like the appearance which deceives the African traveller, of an imaginary lake, whose deluding resemblance served as a barrier to her residence. Here she dwelt not alone, but in the midst of a numerous retinue, and a splendid court of knights and damsels.

The queen, after her double loss, retired to a convent, where she was joined by the widow of Bohort, for this good king had died of grief on hearing of the death of his brother Ban. His two sons, Lionel and Bohort, were rescued by a faithful knight, and arrived in the shape of greyhounds at the palace of the lake, where, having resumed their natural form, they were educated along with their cousin Launcelot.

The fairy, when her pupil had attained the age of eighteen, conveyed him to the court of Arthur, for the purpose of demanding his admission to the honor of knighthood; and at the first appearance of the youthful candidate the graces of his person, which were not inferior to his courage and skill in arms, made an instantaneous and indelible impression on the heart of Guenever, while her charms inspired him with an equally ardent and constant passion. The mutual attachment of these lovers exerted, from that time forth, an influence over the whole history of Arthur. For the sake of Guenever Launcelot achieved the conquest of Northumberland, defeated Gallehaut, King of the Marches, who afterwards become his most faithful friend and ally, exposed himself in numberless encounters, and brought hosts of prisoners to the feet of his sovereign.

After King Arthur was come from Rome into England all the knights of the Table Round resorted unto him, and made him many jousts and tournaments. And in especial Sir Launcelot of the Lake, in all tournaments and jousts and deeds of arms, both for life and death, passed all other knights, and was never overcome, except it were by treason or enchantment; and he increased marvellously in worship, wherefore Queen Guenever had him in great favor, above all other knights. And for certain he loved the queen again above all other ladies; and for her he did many deeds of arms, and saved her from peril through his noble chivalry. Thus Sir Launcelot rested him long with play and game, and then he thought to prove himself in strange adventures; so he bade his nephew, Sir Lionel, to make him ready,—

"for we two will seek adventures." So they mounted on their horses, armed at all sights, and rode into a forest, and so into a deep plain. And the weather was hot about noon, and Sir Launcelot had great desire to sleep. Then Sir Lionel espied a great apple-tree that stood by a hedge, and he said: "Brother, yonder is a fair shadow,—there may we rest us and our horses." "It is well said," replied Sir Launcelot. So they there alighted, and Sir Launcelot laid him down, and his helm under his head, and soon was asleep passing fast. And Sir Lionel waked while he slept. And presently there came three knights riding as fast as ever they might ride, and there followed them but one knight. And Sir Lionel thought he never saw so great a knight before. So within a while this great knight overtook one of those knights, and smote him so that he fell to the earth. Then he rode to the second knight and smote him, and so he did to the third knight. Then he alighted down, and bound all the three knights fast with their own bridles. When Sir Lionel saw him do thus he thought to assay him, and made him ready, silently, not to awake Sir Launcelot, and rode after the strong knight, and bade him turn. And the other smote Sir Lionel so hard that horse and man fell to the earth; and then he alighted down, and bound Sir Lionel, and threw him across his own horse; and so he served them all four, and rode with them away to his own castle. And when he came there, he put them in a deep prison, in which were many more knights in great distress.

Now while Sir Launcelot lay under the apple-tree sleeping there came by him four queens of great estate. And that the heat should not grieve them, there rode four knights about them, and bare a cloth of green silk, on four spears, betwixt them and the sun. And the queens rode on four white mules.

Thus as they rode they heard by them a great horse grimly neigh. Then they were aware of a sleeping knight, that lay all armed under an apple-tree; and as the queens looked on his face they knew it was Sir Launcelot. Then they began to strive for that knight, and each one said she would have him for her love. "We will not strive," said Morgane le Fay, that was King Arthur's sister, "for I will put an enchantment upon him, that he shall not wake for six hours, and we will take him away to my castle; and then when he is surely within my hold I will take the enchantment from him, and then let him choose which of us he will have for his love." So the enchantment was cast upon Sir Launcelot. And then they laid him upon his shield, and bare him so on horseback between two knights, and brought him unto the castle and laid him in a chamber, and at night they sent him his supper.

And on the morning came early those four queens, richly dight, and bade him good morning, and he them again. "Sir knight," they said, "thou must understand that thou art our prisoner; and we know thee well, that thou art Sir Launcelot of the Lake, King Ban's son, and that thou art the noblest knight living. And we know well that there can no lady have thy love but one, and that is Queen Guenever; and now thou shalt lose her forever, and she thee; and therefore it behooveth thee now to choose one of us. I am the Queen Morgane le Fay, and here is the Queen of North Wales, and the Queen of Eastland, and the Queen of the Isles. Now choose one of us which thou wilt have, for if thou choose not in this prison thou shalt die." "This is a hard case," said Sir Launcelot, "that either I must die or else choose one of you; yet had I liever to die in this prison with worship than have to have one of you for my paramour, for ye be false enchantresses." "Well," said the queens, "is this your answer, that ye will refuse us?" "Yea, on my life it is," said Sir Launcelot. Then they departed, making great sorrow.

Then at noon came a damsel unto him with his dinner, and asked him, "What cheer?" "Truly, fair damsel," said Sir Launcelot, "never so ill." "Sir," said she, "if you will be ruled by me, I will help you out of this distress. If ye will promise me to help my father on Tuesday next, who hath made a tournament betwixt him and the king of North Wales; for the last Tuesday my father lost the field." "Fair maiden," said Sir Launcelot, "tell me what is your father's name, and then will I give you an answer." "Sir knight," she said, "my father is King Bagdemagus." "I know him well," said Sir Launcelot, "for a noble king and a good knight, and, by the faith of my body, I will be ready to do your father and you service at that day."

So she departed, and came on the next morning early and

found him ready, and brought him out of twelve locks, and
brought him to his own horse, and lightly he saddled him,
and so rode forth.

And on the Tuesday next he came to a little wood where
the tournament should be. And there were scaffolds and
holds, that lords and ladies might look on, and give the
prize. Then came into the field the king of North Wales,
with eightscore helms, and King Bagdemagus came with
fourscore helms. And then they couched their spears, and
came together with a great dash, and there were overthrown
at the first encounter twelve of King Bagdemagus's party
and six of the king of North Wales's party, and King Bagdemagus's party had the worse.

With that came Sir Launcelot of the Lake, and thrust in
with his spear in the thickest of the press; and he smote
down five knights ere he held his hand; and he smote
down the king of North Wales, and he brake his thigh in
that fall. And then the knights of the king of North Wales
would joust no more; and so the gree was given to King
Bagdemagus.

And Sir Launcelot rode forth with King Bagdemagus
unto his castle; and there he had passing good cheer, both
with the king and with his daughter. And on the morn he took
his leave, and told the king he would go and seek his brother,
Sir Lionel, that went from him when he slept. So he departed, and by adventure he came to the same forest where
he was taken sleeping. And in the highway he met a damsel
riding on a white palfrey, and they saluted each other. "Fair
damsel," said Sir Launcelot, "know ye in this country any
adventures?" "Sir Knight," said the damsel, "here are adventures near at hand, if thou durst pursue them." "Why should
I not prove adventures?" said Sir Launcelot, "since for that
came I hither." "Sir," said she, "hereby dwelleth a knight
that will not be overmatched for any man I know, except
thou overmatch him. His name is Sir Turquine, and, as I
understand, he is a deadly enemy of King Arthur, and he
has in his prison good knights of Arthur's court three score
and more, that he hath won with his own hands." "Damsel,"
said Launcelot, "I pray you bring me unto this knight." So
she told him, "Hereby, within this mile, is his castle, and by
it on the left hand is a ford for horses to drink of, and over
that ford there groweth a fair tree, and on that tree hang

many shields that good knights wielded aforetime, that are now prisoners: and on the tree hangeth a basin of copper and latten, and if thou strike upon that basin thou shalt hear tidings." And Sir Launcelot departed, and rode as the damsel had shown him, and shortly he came to the ford, and the tree where hung the shields and basin. And among the shields he saw Sir Lionel's and Sir Hector's shield, besides many others of knights that he knew.

Then Sir Launcelot struck on the basin with the butt of his spear; and long he did so, but he saw no man. And at length he was ware of a great knight that drove a horse before him, and across the horse there lay an armed knight bounden. And as they came near Sir Launcelot thought he should know the captive knight. Then Sir Launcelot saw that it was Sir Gaheris, Sir Gawain's brother, a knight of the Table Round. "Now, fair knight," said Sir Launcelot, "put that wounded knight off the horse, and let him rest awhile, and let us two prove our strength. For, as it is told me, thou hast done great despite and shame unto knights of the Round Table, therefore now defend thee." "If thou be of the Table Round," said Sir Turquine, "I defy thee and all thy fellowship." "That is overmuch said," said Sir Launcelot.

Then they put their spears in the rests, and came together with their horses as fast as they might run. And each smote the other in the middle of their shields, so that their horses fell under them, and the knights were both staggered; and as soon as they could clear their horses, they drew out their swords and came together eagerly, and each gave the other many strong strokes, for neither shield nor harness might withstand their strokes. So within a while both had grimly wounds, and bled grievously. Then at the last they were breathless both, and stood leaning upon their swords. "Now, fellow," said Sir Turquine, "thou art the stoutest man that ever I met with, and best breathed; and so be it thou be not the knight that I hate above all other knights, the knight that slew my brother, Sir Caradoc, I will gladly accord with thee; and for thy love I will deliver all the prisoners that I have."

"What knight is he that thou hatest so above others?" "Truly," said Sir Turquine, "his name is Sir Launcelot of the Lake." "I am Sir Launcelot of the Lake, King Ban's son of Benwick, and very knight of the Table Round; and now I defy thee do thy best." "Ah," said Sir Turquine, "Launcelot, thou art to me the most welcome that ever was knight; for we shall never part till the one of us be dead." And then they hurtled together like two wild bulls, rashing and lashing with their swords and shields, so that sometimes they fell, as it were, headlong. Thus they fought two hours and more, till the ground where they fought was all be-purpled with blood.

Then at the last Sir Turquine waxed sore faint, and gave somewhat aback, and bare his shield full low for weariness. That spied Sir Launcelot, and leapt then upon him fiercely as a lion, and took him by the beaver of his helmet, and drew him down on his knees. And he rased off his helm, and smote his neck in sunder.

And Sir Gaheris, when he saw Sir Turquine slain, said, "Fair lord, I pray you tell me your name, for this day I say ye are the best knight in the world, for ye have slain this day in my sight the mightiest man and the best knight except you that ever I saw." "Sir, my name is Sir Launcelot du Lac, that ought to help you of right for King Arthur's sake, and in especial for Sir Gawain's sake, your own dear brother. Now I pray you, that ye go into yonder castle, and set free all the prisoners ye find there, for I am sure ye shall find there many knights of the Table Round, and especially my brother Sir Lionel. I pray you greet them all from me, and tell them I bid them take there such stuff as they find; and tell my brother to go unto the court and abide me there, for by the feast of Pentecost I think to be there; but at this time I may not stop, for I have adventures on hand." So he departed, and Sir Gaheris rode into the castle, and took the keys from the porter, and hastily opened the prison door and let out all the prisoners. There was Sir Kay, Sir Brandeles, and Sir Galynde, Sir Bryan and Sir Alyduke, Sir Hector de Marys and Sir Lionel, and many more. And when they saw Sir Gaheris, they all thanked him, for they thought, because he was wounded, that he had slain Sir Turquine. "Not so," said Sir Gaheris; "it was Sir Launcelot that slew him, right worshipfully; I saw it with mine eyes."

Sir Launcelot rode till at nightfall he came to a fair castle, and therein he found an old gentlewoman, who lodged him with goodwill, and there he had good cheer for him and his horse. And when time was, his host brought him to a fair chamber over the gate to his bed. Then Sir Launcelot unarmed him, and set his harness by him, and went to bed, and anon he fell asleep. And soon after, there came one on horseback and knocked at the gate in great haste; and when Sir Launcelot heard this, he arose and looked out of the window, and saw by the moonlight three knights riding after that one man, and all three lashed on him with their swords, and that one knight turned on them knightly again and defended himself. "Truly," said Sir Launcelot, "yonder one knight will I help, for it is shame to see three knights on one." Then he took his harness and went out at the window by a sheet down to the four knights; and he said aloud, "Turn you knights unto me, and leave your fighting with that knight." Then the knights left Sir Kay, for it was he they were upon, and turned unto Sir Launcelot, and struck many great strokes at Sir Launcelot, and assailed him on every side. Then Sir Kay addressed him to help Sir Launcelot, but he said, "Nay, sir, I will none of your help; let me alone with them." So Sir Kay suffered him to do his will, and stood one side. And within six strokes, Sir Launcelot had stricken them down.

Then they all cried, "Sir knight, we yield us unto you." "As to that," said Sir Launcelot, "I will not take your yielding unto me. If so be ye will yield you unto Sir Kay the seneschal, I will save your lives, but else not." "Fair knight," then they said, "we will do as thou commandest us." "Then shall ye," said Sir Launcelot, "on Whitsunday next, go unto the court of King Arthur, and there shall ye yield you unto Queen Guenever, and say that Sir Kay sent you thither to be her prisoners." "Sir," they said, "it shall be done, by the faith of our bodies"; and then they swore, every knight upon his sword. And so Sir Launcelot suffered them to depart.

On the morn Sir Launcelot rose early and left Sir Kay sleeping; and Sir Launcelot took Sir Kay's armor and his shield, and armed him, and went to the stable and took his horse, and so he departed. Then soon after arose Sir Kay and missed Sir Launcelot. And then he espied that he had taken his armor and his horse. "Now, by my faith, I know well," said Sir Kay, "that he will grieve some of King Arthur's knights, for they will deem that it is I, and will be bold to meet him. But by cause of his armor I am sure I shall ride in peace." Then Sir Kay thanked his host and departed.

Sir Launcelot rode in a deep forest, and there he saw four knights under an oak, and they were of Arthur's court. There was Sir Sagramour le Desirus and Hector de Marys, and Sir Gawain and Sir Uwaine. As they spied Sir Launcelot, they judged by his arms it had been Sir Kay. "Now, by my faith," said Sir Sagramour, "I will prove Sir Kay's might"; and got his spear in his hand, and came toward Sir Launcelot. Therewith Sir Launcelot couched his spear against him, and smote Sir Sagramour so sore that horse and man fell both to the earth. Then said Sir Hector, "Now shall ye see what I may do with him." But he fared worse than Sir Sagramour, for Sir Launcelot's spear went through his shoulder and bare him from his horse to the ground. "By my faith," said Sir Uwaine, "yonder is a strong knight, and I fear he hath slain Sir Kay, and taken his armor." And therewith Sir Uwaine took his spear in hand, and rode toward Sir Launcelot; and Sir Launcelot met him on the plain and gave him such a buffet that he was staggered, and wist not where he was. "Now see I well," said Sir Gawain, "that I must encounter with that knight." Then he adjusted his shield, and took a good spear in his hand, and Sir Launcelot knew him well. Then they let run their horses with all their mights, and each knight smote the other in the middle of his shield. But Sir Gawain's spear broke, and Sir Launcelot charged so sore upon him that his horse fell over backward. Then Sir Launcelot rode away smiling with himself, and he said, "Good luck be with him that made this spear, for never came a better into my hand." Then the four knights went each to the other and comforted one another. "What say ye to this adventure," said Sir Gawain, "that one spear hath felled us all four?" "I dare lay my head it is Sir Launcelot," said Sir Hector; "I know it by his riding."

And Sir Launcelot rode through many strange countries, till, by fortune, he came to a fair castle; and as he passed beyond the castle, he thought he heard two bells ring. And then he perceived how a falcon came flying over his head toward a high elm; and she had long lunys [1] about her feet, and she flew unto the elm to take her perch, and the lunys

---

[1] *Lunys*, the string with which the falcon is held.

got entangled in a bough; and when she would have taken her flight, she hung by the legs fast, and Sir Launcelot saw how she hung and beheld the fair falcon entangled, and he was sorry for her. Then came a lady out of the castle and cried aloud, "O Launcelot, Launcelot, as thou art the flower of all knights, help me to get my hawk; for if my hawk be lost, my lord will slay me, he is so hasty." "What is your lord's name?" said Sir Launcelot. "His name is Sir Phelot, a knight that belongeth to the king of North Wales." "Well, fair lady, since ye know my name, and require me of knighthood to help you, I will do what I may to get your hawk; and yet, in truth, I am an ill climber and the tree is passing high and few boughs to help me." And therewith Sir Launcelot alighted and tied his horse to a tree, and prayed the lady to unarm him. And when he was unarmed, he put off his jerkin, and with might and force he clomb up to the falcon, and tied the lunys to a rotten bough, and threw the hawk down with it; and the lady got the hawk in her hand. Then suddenly there came out of the castle her husband all armed, and with his naked sword in his hand, and said, "O Knight Launcelot, now have I got thee as I would"; and stood at the boll of the tree to slay him. "Ah, lady!" said Sir Launcelot, "why have ye betrayed me?" "She hath done," said Sir Phelot, "but as I commanded her; and therefore there is none other way but thine hour is come, and thou must die." "That were shame unto thee," said Sir Launcelot; "thou an armed knight to slay a naked man by treason." "Thou gettest none other grace," said Sir Phelot, "and therefore help thyself if thou canst." "Alas!" said Sir Launcelot, "that ever a knight should die weaponless!" And therewith he turned his eyes upward and downward; and over his head he saw a big bough leafless, and he brake it off from the trunk. And then he came lower, and watched how his own horse stood; and suddenly he leapt on the further side of his horse from the knight. Then Sir Phelot lashed at him eagerly, meaning to have slain him. But Sir Launcelot put away the stroke with the big bough, and smote Sir Phelot therewith on the side of the head, so that he fell down in a swoon to the ground. Then Sir Launcelot took his sword out of his hand and struck his head from the body. Then said the lady, "Alas! why hast thou slain my husband?" "I am not the cause," said Sir Launcelot, "for with falsehood ye would have slain me, and now it is fallen on yourselves." Thereupon Sir Launcelot got all his armor and put it upon him hastily for fear of more resort, for the knight's castle was so nigh. And as soon as he might, he took his horse and departed, and thanked God he had escaped that adventure.

And two days before the feast of Pentecost, Sir Launcelot came home; and the king and all the court were passing glad of his coming. And when Sir Gawain, Sir Uwaine, Sir Sagramour, and Sir Hector de Marys saw Sir Launcelot in Sir Kay's armor, then they wist well it was he that smote them down, all with one spear. Then there was laughing and merriment among them; and from time to time came all the knights that Sir Turquine had prisoners, and they all honoured and worshipped Sir Launcelot. Then Sir Gaheris said, "I saw all the battle from the beginning to the end," and he told King Arthur all how it was. Then Sir Kay told the king how Sir Launcelot had rescued him, and how he "made the knights yield to me, and not to him." And there they were, all three, and confirmed it all. "And by my faith," said Sir Kay, "because Sir Launcelot took my harness and left me his, I rode in peace, and no man would have to do with me."

And so at that time Sir Launcelot had the greatest name of any knight of the world, and most was he honored of high and low.

6. THE STORY OF LAUNCELOT: THE LADY OF SHALOTT

King Arthur proclaimed a solemn tournament to be held at Winchester. The king, not less impatient than his knights for this festival, set off some days before to superintend the preparations, leaving the queen with her court at Camelot. Sir Launcelot, under pretence of indisposition, remained behind also. His intention was to attend the tournament in disguise; and having communicated his project to Guenever, he mounted his horse, set off without any attendant, and, counterfeiting the feebleness of age, took the most unfrequented road to Winchester, and passed unnoticed as an old knight who was going to be a spectator of the sports. Even Arthur and Gawain, who happened to behold him from the windows of a castle under which he passed, were the dupes of his disguise. But an accident betrayed him. His horse happened to stumble, and the hero, forgetting for a moment his assumed character, recovered the animal with a strength and agility so peculiar to himself, that they instantly recognized the inimitable Launcelot. They suffered him, however, to proceed on his journey without interruption, convinced that his extraordinary feats of arms must discover him at the approaching festival.

In the evening Launcelot was magnificently entertained as a stranger knight at the neighboring castle of Shalott. The lord of this castle had a daughter of exquisite beauty, and two sons lately received into the order of knighthood, one of whom was at that time ill in bed, and thereby prevented from attending the tournament, for which both brothers had long made preparations. Launcelot offered to attend the other, if he were permitted to borrow the armor of the invalid, and the lord of Shalott, without knowing the name of his guest, being satisfied from his appearance that his son could not have a better assistant in arms, most thankfully accepted the offer. In the meantime the young lady, who had been much struck by the first appearance of the stranger knight, continued to survey him with increased attention, and before the conclusion of supper, became so deeply enamored of him, that, after frequent changes of color, and other symptoms which Sir Launcelot could not possibly mistake, she was obliged to retire to her chamber, and seek relief in tears. Sir Launcelot hastened to convey to her, by means of her brother, the information that his heart was already disposed of, but that it would be his pride and pleasure to act as her knight at the approaching tournament. The lady, obliged to be satisfied with that courtesy, presented him her scarf to be worn at the tournament.

Launcelot set off in the morning with the young knight, who, on their approaching Winchester, carried him to the castle of a lady, sister to the lord of Shalott, by whom they were hospitably entertained. The next day they put on their armor, which was perfectly plain, and without any device, as was usual to youths during the first year of knighthood, their shields being only painted red, as some color was necessary to enable them to be recognized by their attendants. Launcelot wore on his crest the scarf of the maid of Shalott, and, thus equipped, proceeded to the tournament, where the knights were divided into two companies, the one commanded by Sir Galehaut, the other by King Arthur. Having surveyed the combat for a short time from without the lists, and observed that Sir Galehaut's party began to give way, they joined the press and attacked the royal knights, the young man choosing such adversaries as were suited to his strength, while his companion selected the principal champions of the Round Table, and successively overthrew Gawain, Bohort, and Lionel. The astonishment of the spectators was extreme, for it was thought that no one but Launcelot could possess such invincible force; yet the favor on his crest seemed to preclude the possibility of his being thus disguised, for Launcelot had never been known to wear the badge of any but his sovereign lady. At length Sir Hector, Launcelot's brother, engaged him, and, after a dreadful combat, wounded him dangerously in the head, but was himself completely stunned by a blow on the helmet, and felled to the ground; after which the conqueror rode off at full speed, attended by his companion.

They returned to the castle of Shalott, where Launcelot was attended with the greatest care by the good earl, by his two sons, and, above all, by his fair daughter, whose medical skill probably much hastened the period of his recovery. His health was almost completely restored, when Sir Hector, Sir Bohort, and Sir Lionel, who, after the return of the court to Camelot, had undertaken the quest of their relation, discovered him walking on the walls of the castle. Their meeting was very joyful; they passed three days in the castle amidst constant festivities, and bantered each other on the events of the tournament. Launcelot, though he began by vowing vengeance against the author of his wound, yet ended by declaring that he felt rewarded for the pain by the pride he took in witnessing his brother's extraordinary prowess. He then dismissed them with a message to the queen, promising to follow immediately, it being necessary that he should first take a formal leave of his kind hosts, as well as of the fair maid of Shalott.

The young lady, after vainly attempting to detain him by her tears and solicitations, saw him depart without leaving her any ground for hope.

It was early summer when the tournament took place; but some months had passed since Launcelot's departure, and winter was now near at hand. The health and strength of the Lady of Shalott had gradually sunk, and she felt that she could not live apart from the object of her affections. She left the castle, and, descending to the river's brink, placed herself in a boat, which she loosed from its moorings, and suffered to bear her down the current toward Camelot.

One morning, as Arthur and Sir Lionel looked from the window of the tower, the walls of which were washed by a river, they descried a boat richly ornamented, and covered with an awning of cloth of gold, which appeared to be floating down the stream without any human guidance. It struck the shore while they watched it, and they hastened down to examine it. Beneath the awning they discovered the dead body of a beautiful woman, in whose features Sir Lionel easily recognized the lovely maid of Shalott. Pursuing their search, they discovered a purse richly embroidered with gold and jewels, and within the purse a letter, which Arthur opened, and found addressed to himself and all the knights of the Round Table, stating that Launcelot of the Lake, the most accomplished of knights and most beautiful of men, but at the same time the most cruel and inflexible, had by his rigor produced the death of the wretched maiden, whose love was no less invincible than his cruelty.

The king immediately gave orders for the interment of the lady, with all the honors suited to her rank, at the same time explaining to the knights the history of her affection for Launcelot, which moved the compassion and regret of all.

7. THE STORY OF LAUNCELOT: QUEEN GUENEVER'S PERIL

It happened at this time that Queen Guenever was thrown into great peril of her life. A certain squire who was in her immediate service, having some cause of animosity to Sir Gawain, determined to destroy him by poison at a public entertainment. For this purpose he concealed the poison in an apple of fine appearance, which he placed on the top of several others, and put the dish before the queen, hoping that, as Sir Gawain was the knight of greatest dignity, she would present the apple to him. But it happened that a Scottish knight of high distinction, who arrived on that day, was seated next to the queen, and to him, as a stranger, she presented the apple, which he had no sooner eaten than he was seized with dreadful pain, and fell senseless. The whole court was of course thrown into confusion; the knights rose from table, darting looks of indignation at the wretched queen, whose tears and protestations were unable to remove their suspicions. In spite of all that could be done the knight died, and nothing remained but to order a magnificent funeral and monument for him, which was done.

Some time after, Sir Mador, brother of the murdered knight, arrived at Arthur's court in quest of him. While hunting in the forest he by chance came to the spot where the monument was erected, read the inscription, and returned to court determined on immediate and signal vengeance. He rode into the hall, loudly accused the queen of treason, and insisted on her being given up to punishment, unless she should find, by a certain day, a knight hardy enough to risk his life in support of her innocence. Arthur, powerful as he was, did not dare to deny the appeal, but was compelled, with a heavy heart, to accept it, and Mador sternly took his departure, leaving the royal couple plunged in terror and anxiety.

During all this time Launcelot was absent, and no one

knew where he was. He had fled in anger from his fair mistress, upon being reproached by her with his passion for the Lady of Shalott, which she had hastily inferred from his wearing her scarf at the tournament. He took up his abode with a hermit in the forest, and resolved to think no more of the cruel beauty, whose conduct he thought must flow from a wish to get rid of him. Yet calm reflection had somewhat cooled his indignation, and he had begun to wish, though hardly able to hope, for a reconciliation, when the news of Sir Mador's challenge fortunately reached his ears. The intelligence revived his spirits, and he began to prepare with the utmost cheerfulness for a contest which, if successful, would insure him at once the affection of his mistress and the gratitude of his sovereign.

The sad fate of the Lady of Shalott had ere this completely acquitted Launcelot in the queen's mind of all suspicion of his fidelity, and she lamented most grievously her foolish quarrel with him, which now, at her time of need, deprived her of her most efficient champion.

As the day appointed by Sir Mador was fast approaching, it became necessary that she should procure a champion for her defence; and she successively adjured Sir Hector, Sir Lionel, Sir Bohort, and Sir Gawain to undertake the battle. She fell on her knees before them, called Heaven to witness her innocence of the crime alleged against her, but was sternly answered by all that they could not fight to maintain the innocence of one whose act, and the fatal consequences of it, they had seen with their own eyes. She retired, therefore, dejected and disconsolate; but the sight of the fatal pile on which, if guilty, she was doomed to be burned, exciting her to fresh effort, she again repaired to Sir Bohort, threw herself at his feet, and, piteously calling on him for mercy, fell into a swoon. The brave knight was not proof against this. He raised her up, and hastily promised that he would undertake her cause, if no other or better champion should present himself. He then summoned his friends, and told them his resolution; and as a mortal combat with Sir Mador was a most fearful enterprise, they agreed to accompany him in the morning to the hermitage in the forest, where he proposed to receive absolution from the hermit, and to make his peace with Heaven, before he entered the lists. As they approached the hermitage, they espied a knight riding in the forest, whom they at once recognized as Sir Launcelot. Overjoyed at the meeting, they quickly, in answer to his questions, confirmed the news of the queen's imminent danger, and received his instructions to return to court, to comfort her as well as they could, but to say nothing of his intention of undertaking her defence, which he meant to do in the character of an unknown adventurer.

On their return to the castle they found that mass was finished, and had scarcely time to speak to the queen before they were summoned into the hall to dinner. A general gloom was spread over the countenances of all the guests. Arthur himself was unable to conceal his dejection, and the wretched Guenever, motionless and bathed in tears, sat in trembling expectation of Sir Mador's appearance. Nor was it long ere he stalked into the hall, and with a voice of thunder, rendered more impressive by the general silence, demanded instant justice on the guilty party. Arthur replied with dignity, that little of the day was yet spent, and that perhaps a champion might yet be found capable of satisfying his thirst for battle. Sir Bohort now rose from table, and, shortly returning in complete armor, resumed his place, after receiving the embraces and thanks of the king, who now began to resume some degree of confidence. Sir Mador, growing impatient, again repeated his denunciations of vengeance, and insisted that the combat should no longer be postponed.

In the height of the debate there came riding into the hall a knight mounted on a black steed, and clad in black armor, with his visor down, and lance in hand. "Sir," said the king, "is it your will to alight and partake of our cheer?" "Nay, sir," he replied; "I come to save a lady's life. The queen hath ill bestowed her favors, and honored many a knight, that in her hour of need she should have none to take her part. Thou that darest accuse her of treachery stand forth, for to-day shalt thou need all thy might."

Sir Mador, though surprised, was not appalled by the stern challenge and formidable appearance of his antagonist, but prepared for the encounter. At the first shock both were unhorsed. They then drew their swords, and commenced a combat which lasted from noon till evening, when Sir Mador, whose strength began to fail, was felled to the ground by Launcelot, and compelled to sue for mercy. The

victor, whose arm was already raised to terminate the life
of his opponent, instantly dropped his sword, courteously
lifted up the fainting Sir Mador, frankly confessing that he
had never before encountered so formidable an enemy. The
other, with similar courtesy, solemnly renounced all further
projects of vengeance for his brother's death; and the two
knights, now become fast friends, embraced each other with
the greatest cordiality. In the meantime Arthur, having recognized Sir Launcelot, whose helmet was now unlaced,
rushed down into the lists, followed by all his knights, to
welcome and thank his deliverer. Guenever swooned with
joy, and the place of combat suddenly exhibited a scene of
the most tumultuous delight.

The general satisfaction was still further increased by the
discovery of the real culprit. Having accidentally incurred
some suspicion, he confessed his crime, and was publicly
punished in the presence of Sir Mador.

The court now returned to the castle, which, with the
title of "La Joyeuse Garde" bestowed upon it in memory of
the happy event, was conferred on Sir Launcelot by Arthur,
as a memorial of his gratitude.

8. THE STORY OF TRISTRAM
OF LYONESSE

Meliadus was king of Leonois, or Lyonesse, a country famous in the annals of romance, which adjoined the kingdom of Cornwall, but has now disappeared from the map,
having been, it is said, overwhelmed by the ocean. Meliadus
was married to Isabella, sister of Mark, king of Cornwall. A
fairy fell in love with him, and drew him away by enchantment while he was engaged in hunting. His queen set out in
quest of him, but was taken ill on her journey, and died,
leaving an infant son, whom, from the melancholy circumstances of his birth, she called Tristram.

Gouvernail, the queen's squire, who had accompanied
her, took charge of the child, and restored him to his father,

who had at length burst the enchantments of the fairy, and returned home.

Meliadus, after seven years, married again, and the new queen, being jealous of the influence of Tristram with his father, laid plots for his life, which were discovered by Gouvernail, who, in consequence, fled with the boy to the court of the king of France, where Tristram was kindly received, and grew up improving in every gallant and knightly accomplishment, adding to his skill in arms the arts of music and of chess. In particular, he devoted himself to the chase and to all woodland sports, so that he became distinguished above all other chevaliers of the court for his knowledge of all that relates to hunting. No wonder that Belinda, the king's daughter, fell in love with him; but as he did not return her passion, she, in a sudden impulse of anger, excited her father against him, and he was banished the kingdom. The princess soon repented of her act, and in despair destroyed herself, having first written a most tender letter to Tristram, sending him at the same time a beautiful and sagacious dog, of which she was very fond, desiring him to keep it as a memorial of her. Meliadus was now dead, and as his queen, Tristram's stepmother, held the throne, Gouvernail was afraid to carry his pupil to his native country, and took him to Cornwall, to his uncle Mark, who gave him a kind reception.

King Mark resided at the castle of Tintadel, already mentioned in the history of Uther and Iguerne. In this court Tristram became distinguished in all the exercises incumbent on a knight; nor was it long before he had an opportunity of practically employing his valor and skill. Moraunt, a celebrated champion, brother to the queen of Ireland, arrived at the court, to demand tribute of King Mark. The knights of Cornwall are in ill repute, in romance, for their cowardice, and they exhibited it on this occasion. King Mark could find no champion who dared to encounter the Irish knight, till his nephew Tristram, who had not yet received the honors of knighthood, craved to be admitted to the order, offering at the same time to fight the battle of Cornwall against the Irish champion. King Mark assented with reluctance; Tristram received the accolade, which conferred knighthood upon him; and the place and time were assigned for the encounter.

Without attempting to give the details of this famous combat, the first and one of the most glorious of Tristram's exploits, we shall only say that the young knight, though severely wounded, cleft the head of Moraunt, leaving a portion of his sword in the wound. Moraunt, half dead with his wound and the disgrace of his defeat, hastened to hide himself in his ship, sailed away with all speed for Ireland, and died soon after arriving in his own country.

The kingdom of Cornwall was thus delivered from its tribute. Tristram, weakened by loss of blood, fell senseless. His friends flew to his assistance. They dressed his wounds, which in general healed readily; but the lance of Moraunt was poisoned, and one wound which it made yielded to no remedies, but grew worse day by day. The surgeons could do no more. Tristram asked permission of his uncle to depart, and seek for aid in the kingdom of Loegria (England). With his consent he embarked, and, after tossing for many days on the sea, was driven by the winds to the coast of Ireland. He landed, full of joy and gratitude that he had escaped the peril of the sea; took his rote,[1] and began to play. It was a summer evening, and the king of Ireland and his daughter, the beautiful Isoude, were at a window which overlooked the sea. The strange harper was sent for, and conveyed to the palace, where, finding that he was in Ireland, whose champion he had lately slain, he concealed his name, and called himself Tramtris. The queen undertook his cure, and by a medicated bath gradually restored him to health. His skill in music and in games occasioned his being frequently called to court, and he became instructor of the Princess Isoude in minstrelsy and poetry, who profited so well under his care, that she soon had no equal in the kingdom, except her instructor.

At this time a tournament was held, at which many knights of the Round Table, and others, were present. On the first day a Saracen prince, named Palamedes, obtained the advantage over all. They brought him to the court, and gave him a feast, at which Tristram, just recovering from his wound, was present. The fair Isoude appeared on this occasion in all her charms. Palamedes could not behold them without emotion, and made no effort to conceal his

---

[1] A musical instrument.

love. Tristram perceived it, and the pain he felt from jealousy taught him how dear the fair Isoude had already become to him.

Next day the tournament was renewed. Tristram, still feeble from his wound, rose during the night, took his arms, and concealed them in a forest near the place of the contest, and, after it had begun, mingled with the combatants. He overthrew all that encountered him, in particular Palamedes, whom he brought to the ground with a stroke of his lance, and then fought him hand to hand, bearing off the prize of the tourney. But his exertions caused his wound to reopen; he bled fast, and in this sad state, yet in triumph, they bore him to the palace. The fair Isoude devoted herself to his relief with an interest which grew more vivid day by day; and her skilful care soon restored him to health.

It happened one day that a damsel of the court, entering the closet where Tristram's arms were deposited, perceived that a part of the sword had been broken off. It occurred to her that the missing portion was like that which was left in the skull of Moraunt, the Irish champion. She imparted her thought to the queen, who compared the fragment taken from her brother's wound with the sword of Tristram, and was satisfied that it was part of the same, and that the weapon of Tristram was that which reft her brother's life. She laid her griefs and resentment before the king, who satisfied himself with his own eyes of the truth of her suspicions. Tristram was cited before the whole court, and reproached with having dared to present himself before them after having slain their kinsman. He acknowledged that he had fought with Moraunt to settle the claim for tribute, and said that it was by force of winds and waves alone that he was thrown on their coast. The queen demanded vengeance for the death of her brother; the fair Isoude trembled and grew pale, but a murmur rose from all the assembly that the life of one so handsome and so brave should not be taken for such a cause, and generosity finally triumphed over resentment in the mind of the king. Tristram was dismissed in safety, but commanded to leave the kingdom without delay, and never to return thither under pain of death. Tristram went back, with restored health, to Cornwall.

King Mark made his nephew give him a minute recital of his adventures. Tristram told him all minutely; but when he

came to speak of the fair Isoude, he described her charms
with a warmth and energy such as none but a lover could
display. King Mark was fascinated with the description,
and, choosing a favorable time, demanded a boon [1] of his
nephew, who readily granted it. The king made him swear
upon the holy reliques that he would fulfil his commands.
Then Mark directed him to go to Ireland, and obtain for
him the fair Isoude to be queen of Cornwall.

Tristram believed it was certain death for him to return
to Ireland; and how could he act as ambassador for his
uncle in such a cause? Yet, bound by his oath, he hesitated
not for an instant. He only took the precaution to change
his armor. He embarked for Ireland; but a tempest drove
him to the coast of England, near Camelot, where King
Arthur was holding his court, attended by the knights of the
Round Table, and many others, the most illustrious in the
world.

Tristram kept himself unknown. He took part in many
jousts; he fought many combats, in which he covered himself with glory. One day he saw among those recently arrived the king of Ireland, father of the fair Isoude. This
prince, accused of treason against his liege sovereign, Arthur, came to Camelot to free himself of the charge. Blaanor, one of the most redoubtable warriors of the Round
Table, was his accuser, and Argius, the king, had neither
youthful vigor nor strength to encounter him. He must
therefore seek a champion to sustain his innocence. But the
knights of the Round Table were not at liberty to fight
against one another, unless in a quarrel of their own. Argius
heard of the great renown of the unknown knight; he also
was witness of his exploits. He sought him, and conjured
him to adopt his defence, and on his oath declared that he
was innocent of the crime of which he was accused. Tristram readily consented, and made himself known to the

---

[1] "Good faith was the very corner-stone of chivalry. Whenever a knight's
word was pledged (it mattered not how rashly), it was to be redeemed at
any price. Hence the sacred obligation of the *boon granted* by a knight to
his suppliant. Instances without number occur in romance, in which a
knight, by rashly granting an indefinite boon, was obliged to do or suffer
something extremely to his prejudice. But it is not in romance alone that
we find such singular instances of adherence to an indefinite promise.
The history of the times presents authentic transactions equally embarras-
sing and absurd."—SCOTT, *note of Sir Tristram.*

king, who on his part promised to reward his exertions, if successful, with whatever gift he might ask.

Tristram fought with Blaanor, and overthrew him, and held his life in his power. The fallen warrior called on him to use his right of conquest, and strike the fatal blow. "God forbid," said Tristram, "that I should take the life of so brave a knight!" He raised him up and restored him to his friends. The judges of the field decided that the king of Ireland was acquitted of the charge against him, and they led Tristram in triumph to his tent. King Argius, full of gratitude, conjured Tristram to accompany him to his kingdom. They departed together, and arrived in Ireland; and the queen, forgetting her resentment for her brother's death, exhibited to the preserver of her husband's life nothing but gratitude and good-will.

How happy a moment for Isoude, who knew that her father had promised his deliverer whatever boon he might ask. But the unhappy Tristram gazed on her with despair, at the thought of the cruel oath which bound him. His magnanimous soul subdued the force of his love. He revealed the oath which he had taken, and with trembling voice demanded the fair Isoude for his uncle.

Argius consented, and soon all was prepared for the departure of Isoude. Brengwain, her favorite maid-of-honor, was to accompany her. On the day of departure the queen took aside this devoted attendant, and told her that she had observed that her daughter and Tristram were attached to one another, and that to avert the bad effects of this inclination she had procured from a powerful fairy a potent philter (love-draught), which she directed Brengwain to adminster to Isoude and to King Mark on the evening of their marriage.

Isoude and Tristram embarked together. A favorable wind filled the sails and promised them a fortunate voyage. The lovers gazed upon one another, and could not repress their sighs. Love seemed to light up all his fires on their lips, as in their hearts. The day was warm; they suffered from thirst. Isoude first complained. Tristram descried the bottle containing the love-draught, which Brengwain had been so imprudent as to leave in sight. He took it, gave some of it to the charming Isoude, and drank the remainder himself. The dog Houdain licked the cup. The ship arrived in Cornwall, and Isoude was married to King Mark. The old monarch was delighted with his bride, and his gratitude to Tristram was unbounded. He loaded him with honors, and made him chamberlain of his palace, thus giving him access to the queen at all times.

In the midst of the festivities of the court which followed the royal marriage, an unknown minstrel one day presented himself, bearing a harp of peculiar construction. He excited the curiosity of King Mark by refusing to play upon it till he should grant him a boon. The king having promised to grant his request, the minstrel, who was none other than the Saracen knight, Sir Palamedes, the lover of the fair Isoude, sung to the harp a lay, in which he demanded Isoude as the promised gift. King Mark could not by the laws of knighthood withhold the boon. The lady was mounted on her horse and led away by her triumphant lover. Tristram, it is needless to say, was absent at the time, and did not return until their departure. When he heard what had taken place, he seized his rote, and hastened to the shore, where Isoude and her new master had already embarked. Tristram played upon his rote, and the sound reached the ears of Isoude, who became so deeply affected that Sir Palamedes was induced to return with her to land, that they might see the unknown musician. Tristram watched his opportunity, seized the lady's horse by the bridle, and plunged with her into the forest, tauntingly informing his rival that "what he had got by the harp he had lost by the rote." Palamedes pursued, and a combat was about to commence, the result of which must have been fatal to one or other of these gallant knights; but Isoude stepped between them, and, addressing Palamedes, said, "You tell me that you love me; you will not then deny me the request I am about to make?" "Lady," he replied, "I will perform your bidding." "Leave, then," said she, "this contest, and repair to King Arthur's court, and salute Queen Guenever for me; tell her that there are in the world but two ladies, herself and I, and two lovers, hers and mine; and come thou not in future in any place where I am." Palamedes burst into tears. "Ah, lady," said he, "I will obey you; but I beseech you that you will not forever steel your heart against me." "Palamedes," she replied, "may I never taste of joy again if I ever quit my first love." Palamedes then went his way. The lovers remained a week in concealment, after which Tristram restored Isoude to her husband, advising him in future to reward minstrels in some other way.

The king showed much gratitude to Tristram, but in the bottom of his heart he cherished bitter jealousy of him. One day Tristram and Isoude were alone together in her private chamber. A base and cowardly knight of the court, named Andret, spied them through a keyhole. They sat at a table of chess, but were not attending to the game. Andret brought the king, having first raised his suspicions, and placed him so as to watch their motions. The king saw enough to confirm his suspicions, and he burst into the apartment with his sword drawn, and had nearly slain Tristram before he was put on his guard. But Tristram avoided the blow, drew his sword, and drove before him the cowardly monarch, chasing him through all the apartments of the palace, giving him frequent blows with the flat of his sword, while he cried in vain to his knights to save him. They were not inclined, or did not dare to interpose in his behalf.

9. TRISTRAM AND ISOUDE

After this affair Tristram was banished from the kingdom, and Isoude shut up in a tower which stood on the bank of a river. Tristram could not resolve to depart without some further communication with his beloved; so he concealed himself in the forest, till at last he contrived to attract her attention by means of twigs, which he curiously peeled and sent down the stream under her window. By this means many secret interviews were obtained. Tristram dwelt in the forest, sustaining himself by game, which the dog Houdain ran down for him; for this faithful animal was unequalled in the chase, and knew so well his master's wish for concealment that in the pursuit of his game he never barked. At length Tristram departed, but left Houdain with Isoude, as a remembrancer of him.

Sir Tristram wandered through various countries, achieving the most perilous enterprises, and covering himself with glory, yet unhappy at the separation from his beloved Isoude. Sir Tristram rode through a forest, and saw ten men fighting, and one man did battle against nine. So he rode to the knights and cried to them, bidding them cease their battle, for they did themselves great shame, so many knights to fight against one. Then answered the master of the knights (his name was Sir Breuse sans Pitié, who was at that time the most villainous knight living): "Sir knight, what have ye to do to meddle with us? If ye be wise, depart on your way as you came, for this knight shall not escape us." "That were pity," said Sir Tristram, "that so good a knight should be slain so cowardly; therefore I warn you I will succor him with all my puissance."

Then Sir Tristram alighted off his horse, because they were on foot, that they should not slay his horse. And he smote on the right hand and on the left so vigorously, that well-nigh at every stroke he struck down a knight. At last they fled, with Breuse sans Pitié, into the tower, and shut Sir Tristram without the gate. Then Sir Tristram returned back to the rescued knight, and found him sitting under a tree, sore wounded. "Fair knight," said he, "how is it with you?" "Sir knight," said Sir Palamedes, for he it was, "I thank you for your great goodness, for ye have rescued me from death." "What is your name?" said Sir Tristram. He said, "My name is Sir Palamedes." "Say ye so?" said Sir Tristram; "now know that thou art the man in the world that I most hate; therefore make thee ready, for I will do battle with thee." "What is your name?" said Sir Palamedes. "My name is Sir Tristram, your mortal enemy." "It may be so," said Sir Palamedes; "but you have done overmuch for me this day, that I should fight with you. Moreover, it will be no honor for you to have to do with me, for you are fresh and I am wounded. Therefore, if you will needs have to do with me, assign me a day, and I shall meet you without fail." "You say well," said Sir Tristram; "now I assign you to meet me in the meadow by the river of Camelot, where Merlin set the monument." So they were agreed. Then they departed, and took their ways diverse. Sir Tristram passed through a great forest into a plain, till he came to a priory, and there he reposed him with a good man six days.

Then departed Sir Tristram, and rode straight into Camelot to the monument of Merlin, and there he looked about him for Sir Palamedes. And he perceived a seemly knight, who came riding against him all in white, with a covered shield. When he came nigh, Sir Tristram said aloud, "Welcome, sir knight, and well and truly have you kept your promise." Then they made ready their shields and spears, and came together with all the might of their horses, so fiercely, that both the horses and the knights fell to the earth. And as soon as they might, they quitted their horses, and struck together with bright swords as men of might, and each wounded the other wonderfully sore, so that the blood ran out upon the grass. Thus they fought for the space of four hours, and never one would speak to the other one word. Then at last spake the white knight, and said, "Sir, thou fightest wonderful well, as ever I saw knight; therefore, if it please you, tell me your name." "Why dost thou ask my name?" said Sir Tristram; "art thou not Sir Palamedes?" "No, fair knight," said he, "I am Sir Launcelot of the Lake." "Alas!" said Sir Tristram, "what have I done? for you are the man of the world that I love best." "Fair knight," said Sir Launcelot, "tell me your name." "Truly," said he, "my name is Sir Tristram de Lyonesse." "Alas! alas!" said Sir Launcelot, "what adventure has befallen me!" And therewith Sir Launcelot kneeled down, and yielded him up his sword; and Sir Tristram kneeled down, and yielded him up his sword; and so either gave other the degree. And then they both went to the stone, and sat them down upon it, and took off their helms, and each kissed the other a hundred times. And then anon they rode toward Camelot, and on the way they met with Sir Gawain and Sir Gaheris, that had made promise to Arthur never to come again to the court till they had brought Sir Tristram with them.

"Return again," said Sir Launcelot, "for your quest is done; for I have met with Sir Tristram. Lo, here he is in his own person." Then was Sir Gawain glad, and said to Sir Tristram, "Ye are welcome." With this came King Arthur, and when he wist there was Sir Tristram, he ran unto him, and took him by the hand, and said, "Sir Tristram, ye are as welcome as any knight that ever came to this court." Then Sir Tristram told the king how he came thither for to have had to do with Sir Palamedes, and how he had rescued him

from Sir Breuse sans Pitié and the nine knights. Then King
Arthur took Sir Tristram by the hand, and went to the
Table Round, and Queen Guenever came, and many ladies
with her, and all the ladies said with one voice, "Welcome,
Sir Tristram." "Welcome," said the knights. "Welcome,"
said Arthur, "for one of the best knights, and the gentlest of
the world, and the man of most worship; for of all manner
of hunting thou bearest the prize, and of all measures of
blowing thou art the beginning, and of all the terms of
hunting and hawking ye are the inventor, and of all instruments of music ye are the best skilled; therefore, gentle
knight," said Arthur, "ye are welcome to this court." And
then King Arthur made Sir Tristram knight of the Table
Round with great nobley and feasting as can be thought.

The Round Table had been made by the famous enchanter Merlin, and on it he had exerted all his skill and
craft. Of the seats which surrounded it he had constructed
thirteen, in memory of the thirteen Apostles. Twelve of
these seats only could be occupied, and they only by knights
of the highest fame; the thirteenth represented the seat of
the traitor Judas. It remained always empty. It was called
the *perilous seat* ever since a rash and haughty Saracen
knight had dared to place himself in it, when the earth
opened and swallowed him up.

A magic power wrote upon each seat the name of the
knight who was entitled to sit in it. No one could succeed
to a vacant seat unless he surpassed in valor or glorious
deeds the knight who had occupied it before him; without
this qualification he would be violently repelled by a hidden
force. Thus proof was made of all those who presented
themselves to replace any companions of the order who had
fallen.

One of the principal seats, that of Moraunt of Ireland,
had been vacant ten years, and his name still remained over
it ever since the time when that distinguished champion fell
beneath the sword of Sir Tristram. Arthur now took Tristram by the hand and led him to that seat. Immediately the
most melodious sounds were heard, and exquisite perfumes
filled the place; the name of Moraunt disappeared, and that
of Tristram blazed forth in light. The rare modesty of Tristram had now to be subjected to a severe task; for the clerks
charged with the duty of preserving the annals of the Round

Table attended, and he was required by the law of his order to declare what feats of arms he had accomplished to entitle him to take that seat. This ceremony being ended, Tristram received the congratulations of all his companions. Sir Launcelot and Guenever took occasion to speak to him of the fair Isoude, and to express their wish that some happy chance might bring her to the kingdom of Loegria.

While Tristram was thus honored and caressed at the court of King Arthur, the most gloomy and malignant jealousy harassed the soul of Mark. He could not look upon Isoude without remembering that she loved Tristram, and the good fortune of his nephew goaded him to thoughts of vengeance. He at last resolved to go disguised into the kingdom of Loegria, attack Tristram by stealth, and put him to death. He took with him two knights, brought up in his court, who he thought were devoted to him; and, not willing to leave Isoude behind, named two of her maidens to attend her, together with her faithful Brengwain, and made them accompany him.

Having arrived in the neighborhood of Camelot, Mark imparted his plan to his two knights, but they rejected it with horror; nay, more, they declared that they would no longer remain in his service; and left him, giving him reason to suppose that they should repair to the court to accuse him before Arthur. It was necessary for Mark to meet and rebut their accusation; so, leaving Isoude in an abbey, he pursued his way alone to Camelot.

Mark had not ridden far when he encountered a party of knights of Arthur's court, and would have avoided them, for he knew their habit of challenging to a joust every stranger knight whom they met. But it was too late. They had seen his armor, and recognized him as a Cornish knight, and at once resolved to have some sport with him. It happened they had with them, Daguenet, King Arthur's fool, who, though deformed and weak of body, was not wanting in courage. The knights as Mark approached laid their plan that Daguenet should personate Sir Launcelot of the Lake, and challenge the Cornish knight. They equipped him in armor belonging to one of their number who was ill, and sent him forward to the cross-road to defy the strange knight. Mark, who saw that his antagonist was by no means formidable in appearance, was not disinclined to the combat; but when the dwarf rode towards him, calling out that he was Sir Launcelot of the Lake, his fears prevailed, he put spurs to his horse, and rode away at full speed, pursued by the shouts and laughter of the party.

Meanwhile, Isoude, remaining at the abbey with her faithful Brengwain, found her only amusement in walking occasionally in a forest adjoining the abbey. There, on the brink of a fountain girdled with trees, she thought of her love, and sometimes joined her voice and her harp in lays reviving the memory of its pains or pleasures. One day the caitiff knight, Breuse the Pitiless, heard her voice, concealed himself, and drew near. She sang:—

"Sweet silence, shadowy bower, and verdant lair,
    Ye court my troubled spirit to repose,
Whilst I, such dear remembrance rises there,
    Awaken every echo with my woes.

"Within these woods, by Nature's hand arrayed,
    A fountain springs, and feeds a thousand flowers;
Ah! how my groans do all its murmurs aid!
    How my sad eyes do swell it with their showers!

"What doth my knight the while? to him is given
    A double meed; in love and arms' emprise,
Him the Round Table elevates to heaven!
    Tristram! ah me! he hears not Isoude's cries."

Breuse the Pitiless, who, like most other caitiffs, had felt the weight of Tristram's arm, and hated him accordingly, at hearing his name breathed forth by the beautiful song-stress, impelled by a double impulse, rushed forth from his concealment and laid hands on his victim. Isoude fainted, and Brengwain filled the air with her shrieks. Breuse carried Isoude to the place where he had left his horse; but the animal had got away from his bridle, and was at some distance. He was obliged to lay down his fair burden, and go in pursuit of his horse. Just then a knight came up, drawn by the cries of Brengwain, and demanded the cause of her distress. She could not speak, but pointed to her mistress lying insensible on the ground.

Breuse had by this time returned, and the cries of Brengwain, renewed at seeing him, sufficiently showed the stranger the cause of the distress. Tristram spurred his horse towards Breuse, who, not unprepared, ran to the encounter. Breuse was unhorsed, and lay motionless, pretending to be dead; but when the stranger knight left him to attend to the distressed damsels, he mounted his horse, and made his escape.

The knight now approached Isoude, gently raised her head, drew aside the golden hair which covered her countenance, gazed thereon for an instant, uttered a cry, and fell back insensible. Brengwain came; her caress soon restored her mistress to life, and they then turned their attention to the fallen warrior. They raised his visor, and discovered the countenance of Sir Tristram. Isoude threw herself on the body of her lover, and bedewed his face with her tears. Their warmth revived the knight, and Tristram, on awaking, found himself in the arms of his dear Isoude.

It was the law of the Round Table that each knight after his admission should pass the next ten days in quest of adventures, during which time his companions might meet him in disguised armor, and try their strength with him. Tristram had now been out seven days, and in that time had encountered many of the best knights of the Round Table, and acquitted himself with honor. During the remaining three days Isoude remained at the abbey, under his protection, and then set out with her maidens, escorted by Sir Tristram, to rejoin King Mark at the court of Camelot.

This happy journey was one of the brightest epochs in the lives of Tristram and Isoude. They arrived at Camelot, where Sir Launcelot received them most cordially. Isoude was introduced to King Arthur and Queen Gueneyer, who welcomed her as a sister. As King Mark was held in arrest under the accusation of the two Cornish knights, Queen Isoude could not rejoin her husband, and Sir Launcelot placed his castle of La Joyeuse Garde at the disposal of his friends, who there took up their abode.

King Mark, who found himself obliged to confess the truth of the charge against him, or to clear himself by combat with his accusers, preferred the former, and King Arthur, as his crime had not been perpetrated, remitted the penalty, only enjoining upon him, under pain of his signal displeasure, to lay aside all thoughts of vengeance against his nephew. In the presence of the king and his court, all parties were formally reconciled; Mark and his queen departed for their home, and Tristram remained at Arthur's court.

10. THE END OF THE STORY OF SIR TRISTRAM

While Sir Tristram and the fair Isoude abode yet at La Joyeuse Garde, Sir Tristram rode forth one day, without armor, having no weapon but his spear and his sword. And as he rode he came to a place where he saw two knights in battle, and one of them had gotten the better, and the other lay overthrown. The knight who had the better was Sir Palamedes. When Sir Palamedes knew Sir Tristram, he cried out, "Sir Tristram, now we be met, and ere we depart we will redress our old wrongs." "As for that," said Sir Tristram, "there never yet was Christian man that might make his boast that I ever fled from him, and thou that art a Saracen shalt never say that of me." And therewith Sir Tristram made his horse to run, and with all his might came straight upon Sir Palamedes, and broke his spear upon him. Then he drew his sword and struck at Sir Palamedes six great strokes, upon his helm. Sir Palamedes saw that Sir Tristram had not his armor on, and he marvelled at his rashness and his great folly; and said to himself, "If I meet and slay him I am ashamed wheresoever I go." Then Sir Tristram cried out and said, "Thou coward knight, why wilt thou not do battle with me? for have thou no doubt I shall endure all thy malice." "Ah, Sir Tristram!" said Sir Palamedes, "thou knowest I may not fight with thee for shame; for thou art here naked, and I am armed; now I require that thou answer me a question that I shall ask you." "Tell me what it is," said Sir Tristram. "I put the case," said Sir Palamedes, "that you were well armed, and I naked as ye be; what would you do to me now, by your true knighthood?" "Ah!" said Sir Tristram, "now I understand thee well, Sir Palamedes; and, as

God me bless, what I shall say shall not be said for fear that I have of thee. But if it were so, thou shouldest depart from me, for I would not have to do with thee." "No more will I with thee," said Sir Palamedes, "and therefore ride forth on thy way." "As for that, I may choose," said Sir Tristram, "either to ride or to abide. But, Sir Palamedes, I marvel at one thing,—that thou art so good a knight, yet that thou wilt not be christened." "As for that," said Sir Palamedes, "I may not yet be christened, for a vow which I made many years ago; yet in my heart I believe in our Saviour and his mild mother Mary; but I have yet one battle to do, and when that is done I will be christened, with a good will." "By my head," said Sir Tristram, "as for that one battle, thou shalt seek it no longer; for yonder is a knight, whom you have smitten down. Now help me to be clothed in his armor, and I will soon fulfil thy vow." "As ye will," said Sir Palamedes, "so shall it be." So they rode both unto that knight that sat on a bank; and Sir Tristram saluted him, and he full weakly saluted him again. "Sir," said Sir Tristram, "I pray you to lend me your whole armor; for I am unarmed, and I must do battle with this knight." "Sir," said the hurt knight, "you shall have it, with a right good will." Then Sir Tristram unarmed Sir Galleron, for that was the name of the hurt knight, and he as well as he could helped to arm Sir Tristram. Then Sir Tristram mounted upon his own horse, and in his hand he took Sir Galleron's spear. Thereupon Sir Palamedes was ready, and so they came hurtling together, and each smote the other in the midst of their shields. Sir Palamedes' spear broke, and Sir Tristram smote down the horse. Then Sir Palamedes leapt from his horse, and drew out his sword. That saw Sir Tristram, and therewith he alighted and tied his horse to a tree. Then they came together as two wild beasts, lashing the one on the other, and so fought more than two hours; and often Sir Tristram smote such strokes at Sir Palamedes that he made him to kneel, and Sir Palamedes broke away Sir Tristram's shield, and wounded him. Then Sir Tristram was wroth out of measure, and he rushed to Sir Palamedes and wounded him passing sore through the shoulder, and by fortune smote Sir Palamedes' sword out of his hand. And if Sir Palamedes had stooped for his sword, Sir Tristram had slain him. Then Sir Palamedes stood and beheld his sword with a full sorrowful heart. "Now," said Sir Tristram, "I have thee at a vantage, as thou hadst me to-day; but it shall never be said, in court, or among good knights, that Sir Tristram did slay any knight that was weaponless: therefore take thou thy sword, and let us fight this battle to the end." Then spoke Sir Palamedes to Sir Tristram: "I have no wish to fight this battle any more. The offence that I have done unto you is not so great but that, if it please you, we may be friends. All that I have offended is for the love of the queen, La Belle Isoude, and I dare maintain that she is peerless among ladies; and for that offence ye have given me many grievous and sad strokes, and some I have given you again. Wherefore I require you, my lord Sir Tristram, forgive me all that I have offended you, and this day have me unto the next church; and first I will be clean confessed, and after that see you that I be truly baptized, and then we will ride together unto the court of my lord, King Arthur, so that we may be there at the feast of Pentecost." "Now take your horse," said Sir Tristram, "and as you have said, so shall it be done." So they took their horses, and Sir Galleron rode with them. When they came to the church of Carlisle, the bishop commanded to fill a great vessel with water; and when he had hallowed it, he then confessed Sir Palamedes clean, and christened him; and Sir Tristram and Sir Galleron were his godfathers. Then soon after they departed, and rode toward Camelot, where the noble King Arthur and Queen Guenever were keeping a court royal. And the king and all the court were glad that Sir Palamedes was christened. Then Sir Tristram returned again to La Joyeuse Garde, and Sir Palamedes went his way.

Not long after these events Sir Gawain returned from Brittany, and related to King Arthur the adventure which befell him in the forest of Breciliande,—how Merlin had there spoken to him, and enjoined him to charge the king to go without delay upon the quest of the Holy Greal. While King Arthur deliberated, Tristram determined to enter upon the quest, and the more readily, as it was well known to him that this holy adventure would, if achieved, procure him the pardon of all his sins. He immediately departed for the kingdom of Brittany, hoping there to obtain from Merlin counsel as to the proper course to pursue to insure success.

On arriving in Brittany Tristram found King Hoel engaged in a war with a rebellious vassal, and hard pressed by his enemy. His best knights had fallen in a late battle, and he knew not where to turn for assistance. Tristram volunteered his aid. It was accepted; and the army of Hoel, led by Tristram, and inspired by his example, gained a complete victory. The king, penetrated by the most lively sentiments of gratitude, and having informed himself of Tristram's birth, offered him his daughter in marriage. The princess was beautiful and accomplished, and bore the same name with the Queen of Cornwall; but this one is designated by the Romancers as Isoude of the White Hands, to distinguish her from Isoude the Fair.

How can we describe the conflict that agitated the heart of Tristram? He adored the first Isoude, but his love for her was hopeless, and not unaccompanied by remorse. Moreover, the sacred quest on which he had now entered demanded of him perfect purity of life. It seemed as if a happy destiny had provided for him, in the charming princess Isoude of the White Hands, the best security for all his good resolutions. This last reflection determined him. They were married, and passed some months in tranquil happiness at the court of King Hoel. The pleasure which Tristram felt in his wife's society increased day by day. An inward grace seemed to stir within him from the moment when he took the oath to go on the quest of the Holy Greal; it seemed even to triumph over the power of the magic love-potion.

The war, which had been quelled for a time, now burst out anew. Tristram, as usual, was foremost in every danger. The enemy was worsted in successive conflicts, and at last shut himself up in his principal city. Tristram led on the attack of the city. As he mounted a ladder to scale the walls, he was struck on the head by a fragment of rock, which the besieged threw down upon him. It bore him to the ground, where he lay insensible.

As soon as he recovered consciousness, he demanded to be carried to his wife. The princess, skilled in the art of surgery, would not suffer any one but herself to touch her beloved husband. Her fair hands bound up his wounds; Tristram kissed them with gratitude, which began to grow into love. At first the devoted cares of Isoude seemed to meet with great success; but after awhile these flattering appearances vanished, and, in spite of all her care, the malady grew more serious day by day.

In this perplexity, an old squire of Tristram's reminded his master that the princess of Ireland, afterward queen of Cornwall, had once cured him under circumstances quite as discouraging. He called Isoude of the White Hands to him, told her of his former cure, added that he believed that the Queen Isoude could heal him, and that he felt sure that she would come to his relief if sent for.

Isoude of the White Hands consented that Gesnes, a trusty man and skilful navigator, should be sent to Cornwall. Tristram called him, and, giving him a ring, "Take this," he said, "to the Queen of Cornwall. Tell her that Tristram, near to death, demands her aid. If you succeed in bringing her with you, place white sails to your vessel on your return, that we may know of your success when the vessel first heaves in sight. But if Queen Isoude refuses, put on black sails; they will be the presage of my impending death."

Gesnes performed his mission successfully. King Mark happened to be absent from his capital, and the queen readily consented to return with the bark to Brittany. Gesnes clothed his vessel in the whitest of sails, and sped his way back to Brittany.

Meantime the wound of Tristram grew more desperate day by day. His strength, quite prostrated, no longer permitted him to be carried to the seaside daily, as had been his custom from the first moment when it was possible for the bark to be on the way homeward. He called a young damsel, and gave her in charge to keep watch in the direction of Cornwall, and to come and tell him the color of the sails of the first vessel she should see approaching.

When Isoude of the White Hands consented that the queen of Cornwall should be sent for, she had not known all the reasons which she had for fearing the influence which renewed intercourse with that princess might have on her own happiness. She had now learned more, and felt the danger more keenly. She thought, if she could only keep the knowledge of the queen's arrival from her husband she might employ in his service any resources which her skill could supply, and still avert the dangers which she apprehended. When the vessel was seen approaching, with its white sails sparkling in the sun, the damsel, by command of her mistress, carried word to Tristram that the sails were black.

Tristram, penetrated with inexpressible grief, breathed a profound sigh, turned away his face, and said, "Alas, my beloved! we shall never see one another again!" Then he commended himself to God, and breathed his last.

The death of Tristram was the first intelligence which the queen of Cornwall heard on landing. She was conducted almost senseless into the chamber of Tristram, and expired holding him in her arms.

Tristram, before his death, had requested that his body should be sent to Cornwall, and that his sword, with a letter he had written, should be delivered to King Mark. The remains of Tristram and Isoude were embarked in a vessel, along with the sword, which was presented to the king of Cornwall. He was melted with tenderness when he saw the weapon which slew Moraunt of Ireland,—which had so often saved his life, and redeemed the honor of his kingdom. In the letter Tristram begged pardon of his uncle, and related the story of the amorous draught.

Mark ordered the lovers to be buried in his own chapel. From the tomb of Tristram there sprung a vine, which went along the walls, and descended into the grave of the queen. It was cut down three times, but each time sprung up again more vigorous than before, and this wonderful plant has ever since shaded the tombs of Tristram and Isoude.

11. THE STORY OF PERCEVAL

"—Sir Percivale,
Whom Arthur and his knighthood called the Pure."
—TENNYSON

The father and two elder brothers of Perceval had fallen in battle or tournaments, and hence, as the last hope of his family, his mother retired with him into a solitary region, where he was brought up in total ignorance of arms and chivalry. He was allowed no weapon but "a lyttel Scots spere," which was the only thing of all "her lordes faire gere" that his mother carried to the wood with her. In the use of this he became so skilful that he could kill with it not only the animals of the chase for her table, but even birds on the wing. At length, however, Perceval was roused to a desire of military renown by seeing in the forest five knights who were in complete armor. He said to his mother, "Mother, what are those yonder?" "They are angels, my son," said she. "By my faith, I will go and become an angel with them." And Perceval went to the road and met them. "Tell me, good lad," said one of them, "sawest thou a knight pass this way either to-day or yesterday?" "I know not," said he, "what a knight is." "Such an one as I am," said the knight. "If thou wilt tell me what I ask thee, I will tell thee what thou askest me." "Gladly will I do so," said Sir Owain, for that was the knight's name. "What is this?" demanded Perceval, touching the saddle. "It is a saddle," said Owain. Then he asked about all the accoutrements which he saw upon the men and the horses, and about the arms, and what they were for, and how they were used. And Sir Owain showed him all those things fully. And Perceval in return gave him such information as he had.

Then Perceval returned to his mother, and said to her, "Mother, those were not angels, but honorable knights." Then his mother swooned away. And Perceval went to the place where they kept the horses that carried firewood and provisions for the castle, and he took a bony, piebald horse, which seemed to him the strongest of them. And he pressed a pack into the form of a saddle, and with twisted twigs he imitated the trappings which he had seen upon the horses. When he came again to his mother the countess had recovered from her swoon. "My son," said she, "desirest thou to ride forth?" "Yes, with thy leave," said he. "Go forward then," she said, "to the court of Arthur, where there are the best and the noblest and the most bountiful of men, and tell him thou art Perceval, the son of Pelenore, and ask of him to bestow knighthood on thee. And whenever thou seest a church, repeat there thy pater-noster; and if thou see meat and drink, and hast need of them, thou mayest take them. If thou hear an outcry of one in distress, proceed toward it,

especially if it be the cry of a woman, and render her what
service thou canst. If thou see a fair jewel, win it, for thus
shalt thou acquire fame; yet freely give it to another, for
thus thou shalt obtain praise. If thou see a fair woman, pay
court to her, for thus thou wilt obtain love."

After this discourse Perceval mounted the horse, and,
taking a number of sharp-pointed sticks in his hand, he rode
forth. And he rode far in the woody wilderness without
food or drink. At last he came to an opening in the wood,
where he saw a tent, and as he thought it might be a church
he said his pater-noster to it. And he went toward it; and the
door of the tent was open. And Perceval dismounted and
entered the tent. In the tent he found a maiden sitting, with
a golden frontlet on her forehead and a gold ring on her
hand. And Perceval said, "Maiden, I salute you, for my
mother told me whenever I met a lady I must respectfully
salute her." Perceiving in one corner of the tent some food,
two flasks full of wine, and some boar's flesh roasted, he
said, "My mother told me, whenever I saw meat and drink
to take it." And he ate greedily, for he was very hungry.
"Sir, thou hadst best go quickly from here, for fear that my
friends should come, and evil should befall you." But Perceval said, "My mother told me wheresoever I saw a fair jewel
to take it," and he took the gold ring from her finger, and
put it on his own; and he gave the maiden his own ring in
exchange for hers; then he mounted his horse and rode
away.

Perceval journeyed on till he arrived at Arthur's court.
And it so happened that just at that time an uncourteous
knight had offered Queen Guenever a gross insult. For when
her page was serving the queen with a golden goblet, this
knight struck the arm of the page and dashed the wine in the
queen's face and over her stomacher. Then he said, "If any
have boldness to avenge this insult to Guenever, let him follow me to the meadow." So the knight took his horse and
rode to the meadow, carrying away the golden goblet. And
all the household hung down their heads, and no one offered
to follow the knight to take vengeance upon him. For it
seemed to them that no one would have ventured on so daring an outrage unless he possessed such powers, through
magic or charms, that none could be able to punish him.
Just then, behold, Perceval entered the hall upon the bony,

piebald horse, with his uncouth trappings. In the centre of
the hall stood Kay the seneschal. "Tell me, tall man," said
Perceval, "is that Arthur yonder?" "What wouldst thou with
Arthur?" asked Kay. "My mother told me to go to Arthur
and receive knighthood from him." "By my faith," said he,
"thou art all too meanly equipped with horse and with
arms." Then all the household began to jeer and laugh at
him. But there was a certain damsel who had been a whole
year at Arthur's court, and had never been known to smile.
And the king's fool [1] had said that this damsel would not
smile till she had seen him who would be the flower of chivalry. Now this damsel came up to Perceval and told him,
smiling, that, if he lived, he would be one of the bravest and
best of knights. "Truly," said Kay, "thou art ill taught to remain a year at Arthur's court, with choice of society, and
smile on no one, and now before the face of Arthur and all
his knights to call such a man as this the flower of knighthood"; and he gave her a box on the ear, that she fell senseless to the ground. Then said Kay to Perceval, "Go after
the knight who went hence to the meadow, overthrow him
and recover the golden goblet, and possess thyself of his
horse and arms, and thou shalt have knighthood." "I will
do so, tall man," said Perceval. So he turned his horse's head
toward the meadow. And when he came there, the knight
was riding up and down, proud of his strength and valor
and noble mien. "Tell me," said the knight, "didst thou see
any one coming after me from the court?" "The tall man
that was there," said Perceval, "told me to come and overthrow thee, and to take from thee the goblet and thy horse
and armor for myself." "Silence!" said the knight; "go back
to the court, and tell Arthur either to come himself, or to
send some other to fight with me; and unless he do so
quickly, I will not wait for him." "By my faith," said Perceval, "choose thou whether it shall be willingly or unwillingly, for I will have the horse and the arms and the goblet."
Upon this the knight ran at him furiously, and struck him a
violent blow with the shaft of his spear, between the neck

---

[1] A fool was a common appendage of the courts of those days when this
romance was written. A fool was the ornament held in next estimation to
a dwarf. He wore a white dress with a yellow bonnet, and carried a bell
or *bawble* in his hand. Though called a fool, his words were often weighed
and remembered as if there were a sort of oracular meaning in them.

and the shoulder. "Ha, ha, lad!" said Perceval, "my mother's servants were not used to play with me in this wise; so thus will I play with thee." And he threw at him one of his sharp-pointed sticks, and it struck him in the eye, and came out at the back of his head, so that he fell down lifeless.

But at the court of Arthur, Sir Owain said to Kay, "Verily, thou wert ill advised when thou didst send that madman after the knight. For one of two things must befall him. He must either be overthrown or slain. If he is overthrown by the knight, he will be counted by him to be an honorable person of the court, and an eternal disgrace will it be to Arthur and his warriors. And if he is slain, the disgrace will be the same, and moreover his sin will be upon him; therefore will I go to see what has befallen him." So Sir Owain went to the meadow, and he found Perceval dragging the man about. "What art thou doing thus?" said Sir Owain. "This iron coat," said Perceval, "will never come off him; not by my efforts, at any rate." And Sir Owain unfastened his armor and his clothes. "Here, my good soul," said he, "is a horse and armor better than thine. Take them joyfully, and come with me to Arthur to receive the order of knighthood, for thou dost merit it." And Owain helped Perceval to put it on, and taught him how to put his foot in the stirrup, and use the spur; for Perceval had never used stirrup nor spur, but rode without saddle, and urged on his horse with a stick. Then Owain would have had him return to the court to receive the praise that was his due; but Perceval said, "I will not come to the court till I have encountered the tall man that is there, to revenge the injury he did to the maiden. But take thou the goblet to Queen Guenever, and tell King Arthur that, wherever I am, I will be his vassal, and will do him what profit and service I can." And Sir Owain went back to the court, and related all these things to Arthur and Guenever, and to all the household.

And Perceval rode forward. And as he proceeded, behold a knight met him. "Whence comest thou?" said the knight. "I come from Arthur's court," said Perceval. "Art thou one of his men?" asked he. "Yes, by my faith," he answered. "A good service, truly, is that of Arthur." "Wherefore sayest thou so?" said Perceval. "I will tell thee," said he. "I have always been Arthur's enemy, and all such of his men as I have ever encountered I have slain." And without further

parlance they fought, and it was not long before Perceval
brought him to the ground, over his horse's crupper. Then
the knight besought his mercy. "Mercy thou shalt have,"
said Perceval, "if thou wilt make oath to me that thou wilt
go to Arthur's court and tell him that it was I that overthrew thee, for the honor of his service; and say that I will
never come to the court until I have avenged the insult
offered to the maiden." The knight pledged him his faith of
this, and proceeded to the court of Arthur and said as he
had promised, and conveyed the threat to Sir Kay.

And Perceval rode forward. And within that week he encountered sixteen knights, and overthrew them all shame-
fully. And they all went to Arthur's court, taking with them
the same message which the first knight had conveyed from
Perceval, and the same threat which he had sent to Sir Kay.
And thereupon Sir Kay was reproved by Arthur; and Sir
Kay was greatly grieved thereat.

And Perceval rode forward. And he came to a lake, on
the side of which was a fair castle, and on the border of the
lake he saw a hoary-headed man sitting upon a velvet
cushion, and his attendants were fishing in the lake. When
the hoary-headed man beheld Perceval approaching, he
arose and went into the castle. Perceval rode to the castle,
and the door was open, and he entered the hall. And the
hoary-headed man received Perceval courteously, and asked
him to sit by him on the cushion. When it was time, the
tables were set, and they went to meat. And when they had
finished their meat, the hoary-headed man asked Perceval if
he knew how to fight with the sword. "I know not," said
Perceval, "but were I to be taught, doubtless I should."
"Whoever can play well with the cudgel and shield will also
be able to fight with a sword." And the man had two sons;
the one had yellow hair and the other auburn. "Arise,
youths," said the old man, "and play with the cudgel and
the shield." And so did they. "Tell me, my son," said the
man, "which of the youths thinkest thou plays best?" "I
think," said Perceval, "that the yellow-haired youth could
draw blood if he chose." "Arise thou, then, and take the
cudgel and the shield from the hand of the youth with the
auburn hair, and draw blood from the yellow-haired youth
if thou canst." So Perceval arose, and he lifted up his arm,
and struck him such a mighty blow that he cut his forehead

open from one side to the other. "Ah, my life," said the old man, "come, now, and sit down, for thou wilt become the best fighter with the sword of any in this island; and I am thy uncle, thy mother's brother; I am called King Pecheur.[1] Thou shalt remain with me a space, in order to learn the manners and customs of different countries, and courtesy and noble bearing. And this do thou remember: if thou seest aught to cause thy wonder, ask not the meaning of it; if no one has the courtesy to inform thee, the reproach will not fall upon thee, but upon me that am thy teacher." While Perceval and his uncle discoursed together, Perceval beheld two youths enter the hall, bearing a golden cup and a spear of mighty size, with blood dropping from its point to the ground. And when all the company saw this, they began to weep and lament. But for all that, the man did not break off his discourse with Perceval. And as he did not tell him the meaning of what he saw, he forbore to ask him concerning it. Now the cup that Perceval saw was the Sangreal, and the spear the sacred spear; and afterwards King Pecheur removed with those sacred relics into a far country. .

One evening Perceval entered a valley, and came to a hermit's cell; and the hermit welcomed him gladly, and there he spent the night. And in the morning he arose, and when he went forth, behold! a shower of snow had fallen in the night, and a hawk had killed a wild-fowl in front of the cell. And the noise of the horse had scared the hawk away, and a raven alighted on the bird. And Perceval stood and compared the blackness of the raven and the whiteness of the snow and the redness of the blood to the hair of the lady that best he loved, which was blacker than jet, and to her skin, which was whiter than the snow, and to the two red spots upon her cheeks, which were redder than the blood upon the snow.

Now Arthur and his household were in search of Perceval, and by chance they came that way. "Know ye," said Arthur, "who is the knight with the long spear that stands by the brook up yonder?" "Lord," said one of them, "I will go and learn who he is." So the youth came to the place where Perceval was, and asked him what he did thus, and who he was. But Perceval was so intent upon his thought

---

[1] The word means both *fisher* and *sinner*.

that he gave him no answer. Then the youth thrust at Perceval with his lance; and Perceval turned upon him and struck him to the ground. And when the youth returned to the king, and told how rudely he had been treated, Sir Kay said, "I will go myself." And when he greeted Perceval, and got no answer, he spoke to him rudely and angrily. And Perceval thrust at him with his lance, and cast him down so that he broke his arm and his shoulder-blade. And while he lay thus stunned, his horse returned back at a wild and prancing pace.

Then said Sir Gawain, surnamed the Golden-Tongued, because he was the most courteous knight in Arthur's court: "It is not fitting that any should disturb an honorable knight from his thought unadvisedly; for either he is pondering some damage that he has sustained, or he is thinking of the lady he best loves. If it seem well to thee, lord, I will go and see if this knight has changed from his thought, and if he has, I will ask him courteously to come and visit thee."

And Perceval was resting on the shaft of his spear, pondering the same thought, and Sir Gawain came to him, and said, "If I thought it would be as agreeable to thee as it would be to me, I would converse with thee. I have also a message from Arthur unto thee, to pray thee to come and visit him. And two men have been before on this errand." "That is true," said Perceval, "and uncourteously they came. They attacked me, and I was annoyed thereat." Then he told him the thought that occupied his mind, and Gawain said, "This was not an ungentle thought, and I should marvel if it were pleasant for thee to be drawn from it." Then said Perceval, "Tell me, is Sir Kay in Arthur's court?" "He is," said Gawain; "and truly he is the knight who fought with thee last." "Verily," said Perceval, "I am not sorry to have thus avenged the insult to the smiling maiden." Then Perceval told him his name, and said, "Who art thou?" And he replied, "I am Gawain." "I am right glad to meet thee," said Perceval, "for I have everywhere heard of thy prowess and uprightness; and I solicit thy fellowship." "Thou shalt have it, by my faith; and grant me thine," said he. "Gladly will I do so," answered Perceval.

So they went together to Arthur, and saluted him. "Behold, lord," said Gawain, "him whom thou hast sought so long." "Welcome unto thee, chieftain," said Arthur. And hereupon there came the queen and her handmaidens, and Perceval saluted them. And they were rejoiced to see him, and bade him welcome. And Arthur did him great honor and respect, and they returned toward Caerleon.

12. THE QUEST OF THE SANGREAL

"—The cup itself from which our Lord
Drank at the last sad supper with His own.
This from the blessed land of Aromat,
After the day of darkness, when the dead
Went wandering over Moriah—the good saint,
Arimathean Joseph, journeying, brought
To Glastonbury, where the winter thorn
Blossoms at Christmas, mindful of our Lord,
And there awhile abode; and if a man
Could touch or see it, he was healed at once,
By faith, of all his ills. But then the times
Grew to such evil that the holy cup
Was caught away to Heaven, and disappeared."
—TENNYSON

The Sangreal was the cup from which our Saviour drank at his last supper. He was supposed to have given it to Joseph of Arimathea, who carried it to Europe, together with the spear with which the soldier pierced the Saviour's side. From generation to generation one of the descendants of Joseph of Arimathea had been devoted to the guardianship of these precious relics; but on the sole condition of leading a life of purity in thought, word, and deed. For a long time the Sangreal was visible to all pilgrims, and its presence conferred blessings upon the land in which it was preserved. But at length one of those holy men to whom its guardianship had descended so far forgot the obligation of his sacred office as to look with unhallowed eye upon a young female pilgrim whose robe was accidentally loosened as she knelt before him. The sacred lance instantly punished his frailty, spontaneously falling upon him, and inflicting a deep wound. The marvellous wound could by no means be healed, and the guardian of the Sangreal was ever after called "Le Roi Pecheur,"—the Sinner King. The Sangreal withdrew its visible presence from the crowds who came to worship, and an iron age succeeded to the happiness which its presence had diffused among the tribes of Britain.

We have told in the history of Merlin how that great prophet and enchanter sent a message to King Arthur by Sir Gawain, directing him to undertake the recovery of the Sangreal, informing him at the same time that the knight who should accomplish that sacred quest was already born, and of a suitable age to enter upon it. Sir Gawain delivered his message, and the king was anxiously revolving in his mind how best to achieve the enterprise, when, at the vigil of Pentecost, all the fellowship of the Round Table being met together at Camelot, as they sat at meat, suddenly there was heard a clap of thunder, and then a bright light burst forth, and every knight, as he looked on his fellow, saw him, in seeming, fairer than ever before. All the hall was filled with sweet odors, and every knight had such meat and drink as he best loved. Then there entered into the hall the Holy Greal, covered with white samite, so that none could see it, and it passed through the hall suddenly and disappeared. During this time no one spoke a word, but when they had recovered breath to speak, King Arthur said, "Certainly we ought greatly to thank the Lord for what He hath showed us this day." Then Sir Gawain rose up, and made a vow that for twelve months and a day he would seek the Sangreal, and not return till he had seen it, if so he might speed. When they of the Round Table heard Sir Gawain say so, they arose, the most part of them, and vowed the same. When King Arthur heard this he was greatly displeased, for he knew well that they might not gainsay their vows. "Alas!" said he to Sir Gawain, "you have nigh slain me with the vow and promise that ye have made, for ye have bereft me of the fairest fellowship that ever was seen together in any realm of the world; for when they shall depart hence, I am sure that all shall never meet more in this world."

Sir Galahad

At that time there entered the hall a good old man, and with him he brought a young knight, and these words he said: "Peace be with you, fair lords." Then the old man said unto King Arthur, "Sir, I bring you here a young knight that is of kings' lineage, and of the kindred of Joseph of Arimathea, being the son of Dame Elaine, the daughter of King Pelles, king of the foreign country." Now the name of the young knight was Sir Galahad, and he was the son of Sir Launcelot du Lac; but he had dwelt with his mother, at the court of King Pelles, his grandfather, till now he was old enough to bear arms, and his mother had sent him in the charge of a holy hermit to King Arthur's court. Then Sir Launcelot beheld his son, and had great joy of him. And Sir Bohort told his fellows, "Upon my life, this young knight shall come to great worship." The noise was great in all the court, so that it came to the queen. And she said, "I would fain see him, for he must needs be a noble knight, for so is his father." And the queen and her ladies all said that he resembled much unto his father; and he was seemly and demure as a dove, with all manner of good features, that in the whole world men might not find his match. And King Arthur said, "God make him a good man, for beauty faileth him not, as any that liveth."

Then the hermit led the young knight to the Siege Perilous; and he lifted up the cloth, and found there letters that said, "This is the seat of Sir Galahad, the good knight"; and he made him sit in that seat. And all the knights of the Round Table marvelled greatly at Sir Galahad, seeing him sit securely in that seat, and said, "This is he by whom the Sangreal shall be achieved, for there never sat one before in that seat without being mischieved."

On the next day the king said, "Now, at this quest of the Sangreal shall all ye of the Round Table depart, and never shall I see you again all together; therefore I will that ye all repair to the meadow of Camelot, for to joust and tourney yet once more before ye depart." But all the meaning of the king was to see Sir Galahad proved. So then were they all assembled in the meadow. Then Sir Galahad, by request of the king and queen, put on his harness and his helm, but shield would he take none for any prayer of the king. And the queen was in a tower, with all her ladies, to behold that tournament. Then Sir Galahad rode into the midst of the meadow; and there he began to break spears marvellously, so that all men had wonder of him, for he surmounted all knights that encountered with him, except two, Sir Launcelot and Sir Perceval. Then the king, at the queen's request, made him to alight, and presented him to the queen; and she said, "Never two men resembled one another more than he and Sir Launcelot, and therefore it is no marvel that he is like him in prowess."

Then the king and the queen went to the minster, and the knights followed them. And after the service was done, they put on their helms and departed, and there was great sorrow. They rode through the streets of Camelot, and there was weeping of the rich and poor; and the king turned away, and might not speak for weeping. And so they departed, and every knight took the way that him best liked.

Sir Galahad rode forth without shield, and rode four days, and found no adventure. And on the fourth day he came to a white abbey; and there he was received with great reverence, and led to a chamber. He met there two knights, King Bagdemagus and Sir Uwaine, and they made of him great solace. "Sirs," said Sir Galahad, "what adventure brought you hither?" "Sir," said they, "it is told us that within this place is a shield, which no man may bear unless he be worthy; and if one unworthy should attempt to bear it, it shall surely do him a mischief." Then King Bagdemagus said, "I fear not to bear it, and that shall ye see tomorrow."

So on the morrow they arose, and heard mass; then King Bagdemagus asked where the adventurous shield was. Anon a monk led him behind an altar, where the shield hung, as white as snow; but in the midst there was a red cross. Then King Bagdemagus took the shield, and bare it out of the minster; and he said to Sir Galahad, "If it please you, abide here till ye know how I shall speed."

Then King Bagdemagus and his squire rode forth; and when they had ridden a mile or two, they saw a goodly knight come towards them, in white armor, horse and all; and he came as fast as his horse might run, with his spear in the rest; and King Bagdemagus directed his spear against him, and broke it upon the white knight, but the other struck him so hard that he broke the mails, and thrust him through the right shoulder, for the shield covered him not, and so he bare him from his horse. Then the white knight turned his horse and rode away.

Then the squire went to King Bagdemagus, and asked him whether he were sore wounded or not. "I am sore wounded," said he, "and full hardly shall I escape death." Then the squire set him on his horse, and brought him to an abbey; and there he was taken down softly, and unarmed, and laid in a bed, and his wound was looked to, for he lay there long, and hardly escaped with his life. And the squire brought the shield back to the abbey.

The next day Sir Galahad took the shield, and within a while he came to the hermitage, where he met the white knight, and each saluted the other courteously. "Sir," said Sir Galahad, "can you tell me the marvel of the shield?" "Sir," said the white knight, "that shield belonged of old to the gentle knight, Joseph of Arimathea; and when he came to die, he said, 'Never shall man bear this shield about his neck but he shall repent it, unto the time that Sir Galahad, the good knight, bear it, the last of my lineage, the which shall do many marvellous deeds.'" And then the white knight vanished away.

Sir Gawain

After Sir Gawain departed, he rode many days, both toward and forward, and at last he came to the abbey where Sir Galahad took the white shield. And they told Sir Gawain of the marvellous adventure that Sir Galahad had done. "Truly," said Sir Gawain, "I am not happy that I took not the way that he went, for, if I may meet with him, I will not part from him lightly, that I may partake with him all the marvellous adventures which he shall achieve." "Sir," said one of the monks, "he will not be of your fellowship." "Why?" said Sir Gawain. "Sir," said he, "because ye be sinful, and he is blissful." Then said the monk, "Sir Gawain, thou must do penance for thy sins." "Sir, what penance shall I do?" "Such as I will show," said the good man. "Nay," said Sir Gawain, "I will do no penance, for we knights adventurous often suffer great woe and pain." "Well," said the good man; and he held his peace. And Sir Gawain departed.

Now it happened, not long after this, that Sir Gawain and Sir Hector rode together, and they came to a castle where was a great tournament. And Sir Gawain and Sir Hector joined themselves to the party that seemed the weaker, and they drove before them the other party. Then suddenly came into the lists a knight, bearing a white shield with a red cross, and by adventure he came by Sir Gawain, and he smote him so hard that he clave his helm and wounded his head, so that Sir Gawain fell to the earth. When Sir Hector saw that, he knew that the knight with the white shield was Sir Galahad, and he thought it no wisdom to abide with him, and also for natural love, that he was his uncle. Then Sir Galahad retired privily, so that none knew where he had gone. And Sir Hector raised up Sir Gawain, and said, "Sir, me seemeth your quest is done." "It is done," said Sir Gawain; "I shall seek no further." Then Gawain was borne into the castle, and unarmed, and laid in a rich bed, and a leech found to search his wound. And Sir Gawain and Sir Hector abode together, for Sir Hector would not away until Sir Gawain were whole.

Now Sir Galahad, after that the white knight had vanished away, rode till he came to a waste forest, and there he met with Sir Launcelot and Sir Perceval, but they knew him not, for he was new disguised. Right so, Sir Launcelot his father dressed his spear, and brake it upon Sir Galahad, and Sir Galahad smote him so again, that he smote down horse and man. And then he drew his sword, and dressed him to Sir Perceval, and smote him so on the helm that it rove to the coif of steel, and had not the sword swerved Sir Perceval had been slain, and with the stroke he fell out of his saddle. This joust was done before the hermitage where a recluse dwelled. And when she saw Sir Galahad ride, she said, "God be with thee, best knight of the world. Ah, certes," she said all aloud, that Launcelot and Perceval might hear it, "and yonder two knights had known thee as well as I do, they would not have encountered with thee." When Sir Galahad heard her say so he was sore adread to be known: therewith he smote his horse with his spurs, and rode at a great pace away from them. Then perceived they both that he was Sir Galahad, and up they got on their horses, and rode fast after him, but in a while he was out of their sight. And then they turned again with heavy cheer. "Let us spere some tidings," said Sir Perceval, "at yonder recluse." "Do as ye list," said Sir Launcelot. When Sir Perceval came to the recluse, she knew him well enough, and Sir Launcelot both.

But Sir Launcelot rode overthwart and endlong in a wild forest, and held no path, but as wild adventure led him. And at the last he came to a stony cross, which departed two ways in waste land, and by the cross was a stone that was of marble, but it was so dark that Sir Launcelot might not wit what it was. Then Sir Launcelot looked by him, and saw an old chapel, and there he thought to have found people. And Sir Launcelot tied his horse to a tree, and there he did off his shield, and hung it upon a tree. And then he went to the chapel door, and found it waste and broken. And within he found a fair altar full richly arrayed with cloth of clean silk, and there stood a fair, clean candlestick which bare six great candles, and the candlestick was of silver. And when Sir Launcelot saw this light, he had great will for to enter into the chapel, but he could find no place where he might enter: then was he passing heavy and dismayed. And he returned and came again to his horse, and took off his saddle and his bridle, and let him pasture; and unlaced his helm, and ungirded his sword, and laid him down to sleep upon his shield before the cross.

And as he lay, half waking and half sleeping, he saw come by him two palfreys, both fair and white, which bare a litter, on which lay a sick knight. And when he was nigh the cross, he there abode still. And Sir Launcelot heard him say, "O sweet Lord, when shall this sorrow leave me, and when shall the holy vessel come by me whereby I shall be healed?" And thus a great while complained the knight, and Sir Launcelot heard it. Then Sir Launcelot saw the candlestick, with the lighted tapers, come before the cross, but he could see nobody that brought it. Also there came a salver of silver and the holy vessel of the Sangreal; and therewith the sick knight sat him upright, and held up both his hands, and said, "Fair, sweet Lord, which is here within the holy vessel, take heed to me, that I may be whole of this great malady." And therewith, upon his hands and upon his knees, he went so nigh that he touched the holy vessel and

kissed it. And anon he was whole. Then the holy vessel
went into the chapel again, with the candlestick and the
light, so that Sir Launcelot wist not what became of it.

Then the sick knight rose up and kissed the cross; and
anon his squire brought him his arms, and asked his lord
how he did. "I thank God right heartily," said he, "for,
through the holy vessel, I am healed. But I have great marvel of this sleeping knight, who hath had neither grace nor
power to awake during the time that the holy vessel hath
been here present." "I dare it right well say," said the
squire, "that this same knight is stained with some manner
of deadly sin, whereof he was never confessed." So they departed.

Then anon Sir Launcelot waked, and set himself upright,
and bethought him of what he had seen, and whether it
were dreams or not. And he was passing heavy, and wist
not what to do. And he said: "My sin and my wretched-
ness hath brought me into great dishonor. For when I
sought worldly adventures and worldly desires, I ever
achieved them, and had the better in every place, and never
was I discomfited in any quarrel, were it right or wrong.
And now I take upon me the adventure of holy things, I see
and understand that mine old sin hindereth me, so that I
had no power to stir nor to speak when the holy blood appeared before me." So thus he sorrowed till it was day, and
heard the fowls of the air sing. Then was he somewhat comforted.

Then he departed from the cross into the forest. And
there he found a hermitage, and a hermit therein, who was
going to mass. So when mass was done, Sir Launcelot called
the hermit to him, and prayed him for charity to hear his
confession. "With a good will," said the good man. And
then he told that good man all his life, and how he had
loved a queen unmeasurably many years. "And all my great
deeds of arms that I have done, I did the most part for the
queen's sake, and for her sake would I do battle, were it
right or wrong, and never did I battle all only for God's
sake, but for to win worship, and to cause me to be better
beloved; and little or naught I thanked God for it. I pray
you counsel me."

"I will counsel you," said the hermit, "if ye will insure
me that ye will never come in that queen's fellowship as

much as ye may forbear." And then Sir Launcelot promised the hermit, by his faith, that he would no more come in her company. "Look that your heart and your mouth accord," said the good man, "and I shall insure ye that ye shall have more worship than ever ye had."

Then the good man enjoined Sir Launcelot such penance as he might do, and he assoiled Sir Launcelot, and made him abide with him all that day. And Sir Launcelot repented him greatly.

Sir Perceval

Sir Perceval departed, and rode till the hour of noon; and he met in a valley about twenty men of arms. And when they saw Sir Perceval, they asked him whence he was; and he answered, "Of the court of King Arthur." Then they cried all at once, "Slay him." But Sir Perceval smote the first to the earth, and his horse upon him. Then seven of the knights smote upon his shield all at once, and the remnant slew his horse, so that he fell to the earth. So had they slain him or taken him, had not the good knight Sir Galahad, with the red cross, come there by adventure. And when he saw all the knights upon one, he cried out, "Save me that knight's life." Then he rode toward the twenty men of arms as fast as his horse might drive, with his spear in the rest, and smote the foremost horse and man to the earth. And when his spear was broken, he set his hand to his sword, and smote on the right hand and on the left, that it was marvel to see; and at every stroke he smote down one, or put him to rebuke, so that they would fight no more, but fled to a thick forest, and Sir Galahad followed them. And when Sir Perceval saw him chase them so, he made great sorrow that his horse was slain. And he wist well it was Sir Galahad. Then he cried aloud, "Ah, fair knight, abide, and suffer me to do thanks unto thee; for right well have ye done for me." But Sir Galahad rode so fast, that at last he passed out of his sight. When Sir Perceval saw that he would not turn, he said, "Now am I a very wretch, and most unhappy above all other knights." So in this sorrow he abode all that day till it was night; and then he was faint, and laid him down and slept till midnight; and then he awaked, and saw before him a woman, who said unto him, "Sir Perceval, what dost thou here?" He answered, "I do neither good, nor great ill." "If thou wilt promise me," said she, "that thou wilt fulfil my will when I summon thee, I will lend thee my own horse, which shall bear thee whither thou wilt." Sir Perceval was glad of her proffer, and insured her to fulfil all her desire. "Then abide me here, and I will go fetch you a horse." And so she soon came again, and brought a horse with her that was inky black. When Perceval beheld that horse, he marvelled, it was so great and so well apparelled. And he leapt upon him, and took no heed of himself. And he thrust him with his spurs, and within an hour and less he bare him four days' journey thence, until he came to a rough water, which roared, and his horse would have bare him into it. And when Sir Perceval came nigh the brim, and saw the water so boisterous, he doubted to overpass it. And then he made the sign of the cross on his forehead. When the fiend felt him so charged, he shook off Sir Perceval, and went into the water crying and roaring; and it seemed unto him that the water burned. Then Sir Perceval perceived it was a fiend that would have brought him unto his perdition. Then he commended himself unto God, and prayed our Lord to keep him from all such temptations; and so he prayed all that night till it was day. Then he saw that he was in a wild place, that was closed with the sea nigh all about. And Sir Perceval looked forth over the sea, and saw a ship come sailing toward him; and it came and stood still under the rock. And when Sir Perceval saw this, he hied him thither, and found the ship covered with silk; and therein was a lady of great beauty, and clothed so richly that none might be better.

And when she saw Sir Perceval she saluted him, and Sir Perceval returned her salutation. Then he asked her of her country and her lineage. And she said, "I am a gentlewoman that am disinherited, and was once the richest woman of the world." "Damsel," said Sir Perceval, "who hath disinherited you? for I have great pity of you." "Sir," said she, "my enemy is a great and powerful lord, and aforetime he made much of me, so that of his favor and of my beauty I had a little pride more than I ought to have had. Also I said a word that pleased him not. So he drove me from his company and from mine heritage. Therefore I know no good

knight nor good man but I get him on my side if I may.
And, for that I know that thou art a good knight, I beseech
thee to help me."

Then Sir Perceval promised her all the help that he might,
and she thanked him.

And at that time the weather was hot and she called to
her a gentlewoman, and bade her bring forth a pavilion.
And she did so, and pitched it upon the gravel. "Sir," said
she, "now may ye rest you in this heat of the day." Then he
thanked her, and she put off his helm and his shield, and
there he slept a great while. Then he awoke, and asked her
if she had any meat, and she said yea, and so there was set
upon the table all manner of meats that he could think on.
Also he drank there the strongest wine that ever he drank,
and therewith he was a little chafed more than he ought to
be. With that he beheld the lady, and he thought she was
the fairest creature that ever he saw. And then Sir Perceval
proffered her love, and prayed her that she would be his.
Then she refused him in a manner, for the cause he should
be the more ardent on her, and ever he ceased not to pray
her of love. And when she saw him well enchafed, then
she said, "Sir Perceval, wit ye well I shall not give ye my
love unless you swear from henceforth you will be my true
servant, and do no thing but that I shall command you. Will
you insure me this, as ye be a true knight?" "Yea," said he,
"fair lady, by the faith of my body." And as he said this,
by adventure and grace, he saw his sword lie on the ground
naked, in whose pommel was a red cross, and the sign of
the crucifix thereon. Then he made the sign of the cross
upon his forehead, and therewith the pavilion shrivelled
up, and changed into a smoke and a black cloud. And the
damsel cried aloud, and hasted into the ship, and so she
went with the wind roaring and yelling that it seemed all
the water burned after her. Then Sir Perceval made great
sorrow, and called himself a wretch, saying, "How nigh
was I lost!" Then he took his arms, and departed thence.

13. THE END OF THE QUEST

Sir Bohort

When Sir Bohort departed from Camelot he met with a religious man, riding upon an ass; and Sir Bohort saluted him. "What are ye?" said the good man. "Sir," said Sir Bohort, "I am a knight that fain would be counselled in the quest of the Sangreal." So rode they both together till they came to a hermitage; and there he prayed Sir Bohort to dwell that night with him. So he alighted, and put away his armor, and prayed him that he might be confessed. And they went both into the chapel, and there he was clean confessed. And they ate bread and drank water together. "Now," said the good man, "I pray thee that thou eat none other till thou sit at the table where the Sangreal shall be." "Sir," said Sir Bohort, "but how know ye that I shall sit there?" "Yea," said the good man, "that I know well; but there shall be few of your fellows with you." Then said Sir Bohort, "I agree me thereto." And the good man, when he had heard his confession, found him in so pure a life and so stable that he marvelled thereof.

With that Sir Bohort heard a voice say, "Sir Bohort, take thy way anon, right to the sea, for Sir Perceval abideth thee there." So Sir Bohort departed, and rode the nearest way to the sea. And at last he came to an abbey that was nigh the sea. That night he rested him there, and in his sleep there came a voice unto him and bade him go to the seashore. He started up, and made the sign of the cross on his forehead, and armed himself, and made ready his horse and mounted him, and at a broken wall he rode out, and came to the sea-shore. And there he found a ship, covered all with white samite. And he entered into the ship; but it was anon so dark that he might see no man, and he laid him down and slept till it was day. Then he awaked, and saw in the middle of the ship a knight all armed, save his helm. And then he knew it was Sir Perceval de Galis, and each

made of other right great joy. Then said Sir Perceval, "We
lack nothing now but the good knight Sir Galahad."

Of Sir Launcelot Again

It befell upon a night Sir Launcelot arrived before a castle, which was rich and fair. And there was a postern that
opened toward the sea, and was open without any keeping,
save two lions kept the entry; and the moon shined clear.
Anon Sir Launcelot heard a voice that said, "Launcelot,
enter into the castle, where thou shalt see a great part of
thy desire." So he went unto the gate, and saw the two lions;
then he set hands to his sword, and drew it. Then there came
suddenly as it were a stroke upon the arm, so sore that the
sword fell out of his hand, and he heard a voice that said,
"O man of evil faith, wherefore believest thou more in thy
armor than in thy Maker?" Then said Sir Launcelot, "Fair
Lord, I thank thee of thy great mercy, that thou reprovest
me of my misdeed; now see I well that thou holdest me for
thy servant." Then he made a cross on his forehead, and
came to the lions; and they made semblance to do him
harm, but he passed them without hurt, and entered into the
castle, and he found no gate nor door but it was open. But
at the last he found a chamber whereof the door was shut;
and he set his hand thereto, to have opened it, but he might
not. Then he listened, and heard a voice which sung so
sweetly that it seemed none earthly thing; and the voice
said, "Joy and honor be to the Father of heaven." Then
Sir Launcelot kneeled down before the chamber, for well
he wist that there was the Sangreal in that chamber. Then
said he, "Fair, sweet Lord, if ever I did anything that
pleased thee for thy pity show me something of that which
I seek." And with that he saw the chamber door open, and
there came out a great clearness, that the house was as
bright as though all the torches of the world had been there.
So he came to the chamber door, and would have entered;
and anon a voice said unto him, "Stay, Sir Launcelot, and
enter not." And he withdrew him back, and was right heavy
in his mind. Then looked he in the midst of the chamber,
and saw a table of silver, and the holy vessel, covered with
red samite, and many angels about it; whereof one held a

candle of wax burning, and another held a cross, and the ornaments of the altar. Then, for very wonder and thankfulness, Sir Launcelot forgot himself, and he stepped forward and entered the chamber. And suddenly a breath that seemed intermixed with fire smote him so sore in the visage, that therewith he fell to the ground, and had no power to rise. Then felt he many hands about him, which took him up, and bare him out of the chamber, without any amending of his swoon, and left him there, seeming dead to all the people. So on the morrow, when it was fair daylight, and they within were arisen, they found Sir Launcelot lying before the chamber door. And they looked upon him and felt his pulse, to know if there were any life in him. And they found life in him, but he might neither stand nor stir any member that he had. So they took him and bare him into a chamber, and laid him upon a bed, far from all folk, and there he lay many days. Then the one said he was alive, and others said nay. But said an old man, "He is as full of life as the mightiest of you all, and therefore I counsel you that he be well kept till God bring him back again." And after twenty-four days he opened his eyes; and when he saw folk, he made great sorrow, and said, "Why have ye wakened me? for I was better at ease than I am now." "What have ye seen?" said they about him. "I have seen," said he, "great marvels that no tongue can tell, and more than any heart can think." Then they said, "Sir, the quest of the Sangreal is achieved right now in you, and never shall ye see more of it than ye have seen." "I thank God," said Sir Launcelot, "of His great mercy, for that I have seen, for it sufficeth me." Then he rose up and clothed himself; and when he was so arrayed, they marvelled all, for they knew it was Sir Launcelot, the good knight. And, after four days, he took his leave of the lord of the castle, and of all the fellowship that were there, and thanked them for their great labor and care of him. Then he departed, and turned to Camelot, where he found King Arthur and Queen Guenever; but many of the knights of the Round Table were slain and destroyed, more than half. Then all the court was passing glad of Sir Launcelot; and he told the king all his adventures that had befallen him since he departed.

Sir Galahad

Now, when Sir Galahad had rescued Perceval from the
twenty knights, he rode into a vast forest, wherein he abode
many days. Then he took his way to the sea, and it befell
him that he was benighted in a hermitage. And the good
man was glad when he saw he was a knight-errant. And
when they were at rest, there came a gentlewoman knock-
ing at the door; and the good man came to the door to wit
what she would. Then she said, "I would speak with the
knight which is with you." Then Galahad went to her, and
asked her what she would. "Sir Galahad," said she, "I will
that ye arm you, and mount upon your horse, and follow
me; for I will show you the highest adventure that ever
knight saw." Then Galahad armed himself and commended himself to God, and bade the damsel go before,
and he would follow where she led.

So she rode as fast as her palfrey might bear her, till
she came to the sea; and there they found the ship where
Sir Bohort and Sir Perceval were, who cried from the ship,
"Sir Galahad, you are welcome; we have awaited you long."
And when he heard them, he asked the damsel who they
were. "Sir," said she, "leave your horse here, and I shall
leave mine, and we will join ourselves to their company."
So they entered into the ship, and the two knights received
them both with great joy. For they knew the damsel, that
she was Sir Perceval's sister. Then the wind arose and drove
them through the sea all that day and the next, till the ship
arrived between two rocks, passing great and marvellous;
but there they might not land, for there was a whirlpool;
but there was another ship, and upon it they might go without danger. "Go we thither," said the gentlewoman, "and
there shall we see adventures, for such is our Lord's will."
Then Sir Galahad blessed him, and entered therein, and
then next the gentlewoman, and then Sir Bohort and Sir
Perceval. And when they came on board, they found there
the table of silver, and the Sangreal, which was covered
with red samite. And they made great reverence thereto,
and Sir Galahad prayed a long time to our Lord, that at
what time he should ask to pass out of this world, he should
do so; and a voice said to him, "Galahad, thou shalt have

thy request; and when thou askest the death of thy body thou shalt have it, and then shalt thou find the life of thy soul."

And anon the wind drove them across the sea, till they came to the city of Sarras. Then they took out of the ship the table of silver, and he took it to Sir Perceval and Sir Bohort to go before, and Sir Galahad came behind, and right so they came to the city, and at the gate of the city they saw an old man, crooked. Then Sir Galahad called him and bade him help bear this heavy thing. "Truly," said the old man, "it is ten years ago that I might not go save with crutches." "Care thou not," said Sir Galahad, "but arise up and show thy good will." And so he assayed and found himself as whole as ever he was. Then ran he to the table and took one part against Sir Galahad. And anon arose there a great noise in the city, that a cripple was made whole by knights marvellous that entered into the city. Then anon after, the three knights went to the water, and brought up into the palace Sir Perceval's sister. And when the king of the city, which was cleped Estorause, saw the fellowship, he asked them of whence they were, and what thing it was they had brought upon the table of silver. And they told him the truth of the Sangreal, and the power which God had set there. Then the king was a tyrant, and was come of the line of Paynims, and took them and put them in prison in a deep hole.

But as soon as they were there, our Lord sent them the Sangreal, through whose grace they were always filled while that they were in prison. So at the year's end it befell that this king Estorause lay sick, and felt that he should die. Then he sent for the three knights, and they came afore him, and he cried them mercy of that he had done to them, and they forgave it him goodly, and he died anon. When the king was dead, all the city was dismayed, and wist not who might be their king. Right so they were in council, there came a voice among them, and bade them choose the youngest knight of them three to be their king, "for he shall well maintain you and all yours." So they made Sir Galahad king by all the assent of the whole city, and else they would have slain him. And when he was come to behold the land, he had made about the table of silver a chest of gold and of precious stones that covered the holy vessel, and every

day early the three fellows would come afore it and make
their prayers. Now at the year's end, and the next day after
Sir Galahad had borne the crown of gold, he rose up early,
and his fellows, and came to the palace, and saw before
them the holy vessel, and a man kneeling on his knees, in
likeness of a bishop, that had about him a great fellowship
of angels, as it had been Jesus Christ himself. And then he
arose and began a mass of Our Lady. And when he came
to the sacrament of the mass, and had done, anon he called
Sir Galahad, and said to him, "Come forth, the servant of
Jesus Christ, and thou shalt see that thou hast much desired to see." And then he began to tremble right hard,
when the deadly flesh began to behold the spiritual things.
Then he held up his hands toward heaven, and said, "Lord,
I thank thee, for now I see that that hath been my desire
many a day. Now, blessed Lord, would I not longer live;
if it might please thee, Lord." And therewith the good man
took our Lord's body betwixt his hands, and proffered it to
Sir Galahad, and he received it right gladly and meekly.
"Now, wottest thou what I am?" said the good man. "Nay,"
said Sir Galahad. "I am Joseph of Arimathea, which our Lord
hath sent here to bear thee fellowship. And wottest thou
wherefore that he hath sent me more than any other? For
thou hast resembled me in two things, in that thou hast
seen the marvels of the Sangreal, and in that thou hast been
a clean maiden as I have been and am." And when he had
said these words Sir Galahad went to Sir Perceval and kissed
him, and commended him to God. And so he went to Sir
Bohort and kissed him, and commended him to God, and
said, "Fair lord, salute me to my lord Sir Launcelot, my
father, and as soon as ye see him bid him remember of this
unstable world." And therewith he kneeled down before
the table and made his prayers, and then suddenly his soul
departed to Jesus Christ, and a great multitude of angels
bare his soul up to heaven, that the two fellows might well
behold it. Also the two fellows saw come from heaven a
hand, but they saw not the body; and then it came right to
the vessel, and took it and the spear, and so bare it up to
heaven. Sithen there was never man so hardy to say that he
had seen the Sangreal.

When Sir Perceval and Sir Bohort saw Sir Galahad dead
they made as much sorrow as ever did two men; and if they

had not been good men they might lightly have fallen into despair. And the people of the country and of the city were right heavy. And then he was buried. And as soon as he was buried Sir Perceval yielded him to an hermitage out of the city, and took a religious clothing; and Sir Bohort was always with him, but never changed he his secular clothing, for that he purposed to go again into the realm of Loegria. Thus a year and two months lived Sir Perceval in the hermitage a full holy life, and then he passed out of this world. And Sir Bohort let bury him by his sister and by Sir Galahad.

And when Sir Bohort saw that he was in so far countries as in the parts of Babylon, he departed from Sarras, and armed him, and came to the sea, and entered into a ship, and so it befell him in good adventure he came into the realm of Loegria. And he rode so fast till he came to Camelot, where the king was. And then was there great joy made of him in the court, for they wend all he had been dead, forasmuch as he had been so long out of the country. And when they had eaten, the king made great clerks to come afore him, that they should chronicle of the high adventures of the good knights. Then Sir Bohort told him of the adventures of the Sangreal, such as had befallen him and his three fellows, that was Sir Launcelot, Sir Perceval, and Sir Galahad. Then Sir Launcelot told the adventures of the Sangreal that he had seen. All this was made in great books, and put in almeries in Salisbury. And anon Sir Bohort said to Sir Launcelot, "Galahad, your own son, saluted you by me, and after you King Arthur, and all the court, and so did Sir Perceval; for I buried them with mine own hands in the city of Sarras. Also, Sir Launcelot, Galahad prayeth you to remember of this uncertain world, as ye behight him when ye were together more than half a year." "This is true," said Sir Launcelot; "now I trust to God his prayer shall avail me." Then Sir Launcelot took Sir Bohort in his arms, and said, "Gentle cousin, ye are right welcome to me, and all that ever I may do for you and for yours, ye shall find my poor body ready at all times whiles the spirit is in it, and that I promise you faithfully, and never to fail. And wit ye well, gentle cousin Sir Bohort, that ye and I will never part in sunder whilst our lives may last." "Sir," said he, "I will as ye will."

Thus endeth the history of the Sangreal, which is a story chronicled as one of the truest and holiest that is in this world.

14. SIR AGRIVAIN'S TREASON

So after the quest of the Sangreal was fulfilled, and all the knights that were left alive were come again to the Table Round, there was great joy in the court, and in especial King Arthur and Queen Guenever made great joy of the remnant that were come home, and passing glad were the king and the queen of Sir Launcelot and of Sir Bohort, for they had been passing long away in the quest of the Sangreal.

Then Sir Launcelot began to resort unto Queen Guenever again, and forgot the promise that he made in the quest; so that many in the court spoke of it, and in especial Sir Agrivain, Sir Gawain's brother, for he was ever open-mouthed. So it happened Sir Gawain and all his brothers were in King Arthur's chamber, and then Sir Agrivain said thus openly, "I marvel that we all are not ashamed to see and to know so noble a knight as King Arthur so to be shamed by the conduct of Sir Launcelot and the queen." Then spoke Sir Gawain, and said, "Brother, Sir Agrivain, I pray you and charge you move not such matters any more before me, for be ye assured I will not be of your counsel." "Neither will we," said Sir Gaheris and Sir Gareth. "Then will I," said Sir Modred. "I doubt you not," said Sir Gawain, "for to all mischief ever were ye prone; yet I would that ye left all this, for I know what will come of it." "Fall of it what fall may," said Sir Agrivain, "I will disclose it to the king." With that came to them King Arthur. "Now, brothers, hold your peace," said Sir Gawain. "We will not," said Sir Agrivain. Then said Sir Gawain, "I will not hear your tales, nor be of your counsel." "No more will I," said Sir Gareth and Sir Gaheris, and therewith they departed, making great sorrow.

Then Sir Agrivain told the king all that was said in the

court of the conduct of Sir Launcelot and the queen, and
it grieved the king very much. But he would not believe it
to be true without proof. So Sir Agrivain laid a plot to en-
trap Sir Launcelot and the queen, intending to take them
together unawares. Sir Agrivain and Sir Modred led a party
for this purpose, but Sir Launcelot escaped from them, having slain Sir Agrivain and wounded Sir Modred. Then Sir
Launcelot hastened to his friends, and told them what had
happened, and withdrew with them to the forest; but he
left spies to bring him tidings of whatever might be done.

So Sir Launcelot escaped, but the queen remained in the
king's power, and Arthur could no longer doubt of her guilt.
And the law was such in those days that they who committed such crimes, of what estate or condition soever they
were, must be burned to death, and so it was ordained for
Queen Guenever. Then said King Arthur to Sir Gawain,
"I pray you make you ready, in your best armor, with your
brethren, Sir Gaheris and Sir Gareth, to bring my queen
to the fire, there to receive her death." "Nay, my most noble
lord," said Sir Gawain, "that will I never do; for know thou
well, my heart will never serve me to see her die, and it
shall never be said that I was of your counsel in her death."
Then the king commanded Sir Gaheris and Sir Gareth to
be there, and they said, "We will be there, as ye command
us, sire, but in peaceable wise, and bear no armor upon us."

So the queen was led forth, and her ghostly father was
brought to her to shrive her, and there was weeping and
wailing of many lords and ladies. And one went and told
Sir Launcelot that the queen was led forth to her death.
Then Sir Launcelot and the knights that were with him
fell upon the troop that guarded the queen, and dispersed
them, and slew all who withstood them. And in the confusion Sir Gareth and Sir Gaheris were slain, for they were
unarmed and defenceless. And Sir Launcelot carried away
the queen to his castle of La Joyeuse Garde.

Then there came one to Sir Gawain and told him how
that Sir Launcelot had slain the knights and carried away
the queen. "O Lord, defend my brethren!" said Sir Gawain. "Truly," said the man, "Sir Gareth and Sir Gaheris
are slain." "Alas!" said Sir Gawain, "now is my joy gone."
And then he fell down and swooned, and long he lay there
as he had been dead.

When he arose out of his swoon Sir Gawain ran to the king, crying, "O King Arthur, mine uncle, my brothers are slain." Then the king wept and he both. "My king, my lord, and mine uncle," said Sir Gawain, "bear witness now that I make you a promise that I shall hold by my knighthood, that from this day I will never fail Sir Launcelot until the one of us have slain the other. I will seek Sir Launcelot throughout seven kings' realms, but I shall slay him or he shall slay me." "Ye shall not need to seek him," said the king, "for, as I hear, Sir Launcelot will abide me and you in the Joyeuse Garde; and much people draweth unto him, as I hear say." "That may I believe," said Gawain, "but, my lord, summon your friends, and I will summon mine." "It shall be done," said the king. So then the king sent letters and writs throughout all England, both in the length and breadth, to summon all his knights. And unto Arthur drew many knights, dukes, and earls, so that he had a great host. Thereof heard Sir Launcelot, and collected all whom he could; and many good knights held with him, both for his sake and for the queen's sake. But King Arthur's host was too great for Sir Launcelot to abide him in the field; and he was full loath to do battle against the king. So Sir Launcelot drew him to his strong castle, with all manner of provisions. Then came King Arthur and Sir Gawain, and laid siege all about La Joyeuse Garde, both the town and the castle; but in no wise would Sir Launcelot ride out of his castle, neither suffer any of his knights to issue out, until many weeks were past.

Then it befell upon a day in harvest-time Sir Launcelot looked over the wall, and spake aloud to King Arthur and Sir Gawain, "My lords both, all is vain that ye do at this siege, for here ye shall win no worship, but only dishonor; for if I list to come out, and my good knights, I shall soon make an end of this war." "Come forth," said Arthur, "if thou darest, and I promise thee I shall meet thee in the midst of the field." "God forbid me," said Sir Launcelot, "that I should encounter with the most noble king that made me knight." "Fie upon thy fair language," said the king, "for know thou well that I am thy mortal foe, and ever will be to my dying day." And Sir Gawain said, "What cause hadst thou to slay my brother, Sir Gaheris, who bore no arms against thee, and Sir Gareth, whom thou madest knight, and

who loved thee more than all my kin? Therefore know thou
well I shall make war to thee all the while that I may live."

When Sir Bohort, Sir Hector de Marys, and Sir Lionel
heard this outcry they called to them Sir Palamedes, and
Sir Saffire his brother, and Sir Lawayn, with many more,
and all went to Sir Launcelot. And they said, "My lord,
Sir Launcelot, we pray you, if you will have our service,
keep us no longer within these walls, for know well all
your fair speech and forbearance will not avail you."
"Alas!" said Sir Launcelot, "to ride forth and to do battle
I am full loath." Then he spake again unto the king and Sir
Gawain, and willed them to keep out of the battle; but they
depised his words. So then Sir Launcelot's fellowship came
out of the castle in full good array. And always Sir Launcelot charged all his knights, in any wise, to save King Arthur and Sir Gawain.

Then came forth Sir Gawain from the king's host, and
offered combat, and Sir Lionel encountered with him, and
there Sir Gawain smote Sir Lionel through the body, that
he fell to the earth as if dead. Then there began a great
conflict, and much people were slain; but ever Sir Launcelot did what he might to save the people on King Arthur's
party, and ever King Arthur followed Sir Launcelot to slay
him; but Sir Launcelot suffered him, and would not strike
again. Then Sir Bohort encountered with King Arthur,
and smote him down; and he alighted and drew his sword,
and said to Sir Launcelot, "Shall I make an end of this
war?" for he meant to have slain King Arthur. "Not so,"
said Sir Launcelot, "touch him no more, for I will never
see that most noble king that made me knight either slain
or shamed;" and therewith Sir Launcelot alighted off his
horse and took up the king, and horsed him again, and said
thus: "My lord Arthur, for God's love, cease this strife."
And King Arthur looked upon Sir Launcelot, and his tears
burst from his eyes, thinking on the great courtesy that was
in Sir Launcelot more than in any other man; and therewith the king rode his way. Then anon both parties withdrew to repose them, and buried the dead.

But the war continued, and it was noised abroad through
all Christendom, and at last it was told afore the pope; and
he, considering the great goodness of King Arthur, and of
Sir Launcelot, called unto him a noble clerk, which was the

Bishop of Rochester, who was then in his dominions, and sent him to King Arthur, charging him that he take his queen, dame Guenever, unto him again, and make peace with Sir Launcelot.

So, by means of this bishop, peace was made for the space of one year; and King Arthur received back the queen, and Sir Launcelot departed from the kingdom with all his knights, and went to his own country. So they shipped at Cardiff, and sailed unto Benwick, which some men call Bayonne. And all the people of those lands came to Sir Launcelot, and received him home right joyfully. And Sir Launcelot stablished and garnished all his towns and castles, and he greatly advanced all his noble knights, Sir Lionel and Sir Bohort, and Sir Hector de Marys, Sir Blanor, Sir Lawayne, and many others, and made them lords of lands and castles; till he left himself no more than any one of them.

But when the year was passed, King Arthur and Sir Gawain came with a great host, and landed upon Sir Launcelot's lands, and burnt and wasted all that they might overrun. Then spake Sir Bohort and said, "My lord, Sir Launcelot, give us leave to meet them in the field, and we shall make them rue the time that ever they came to this country." Then said Sir Launcelot, "I am full loath to ride out with my knights for shedding of Christian blood; so we will yet awhile keep our walls, and I will send a messenger unto my lord Arthur, to propose a treaty; for better is peace than always war." So Sir Launcelot sent forth a damsel, and a dwarf with her, requiring King Arthur to leave his warring upon his lands; and so she started on a palfrey, and the dwarf ran by her side. And when she came to the pavilion of King Arthur, she alighted, and there met her a gentle knight, Sir Lucan the butler, and said, "Fair damsel, come ye from Sir Launcelot du Lac?" "Yea, sir," she said, "I come hither to speak with the king." "Alas!" said Sir Lucan, "my lord Arthur would be reconciled to Sir Launcelot, but Sir Gawain will not suffer him." And with this Sir Lucan led the damsel to the king, where he sat with Sir Gawain, to hear what she would say. So when she had told her tale, the tears ran out of the king's eyes; and all the lords were forward to advise the king to be accorded with Sir Launcelot, save only Sir Gawain; and he said,

"My lord, mine uncle, what will ye do? Will you now turn back, now you are so far advanced upon your journey? If ye do, all the world will speak shame of you." "Nay," said King Arthur, "I will do as ye advise me; but do thou give the damsel her answer, for I may not speak to her for pity."

Then said Sir Gawain, "Damsel, say ye to Sir Launcelot, that it is waste labor to sue to mine uncle for peace, and say that I, Sir Gawain, send him word that I promise him, by the faith I owe unto God and to knighthood, I shall never leave him till he have slain me or I him." So the damsel returned; and when Sir Launcelot had heard this answer, the tears ran down his cheeks.

Then it befell on a day Sir Gawain came before the gates, armed at all points, and cried with a loud voice, "Where art thou now, thou false traitor, Sir Launcelot? Why hidest thou thyself within holes and walls like a coward? Look out now, thou traitor knight, and I will avenge upon thy body the death of my three brethren." All this language heard Sir Launcelot, and the knights which were about him; and they said to him, "Sir Launcelot, now must ye defend you like a knight, or else be shamed for ever, for you have slept overlong and suffered overmuch." Then Sir Launcelot spoke on high unto King Arthur, and said, "My lord Arthur, now I have forborne long, and suffered you and Sir Gawain to do what ye would, and now must I needs defend myself, inasmuch as Sir Gawain hath appealed me of treason." Then Sir Launcelot armed him and mounted upon his horse, and the noble knights came out of the city, and the host without stood all apart; and so the covenant was made that no man should come near the two knights, nor deal with them, till one were dead or yielded.

Then Sir Gawain and Sir Launcelot departed a great way in sunder, and then they came together with all their horses' might as they might run, and either smote the other in the midst of their shields, but the knights were so strong, and their spears so big, that their horses might not endure their buffets, and so the horses fell to the earth. And then they avoided their horses, and dressed their shields afore them. Then they stood together, and gave many sad strokes on divers places of their bodies, that the blood burst out on many sides and places. Then had Sir Gawain such a grace and gift that an holy man had given to him, that every day in the year, from morning till high noon, his might increased those three hours as much as thrice his strength, and that caused Sir Gawain to win great honor. And for his sake King Arthur made an ordinance that all manner of battles for any quarrels that should be done before King Arthur should begin at Underne,[1] and all was done for Sir Gawain's love, that by likelihood if that Sir Gawain were on the one part he should have the better in battle, whilst his strength endured three hours, but there were few knights that time living that knew this advantage that Sir Gawain had, but King Arthur only. Thus Sir Launcelot fought with Sir Gawain, and when Sir Launcelot felt his might evermore increase, Sir Launcelot wondered and dread him sore to be ashamed. For Sir Launcelot thought when he felt Sir Gawain double his strength, that he had been a fiend, and no earthly man; wherefore Sir Launcelot traced and traversed, and covered himself with his shield, and kept his might and his braid during three hours; and that while Sir Gawain gave him many sad brunts and many sad strokes, that all the knights that beheld Sir Launcelot marvelled how he might endure him, but full little understood they that travail that Sir Launcelot had for to endure him. And then when it was past noon Sir Gawain had no more but his own might. Then Sir Launcelot felt him so come down; then he stretched him up, and stood near Sir Gawain, and said thus: "My lord Sir Gawain, now I fear ye have done; now my lord Sir Gawain, I must do my part, for many great and grievous strokes I have endured you this day with great pain." Then Sir Launcelot doubled his strokes, and gave Sir Gawain such a buffet on the helmet that he fell down on his side, and Sir Launcelot withdrew from him. "Why turnest thou thee?" said Sir Gawain; "now turn again, false traitor knight, and slay me; for an thou leave me thus, when I am whole, I shall do battle with thee again." "I shall endure you, sir, by God's grace, but wit thou well, Sir Gawain, I will never smite a felled knight." And so Sir Launcelot went into the city, and Sir Gawain was borne into one of King Arthur's pavilions, and leeches were brought to him, and he was searched and salved with soft ointments. And then Sir Launcelot said, "Now have good day, my lord the

---

[1] Underne. The third hour in the day, nine o'clock.

king, for, wit you well, ye win no worship at these walls;
and if I would my knights out bring, there should many a
man die. Therefore, my lord Arthur, remember you of old
kindness, and however I fare, Jesus be your guide in all
places."

Thus the siege endured, and Sir Gawain lay helpless near
a month; and when he was near recovered, came tidings
unto King Arthur that made him return with all his host to
England.

15. MORTE D'ARTHUR

"And now the whole ROUND TABLE is dissolved,
Which was an image of the mighty world,
And I, the last, go forth companionless;
And the days darken round me, and the years
Among new men, strange faces, other minds."
—TENNYSON

Sir Modred was left ruler of all England, and he caused
letters to be written, as if from beyond sea, that King Arthur was slain in battle. So he called a Parliament, and
made himself be crowned king; and he took the queen,
Guenever, and said plainly that he would wed her, but she
escaped from him, and took refuge in the Tower of London. And Sir Modred went and laid siege about the Tower
of London, and made great assaults thereat, but all might
not avail him. Then came word to Sir Modred that King
Arthur had raised the siege of Sir Launcelot, and was coming home. Then Sir Modred summoned all the barony of the
land; and much people drew unto Sir Modred, and said they
would abide with him for better and for worse; and he drew
a great host to Dover, for there he heard say that King
Arthur would arrive.

And as Sir Modred was at Dover with his host, came
King Arthur, with a great number of ships and galleys, and
there was Sir Modred awaiting upon the landing. Then was
there launching of great boats and small, full of noble men

of arms, and there was much slaughter of gentle knights on
both parts. But King Arthur was so courageous, there might
no manner of knights prevent him to land, and his knights
fiercely followed him; and so they landed, and put Sir Modred aback so that he fled, and all his people. And when
the battle was done, King Arthur commanded to bury his
people that were dead. And then was noble Sir Gawain
found, in a great boat, lying more than half dead. And
King Arthur went to him, and made sorrow out of measure. "Mine uncle," said Sir Gawain, "know thou well my
death-day is come, and all is through mine own hastiness
and wilfulness, for I am smitten upon the old wound which
Sir Launcelot gave me, of the which I feel I must die. And
had Sir Launcelot been with you as of old, this war had
never begun, and of all this I am the cause." Then Sir
Gawain prayed the king to send for Sir Launcelot, and to
cherish him above all other knights. And so, at the hour of
noon, Sir Gawain yielded up his spirit, and then the king
bade inter him in a chapel within Dover Castle; and there
all men may see the skull of him, and the same wound is
seen that Sir Launcelot gave him in battle.

Then was it told the king that Sir Modred had pitched
his camp upon Barrendown; and the king rode thither, and
there was a great battle betwixt them, and King Arthur's
party stood best, and Sir Modred and his party fled unto
Canterbury.

And there was a day assigned betwixt King Arthur and
Sir Modred that they should meet upon a down beside
Salisbury, and not far from the seaside, to do battle yet
again. And at night, as the king slept, he dreamed a wonderful dream. It seemed him verily that there came Sir
Gawain unto him, with a number of fair ladies with him.
And when King Arthur saw him, he said, "Welcome, my
sister's son; I weened thou hadst been dead; and now I see
thee alive, great is my joy. But, O fair nephew, what be
these ladies that hither be come with you?" "Sir," said Sir
Gawain, "all these be ladies for whom I have fought when
I was a living man; and because I did battle for them in
righteous quarrel, they have given me grace to bring me
hither unto you, to warn you of your death, if ye fight to-
morrow with Sir Modred. Therefore take ye treaty, and
proffer you largely for a month's delay; for within a month

shall come Sir Launcelot and all his noble knights, and rescue you worshipfully, and slay Sir Modred and all that hold with him." And then Sir Gawain and all the ladies vanished. And anon the king called to fetch his noble lords and wise bishops unto him. And when they were come, the king told them his vision, and what Sir Gawain had told him. Then the king sent Sir Lucan the butler, and Sir Bedivere, with two bishops, and charged them in any wise to take a treaty for a month and a day with Sir Modred. So they departed, and came to Sir Modred; and so, at the last, Sir Modred was agreed to have Cornwall and Kent, during Arthur's life, and all England after his death.

Then it was agreed that King Arthur and Sir Modred should meet betwixt both their hosts, and each of them should bring fourteen persons, and then and there they should sign the treaty. And when King Arthur and his knights were prepared to go forth, he warned all his host, "If so be ye see any sword drawn, look ye come on fiercely, and slay whomsoever withstandeth, for I in no wise trust that traitor, Sir Modred." In likewise Sir Modred warned his host. So they met, and were agreed and accorded thoroughly. And wine was brought, and they drank. Right then came an adder out of a little heath-bush, and stung a knight on the foot. And when the knight felt him sting, he looked down and saw the adder, and then he drew his sword to slay the adder, and thought of no other harm. And when the host on both sides saw that sword drawn, they blew trumpets and horns, and shouted greatly. And King Arthur took his horse, and rode to his party, saying, "Alas, this unhappy day!" And Sir Modred did in like wise. And never was there a more doleful battle in Christian land. And ever King Arthur rode throughout the battle, and did full nobly, as a worthy king should, and Sir Modred that day did his devoir, and put himself in great peril. And thus they fought all the long day, till the most of all the noble knights lay dead upon the ground. Then the king looked about him, and saw of all his host were left alive but two knights, Sir Lucan the butler, and Sir Bedivere his brother, and they were full sore wounded.

Then King Arthur saw where Sir Modred leaned upon his sword among a great heap of dead men. "Now give me my spear," said Arthur unto Sir Lucan, "for yonder I espy the traitor that hath wrought all this woe." "Sir, let him be," said Sir Lucan; "for if ye pass this unhappy day ye shall be right well revenged upon him. Remember what the sprite of Sir Gawain told you, and leave off now, for ye have won the field; and if ye leave off now this evil day of destiny is past." "Betide me life, betide me death," said King Arthur, "he shall not now escape my hands." Then the king took his spear in both hands, and ran toward Sir Modred, crying, "Traitor, now is thy death-day come." And there King Arthur smote Sir Modred under the shield, with a thrust of his spear through the body. And when Sir Modred felt that he had his death-wound, with the might that he had he smote King Arthur, with his sword holden in both his hands, on the side of the head, that the sword pierced the helmet and the brain-pan; and then Sir Modred fell stark dead upon the earth. And the noble Arthur fell in a swoon to the earth. And Sir Lucan the butler and Sir Bedivere raised him up, and gently led him betwixt them both to a little chapel not far from the seaside. And when the king was there he thought him well eased. Then heard they people cry in the field. And Sir Lucan went to see what that cry betokened; and he saw by the moonlight that pillers [1] and robbers were come to rob the dead. And he returned, and said to the king, "By my rede, it is best that we bring you to some town." "I would it were so," said the king. And when the king tried to go he fainted. Then Sir Lucan took up the king on the one part, and Sir Bedivere on the other part; and in the lifting Sir Lucan fell in a swoon to the earth, for he was grievously wounded. And then the noble knight's heart burst. And when the king awoke he beheld Sir Lucan, how he lay foaming at the mouth, and speechless. "Alas!" said the king, "this is to me a full heavy sight, to see this noble duke so die for my sake; for he would have holpen me that had more need of help than I, and he would not complain, his heart was so set to help me." Then Sir Bedivere wept for his brother. "Leave this mourning and weeping," said the king, "for wit thou well, if I might live myself, the death of Sir Lucan would grieve me evermore; but my time hieth fast. Therefore," said Arthur unto Sir Bedivere, "take thou Excalibar, my good

---

[1] Plunderers: the word is not now used.

sword, and go with it to yonder waterside; and when thou comest there I charge thee throw my sword in that water, and come again and tell me what thou there seest." "My lord," said Sir Bedivere, "your commandment shall be done." So Sir Bedivere departed, and by the way he beheld that noble sword, that the pommel and the haft were all of precious stones; and then he said to himself, "If I throw this rich sword into the water no good shall come thereof, but only harm and loss." And then Sir Bedivere hid Excalibur under a tree. And so, as soon as he might, he came again unto the king. "What sawest thou there?" said the king. "Sir," he said, "I saw nothing." "Alas! thou hast deceived me," said the king. "Go thou lightly again, and as thou love me, spare not to throw it in." Then Sir Bedivere went again, and took the sword in his hand to throw it; but again it beseemed him but sin and shame to throw away that noble sword, and he hid it away again, and returned, and told the king he had done his commandment. "What sawest thou there?" said the king. "Sir," he said, "I saw nothing but waters deep and waves wan." "Ah, traitor untrue!" said King Arthur, "now hast thou betrayed me twice. And yet thou art named a noble knight, and hast been lief and dear to me. But now go again, and do as I bid thee, for thy long tarrying putteth me in jeopardy of my life." Then Sir Bedivere went to the sword, and lightly took it up, and went to the water-side, and he bound the girdle about the hilt, and then he threw the sword as far into the water as he might. And there came an arm and a hand out of the water and met it, and caught it, and shook it thrice and brandished it, and then vanished away the hand with the sword in the water.

Then Sir Bedivere came again to the king, and told him what he saw. "Help me hence," said the king, "for I fear I have tarried too long." Then Sir Bedivere took the king on his back, and so went with him to that water-side; and when they came there, even fast by the bank there rode a little barge with many fair ladies in it, and among them was a queen; and all had black hoods, and they wept and shrieked when they saw King Arthur.

"Now put me in the barge," said the king. And there received him three queens with great mourning, and in one of their laps King Arthur laid his head. And the queen said, "Ah, dear brother, why have ye tarried so long? Alas! this wound on your head hath caught overmuch cold." And then they rowed from the land, and Sir Bedivere beheld them go from him. Then he cried: "Ah, my lord Arthur, will ye leave me here alone among mine enemies?" "Comfort thyself," said the king, "for in me is no further help; for I will to the Isle of Avalon, to heal me of my grievous wound." And as soon as Sir Bedivere had lost sight of the barge he wept and wailed; then he took the forest, and went all that night, and in the morning he was ware of a chapel and a hermitage.

Then went Sir Bedivere thither; and when he came into the chapel he saw where lay an hermit on the ground, near a tomb that was newly graven. "Sir," said Sir Bedivere, "what man is there buried that ye pray so near unto?" "Fair son," said the hermit, "I know not verily. But this night there came a number of ladies, and brought hither one dead, and prayed me to bury him." "Alas!" said Sir Bedivere, "that was my lord, King Arthur." Then Sir Bedivere swooned; and when he awoke he prayed the hermit he might abide with him, to live with fasting and prayers. "Ye are welcome," said the hermit. So there bode Sir Bedivere with the hermit; and he put on poor clothes, and served the hermit full lowly in fasting and in prayers.

Thus of Arthur I find never more written in books that he authorized, nor more of the very certainty of his death; but thus was he led away in a ship, wherein were three queens; the one was King Arthur's sister, Queen Morgane le Fay; the other was Viviane, the Lady of the Lake; and the third was the queen of North Galis. And this tale Sir Bedivere, knight of the Table Round, made to be written.

Yet some men say that King Arthur is not dead, but hid away into another place, and men say that he shall come again and reign over England. But many say that there is written on his tomb this verse:—

"*Hic jacet Arthurus, Rex quondam, Rexque futurus.*"
Here Arthur lies, King once and King to be.

And when Queen Guenever understood that King Arthur was slain, and all the noble knights with him, she stole away, and five ladies with her; and so she went to Almes-

bury, and made herself a nun, and ware white clothes and
black, and took great penance as ever did sinful lady, and
lived in fasting, prayers, and alms-deeds. And there she
was abbess and ruler of the nuns. Now turn we from her,
and speak of Sir Launcelot of the Lake.

When Sir Launcelot heard in his country that Sir Modred
was crowned king of England and made war against his own
uncle, King Arthur, then was Sir Launcelot wroth out of
measure, and said to his kinsmen: "Alas, that double traitor,
Sir Modred! now it repenteth me that ever he escaped out
of my hands." Then Sir Launcelot and his fellows made
ready in all haste, with ships and galleys, to pass into England; and so he passed over till he came to Dover, and there
he landed with a great army. Then Sir Launcelot was told
that King Arthur was slain. "Alas!" said Sir Launcelot,
"this is the heaviest tidings that ever came to me." Then he
called the kings, dukes, barons, and knights, and said thus:
"My fair lords, I thank you all for coming into this country with me, but we came too late, and that shall repent
me while I live. But since it is so," said Sir Launcelot, "I
will myself ride and seek my lady, Queen Guenever, for I
have heard say she hath fled into the west; therefore ye shall
abide me here fifteen days, and if I come not within that
time, then take your ships and your host and depart into
your country."

So Sir Launcelot departed and rode westerly, and there
he sought many days; and at last he came to a nunnery, and
was seen of Queen Guenever as he walked in the cloister;
and when she saw him, she swooned away. And when she
might speak, she bade him to be called to her. And when
Sir Launcelot was brought to her, she said: "Sir Launcelot,
I require thee and beseech thee, for all the love that ever
was betwixt us, that thou never see me more, but return to
thy kingdom and take thee a wife, and live with her with
joy and bliss; and pray for me to my Lord, that I may get
my soul's health." "Nay, madam," said Sir Launcelot, "wit
you well that I shall never do; but the same destiny that ye
have taken you to will I take me unto, for to please and
serve God." And so they parted, with tears and much lamentation; and the ladies bare the queen to her chamber, and
Sir Launcelot took his horse and rode away, weeping.

And at last Sir Launcelot was ware of a hermitage and

a chapel, and then he heard a little bell ring to mass; and thither he rode and alighted, and tied his horse to the gate, and heard mass. And he that sang the mass was the hermit with whom Sir Bedivere had taken up his abode; and Sir Bedivere knew Sir Launcelot, and they spake together after mass. But when Sir Bedivere had told his tale, Sir Launcelot's heart almost burst for sorrow. Then he kneeled down, and prayed the hermit to shrive him, and besought that he might be his brother. Then the hermit said, "I will gladly"; and then he put a habit upon Sir Launcelot, and there he served God day and night, with prayers and fastings.

And the great host abode at Dover till the end of the fifteen days set by Sir Launcelot, and then Sir Bohort made them to go home again to their own country; and Sir Bohort, Sir Hector de Marys, Sir Blanor, and many others, took on them to ride through all England to seek Sir Launcelot. So Sir Bohort by fortune rode until he came to the same chapel where Sir Launcelot was; and when he saw Sir Launcelot in that manner of clothing, he prayed the hermit that he might be in that same. And so there was a habit put upon him, and there he lived in prayers and fasting. And within half a year came others of the knights, their fellows, and took such a habit as Sir Launcelot and Sir Bohort had. Thus they endured in great penance six years.

And upon a night there came a vision to Sir Launcelot, and charged him to haste him toward Almesbury, and "by the time thou come there, thou shalt find Queen Guenever dead." Then Sir Launcelot rose up early, and told the hermit thereof. Then said the hermit, "It were well that ye disobey not this vision." And Sir Launcelot took his seven companions with him, and on foot they went from Glastonbury to Almesbury, which is more than thirty miles. And when they were come to Almesbury, they found that Queen Guenever died but half an hour before. Then Sir Launcelot saw her visage, but he wept not greatly, but sighed. And so he did all the observance of the service himself, both the "dirige" at night, and at morn he sang mass. And there was prepared an horse-bier, and Sir Launcelot and his fellows followed the bier on foot from Almesbury until they came to Glastonbury; and she was wrapped in cered clothes, and laid in a coffin of marble. And when she was put in the earth, Sir Launcelot swooned, and lay long as one dead.

And Sir Launcelot never after ate but little meat, nor drank; but continually mourned. And within six weeks Sir Launcelot fell sick; and he sent for the hermit and all his true fellows, and said, "Sir hermit, I pray you give me all my rights that a Christian man ought to have." "It shall not need," said the hermit and all his fellows; "it is but heaviness of your blood, and to-morrow morn you shall be well." "My fair lords," said Sir Launcelot, "my careful body will into the earth; I have warning more than now I will say; therefore give me my rights." So when he was houseled and aneled, and had all that a Christian man ought to have, he prayed the hermit that his fellows might bear his body to Joyous Garde. (Some men say it was Alnwick, and some say it was Bamborough.) "It repenteth me sore," said Sir Launcelot, "but I made a vow aforetime that in Joyous Garde I would be buried." Then there was weeping and wringing of hands among his fellows. And that night Sir Launcelot died; and when Sir Bohort and his fellows came to his bedside the next morning, they found him stark dead; and he lay as if he had smiled, and the sweetest savor all about him that ever they knew.

And they put Sir Launcelot into the same horse-bier that Queen Guenever was laid in, and the hermit and they all together went with the body till they came to Joyous Garde. And there they laid his corpse in the body of the quire, and sang and read many psalms and prayers over him. And ever his visage was laid open and naked, that all folks might behold him. And right thus, as they were at their service, there came Sir Hector de Marys, that had seven years sought Sir Launcelot his brother, through all England, Scotland and Wales. And when Sir Hector heard such sounds in the chapel of Joyous Garde, he alighted and came into the quire. And all they knew Sir Hector. Then went Sir Bohort, and told him how there lay Sir Launcelot his brother, dead. Then Sir Hector threw his shield, his sword, and helm from him. And when he beheld Sir Launcelot's visage, it were hard for any tongue to tell the doleful complaints he made for his brother. "Ah, Sir Launcelot!" he said, "there thou liest. And now I dare to say thou wert never matched of none earthly knight's hand. And thou wert the courteousest knight that ever bare shield; and thou wert the truest friend to thy lover that ever bestrode horse; and thou were the truest lover, of a sinful man, that ever loved woman; and thou wert the kindest man that ever struck with sword. And thou wert the goodliest person that ever came among press of knights. And thou wert the meekest man, and the gentlest, that ever ate in hall among ladies. And thou wert the sternest knight to thy mortal foe that ever put spear in the rest." Then there was weeping and dolor out of measure. Thus they kept Sir Launcelot's corpse fifteen days, and then they buried it with great devotion.

Then they went back with the hermit to his hermitage. And Sir Bedivere was there ever still hermit to his life's end. And Sir Bohort, Sir Hector, Sir Blanor and Sir Bleoberis went into the Holy Land. And these four knights did many battles upon the miscreants, the Turks; and there they died upon a Good Friday, as it pleased God.

Thus endeth this noble and joyous book, entitled La Morte d'Arthur; notwithstanding it treateth of the birth, life and acts of the said King Arthur, and of his noble Knights of the Round Table, their marvellous enquests and adventures, the achieving of the Sangreal, and in the end, la Morte d'Arthur, with the dolorous death and departing out of this world of them all. Which book was reduced into English by Sir Thomas Mallory, Knight, and divided into twenty-one books, chaptered and imprinted and finished in the Abbey Westmestre, the last day of July, the year of our Lord MCCCCLXXXV.

Caxton me fieri fecit.

Legends of
Charlemagne
or
Romance of
The Middle Ages

"How Agrican with all his northern powers
Besieged Albracca, as romances tell;
The city of Galaphron, from thence to win
The fairest of her sex, Angelica,
His daughter, loved of many prowest knights,
Both paynim, and the peers of Charlemain."

Paradise Regained

PREFACE

In an age when intellectual darkness enveloped Western
Europe, a constellation of brilliant writers arose in Italy. Of
these, Pulci (born in 1431), Boiardo (1434), and Ariosto
(1474) took for their subjects the romantic fables which had
for many ages been transmitted in the lays of bards and
the legends of monkish chroniclers. These fables they arranged in order, adorned with the embellishments of fancy,
amplified from their own invention, and stamped with immortality. It may safely be asserted, that as long as civilization shall endure, these productions will retain their place
among the most cherished creations of human genius.

In reading these romances, we cannot fail to observe
how the primitive inventions have been used, again and

again, by successive generations of fabulists. The Siren of Ulysses is the prototype of the Siren of Orlando, and the character of Circe reappears in Alcina. The fountains of Love and Hatred may be traced to the story of Cupid and Psyche; and similar effects produced by a magic draught appear in the tale of Tristram and Isoude, and, substituting a flower for the draught, in Shakespeare's "Midsummer Night's Dream." There are many other instances of the same kind which the reader will recognize without our assistance.

The sources whence we derive these stories are, first, the Italian poets named above; next, the "Romans de Chevalerie" of the Comte de Tressan; lastly, certain German collections of popular tales.

1. INTRODUCTION

Those who have investigated the origin of the romantic fables relating to Charlemagne and his peers are of opinion that the deeds of Charles Martel, and perhaps of other Charleses, have been blended in popular tradition with those properly belonging to Charlemagne. It was indeed a most momentous era; and if our readers will have patience, before entering on the perusal of the fabulous annals which we are about to lay before them, to take a rapid survey of the real history of the times, they will find it hardly less romantic than the tales of the poets.

In the century beginning from the year 600, the countries bordering upon the native land of our Saviour, to the east and south, had not yet received his religion. Arabia was the seat of an idolatrous religion resembling that of the ancient Persians, who worshipped the sun, moon, and stars. In Mecca, in the year 571, Mahomet was born, and here, at the age of forty, he proclaimed himself the prophet of God, in dignity as superior to Christ as Christ had been to Moses. Having obtained by slow degrees a considerable number of disciples, he resorted to arms to diffuse his religion. The energy and zeal of his followers, aided by the weakness of the neighboring nations, enabled him and his successors to spread the sway of Arabia and the religion of Mahomet over the countries to the east as far as the Indus, northward over Persia and Asia Minor, westward over Egypt and the southern shores of the Mediterranean, and thence over the principal portion of Spain. All this was done within one hundred years from the Hegira, or flight of Mahomet from Mecca to Medina, which happened in the year 622, and is the era from which Mahometans reckon time, as we do from the birth of Christ.

From Spain the way was open for the Saracens (so the followers of Mahomet were called) into France, the conquest of which, if achieved, would have been followed very probably by that of all the rest of Europe, and would have resulted in the banishment of Christianity from the earth. For Christianity was not at that day universally professed, even by those nations which we now regard as foremost in civilization. Great part of Germany, Britain, Denmark, and Russia were still pagan or barbarous.

At that time there ruled in France, though without the title of king, the first of those illustrious Charleses of whom we have spoken, Charles Martel, the grandfather of Charlemagne. The Saracens of Spain had made incursions into France in 712, and 718, and had retired, carrying with them a vast booty. In 725, Anbessa, who was then the Saracen governor of Spain, crossed the Pyrenees with a numerous army, and took by storm the strong town of Carcassone. So great was the terror excited by this invasion, that the country for a wide extent submitted to the conqueror, and a Mahometan governor for the province was appointed and installed at Narbonne. Anbessa, however, received a fatal wound in one of his engagements, and the Saracens, being thus checked from further advance, retired to Narbonne.

In 732 the Saracens again invaded France under Abdalrahman, advanced rapidly to the banks of the Garonne, and laid siege to Bordeaux. The city was taken by assault and delivered up to the soldiery. The invaders still pressed forward, and spread over the territories of Orleans, Auxerre, and Sens. Their advanced parties were suddenly called in by their chief, who had received information of the rich abbey of St. Martin of Tours, and resolved to plunder and destroy it.

Charles during all this time had done nothing to oppose the Saracens, for the reason that the portion of France over which their incursions had been made was not at that time under his dominion, but constituted an independent kingdom, under the name of Aquitaine, of which Eude was king. But now Charles became convinced of the danger, and prepared to encounter it. Abdalrahman was advancing toward Tours, when intelligence of the approach of Charles, at the head of an army of Franks, compelled him to fall back upon Poitiers, in order to seize an advantageous field of battle.

Charles Martel had called together his warriors from every part of his dominions, and, at the head of such an army as had hardly ever been seen in France, crossed the Loire, probably at Orleans, and, being joined by the remains of the army of Aquitaine, came in sight of the Arabs in the month of October, 732. The Saracens seem to have been aware of the terrible enemy they were now to encounter, and for the first time these formidable conquerors hesitated. The two armies remained in presence during seven days before either ventured to begin the attack; but at length the signal for battle was given by Abdalrahman, and the immense mass of the Saracen army rushed with fury on the Franks. But the heavy line of the Northern warriors remained like a rock, and the Saracens, during nearly the whole day, expended their strength in vain attempts to make an impression upon them. At length, about four o'clock in the afternoon, when Abdalrahman was preparing for a new and desperate attempt to break the line of the Franks, a terrible clamor was heard in the rear of the Saracens. It was King Eude, who, with his Aquitanians, had attacked their camp, and a great part of the Saracen army rushed tumultuously from the field to protect their plunder. In this moment of confusion the line of the Franks advanced, and, sweeping the field before it, carried fearful slaughter amongst the enemy. Abdalrahman made desperate efforts to rally his troops, but when he himself, with the bravest of his officers, fell beneath the swords of the Christians, all order disappeared, and the remains of his army sought refuge in their immense camp, from which Eude and his Aquitanians had been repulsed. It was now late, and Charles, unwilling to risk an attack on the camp in the dark, withdrew his army, and passed the night in the plain, expecting to renew the battle in the morning.

Accordingly, when daylight came, the Franks drew up in order of battle, but no enemy appeared; and when at last they ventured to approach the Saracen camp, they found it empty. The invaders had taken advantage of the night to begin their retreat, and were already on their way back to Spain, leaving their immense plunder behind to fall into the hands of the Franks.

This was the celebrated battle of Tours, in which vast numbers of the Saracens were slain, and only fifteen hundred of the Franks. Charles received the surname of Martel (the Hammer) in consequence of this victory.

The Saracens, notwithstanding this severe blow, continued to hold their ground in the South of France; but Pepin, the son of Charles Martel, who succeeded to his father's power, and assumed the title of king, successively took from them the strong places they held; and in 759, by the capture of Narbonne, their capital, extinguished the remains of their power in France.

Charlemagne, or Charles the Great, succeeded his father, Pepin, on the throne in the year 768. This prince, though the hero of numerous romantic legends, appears greater in history than in fiction. Whether we regard him as a warrior or as a legislator, as a patron of learning or as the civilizer of a barbarous nation, he is entitled to our warmest admiration. Such he is in history; but the romancers represent him as often weak and passionate, the victim of treacherous counsellors, and at the mercy of turbulent barons, on whose prowess he depends for the maintenance of his throne. The historical representation is doubtless the true one, for it is handed down in trustworthy records, and is confirmed by the events of the age. At the height of his power, the French empire extended over what we now call France, Germany, Switzerland, Holland, Belgium, and a great part of Italy.

In the year 800, Charlemagne, being in Rome, whither he had gone with a numerous army to protect the Pope, was crowned by the Pontiff Emperor of the West. On Christmas day Charles entered the Church of St. Peter, as if merely to take his part in the celebration of the mass with the rest of the congregation. When he approached the altar and stooped in the act of prayer, the Pope stepped forward and placed a crown of gold upon his head; and immediately the Roman people shouted, "Life and victory to Charles the August, crowned by God the great and pacific Emperor of the Romans." The Pope then prostrated himself before him, and paid him reverence, according to the custom established in the times of the ancient Emperors, and concluded the ceremony by anointing him with consecrated oil.

Charlemagne's wars were chiefly against the pagan and barbarous people, who, under the name of Saxons, inhabited the countries now called Hanover and Holland. He also led expeditions against the Saracens of Spain; but his wars with the Saracens were not carried on, as the romances assert, in France, but on the soil of Spain. He entered Spain by the Eastern Pyrenees, and made an easy conquest of Barcelona and Pampeluna. But Saragossa refused to open her gates to him, and Charles ended by negotiating, and accepting a vast sum of gold as the price of his return over the Pyrenees.

On his way back, he marched with his whole army through the gorges of the mountains by way of the valleys of Engui, Eno, and Roncesvalles. The chief of this region had waited upon Charlemagne, on his advance, as a faithful vassal of the monarchy; but now, on the return of the Franks, he had called together all the wild mountaineers who acknowledged him as their chief, and they occupied the heights of the mountains under which the army had to pass. The main body of the troops met with no obstruction, and received no intimation of danger; but the rearguard, which was considerably behind, and encumbered with its plunder, was overwhelmed by the mountaineers in the pass of Roncesvalles, and slain to a man. Some of the bravest of the Frankish chiefs perished on this occasion, among whom is mentioned Roland or Orlando, governor of the marches or frontier of Brittany. His name became famous in after times, and the disaster of Roncesvalles and death of Roland became eventually the most celebrated episode in the vast cycle of romance.

Though after this there were hostile encounters between the armies of Charlemagne and the Saracens, they were of small account, and generally on the soil of Spain. Thus the historical foundation for the stories of the romancers is but scanty, unless we suppose the events of an earlier and of a later age to be incorporated with those of Charlemagne's own time.

There is, however, a pretended history, which for a long time was admitted as authentic, and attributed to Turpin, Archbishop of Rheims, a real personage of the time of Charlemagne. Its title is "History of Charles the Great and Orlando." It is now unhesitatingly considered as a collection of popular traditions, produced by some credulous and unscrupulous monk, who thought to give dignity to his romance by ascribing its authorship to a well-known and eminent individual. It introduces its pretended author, Bishop Turpin, in this manner:—

"Turpin, Archbishop of Rheims, the friend and secretary of Charles the Great, excellently skilled in sacred and profane literature, of a genius equally adapted to prose and verse, the advocate of the poor, beloved of God in his life and conversation, who often fought the Saracens, hand to hand, by the Emperor's side, he relates the acts of Charles the Great in one book, and flourished under Charles and his son Louis, to the year of our Lord eight hundred and thirty."

The titles of some of Archbishop Turpin's chapters will show the nature of his history. They are these: "Of the Walls of Pampeluna, that fell of themselves." "Of the War of the holy Facundus, where the Spears grew." (Certain of the Christians fixed their spears, in the evening, erect in the ground, before the castle; and found them, in the morning, covered with bark and branches.) "How the Sun stood still for Three Days, and the Slaughter of Four Thousand Saracens."

Turpin's history has perhaps been the source of the marvellous adventures which succeeding poets and romancers have accumulated around the names of Charlemagne and his Paladins, or Peers. But Ariosto and the other Italian poets have drawn from different sources, and doubtless often from their own invention, numberless other stories which they attribute to the same heroes, not hesitating to quote as their authority "the good Turpin," though his history contains no trace of them;—and the more outrageous the improbability, or rather the impossibility, of their narrations, the more attentive are they to cite "the

Archbishop," generally adding their testimonial to his unquestionable veracity.

The principal Italian poets who have sung the adventures of the peers of Charlemagne are Pulci, Boiardo, and Ariosto. The characters of Orlando, Rinaldo, Astolpho, Gano, and others, are the same in all, though the adventures attributed to them are different. Boiardo tells us of the loves of Orlando, Ariosto of his disappointment and consequent madness, Pulci of his death.

Ogier, the Dane, is a real personage. History agrees with romance in representing him as a powerful lord who, originally from Denmark and a Pagan, embraced Christianity, and took service under Charlemagne. He revolted from the Emperor, and was driven into exile. He afterwards led one of those bands of piratical Norsemen which ravaged France under the reigns of Charlemagne's degenerate successors. The description which an ancient chronicler gives of Charlemagne, as described by Ogier, is so picturesque, that we are tempted to transcribe it. Charlemagne was advancing to the siege of Pavia. Didier, King of the Lombards, was in the city with Ogier, to whom he had given refuge. When they learned that the king was approaching, they mounted a high tower, whence they could see far and wide over the country. "They first saw advancing the engines of war, fit for the armies of Darius or Julius Caesar. 'There is Charlemagne,' said Didier. 'No,' said Ogier. The Lombard next saw a vast body of soldiers, who filled all the plain. 'Certainly Charles advances with that host,' said the king. 'Not yet,' replied Ogier. 'What hope for us,' resumed the king, 'if he brings with him a greater host than that?' At last Charles appeared, his head covered with an iron helmet, his hands with iron gloves, his breast and shoulders with a cuirass of iron, his left hand holding an iron lance, while his right hand grasped his sword. Those who went before the monarch, those who marched at his side, and those who followed him, all had similar arms. Iron covered the fields and the roads; iron points reflected the rays of the sun. This iron, so hard, was borne by a people whose hearts were harder still. The blaze of the weapons flashed terror into the streets of the city."

This picture of Charlemagne in his military aspect would be incomplete without a corresponding one of his "mood of peace." One of the greatest of modern historians, M. Guizot, has compared the glory of Charlemagne to a brilliant meteor, rising suddenly out of the darkness of barbarism to disappear no less suddenly in the darkness of feudalism. But the light of this meteor was not extinguished, and reviving civilization owed much that was permanently beneficial to the great Emperor of the Franks. His ruling hand is seen in the legislation of his time, as well as in the administration of the laws. He encouraged learning; he upheld the clergy, who were the only peaceful and intellectual class, against the encroaching and turbulent barons; he was an affectionate father, and watched carefully over the education of his children, both sons and daughters. Of his encouragement of learning, we will give some particulars.

He caused learned men to be brought from Italy and from other foreign countries, to revive the public schools of France, which had been prostrated by the disorders of preceding times. He recompensed these learned men liberally, and kept some of them near himself, honoring them with his friendship. Of these the most celebrated is Alcuin, an Englishman, whose writings still remain, and prove him to have been both a learned and a wise man. With the assistance of Alcuin, and others like him, he founded an academy or royal school, which should have the direction of the studies of all the schools of the kingdom. Charlemagne himself was a member of this academy on equal terms with the rest. He attended its meetings, and fulfilled all the duties of an academician. Each member took the name of some famous man of antiquity. Alcuin called himself Horace, another took the name of Augustin, a third of Pindar. Charlemagne, who knew the Psalms by heart, and who had an ambition to be, according to his conception, *a king after God's own heart*, received from his brother academicians the name of David.

Of the respect entertained for him by foreign nations an interesting proof is afforded in the embassy sent to him by the Caliph of the Arabians, the celebrated Haroun al Raschid, a prince in character and conduct not unlike to Charlemagne. The ambassadors brought with them, besides other rich presents, a clock, the first that was seen in Europe, which excited universal admiration. It had the form of a twelve-sided edifice with twelve doors. These doors formed niches, in each of which was a little statue representing one of the hours. At the striking of the hour the doors, one for each stroke, were seen to open, and from the doors to issue as many of the little statues, which, following one another, marched gravely round the tower. The motion of the clock was caused by water, and the striking was effected by balls of brass equal to the number of the hours, which fell upon a cymbal of the same metal, the number falling being determined by the discharge of the water, which, as it sunk in the vessel, allowed their escape.

Charlemagne was succeeded by his son Louis, a well-intentioned but feeble prince, in whose reign the fabric reared by Charles began rapidly to crumble. Louis was followed successively by two Charleses, incapable princes, whose weak and often tyrannical conduct is no doubt the source of incidents of that character ascribed in the romances to Charlemagne.

The lawless and disobedient deportment of Charles's paladins, instances of which are so frequent in the romantic legends, was also a trait of the declining empire, but not of that of Charlemagne.

2. THE PEERS, OR PALADINS

The twelve most illustrious knights of Charlemagne were called Peers, for the equality that reigned among them; while the name of Paladins, also conferred on them, implies that they were inmates of the palace and companions of the king. Their names are not always given alike by the romancers, yet we may enumerate the most distinguished of them as follows: Orlando or Roland (the former the Italian, the latter the French form of the name), favorite nephew of Charlemagne; Rinaldo of Montalban, cousin of Orlando; Namo, Duke of Bavaria; Salomon, King of Brittany; Turpin, the Archbishop; Astolpho, of England; Ogier, the Dane; Malagigi, the Enchanter; and Florismart, the friend of Orlando. There were others who are sometimes named as paladins, and the number cannot be strictly limited to twelve. Charlemagne himself must be counted one, and Ganelon, or Gano, of Mayence, the treacherous enemy of all the rest, was rated high on the list by his deluded sovereign, who was completely the victim of his arts.

We shall introduce more particularly to our readers a few of the principal peers, leaving the others to make their own introduction, as they appear in the course of our narrative. We begin with Orlando.

Orlando (Roland)

Milon, or Milone, a knight of great family, and distantly related to Charlemagne, having secretly married Bertha, the Emperor's sister, was banished from France, and excommunicated by the Pope. After a long and miserable wandering on foot as mendicants, Milon and his wife arrived at Sutri, in Italy, where they took refuge in a cave, and in that cave Orlando was born. There his mother continued, deriving a scanty support from the compassion of the neighboring peasants; while Milon, in quest of honor and fortune, went into foreign lands. Orlando grew up among the children of the peasantry, surpassing them all in strength and manly graces. Among his companions in age, though in station far more elevated, was Oliver, son of the governor of the town. Between the two boys a feud arose, that led to a fight, in which Orlando thrashed his rival; but this did not prevent a friendship springing up between the two which lasted through life.

Orlando was so poor that he was sometimes half naked. As he was a favorite of the boys, one day four of them brought some cloth to make him clothes. Two brought white and two red; and from this circumstance Orlando took his coat-of-arms, or *quarterings*.

When Charlemagne was on his way to Rome to receive the imperial crown, he dined in public in Sutri. Orlando and his mother that day had nothing to eat, and Orlando, coming suddenly upon the royal party, and seeing abundance of provisions, seized from the attendants as much as he could carry off, and made good his retreat in spite of their resistance. The Emperor, being told of this incident, was reminded of an intimation he had received in a dream,

and ordered the boy to be followed. This was done by three
of the knights, whom Orlando would have encountered with
a cudgel on their entering the grotto, had not his mother restrained him. When they heard from her who she was, they
threw themselves at her feet, and promised to obtain her
pardon from the Emperor. This was easily effected. Orlando was received into favor by the Emperor, returned
with him to France and so distinguished himself that he
became the most powerful support of the throne and of
Christianity.[1]

Roland and Ferragus

Orlando, or Roland, particularly distinguished himself
by his combat with Ferragus. Ferragus was a giant, and
moreover, his skin was of such impenetrable stuff that no
sword could make any impression upon it. The giant's mode
of fighting was to seize his adversary in his arms and carry
him off, in spite of all the struggles he could make. Roland's utmost skill only availed to keep him out of the
giant's clutches, but all his efforts to wound him with the
sword were useless. After long fighting, Ferragus was so
weary that he proposed a truce, and when it was agreed
upon, he lay down and immediately fell asleep. He slept
in perfect security, for it was against all the laws of chivalry to take advantage of an adversary under such circumstances. But Ferragus lay so uncomfortably for the want
of a pillow, that Orlando took pity upon him, and brought
a smooth stone and placed it under his head. When the
giant woke up, after a refreshing nap, and perceived what
Orlando had done, he seemed quite grateful, became so-
ciable, and talked freely in the usual boastful style of such
characters. Among other things he told Orlando that he
need not attempt to kill him with a sword, for that every
part of his body was invulnerable, except this; and as he
spoke, he put his hand to the vital part, just in the middle
of his breast. Aided by this information, Orlando succeeded,
when the fight was renewed, in piercing the giant in the very
spot he had pointed out, and giving him a death-wound.

[1] It is plain that Shakespeare borrowed from this source the similar incident in his "*As You Like It.*" The names of characters in the play, Orlando, Oliver, Rowland, indicate the same thing.

Great was the rejoicing in the Christian camp, and many the praises showered upon the victorious paladin by the Emperor and all his host.

On another occasion, Orlando encountered a puissant Saracen warrior, and took from him, as the prize of victory, the sword Durindana. This famous weapon had once belonged to the illustrious prince Hector of Troy. It was of the finest workmanship, and of such strength and temper that no armor in the world could stand against it.

A Roland for an Oliver

Guerin de Montglave held the lordship of Vienne, subject to Charlemagne. He had quarrelled with his sovereign, and Charles laid siege to his city, having ravaged the neighboring country. Guerin was an aged warrior, but relied for his defence upon his four sons and two grandsons, who were among the bravest knights of the age. After the siege had continued two months, Charlemagne received tiding that Marsilius, king of Spain, had invaded France, and, finding himself unopposed, was advancing rapidly in the Southern provinces. At this intelligence, Charles listened to the counsel of his peers, and consented to put the quarrel with Guerin to the decision of Heaven, by single combat between two knights, one of each party, selected by lot. The proposal was acceptable to Guerin and his sons. The names of the four, together with Guerin's own, who would not be excused, and of the two grandsons, who claimed their lot, being put into a helmet, Oliver's was drawn forth, and to him, the youngest of the grandsons, was assigned the honor and the peril of the combat. He accepted the award with delight, exulting in being thought worthy to maintain the cause of his family. On Charlemagne's side Roland was the designated champion, and neither he nor Oliver knew who his antagonist was to be.

They met on an island in the Rhone, and the warriors of both camps were ranged on either shore, spectators of the battle. At the first encounter both lances were shivered, but both riders kept their seats, immovable. They dismounted, and drew their swords. Then ensued a combat which seemed so equal, that the spectators could not form an opinion as to the probable issue. Two hours and more the knights continued to strike and parry, to thrust and ward, neither showing any sign of weariness, nor ever being taken at unawares. At length Orlando struck furiously upon Oliver's shield, burying Durindana in its edge so deeply that he could not draw it back, and Oliver, almost at the same moment, thrust so vigorously upon Orlando's breastplate that his sword snapped off at the handle. Thus were the two warriors left weaponless. Scarcely pausing a moment, they rushed upon one another, each striving to throw his adversary to the ground, and failing in that, each snatched at the other's helmet to tear it away. Both succeeded, and at the same moment they stood bareheaded face to face, and Roland recognized Oliver, and Oliver recognized Roland. For a moment they stood still; and the next, with open arms, rushed into one another's embrace. "I am conquered," said Orlando. "I yield me," said Oliver.

The people on the shore knew not what to make of all this. Presently they saw the two late antagonists standing hand in hand, and it was evident the battle was at an end. The knights crowded round them, and with one voice hailed them as equals in glory. If there were any who felt disposed to murmur that the battle was left undecided, they were silenced by the voice of Ogier the Dane, who proclaimed aloud that all had been done that honor required, and declared that he would maintain that award against all gainsayers.

The quarrel with Guerin and his sons being left undecided, a truce was made for four days, and in that time, by the efforts of Duke Namo on the one side, and of Oliver on the other, a reconciliation was effected. Charlemagne, accompanied by Guerin and his valiant family, marched to meet Marsilius, who hastened to retreat across the frontier.

Rinaldo

Rinaldo was one of the four sons of Aymon, who married Aya, the sister of Charlemagne. Thus Rinaldo was nephew to Charlemagne and cousin of Orlando.

When Rinaldo had grown old enough to assume arms, Orlando had won for himself an illustrious name by his exploits against the Saracens, whom Charlemagne and his

brave knights had driven out of France. Orlando's fame
excited a noble emulation in Rinaldo. Eager to go in pursuit of glory, he wandered in the country near Paris, and
one day saw at the foot of a tree a superb horse, fully
equipped and loaded with a complete suit of armor. Rinaldo clothed himself in the armor and mounted the horse,
but took not the sword. On the day when, with his brothers,
he had received the honor of knighthood from the Emperor,
he had sworn never to bind a sword to his side till he had
wrested one from some famous knight.

Rinaldo took his way to the forest of Arden, celebrated
for so many adventures. Hardly had he entered it, when he
met an old man, bending under the weight of years, and
learned from him that the forest was infested with a wild
horse, untamable, that broke and overturned everything
that opposed his career. To attack him, he said, or even
to meet him, was certain death. Rinaldo, far from being
alarmed, showed the most eager desire to combat the animal. This was the horse Bayard, afterwards so famous. He
had formerly belonged to Amadis of Gaul. After the death
of that hero, he had been held under enchantment by the
power of a magician, who predicted that, when the time
came to break the spell, he should be subdued by a knight
of the lineage of Amadis, and not less brave than he.

To win this wonderful horse, it was necessary to conquer
him by force or skill; for from the moment when he should
be thrown down, he would become docile and manageable.
His habitual resort was a cave on the borders of the forest;
but woe be to any one who should approach him, unless
gifted with strength and courage more than mortal. Having
told this, the old man departed. He was not, in fact, an old
man, but Malagigi, the enchanter, cousin of Rinaldo, who,
to favor the enterprises of the young knight, had procured
for him the horse and armor which he so opportunely
found, and now put him in the way to acquire a horse unequalled in the world.

Rinaldo plunged into the forest, and spent many days in
seeking Bayard, but found no traces of him. One day he
encountered a Saracen knight, with whom he made acquaintance, as often happened to knights, by first meeting
him in combat. This knight, whose name was Isolier, was
also in quest of Bayard. Rinaldo succeeded in the encoun-

ter, and so severe was the shock that Isolier was a long time insensible. When he revived, and was about to resume the contest, a peasant who passed by (it was Malagigi) interrupted them with the news that the terrible horse was near at hand, advising them to unite their powers to subdue him, for it would require all their ability.

Rinaldo and Isolier, now become friends, proceeded together to the attack of the horse. They found Bayard, and stood a long time, concealed by the wood, admiring his strength and beauty.

A bright bay in color (whence he was called Bayard), with a silver star in his forehead, and his hind feet white, his body slender, his head delicate, his ample chest filled out with swelling muscles, his shoulders broad and full, his legs straight and sinewy, his thick mane falling over his arching neck,—he came rushing through the forest, regardless of rocks, bushes, or trees, rending everything that opposed his way, and neighing defiance.

He first descried Isolier, and rushed upon him. The knight received him with lance in rest, but the fierce animal broke the spear, and his course was not delayed by it for an instant. The Spaniard adroitly stepped aside, and gave way to the rushing tempest. Bayard checked his career, and turned again upon the knight, who had already drawn his sword. He drew his sword, for he had no hope of taming the horse; that, he was satisfied, was impossible.

Bayard rushed upon him, fiercely rearing, now on this side, now on that. The knight struck him with his sword, where the white star adorned his forehead, but struck in vain, and felt ashamed, thinking that he had struck feebly, for he did not know that the skin of that horse was so tough that the keenest sword could make no impression upon it.

Whistling fell the sword once more, and struck with greater force, and the fierce horse felt it, and drooped his head under the blow, but the next moment turned upon his foe with such a buffet that the Pagan fell stunned and lifeless to the earth.

Rinaldo, who saw Isolier fall, and thought that his life was reft, darted towards the horse, and, with his fist, gave him such a blow on the jaws that the blood tinged his mouth with vermilion. Quicker than an arrow leaves the bow the horse turned upon him, and tried to seize his arm with his teeth.

The knight stepped back, and then, repeating his blow, struck him on the forehead. Bayard turned, and kicked with both his feet with a force that would have shattered a mountain. Rinaldo was on his guard, and evaded his attacks, whether made with head or heels. He kept at his side, avoiding both; but, making a false step, he at last received a terrible blow from the horse's foot, and at the shock almost fainted away. A second such blow would have killed him, but the horse kicked at random, and a second blow did not reach Rinaldo, who in a moment recovered himself. Thus the contest continued until by chance Bayard's foot got caught between the branches of an oak. Rinaldo seized it, and putting forth all his strength and address, threw him on the ground.

No sooner had Bayard touched the ground, than all his rage subsided. No longer an object of terror, he became gentle and quiet, yet with dignity in his mildness.

The paladin patted his neck, stroked his breast, and smoothed his mane, while the animal neighed and showed delight to be caressed by his master. Rinaldo, seeing him now completely subdued, took the saddle and trappings from the other horse, and adorned Bayard with the spoils.

Rinaldo became one of the most illustrious knights of Charlemagne's court,—indeed, the most illustrious, if we except Orlando. Yet he was not always so obedient to the Emperor's commands as he should have been, and every fault he committed was sure to be aggravated by the malice of Gan, Duke of Maganza, the treacherous enemy of Rinaldo and all his house.

At one time Rinaldo had incurred the severe displeasure of Charlemagne, and been banished from court. Seeing no chance of being ever restored to favor, he went to Spain, and entered the service of the Saracen king, Ivo. His brothers, Alardo, Ricardo, and Ricciardetto, accompanied him, and all four served the king so faithfully that they rose to high favor with him. The king gave them land in the mountains on the frontiers of France and Spain, and subjected all the country round to Rinaldo's authority. There was plenty of marble in the mountains, the king furnished workmen, and they built a castle for Rinaldo, surrounded with high walls,

so as to be almost impregnable. Built of white stone, and
placed on the brow of a marble promontory, the castle
shone like a star, and Rinaldo gave it the name of Montalban. Here he assembled his friends, many of whom were
banished men like himself, and the country people furnished them with provisions in return for the protection
the castle afforded. Yet some of Rinaldo's men were lawless, and sometimes the supplies were not furnished in sufficient abundance, so that Rinaldo and his garrison got a
bad name for taking by force what they could not obtain
by gift; and we sometimes find Montalban spoken of as a
nest of freebooters, and its defenders called a beggarly garrison.

Charlemagne's displeasure did not last long, and, at the
time our history commences, Rinaldo and his brothers were
completely restored to the favor of the Emperor, and none
of his cavaliers served him with greater zeal and fidelity
than they, throughout all his wars with the Saracens and
Pagans.

3. THE TOURNAMENT

It was the month of May and the feast of Pentecost. Charlemagne had ordered magnificent festivities, and summoned
to them, besides his paladins and vassals of the crown, all
strangers, Christian or Saracen, then sojourning at Paris.
Among the guests were King Grandonio, from Spain; and
Ferrau, the Saracen, with eyes like an eagle; Orlando and
Rinaldo, the Emperor's nephews; Duke Namo; Astolpho,
of England, the handsomest man living; Malagigi, the Enchanter; and Gano, of Maganza, that wily traitor, who had
the art to make the Emperor think he loved him, while he
plotted against him.

High sat Charlemagne at the head of his vassals and his
paladins, rejoicing in the thought of their number and their
might, while all were sitting and hearing music, and feasting, when suddenly there came into the hall four enormous
giants, having between them a lady of incomparable beauty,

attended by a single knight. There were many ladies present who had seemed beautiful till she made her appearance, but after that they all seemed nothing. Every Christian knight turned his eyes to her, and every Pagan crowded round her, while she, with a sweetness that might have touched a heart of stone, thus addressed the Emperor:—

"High-minded lord, the renown of your worthiness, and of the valor of these your knights, which echoes from sea to sea, encourages me to hope that two pilgrims, who have come from the ends of the world to behold you, will not have encountered their fatigue in vain. And, before I show the motive which has brought us hither, learn that this knight is my brother Uberto, and that I am his sister Angelica. Fame has told us of the jousting this day appointed, and so the prince my brother has come to prove his valor, and to say that, if any of the knights here assembled choose to meet him in the joust, he will encounter them, one by one, at the stair of Merlin, by the Fountain of the Pine. And his conditions are these: No knight who chances to be thrown shall be allowed to renew the combat, but shall remain prisoner to my brother, but if my brother be overthrown he shall depart out of the country, leaving me as the prize of the conqueror."

Now it must be stated that this Angelica and her brother who called himself Uberto, but whose real name was Argalia, were the children of Galafron, king of Cathay, who had sent them to be the destruction of the Christian host; for Argalia was armed with an enchanted lance, which unfailingly overthrew everything it touched, and he was mounted on a horse, a creature of magic, whose swiftness outstripped the wind. Angelica possessed also a ring which was a defence against all enchantments, and when put into the mouth rendered the bearer invisible. Thus Argalia was expected to subdue and take prisoners whatever knights should dare to encounter him; and the charms of Angelica were relied on to entice the paladins to make the fatal venture, while her ring would afford her easy means of escape.

When Angelica ceased speaking, she knelt before the king and awaited his answer, and everybody gazed on her with admiration. Orlando especially felt irresistibly drawn towards her, so that he trembled and changed countenance. Every knight in the hall was infected with the same feeling,

not excepting old white-headed Duke Namo and Charlemagne himself.

All stood for a while in silence, lost in the delight of looking at her. The fiery youth Ferrau could hardly restrain
himself from seizing her from the giants and carrying her
away; Rinaldo turned as red as fire, while Malagigi, who had
discovered by his art that the stranger was not speaking the
truth, muttered softly, as he looked at her, "Exquisite false
creature! I will play thee such a trick for this, as will leave
thee no cause to boast of thy visit."

Charlemagne, to detain her as long as possible before him,
delayed his assent till he had asked her a number of questions, all of which she answered discreetly, and then the
challenge was accepted.

As soon as she was gone, Malagigi consulted his book,
and found out the whole plot of the vile, infidel king Galafron, as we have explained it, so he determined to seek the
damsel and frustrate her designs. He hastened to the appointed spot, and there found the prince and his sister in a
beautiful pavilion, where they lay asleep, while the four
giants kept watch. Malagigi took his book and cast a spell
out of it, and immediately the four giants fell into a deep
sleep. Drawing his sword (for he was a belted knight), he
softly approached the young lady, intending to despatch her
at once; but, seeing her look so lovely, he paused for a moment, thinking there was no need of hurry, as he believed
his spell was upon her, and she could not awake. But the
ring which she wore secured her from the effect of the spell,
and some slight noise, or whatever else it was, caused her at
that moment to awake. She uttered a great cry, and flew to
her brother, and waked him. By the help of her knowledge
of enchantment, they took and bound fast the magician,
and, seizing his book, turned his arts against himself. Then
they summoned a crowd of demons, and bade them seize
their prisoner and bear him to king Galafron, at his great
city of Albracca, which they did, and, on his arrival, he was
locked up in a rock under the sea.

While these things were going on, all was uproar at Paris,
since Orlando insisted upon being the first to try the adventure at the stair of Merlin. This was resented by the other
pretenders to Angelica, and all contested his right to the
precedence. The tumult was stilled by the usual expedient

of drawing lots, and the first prize was drawn by Astolpho. Ferrau, the Saracen, had the second, and Grandonio the third. Next came Berlinghieri, and Otho; then Charles himself, and, as his ill-fortune would have it, after thirty more, the indignant Orlando.

Astolpho, who drew the first lot, was handsome, brave, and rich. But, whether from heedlessness or want of skill, he was an unlucky jouster, and very apt to be thrown, an accident which he bore with perfect good-humor, always ready to mount again and try to mend his fortune, generally with no better success.

Astolpho went forth upon his adventure with great gayety of dress and manner, encountered Argalia, and was immediately tilted out of the saddle. He railed at fortune, to whom he laid all the fault; but his painful feelings were somewhat relieved by the kindness of Angelica, who, touched by his youth and good looks, granted him the liberty of the pavilion, and caused him to be treated with all kindness and respect.

The violent Ferrau had the next chance in the encounter, and was thrown no less speedily than Astolpho; but he did not so easily put up with his mischance. Crying out, "What are the Emperor's engagements to me?" he rushed with his sword against Argalia, who, being forced to defend himself, dismounted and drew his sword, but got so much the worse of the fight that he made a signal of surrender, and, after some words, listened to a proposal of marriage from Ferrau to his sister. The beauty, however, feeling no inclination to match with such a rough and savage-looking person, was so dismayed at the offer, that, hastily bidding her brother to meet her in the forest of Arden, she vanished from the sight of both by means of the enchanted ring. Argalia, seeing this, took to his horse of swiftness, and dashed away in the same direction. Ferrau pursued him, and Astolpho, thus left to himself, took possession of the enchanted lance in place of his own, which was broken, not knowing the treasure he possessed in it, and returned to the tournament. Charlemagne, finding the lady and her brother gone, ordered the jousting to proceed as at first intended, in which Astolpho, by aid of the enchanted lance, unhorsed all comers against him, equally to their astonishment and his own.

The paladin Rinaldo, on learning the issue of the combat

of Ferrau and the stranger, galloped after the fair fugitive
in an agony of love and impatience. Orlando, perceiving his
disappearance, pushed forth in like manner; and, at length,
all three are in the forest of Arden, hunting about for her
who is invisible.

Now in this forest there were two fountains, the one constructed by the sage Merlin, who designed it for Tristram
and the fair Isoude; [1] for such was the virtue of this fountain, that a draught of its waters produced an oblivion of
the love which the drinker might feel, and even produced
aversion for the object formerly beloved. The other fountain was endowed with exactly opposite qualities, and a
draught of it inspired love for the first living object that was
seen after tasting it. Rinaldo happened to come to the first-
mentioned fountain, and, being flushed with heat, dismounted, and quenched in one draught both his thirst and
his passion. So far from loving Angelica as before, he hated
her from the bottom of his heart, became disgusted with
the search he was upon, and, feeling fatigued with his ride,
finding a sheltered and flowery nook, laid himself down and
fell asleep.

Shortly after came Angelica, but, approaching in a different direction, she espied the other fountain, and there
quenched her thirst. Then resuming her way, she came upon
the sleeping Rinaldo. Love instantly seized her, and she
stood rooted to the spot.

The meadow round was all full of lilies of the valley and
wild roses. Angelica, not knowing what to do, at length
plucked a handful of these, and dropped them, one by one,
on the face of the sleeper. He woke up, and, seeing who it
was, received her salutations with averted countenance, remounted his horse, and galloped away. In vain the beautiful
creature followed and called after him, in vain asked him
what she had done to be so despised. Rinaldo disappeared,
leaving her in despair, and she returned in tears to the spot
where she had found him sleeping. There, in her turn, she
herself lay down, pressing the spot of earth on which he
had lain, and, out of fatigue and sorrow, fell asleep.

As Angelica thus lay, fortune conducted Orlando to the
same place. The attitude in which she was sleeping was so

[1] See their story in "The Age of Chivalry."

lovely, that it is not to be conceived, much less expressed. Orlando stood gazing like a man who had been transported to another sphere. "Am I on earth," he exclaimed, "or am I in Paradise? Surely it is I that sleep, and this is my dream."

But his dream was proved to be none in a manner which he little desired. Ferrau, who had slain Argalia, came up, raging with jealousy, and a combat ensued which awoke the sleeper.

Terrified at what she beheld, she rushed to her palfrey, and, while the fighters were occupied with one another, fled away through the forest. The champions continued their fight till they were interrupted by a messenger, who brought word to Ferrau that king Marsilius, his sovereign, was in pressing need of his assistance, and conjured him to return to Spain. Ferrau, upon this, proposed to suspend the combat to which Orlando, eager to pursue Angelica, agreed. Ferrau, on the other hand, departed with the messenger to Spain.

Orlando's quest for the fair fugitive was all in vain. Aided by the powers of magic, she made a speedy return to her own country.

But the thought of Rinaldo could not be banished from her mind, and she determined to set Malagigi at liberty, and to employ him to win Rinaldo, if possible, to make her a return of affection. She accordingly freed him from his dungeon, unlocking his fetters with her own hands, and restored him his book, promising him ample honors and rewards, on condition of his bringing Rinaldo to her feet.

Malagigi accordingly, with the aid of his book, called up a demon, mounted him, and departed. Arrived at his destination, he inveigled Rinaldo into an enchanted bark, which conveyed him, without any visible pilot, to an island where stood an edifice called Joyous Castle. The whole island was a garden. On the western side, close to the sea, was the palace, built of marble, so clear and polished that it reflected the landscape about it. Rinaldo leapt ashore, and soon met a lady, who invited him to enter. The house was as beautiful within as without, full of rooms adorned with azure and gold, and with noble paintings. The lady led the knight into an apartment painted with stories, and opening to the garden, through pillars of crystal, with golden capitals. Here he found a bevy of ladies, three of whom were singing in concert, while another played on an instrument of exquisite accord, and the rest danced round about them. When the ladies beheld him coming, they turned the dance into a circuit round him, and then one of them, in the sweetest manner, said, "Sir Knight, the tables are set, and the hour for the banquet is come"; and, with these words, still dancing, they drew him across the lawn in front of the apartment, to a table that was spread with cloth of gold and fine linen, under a bower of damask roses by the side of a fountain.

Four ladies were already seated there, who rose, and placed Rinaldo at their head, in a chair set with pearls. And truly indeed was he astonished. A repast ensued, consisting of viands the most delicate, and wines as fragrant as they were fine, drunk out of jewelled cups; and, when it drew towards its conclusion, harps and lutes were heard in the distance, and one of the ladies said in the knight's ear: "This house and all that you see in it are yours; for you alone was it built, and the builder is a queen. Happy indeed must you think yourself, for she loves you, and she is the greatest beauty in the world. Her name is Angelica."

The moment Rinaldo heard the name he so detested, he started up, with a changed countenance, and, in spite of all that the lady could say, broke off across the garden, and never ceased hastening till he reached the place where he landed. The bark was still on the shore. He sprang into it, and pushed off, though he saw nobody in it but himself. It was in vain for him to try to control its movements, for it dashed on as if in fury, till it reached a distant shore covered with a gloomy forest. Here Rinaldo, surrounded by enchantments of a very different sort from those which he had lately resisted, was entrapped into a pit.

The pit belonged to a castle called Altaripa, which was hung with human heads, and painted red with blood. As the paladin was viewing the scene with amazement, a hideous old woman made her appearance at the edge of the pit, and told him that he was destined to be thrown to a monster, who was only kept from devastating the whole country by being supplied with living human flesh. Rinaldo said, "Be it so; let me but remain armed as I am, and I fear nothing." The old woman laughed in derision. Rinaldo remained in the pit all night, and the next morning was taken to the place where the monster had his den. It was a court surrounded by a high wall. Rinaldo was shut in with the beast, and a terrible combat ensued. Rinaldo was unable to make any impression on the scales of the monster, while he, on the contrary, with his dreadful claws, tore away plate and mail from the paladin. Rinaldo began to think his last hour was come, and cast his eyes around and above to see if there was any means of escape. He perceived a beam projecting from the wall at the height of some ten feet, and, taking a leap almost miraculous, he succeeded in reaching it, and in flinging himself up across it. Here he sat for hours, the hideous brute continually trying to reach him. All at once, he heard the sound of something coming through the air like a bird, and suddenly Angelica herself alighted on the end of the beam. She held something in her hand towards him, and spoke to him in a loving voice. But the moment Rinaldo saw her, he commanded her to go away, refused all her offers of assistance, and at length declared that, if she did not leave him, he would cast himself down to the monster and meet his fate.

Angelica, saying she would lose her life rather than displease him, departed; but first she threw to the monster a cake of wax she had prepared, and spread around him a rope knotted with nooses. The beast took the bait, and, finding his teeth glued together by the wax, vented his fury in bounds and leaps, and, soon getting entangled in the nooses, drew them tight by his struggles, so that he could scarcely move a limb.

Rinaldo, watching his chance, leapt down upon his back, seized him round the neck, and throttled him, not relaxing his grip till the beast fell dead.

Another difficulty remained to be overcome. The walls were of immense height, and the only opening in them was a grated window of such strength that he could not break the bars. In his distress Rinaldo found a file which Angelica had left on the ground, and, with the help of this, effected his deliverance.

What further adventures he met with will be told in another chapter.

4. THE SIEGE OF ALBRACCA

At the very time when Charlemagne was holding his plenary court and his great tournament, his kingdom was invaded by a mighty monarch, who was moreover so valiant and strong in battle that no one could stand against him. He was named Gradasso, and his kingdom was called Sericane. Now, as it often happens to the greatest and the richest to long for what they cannot have, and thus to lose what they already possess, this king could not rest content without Durindana, the sword of Orlando, and Bayard, the horse of Rinaldo. To obtain these he determined to war upon France, and for this purpose put in array a mighty army.

He took his way through Spain, and, after defeating Marsilius, the king of that country, in several battles, was rapidly advancing on France. Charlemagne, though Marsilius was a Saracen, and had been his enemy, yet felt it needful to succor him in this extremity from a consideration of common danger, and, with the consent of his peers, despatched Rinaldo with a strong body of soldiers against Gradasso.

There was much fighting, with doubtful results, and Gradasso was steadily advancing into France. But, impatient to achieve his objects, he challenged Rinaldo to single combat, to be fought on foot, and upon these conditions: If Rinaldo conquered, Gradasso agreed to give up all his prisoners and return to his own country; but if Gradasso won the day, he was to have Bayard.

The challenge was accepted, and would have been fought had it not been for the arts of Malagigi, who just then returned from Angelica's kingdom with set purpose to win Rinaldo to look with favor upon the fair princess who was dying for love of him. Malagigi drew Rinaldo away from the army, by putting on the semblance of Gradasso, and, after a short contest, pretending to fly before him, by which means Rinaldo was induced to follow him into a boat, in which he was borne away, and entangled in various adventures, as we have already related.

The army, left under the command of Ricciardetto, Rinaldo's brother, was soon joined by Charlemagne and all his peerage, but experienced a disastrous rout, and the Emperor and many of his paladins were taken prisoners. Gradasso, however, did not abuse his victory; he took Charles by the hand, seated him by his side, and told him he warred only for honor. He renounced all conquests, on condition that the Emperor should deliver to him Bayard and Durindana, both of them the property of his vassals, the former of which, as he maintained, was already forfeited to him by Rinaldo's failure to meet him as agreed. To these terms Charlemagne readily acceded.

Bayard, after the departure of his master, had been taken in charge by Ricciardetto, and sent back to Paris, where Astolpho was in command, in the absence of Charlemagne. Astolpho received with great indignation the message despatched for Bayard, and replied by a herald that "he would not surrender the horse of his kinsman Rinaldo, without a contest. If Gradasso wanted the steed, he might come and take him, and that he, Astolpho, was ready to meet him in the field."

Gradasso was only amused at this answer, for Astolpho's fame as a successful warrior was not high, and Gradasso willingly renewed with him the bargain which he had made with Rinaldo. On these conditions the battle was fought. The enchanted lance, in the hands of Astolpho, performed a new wonder; and Gradasso, the terrible Gradasso, was unhorsed.

He kept his word, set free his prisoners, and put his army on the march to return to his own country, renewing his oath, however, not to rest till he had taken from Rinaldo his horse, and from Orlando his sword, or lost his life in the attempt.

Charlemagne, full of gratitude to Astolpho, would have kept him near his person and loaded him with honors, but Astolpho preferred to seek Rinaldo, with the view of restoring to him his horse, and departed from Paris with that design.

Our story now returns to Orlando, whom we left fascinated with the sight of the sleeping beauty, who, however, escaped him while engaged in the combat with Ferrau. Having long sought her in vain through the recesses of the wood, he resolved to follow her to her father's court. Leaving, therefore, the camp of Charlemagne, he travelled long in the direction of the East, making inquiry everywhere, if, perchance, he might get tidings of the fugitive. After many adventures, he arrived one day at a place where many roads crossed, and, meeting there a courier, he asked him for news. The courier replied, that he had been despatched by Angelica to solicit the aid of Sacripant, king of Circassia, in favor of her father Galafron, who was besieged in his city, Albracca, by Agrican, king of Tartary. This Agrican had been an unsuccessful suitor to the damsel, whom he now pursued with arms. Orlando thus learned that he was within a day's journey of Albracca; and feeling now secure of Angelica, he proceeded with all speed to her city.

Thus journeying he arrived at a bridge, under which flowed a foaming river. Here a damsel met him with a goblet, and informed him that it was the usage of this bridge to present the traveller with a cup. Orlando accepted the offered cup and drank its contents. He had no sooner done so that his brain reeled, and he became unconscious of the object of his journey, and of everything else. Under the influence of this fascination he followed the damsel into a magnificent and marvellous palace. Here he found himself in company with many knights, unknown to him and to each other, though if it had not been for the Cup of Oblivion of which they all had partaken, they would have found themselves brothers in arms.

Astolpho, proceeding on his way to seek Rinaldo, splendidly dressed and equipped, as was his wont, arrived in Circassia, and found there a great army encamped under the command of Sacripant, the king of that country, who was leading it to the defence of Galafron, the father of Angelica. Sacripant, much struck by the appearance of Astolpho and his horse, accosted him courteously, and tried to enlist him in his service; but Astolpho, proud of his late victories, scornfully declined his offers, and pursued his way. King Sacripant was too much attracted by his appearance to part with him so easily, and, having laid aside his kingly ornaments, set out in pursuit of him.

Astolpho next day encountered on his way a stranger

knight, named Sir Florismart, Lord of the Sylvan Tower, one of the bravest and best of knights, having as his guide a damsel, young, fair, and virtuous, to whom he was tenderly attached, whose name was Flordelis. Astolpho, as he approached, defied the knight, bidding him yield the lady, or prepare to maintain his right by arms. Florismart accepted the contest, and the knights encountered. Florismart was unhorsed and his steed fell dead, while Bayard sustained no injury by the shock.

Florismart was so overwhelmed with despair at his own disgrace and the sight of the damsel's distress, that he drew his sword, and was about to plunge it into his own bosom. But Astolpho held his hand, told him that he contended only for glory, and was contented to leave him the lady.

While Florismart and Flordelis were vowing eternal gratitude, king Sacripant arrived, and coveting the damsel of the one champion as much as the horse and arms of the other, defied them to the joust. Astolpho met the challenger, whom he instantly overthrew, and presented his courser to Florismart, leaving the king to return to his army on foot.

The friends pursued their route, and erelong Flordelis discovered, by signs which were known to her, that they were approaching the waters of Oblivion, and advised them to turn back, or to change their course. This the knights would not hear of, and, continuing their march, they soon arrived at the bridge where Orlando had been taken prisoner.

The damsel of the bridge appeared as before with the enchanted cup, but Astolpho, forewarned, rejected it with scorn. She dashed it to the ground, and a fire blazed up which rendered the bridge unapproachable. At the same moment the two knights were assailed by sundry warriors, known and unknown, who, having no recollection of anything, joined blindly in defence of their prison-house. Among these was Orlando, at sight of whom Astolpho, with all his confidence not daring to encounter him, turned and fled, owing his escape to the strength and fleetness of Bayard.

Florismart, meanwhile, overlaid by fearful odds, was compelled to yield to necessity, and comply with the usage of the fairy. He drank of the cup, and remained prisoner with the rest. Flordelis, deprived of her two friends, retired from the scene, and devoted herself to untiring efforts to effect her lover's deliverance. Astolpho pursued his way to Albracca, which Agrican was about to besiege. He was kindly welcomed by Angelica, and enrolled among her defenders. Impatient to distinguish himself, he one night sallied forth alone, arrived in Agrican's camp, and unhorsed his warriors right and left by means of the enchanted lance. But he was soon surrounded and overmatched, and made prisoner to Agrican.

Relief was, however, at hand; for as the citizens and soldiers were one day leaning over their walls, they descried a cloud of dust, from which horsemen were seen to prick forth, as it rolled on towards the camp of the beseigers. This turned out to be the army of Sacripant, which immediately attacked that of Agrican, with the view of cutting a passage through his camp to the besieged city. But Agrican, mounted upon Bayard, taken from Astolpho, but not armed with the lance of gold, the virtues of which were unknown to him, performed wonders, and rallied his scattered troops, which had given way to the sudden and unexpected assault. Sacripant, on the other hand, encouraged his men by the most desperate acts of valor, having as an additional incentive to his courage the sight of Angelica, who showed herself upon the city walls.

There she witnessed a single combat between the two leaders, Agrican and Sacripant. In this, at length, her defender appeared to be overmatched, when the Circassians broke the ring, and separated the combatants, who were borne asunder in the rush. Sacripant, severely wounded, profited by the confusion, and escaped into Albracca, where he was kindly received and carefully tended by Angelica.

The battle continuing, the Circassians were at last put to flight, and, being intercepted between the enemy's lines and the town, sought for refuge under the walls. Angelica ordered the drawbridge to be let down, and the gates thrown open to the fugitives. With these Agrican, not distinguished in the crowd, entered the place, driving both Circassians and Cathayans before him, and the portcullis being dropped, he was shut in.

For a time the terror which he inspired put to flight all opposers, but when at last it came to be known that few or none of his followers had effected an entrance with him, the fugitives rallied and surrounded him on all sides. While he was thus apparently reduced to the last extremities, he was saved by the very circumstance which threatened him with destruction. The soldiers of Angelica, closing upon him from all sides, deserted their defences; and his own besieging army entered the city in a part where the wall was broken down.

In this way was Agrican rescued, the city taken, and the inhabitants put to the sword. Angelica, however, with some of the knights who were her defenders, among whom was Sacripant, saved herself in the citadel, which was planted upon a rock.

The fortress was impregnable, but it was scantily victualled, and ill provided with other necessaries. Under these circumstances, Angelica announced to those blockaded with her in the citadel her intention to go in quest of assistance, and, having plighted her promise of a speedy return, she set out, with the enchanted ring upon her finger. Mounted upon her palfrey, the damsel passed through the enemy's lines, and by sunrise was many miles clear of their encampment.

It so happened that her road led her near the fatal bridge of Oblivion, and, as she approached it, she met a damsel weeping bitterly. It was Flordelis, whose lover, Florismart, as we have related, had met the fate of Orlando and many more, and fallen a victim to the enchantress of the cup. She related her adventures to Angelica, and conjured her to lend what aid she might to rescue her lord and his companions. Angelica, accordingly, watching her opportunity and aided by her ring, slipped into the castle unseen, when the door was opened to admit a new victim. Here she speedily disenchanted Orlando and the rest by a touch of her talisman. But Florismart was not there. He had been given up to Falerina, a more powerful enchantress, and was still in durance. Angelica conjured the rescued captives to assist her in the recovery of her kingdom, and all departed together for Albracca.

The arrival of Orlando, with his companions, nine in all, and among the bravest knights of France, changed at once the fortunes of the war. Wherever the great paladin came, pennon and standard fell before him. Agrican in vain attempted to rally his troops. Orlando kept constantly in his front, forcing him to attend to nobody else. The Tartar king at length bethought him of a stratagem. He turned his horse, and made a show of flying in despair. Orlando dashed after him as he desired, and Agrican fled till he reached a green place in a wood, where there was a fountain.

The place was beautiful, and the Tartar dismounted to refresh himself at the fountain, but without taking off his helmet, or laying aside any of his armor. Orlando was quickly at his back, crying out, "So bold, and yet a fugitive! How could you fly from a single arm, and think to escape?"

The Tartar king had leaped on his saddle the moment he saw his enemy, and when the paladin had done speaking, he said, in a mild voice, "Without doubt you are the best knight I ever encountered, and fain would I leave you untouched for your own sake, if you would cease to hinder me from rallying my people. I pretended to fly, in order to bring you out of the field. If you insist upon fighting, I must needs fight and slay you, but I call the sun in the heavens to witness I would rather not. I should be very sorry for your death."

The Count Orlando felt pity for so much gallantry, and he said, "The nobler you show yourself, the more it grieves me to think that, in dying without a knowledge of the true faith, you will be lost in the other world. Let me advise you to save body and soul at once. Receive baptism, and go your way in peace."

Agrican replied: "I suspect you to be the paladin Orlando. If you are, I would not lose this opportunity of fighting with you to be king of Paradise. Talk to me no more about your things of another world for you will preach in vain. Each of us for himself, and let the sword be umpire."

The Saracen drew his sword, boldly advancing upon Orlando, and a combat began, so obstinate and so long, each warrior being a miracle of prowess, that the story says it lasted from noon till night. Orlando then, seeing the stars come out, was the first to propose a respite.

"What are we to do," said he, "now that daylight has left us?"

Agrican answered readily enough, "Let us repose in this meadow, and renew the combat at dawn."

The repose was taken accordingly. Each tied up his horse, and reclined himself on the grass, not far from the other, just as if they had been friends, Orlando by the fountain,

Agrican beneath a pine. It was a beautiful clear night, and, as they talked together before addressing themselves to sleep, the champion of Christendom, looking up at the firmament, said, "That is a fine piece of workmanship, that starry spectacle; God made it all, that moon of silver, and those stars of gold, and the light of day, and the sun,—all for the sake of human kind."

"You wish, I see, to talk of matters of faith," said the Tartar. "Now I may as well tell you at once, that I have no sort of skill in such matters, nor learning of any kind. I never could learn anything when I was a boy. I hated it so that I broke the man's head who was commissioned to teach me; and it produced such an effect on others, that nobody ever afterwards dared so much as show me a book. My boyhood was therefore passed, as it should be, in horsemanship and hunting, and learning to fight. What is the good of a gentleman's poring all day over a book? Prowess to the knight, and preaching to the clergyman, that is my motto."

"I acknowledge," returned Orlando, "that arms are the first consideration of a gentleman; but not at all that he does himself dishonor by knowledge. On the contrary, knowledge is as great an embellishment of the rest of his attainments, as the flowers are to the meadow before us; and as to the knowledge of his Maker, the man that is without it is no better than a stock or a stone or a brute beast. Neither without study can he reach anything of a due sense of the depth and divineness of the contemplation."

"Learned or not learned," said Agrican, "you might show yourself better bred than by endeavoring to make me talk on a subject on which you have me at a disadvantage. If you choose to sleep, I wish you good night; but if you prefer talking, I recommend you to talk of fighting or of fair ladies. And, by the way, pray tell me, are you not that Orlando who makes such a noise in the world? And what is it, pray, that brings you into these parts? Were you ever in love? I suppose you must have been; for to be a knight, and never to have been in love, would be like being a man without a heart in his breast."

The Count replied: "Orlando I am, and in love I am. Love has made me abandon everything, and brought me into these distant regions, and, to tell you all in one word, my heart is in the hands of the daughter of King Galafron.

You have come against him with fire and sword, to get possession of his castles and his dominions; and I have come to help him, for no object in the world but to please his daughter and win her beautiful hand. I care for nothing else in existence."

Now when the Tartar king, Agrican, heard his antagonist speak in this manner, and knew him to be indeed Orlando, and to be in love with Angelica, his face changed color for grief and jealousy, though it could not be seen for the darkness. His heart began beating with such violence that he felt as if he should have died. "Well," said he to Orlando, "we are to fight when it is daylight, and one or other is to be left here, dead on the ground. I have a proposal to make to you,—nay, an entreaty. My love is so excessive for the same lady, that I beg of you to leave her to me. I will owe you my thanks, and give up the siege and put an end to the war. I cannot bear that any one should love her, and that I should live to see it. Why, therefore, should either of us perish? Give her up. Not a soul shall know it."

"I never yet," answered Orlando, "made a promise which I did not keep, and nevertheless I own to you that, were I to make a promise like that, and even swear to keep it, I should not. You might as well ask me to tear away the limbs from my body, and the eyes out of my head. I could as well live without breath itself as cease loving Angelica."

Agrican had hardly patience to let him finish speaking, ere he leapt furiously on horseback, though it was midnight. "Quit her," said he, "or die!"

Orlando seeing the infidel getting up, and not being sure that he would not add treachery to fierceness, had been hardly less quick in mounting for the combat. "Never," exclaimed he; "I never could have quitted her if I would, and now I would not if I could. You must seek her by other means than these."

Fiercely dashed their horses together, in the night-time, on the green mead. Despiteful and terrible were the blows they gave and took by the moonlight. Agrican fought in a rage, Orlando was cooler. And now the struggle had lasted more than five hours, and day began to dawn, when the Tartar king, furious to find so much trouble given him, dealt his enemy a blow sharp and violent beyond conception. It cut the shield in two as if it had been made of wood, and, though blood could not be drawn from Orlando, because he was fated, it shook and bruised him as if it had started every joint in his body.

His *body* only, however, not a particle of his soul. So dreadful was the blow which the paladin gave in return, that not only shield, but every bit of mail on the body of Agrican was broken in pieces, and three of his ribs cut asunder.

The Tartar, roaring like a lion, raised his sword with still greater vehemence than before, and dealt a blow on the paladin's helmet, such as he had never yet received from mortal man. For a moment it took away his senses. His sight failed, his ears tinkled, his frightened horse turned about to fly; and he was falling from the saddle, when the very action of falling threw his head upwards, and thus recalled his recollection.

"What a shame is this!" thought he; "how shall I ever again dare to face Angelica! I have been fighting, hour after hour, with this man, and he is but one, and I call myself Orlando! If the combat last any longer, I will bury myself in a monastery, and never look on sword again."

Orlando muttered with his lips closed and his teeth ground together; and you might have thought that fire instead of breath came out of his nose and mouth. He raised his sword Durindana with both his hands, and sent it down so tremendously on Agrican's shoulder, that it cut through breastplate down to the very haunch, nay, crushed the saddle-bow, though it was made of bone and iron, and felled man and horse to the earth. Agrican turned as white as ashes, and felt death upon him. He called Orlando to come close to him, with a gentle voice, and said, as well as he could: "I believe on Him who died on the cross. Baptize me, I pray thee, with the fountain, before my senses are gone. I have lived an evil life, but need not be rebellious to God in death also. May He who came to save all the rest of the world, save me!" And he shed tears, that great king, though he had been so lofty and fierce.

Orlando dismounted quickly, with his own face in tears. He gathered the king tenderly in his arms, and took and laid him by the fountain, on a marble rim that it had, and then he wept in concert with him heartily, and asked his pardon, and so baptized him in the water of the fountain, and knelt and prayed to God for him with joined hands.

He then paused and looked at him; and when he perceived his countenance changed, and that his whole person
was cold, he left him there on the marble rim of the fountain, all armed as he was, with the sword by his side, and
the crown upon his head.

5. ASTOLPHO IN ABYSSINIA

*The paladin Astolpho has had an adventure with the beauti-
ful sorceress Alcina, who is much like Circe of the Greek
myths. Following this, he is now embarked on a flight over
the countries of the world, mounted upon a Hippogriff.
This beast had the head of an eagle, claws armed with talons, and wings covered with feathers, the rest of his body
being that of a horse. Orlando, meanwhile, has gone mad.
One of the fruits of the adventure which follows is finding
the means to cure Orlando's madness. Another is to procure
relief for Charlemagne who is repelling an invasion of
France.*

The eagle and the falcon have not so swift a flight as the
Hippogriff on which Astolpho rode. It was not long, therefore, before the paladin, directing his course toward the
southeast, arrived over that part of Africa where the great
river Nile has its source. Here he alighted, and found himself in the neighborhood of the capital of Abyssinia, ruled
by Senapus, whose riches and power were immense. His
palace was of surpassing splendor; the bars of the gates,
the hinges and locks, were all of pure gold; in fact this
metal, in that country, is put to all those uses for which we
employ iron. It is so common that they prefer for ornamental purposes rock crystal, of which all the columns were
made. Precious stones of different kinds, rubies, emeralds,
sapphires, and topazes were set in ornamental designs, and
the walls and ceilings were adorned with pearls.

It is in this country those famous balms grow of which
there are some few plants in that part of Judaea called
Gilead. Musk, ambergris, and numerous gums, so precious

in Europe, are here in their native climate. It is said the
Sultan of Egypt pays a vast tribute to the monarch of this
country to hire him not to cut off the source of the Nile,
which he might easily do, and cause the river to flow in some
other direction, thus depriving Egypt of the source of its
fertility.

At the time of Astolpho's arrival in his dominions, this
monarch was in great affliction. In spite of his riches and
the precious productions of his country, he was in danger of
dying of hunger. He was a prey to a flock of obscene birds
called Harpies, which attacked him whenever he sat at meat,
and with their claws snatched, tore, and scattered everything, overturning the vessels, devouring the food, and in-
fecting what they left with their filthy touch. It was said this
punishment was inflicted upon the king because when
young, and filled with pride and presumption, he had attempted to invade with an army the terrestrial paradise,
which is situated on the top of a mountain whence the Nile
draws its source. Nor was this his only punishment. He was
struck blind.

Astolpho, on arriving in the dominions of this monarch,
hastened to pay him his respects. King Senapus received him
graciously, and ordered a splendid repast to be prepared in
honor of his arrival. While the guests were seated at table,
Astolpho filling the place of dignity at the king's right hand,
the horrid scream of the Harpies was heard in the air, and
soon they approached, hovering over the tables, seizing the
food from the dishes, and overturning everything with the
flapping of their broad wings. In vain the guests struck at
them with knives and any weapons which they had, and
Astolpho drew his sword and gave them repeated blows,
which seemed to have no more effect upon them than if
their bodies had been made of tow.

At last Astolpho thought of his horn. He first gave warning to the king and his guests to stop their ears; then blew
a blast. The Harpies, terrified at the sound, flew away as
fast as their wings could carry them. The paladin mounted
his Hippogriff, and pursued them, blowing his horn as often
as he came near them. They stretched their flight towards the
great mountain, at the foot of which there is a cavern, which
is thought to be the mouth of the infernal abodes. Hither
those horrid birds flew, as if to their home. Having seen

them all disappear in the recess, Astolpho cared not to pursue them farther, but, alighting, rolled huge stones into the mouth of the cave, and piled branches of trees therein, so that he effectually barred their passage out, and we have no evidence of their ever having been seen since in the outer air.

After this labor, Astolpho refreshed himself by bathing in a fountain whose pure waters bubbled from a cleft of the rock. Having rested awhile, an earnest desire seized him of ascending the mountain which towered above him. The Hippogriff bore him swiftly upwards, and landed him on the top of the mountain, which he found to be an extensive plain.

A splendid palace rose in the middle of this plain, whose walls shone with such brilliancy that mortal eyes could hardly bear the sight. Astolpho guided the winged horse towards this edifice, and made him poise himself in the air while he took a leisurely survey of this favored spot and its environs. It seemed as if nature and art had striven with one another to see which could do the most for its embellishment.

Astolpho, on approaching the edifice, saw a venerable man advance to meet him. This personage was clothed in a long vesture as white as snow, while a mantle of purple covered his shoulders, and hung down to the ground. A white beard descended to his middle, and his hair, of the same color, overshadowed his shoulders. His eyes were so brilliant, that Astolpho felt persuaded that he was a blessed inhabitant of the heavenly mansions.

The sage, smiling benignantly upon the paladin, who from respect had dismounted from his horse, said to him: "Noble chevalier, know that it is by the Divine will you have been brought to the terrestrial paradise. Your mortal nature could not have borne to scale these heights and reach these seats of bliss if it were not the will of Heaven that you should be instructed in the means to succor Charles, and to sustain the glory of our holy faith. I am prepared to impart the needed counsels; but before I begin, let me welcome you to our sojourn. I doubt not your long fast and distant journey have given you a good appetite."

The aspect of the venerable man filled the prince with admiration; but his surprise ceased when he learned from him that he was that one of the Apostles of our Lord to whom he said, "I will that thou tarry till I come."

St. John, conducting Astolpho, rejoined his companions. These were the patriarch Enoch and the prophet Elijah; neither of whom had yet seen his dying day, but, taken from our lower world, were dwelling in a region of peace and joy, in a climate of eternal spring, till the last trumpet shall sound.

The three holy inhabitants of the terrestrial paradise received Astolpho with the greatest kindness, carried him to a pleasant apartment, and took great care of the Hippogriff, to whom they gave such food as suited him, while to the prince they presented fruits so delicious that he felt inclined to excuse our first parents for their sin in eating them without permission.

Astolpho, having recruited his strength, not only by these excellent fruits, but also by sweet sleep, roused himself at the first blush of dawn, and, as soon as he left his chamber, met the beloved Apostle coming to seek him. St. John took him by the hand, and told him many things relating to the past and the future. Among others, he said, "Son, let me tell you what is now going on in France. Orlando, the illustrious prince who received at his birth the endowment of strength and courage more than mortal, raised up as was Samson of old to be the champion of the true faith, has been guilty of the basest ingratitude in leaving the Christian camp when it most needed the support of his arm, to run after a Saracen princess, whom he would fain marry, though she scorns him. To punish him, his reason has been taken away, so that he runs naked through the land, over mountains and through valleys, without a ray of intelligence. The duration of his punishment has been fixed at three months, and that time having nearly expired, you have been brought hither to learn from us the means by which the reason of Orlando may be restored. True, you will be obliged to make a journey with me, and we must even leave the earth, and ascend to the moon, for it is in that planet we are to seek the remedy for the madness of the paladin. I propose to make our journey this evening, as soon as the moon appears over our head."

As soon as the sun sunk beneath the seas, and the moon presented its luminous disk, the holy man had the chariot brought out in which he was accustomed to make excursions among the stars, the same which was employed long ago to convey Elijah up from earth. The saint made Astolpho seat himself beside him, took the reins, and giving the word to the coursers, they bore them upward with astonishing celerity.

At length they reached the great continent of the Moon. Its surface appeared to be of polished steel, with here and there a spot which, like rust, obscured its brightness. The paladin was astonished to see that the earth, with all its seas and rivers, seemed but an insignificant spot in the distance.

The prince discovered in this region so new to him rivers, lakes, plains, hills, and valleys. Many beautiful cities and castles enriched the landscape. He saw also vast forests, and heard in them the sound of horns and the barking of dogs, which led him to conclude that the nymphs were following the chase.

The knight, filled with wonder at all he saw, was conducted by the saint to a valley, where he stood amazed at the riches strewed all around him. Well he might be so, for that valley was the receptacle of things lost on earth, either by men's fault, or by the effect of time and chance. Let no one suppose we speak here of kingdoms or of treasures; they are the toys of Fortune, which she dispenses in turning her wheel; we speak of things which she can neither give nor take away. Such are reputations, which appear at one time so brilliant, and a short time after are heard of no more. Here, also, are countless vows and prayers for unattainable objects, lovers' sighs and tears, time spent in gaming, dressing, and doing nothing, the leisure of the dull and the intentions of the lazy, baseless projects, intrigues and plots; these and such like things fill all the valley.

Astolpho had a great desire to understand all that he saw, and which appeared to him so extraordinary. Among the rest, he observed a great mountain of blown bladders, from which issued indistinct noises. The saint told him these were the dynasties of Assyrian and Persian kings, once the wonder of the earth, of which now scarce the name remains.

Astolpho could not help laughing when the saint said to him, "All these hooks of silver and gold that you see are the gifts of courtiers to princes, made in the hope of getting something better in return." He also showed him garlands of flowers in which snares were concealed; these were flatteries and adulations, meant to deceive. But nothing was so comical as the sight of numerous grasshoppers which had burst their lungs with chirping. These, he told him, were sonnets, odes, and dedications, addressed by venal poets to great people.

The paladin beheld with wonder what seemed a lake of spilled milk. "It is," said the saint, "the charity done by frightened misers on their death-beds." It would take too long to tell all that the valley contained: meannesses, affectations, pretended virtues, and concealed vices were there in abundance.

Among the rest, Astolpho perceived many days of his own lost, and many imprudent sallies which he had made, and would have been glad not to have been reminded of. But he also saw among so many lost things a great abundance of one thing which men are apt to think they all possess, and do not think it necessary to pray for,—good sense. This commodity appeared under the form of a liquor, most light and apt to evaporate. It was therefore kept in vials, firmly sealed. One of these was labelled, "The sense of the Paladin Orlando."

All the bottles were ticketed, and the sage placed one in Astolpho's hand, which he found was his own. It was more than half full. He was surprised to find there many other vials which contained almost the whole of the wits of many persons who passed among men for wise. Ah, how easy it is to lose one's reason! Some lose theirs by yielding to the sway of the passions; some, in braving tempests and shoals in search of wealth; some, by trusting too much to the promises of the great; some, by setting their hearts on trifles. As might have been expected, the bottles which held the wits of astrologers, inventors, metaphysicians, and above all, of poets, were in general the best filled of all.

Astolpho took his bottle, put it to his nose, and inhaled it all; and Turpin assures us that he was for a long time afterwards as sage as one could wish; but the Archbishop adds, that there was reason to fear that some of the precious fluid afterwards found its way back into the bottle. The paladin took also the bottle which belonged to Orlando. It was a large one, and quite full.

Before quitting the planetary region, Astolpho was conducted to an edifice on the borders of a river. He was shown an immense hall full of bundles of silk, linen, cotton, and wool. A thousand different colors, brilliant or dull, some quite black, were among these skeins. In one part of the hall an old woman was busy winding off yarns from all these different bundles. When she had finished a skein, another ancient dame took it and placed it with others; a third selected from the fleeces spun, and mingled them in due proportions. The paladin inquired what all this might be. "These old women," said the saint, "are the Fates, who spin, measure, and terminate the lives of mortals. As long as the thread stretches in one of those skeins, so long does the mortal enjoy the light of day; but nature and death are on the alert to shut the eyes of those whose thread is spun."

Each one of the skeins had a label of gold, silver, or iron, bearing the name of the individual to whom it belonged. An old man, who, in spite of the burden of years, seemed brisk and active, ran without ceasing to fill his apron with these labels, and carried them away to throw them into the river, whose name was Lethe. When he reached the shore of the river, the old man shook out his apron, and the labels sunk to the bottom. A small number only floated for a time, hardly one in a thousand. Numberless birds, hawks, crows, and vultures hovered over the stream, with clamorous cries, and strove to snatch from the water some of these names; but they were too heavy for them, and after a while the birds were forced to let them drop into the river of oblivion. But two beautiful swans, of snowy whiteness, gathered some few of the names, and returned with them to the shore, where a lovely nymph received them from their beaks, and carried them to a temple placed upon a hill, and suspended them for all time upon a sacred column, on which stood the statue of Immortality.

Astolpho was amazed at all this, and asked his guide to explain it. He replied, "The old man is Time. All the names upon the tickets would be immortal if the old man did not plunge them into the river of oblivion. Those clamorous birds which make vain efforts to save certain of the names are flatterers, pensioners, venal rhymesters, who do their best to rescue from oblivion the unworthy names of their patrons; but all in vain; they may keep them from their fate a little while, but erelong the river of oblivion must swallow them all.

"The swans, that with harmonious strains carry certain names to the temple of Eternal Memory, are the great poets, who save from oblivion worse than death the names of those they judge worthy of immortality. Swans of this kind are rare. Let monarchs know the true breed, and fail not to nourish with care such as may chance to appear in their time."

6. THE WAR IN AFRICA

When Astolpho had descended to the earth with the precious phial, St. John showed him a plant of marvellous virtues, with which he told him he had only to touch the eyes of the king of Abyssinia to restore him to sight. "That important service," said the saint, "added to your having delivered him from the Harpies, will induce him to give you an army wherewith to attack the Africans in their rear, and force them to return from France to defend their own country." The saint also instructed him how to lead his troops in safety across the great deserts, where caravans are often overwhelmed with moving columns of sand. Astolpho, fortified with ample instructions, remounted the Hippogriff, thanked the saint, received his blessing, and took his flight down to the level country.

Keeping the course of the river Nile, he soon arrived at the capital of Abyssinia, and rejoined Senapus. The joy of the king was great when he heard again the voice of the hero who had delivered him from the Harpies. Astolpho touched his eyes with the plant which he had brought from the terrestrial paradise, and restored their sight. The king's gratitude was unbounded. He begged him to name a reward, promising to grant it, whatever it might be. Astolpho asked an army to go to the assistance of Charlemagne, and the king not only granted him a hundred thousand men, but offered to lead them himself.

The night before the day appointed for the departure of the troops, Astolpho mounted his winged horse, and directed his flight towards a mountain, whence the fierce South-wind issues, whose blast raises the sands of the Nubian desert, and whirls them onward in overwhelming clouds. The paladin, by the advice of St. John, had prepared himself with a leather bag, which he placed adroitly, with its mouth open, over the vent which issues this terrible wind. At the first dawn of morning the wind rushed from its cavern to resume its daily course, and was caught in the bag, and securely tied up. Astolpho, delighted with his prize, returned to his army, placed himself at their head, and commenced his march. The Abyssinians traversed without danger or difficulty those vast fields of sand which separate their country from the kingdoms of Northern Africa, for the terrible South-wind, taken completely captive, had not force enough left to blow out a candle.

Senapus was distressed that he could not furnish any cavalry, for his country, rich in camels and elephants, was destitute of horses. This difficulty the saint had foreseen, and had taught Astolpho the means of remedying. He now put those means in operation. Having reached a place whence he beheld a vast plain and the sea, he chose from his troops those who appeared to be the best made and the most intelligent. These he caused to be arranged in squadrons at the foot of a lofty mountain which bordered the plain, and he himself mounted to the summit to carry into effect his great design. Here he found vast quantities of fragments of rock and pebbles. These he set rolling down the mountain's side, and, wonderful to relate, as they rolled they grew in size, made themselves bodies, legs, necks, and long faces. Next they began to neigh, to curvet, to scamper on all sides over the plain. Some were bay, some roan, some dapple, some chestnut. The troops at the foot of the mountain exerted themselves to catch these new-created horses, which they easily did, for the miracle had been so considerate as to provide all the horses with bridles and saddles. Astolpho thus suddenly found himself supplied with an excellent corps of cavalry, not fewer (as Archbishop Turpin asserts) than eighty thousand strong. With these troops Astolpho reduced all the country to subjection, and at last arrived before the walls of Agramant's capital city, Biserta, to which he laid siege.

We will now return to Orlando, whom we last heard of as furiously mad, and doing a thousand acts of violence in his senseless rage. One day he came to the borders of a stream which intercepted his course. He swam across it, for he could swim like an otter, and on the other side saw a peasant watering his horse. He seized the animal, in spite of the resistance of the peasant, and rode it with furious speed till he arrived at the sea-coast, where Spain is divided from Africa by only a narrow strait. At the moment of his arrival, a vessel had just put off to cross the strait. She was full of people who, with glass in hand, seemed to be taking a merry farewell of the land, wafted by a favorable breeze.

The frantic Orlando cried out to them to stop and take him in; but they, having no desire to admit a madman to their company, paid him no attention. The paladin thought this behavior very uncivil; and by force of blows made his horse carry him into the water in pursuit of the ship. The wretched animal soon had only his head above water; but as Orlando urged him forward, nothing was left for the poor beast but either to die or swim over to Africa.

Already Orlando had lost sight of the bark; distance and the swell of the sea completely hid it from his sight. He continued to press his horse forward, till at last it could struggle no more, and sunk beneath him. Orlando, nowise concerned, stretched out his nervous arms, puffing the salt water before his mouth, and carried his head above the waves. Fortunately they were not rough, scarce a breath of wind agitated the surface; otherwise, the invincible Orlando would then have met his death. But fortune, which it is said favors fools, delivered him from this danger, and landed him safe on the shore of Ceuta. Here he rambled along the shore till he came to where the black army of Astolpho held its camp.

Now it happened, just before this time, that a vessel filled with prisoners which Rodomont had taken at the bridge had arrived, and, not knowing of the presence of the Abyssinian army, had sailed right into port, where of course the prisoners and their captors changed places, the former being set at liberty and received with all joy, the latter sent to serve in the galleys. Astolpho thus found himself surrounded with Christian knights, and he and his friends were exchanging greetings and felicitations, when a noise was heard in the camp, and seemed to increase every moment. Astolpho and his friends seized their weapons, mounted their horses, and rode to the quarter whence the noise proceeded. Imagine their astonishment when they saw that the tumult was caused by a single man, perfectly naked, and browned with dirt and exposure, but of a force and fury so terrible that he overturned all that offered to lay hands on him.

Astolpho, Dudon, Oliver, and Florismart gazed at him with amazement. It was with difficulty they knew him. Astolpho, who had been warned of his condition by his holy monitor, was the first to recognize him. As the paladins closed round Orlando, the madman dealt one and another a blow of his fist, which, if they had not been in armor, or he had had any weapon, would probably have despatched them; as it was, Dudon and Astolpho measured their length on the sand. But Florismart seized him from behind, Sansonnet and another grasped his legs, and at last they succeeded in securing him with ropes. They took him to the water-side and washed him well, and then Astolpho, having first bandaged his mouth so that he could not breathe except through his nose, brought the precious phial, uncorked it, and placed it adroitly under his nostrils, when the good Orlando took it all up in one breath. O marvellous prodigy! The paladin recovered in an instant all his intelligence. He felt like one who had awakened from a painful dream, in which he had believed that monsters were about to tear him to pieces. He seemed prostrated, silent, and abashed. Florismart, Oliver, and Astolpho stood gazing upon him, while he turned his eyes around and on himself. He seemed surprised to find himself naked, bound, and stretched on the sea-shore. After a few moments he recognized his friends, and spoke to them in a tone so tender that they hastened to unbind him, and to supply him with garments. Then they exerted themselves to console him, to diminish the weight with which his spirits were oppressed, and to make him forget the wretched condition into which he had been sunk.

7. THE BATTLE OF RONCESVALLES

After the expulsion of the Saracens from France, Charlemagne led his army into Spain, to punish Marsilius, the king of that country, for having sided with the African Saracens in the late war. Charlemagne succeeded in all his attempts, and compelled Marsilius to submit, and pay tribute to France. Our readers will remember Gano, otherwise called Gan, or Ganelon, whom we mentioned in one of our early chapters as an old courtier of Charlemagne, and a deadly enemy of Orlando, Rinaldo, and all their friends. He had great influence over Charles, from equality of age and long intimacy; and he was not without good qualities: he was brave and sagacious, but envious, false, and treacherous. Gan prevailed on Charles to send him as ambassador to Marsilius, to arrange the tribute. He embraced Orlando over and over again at taking leave, using such pains to seem loving and sincere, that his hypocrisy was manifest to every one but the old monarch. He fastened with equal tenderness on Oliver, who smiled contemptuously in his face, and thought to himself, "You may make as many fair speeches as you choose, but you lie." All the other paladins who were present thought the same, and they said as much to the Emperor, adding, that Gan should on no account be sent ambassador to the Spaniards. But Charles was infatuated.

Gan was received with great honor by Mersilius. The king, attended by his lords, came fifteen miles out of Saragossa to meet him, and then conducted him into the city with acclamations. There was nothing for several days but balls, games, and exhibitions of chivalry, the ladies throwing flowers on the heads of the French knights, and the people shouting, "France! Mountjoy and St. Denis!"

After the ceremonies of the first reception, the king and the ambassador began to understand one another. One day they sat together in a garden on the border of a fountain. The water was so clear and smooth it reflected every object around, and the spot was encircled with fruit-trees which quivered with the fresh air. As they sat and talked, as if without restraint, Gan, without looking the king in the face, was enabled to see the expression of his countenance in the water, and governed his speech accordingly. Marsilius was equally adroit, and watched the face of Gan while he addressed him. Marsilius began by lamenting, not as to the ambassador, but as to the friend, the injuries which Charles had done him by invading his dominions, charging him with wishing to take his kingdom from him, and give it to Orlando; till at length he plainly uttered his belief that, if that ambitious paladin were but dead, good men would get their rights.

Gan heaved a sigh, as if he was unwillingly compelled to allow the force of what the king said; but, unable to contain himself long, he lifted up his face, radiant with triumphant wickedness, and exclaimed: "Every word you utter is truth; die he must, and die also must Oliver, who struck me that foul blow at court. Is it treachery to punish affronts like these? I have planned everything,—I have settled everything already with their besotted master. Orlando will come to your borders,—to Roncesvalles,—for the purpose of receiving the tribute. Charles will await him at the foot of the mountains. Orlando will bring but a small band with him: you, when you meet him, will have secretly your whole army at your back. You surround him, and who receives tribute then?"

The new Judas had scarcely uttered these words when his exultation was interrupted by a change in the face of nature. The sky was suddenly overcast, there was thunder and lightning, a laurel was split in two from head to foot, and the Carob-tree under which Gan was sitting, which is said to be the species of tree on which Judas Iscariot hung himself, dropped one of its pods on his head.

Marsilius, as well as Gan, was appalled at this omen; but on assembling his soothsayers they came to the conclusion that the laurel-tree turned the omen against the Emperor, the successor of the Caesars, though one of them renewed the consternation of Gan by saying that he did not understand the meaning of the tree of Judas, and intimating that perhaps the ambassador could explain it. Gan relieved his vexation by anger; the habit of wickedness prevailed over

all other considerations; and the king prepared to march to
Roncesvalles at the head of all his forces.

Gan wrote to Charlemagne to say how humbly and sub-
missively Marsilius was coming to pay the tribute into the
hands of Orlando, and how handsome it would be of the
Emperor to meet him halfway, and so be ready to receive
him after the payment at his camp. He added a brilliant account of the tribute, and the accompanying presents. The
good Emperor wrote in turn to say how pleased he was with
the ambassador's diligence, and that matters were arranged
precisely as he wished. His court, however, had its suspicions still, though they little thought Gan's object in bringing Charles into the neighborhood of Roncesvalles was to
deliver him into the hands of Marsilius, after Orlando
should have been destroyed by him.

Orlando, however, did as his lord and sovereign desired.
He went to Roncesvalles, accompanied by a moderate train
of warriors, not dreaming of the atrocity that awaited him.
Gan, meanwhile, had hastened back to France, in order to
show himself free and easy in the presence of Charles, and
secure the success of his plot; while Marsilius, to make as-
surance double sure, brought into the passes of Roncesvalles
no less than three armies, which were successively to fall on
the paladin in case of the worst, and so extinguish him with
numbers. He had also, by Gan's advice, brought heaps of
wine and good cheer to be set before his victims in the first
instance; "for that," said the traitor, "will render the onset
the more effective, the feasters being unarmed. One thing,
however, I must not forget," added he; "my son Baldwin is
sure to be with Orlando; you must take care of his life for
my sake."

"I give him this vesture off my own body," said the king;
"let him wear it in the battle, and have no fear. My soldiers
shall be directed not to touch him."

Gan went away rejoicing to France. He embraced the
sovereign and the court all round with the air of a man who
had brought them nothing but blessings, and the old king
wept for very tenderness and delight.

"Something is going on wrong, and looks very black,"
thought Malagigi, the good wizard; "Rinaldo is not here,
and it is indispensably necessary that he should be. I must

find out where he is and Ricciardetto too, and send for them with all speed."

Malagigi called up by his art a wise, terrible, and cruel spirit, named Ashtaroth. "Tell me, and tell me truly, of Rinaldo," said Malagigi to the spirit. The demon looked hard at the paladin, and said nothing. His aspect was clouded and violent.

The enchanter, with an aspect still cloudier, bade Ashtaroth lay down that look; and made signs as if he would resort to angrier compulsion; and the devil, alarmed, loosened his tongue, and said, "You have not told me what you desire to know of Rinaldo."

"I desire to know what he has been doing, and where he is."

"He has been conquering and baptizing the world, east and west," said the demon, "and is now in Egypt with Ricciardetto."

"And what has Gan been plotting with Marsilius?" inquired Malagigi; "and what is to come of it?"

"I know not," said the devil. "I was not attending to Gan at the time, and we fallen spirits know not the future. All I discern is that by the signs and comets in the heavens something dreadful is about to happen,—something very strange, treacherous, and bloody;—and that Gan has a seat ready prepared for him in hell."

"Within three days," cried the enchanter, loudly, "bring Rinaldo and Ricciardetto into the pass of Roncesvalles. Do it, and I hereby undertake to summon thee no more."

"Suppose they will not trust themselves with me?" said the spirit.

"Enter Rinaldo's horse, and bring him, whether he trust thee or not."

"It shall be done," returned the demon.

There was an earthquake, and Ashtaroth disappeared.

Marsilius now made his first movement towards the destruction of Orlando, by sending before him his vassal, King Blanchardin, with his presents of wines and other luxuries. The temperate but courteous hero took them in good part, and distributed them as the traitor wished; and then Blanchardin, on pretence of going forward to salute Charlemagne, returned, and put himself at the head of the second army, which was the post assigned him by his liege-lord. King Falseron, whose son Orlando had slain in battle, headed the first army, and King Balugante the third. Marsilius made a speech to them, in which he let them into his design, and concluded by recommending to their good-will the son of his friend Gan, whom they would know by the vest he had sent him, and who was the only soul amongst the Christians they were to spare.

This son of Gan, meanwhile, and several of the paladins, who distrusted the misbelievers, and were anxious at all events to be with Orlando, had joined the hero in the fated valley; so that the little Christian host, considering the tremendous valor of their lord and his friends, were not to be sold for nothing. Rinaldo, alas! the second thunderbolt of Christendom, was destined not to be there in time to meet the issue. The paladins in vain begged Orlando to be on his guard against treachery, and send for a more numerous body of men. The great heart of the Champion of the Faith was unwilling to harbor suspicion as long as he could help it. He refused to summon aid which might be superfluous; neither would he do anything but what his liege-lord had directed. And yet he could not wholly repress a misgiving. A shadow had fallen on his heart, great and cheerful as it was. The anticipations of his friends disturbed him, in spite of the face with which he met them. Perhaps by a certain foresight he felt his death approaching; but he felt bound not to encourage the impression. Besides, time pressed; the moment of the looked-for tribute was at hand, and little combinations of circumstances determine often the greatest events.

King Marsilius was to arrive early next day with the tribute, and Oliver, with the morning sun, rode forth to reconnoitre, and see if he could discover the peaceful pomp of the Spanish court in the distance. He rode up the nearest height, and from the top of it beheld the first army of Marsilius already forming in the passes. "O devil Gan," he exclaimed, "this then is the consummation of thy labors!" Oliver put spurs to his horse, and galloped back down the mountain to Orlando.

"Well," cried the hero, "what news?"

"Bad news," said his cousin, "such as you would not hear of yesterday. Marsilius is here in arms, and all the world is with him."

The paladins pressed round Orlando, and entreated him to sound his horn, in token that he needed help. His only answer was to mount his horse, and ride up the mountain with Sansonetto.

As soon, however, as he cast forth his eyes, and beheld what was round about him, he turned in sorrow, and looked down into Roncesvalles, and said, "O miserable valley! the blood shed in thee this day will color thy name forever."

Orlando's little camp were furious against the Saracens. They armed themselves with the greatest impatience. There was nothing but lacing of helmets and mounting of horses, while good Archbishop Turpin went from rank to rank exhorting and encouraging the warriors of Christ. Orlando and his captains withdrew for a moment of consultation. He fairly groaned for sorrow, and at first had not a word to say; so wretched he felt at having brought his people to die in Roncesvalles. Then he said: "If it had entered into my heart to conceive the king of Spain to be such a villain, never would you have seen this day. He has exchanged with me a thousand courtesies and good words; and I thought that the worse enemies we had been before, the better friends we had become now. I fancied every human being capable of this kind of virtue on a good opportunity, saying, indeed, such base-hearted wretches as can never forgive their very forgivers; and of these I did not suppose him to be one. Let us die, if die we must, like honest and gallant men, so that it shall be said of us, it was only our bodies that died. The reason why I did not sound the horn was partly because I thought it did not become us, and partly because our liege-lord could hardly save us, even if he heard it." And with these words Orlando sprang to his horse, crying, "Away, against the Saracens!" But he had no sooner turned his face, than he wept bitterly, and said, "O Holy Virgin, think not of me, the sinner Orlando, but have pity on these thy servants!"

And now, with a mighty dust, and an infinite sound of horns and tambours which came filling the valley, the first army of the infidels made its appearance, horses neighing, and a thousand pennons flying in the air. King Falseron led them on, saying to his officers: "Let nobody dare to lay a finger on Orlando. He belongs to myself. The revenge of my son's death is mine. I will cut the man down that comes between us."

"Now, friends," said Orlando, "every man for himself, and St. Michael for us all! There is not one here that is not a perfect knight." And he might well say it, for the flower of all France was there, except Rinaldo and Ricciardetto,— every man a picked man, all friends and constant companions of Orlando.

So the captains of the little troop and of the great army sat looking at one another, and singling one another out as the latter came on, and then the knights put spear in rest, and ran for a while two and two in succession, one against the other.

Astolpho was the first to move. He ran against Arlotto of Soria, and thrust his antagonist's body out of the saddle, and his soul into the other world. Oliver encountered Malprimo, and, though he received a thrust which hurt him, sent his lance right through the heart of Malprimo.

Falseron was daunted at this blow. "Truly," thought he, "this is a marvel." Oliver did not press on among the Saracens, his wound was too painful; but Orlando now put himself and his whole band in motion, and you may guess what an uproar ensued. The sound of the rattling of blows and helmets was as if the forge of Vulcan had been thrown open. Falseron beheld Orlando coming so furiously, that he thought him a Lucifer who had burst his chain, and was quite of another mind than when he purposed to have him all to himself. On the contrary, he recommended himself to his gods, and turned away, meaning to wait for a more auspicious season of revenge. But Orlando hailed him, with a terrible voice, saying, "O thou traitor! was this the end to which old quarrels were made up?" Then he dashed at Falseron with a fury so swift, and at the same time with a mastery of his lance so marvellous, that, though he plunged it in the man's body so as instantly to kill him, and then withdrew it, the body did not move in the saddle. The hero himself, as he rushed onwards, was fain to see the end of a stroke so perfect, and turning his horse back, touched the carcass with his sword, and it fell on the instant!

When the infidels beheld their leader dead, such fear fell

upon them that they were for leaving the field to the paladins, but they were unable. Marsilius had drawn the rest of his forces round the valley like a net, so that their shoulders were turned in vain. Orlando rode into the thick of them, and wherever he went thunderbolts fell upon helmets. Oliver was again in the fray, with Walter and Baldwin, Avino and Avolio, while Archbishop Turpin had changed his crosier for a lance, and chased a new flock before him to the mountains.

Yet what could be done against foes without number? Marsilius constantly pours them in. The paladins are as units to thousands. Why tarry the horses of Rinaldo and Ricciardetto?

The horses did not tarry, but fate had been quicker than enchantment. Ashtaroth had presented himself to Rinaldo in Egypt, and, after telling his errand, he and Foul-mouth, his servant, entered the horses of Rinaldo and Ricciardetto, which began to neigh, and snort, and leap with the fiends within them, till off they flew through the air over the pyramids and across the desert, and reached Spain and the scene of action just as Marsilius brought up his third army. The two paladins on their horses dropped right into the midst of the Saracens, and began making such havoc among them that Marsilius, who overlooked the fight from a mountain, thought his soldiers had turned against one another. Orlando beheld it, and guessed it could be no other but his cousins, and pressed to meet them. Oliver coming up at the same moment, the rapture of the whole party is not to be expressed. After a few hasty words of explanation they were forced to turn again upon the enemy, whose numbers seemed perfectly without limit.

Orlando, making a bloody passage towards Marsilius, struck a youth on the head, whose helmet was so strong as to resist the blow, but at the same time flew off. Orlando prepared to strike a second blow, when the youth exclaimed, "Hold! you loved my father; I am Bujaforte!" The paladin had never seen Bujaforte, but he saw the likeness to the good old man, his father, and he dropped his sword. "O Bujaforte," said he, "I loved him indeed; but what does his son do here fighting against his friends?"

Bujaforte could not at once speak for weeping. At length he said: "I am forced to be here by my lord and master,

Marsilius; and I have made a show of fighting, but have not hurt a single Christian. Treachery is on every side of you. Baldwin himself has a vest given him by Marsilius, that everybody may know the son of his friend Gan, and do him no harm."

"Put your helmet on again," said Orlando, "and behave just as you have done. Never will your father's friend be an enemy to the son."

The hero then turned in fury to look for Baldwin, who was hastening towards him, at that moment, with friendliness in his looks.

" 'Tis strange," said Baldwin, "I have done my duty as well as I could, yet nobody will come against me. I have slain right and left, and cannot comprehend what it is that makes the stoutest infidels avoid me."

"Take off your vest," said Orlando, contemptuously, "and you will soon discover the secret, if you wish to know it. Your father has sold us to Marsilius, all but his honorable son."

"If my father," said Baldwin, impetuously tearing off the vest, "has been such a villain, and I escape dying, I will plunge this sword through his heart. But I am no traitor, Orlando, and you do me wrong to say it. Think not I can live with dishonor."

Baldwin spurred off into the fight, not waiting to hear another word from Orlando, who was very sorry for what he had said, for he perceived that the youth was in despair.

And now the fight raged beyond all it had done before; twenty pagans went down for one paladin, but still the paladins fell. Sansonetto was beaten to earth by the club of Grandonio, Walter d'Amulion had his shoulder broken, Berlinghieri and Ottone were slain, and at last Astolpho fell, in revenge of whose death Orlando turned the spot where he died into a lake of Saracen blood. The luckless Bujaforte met Rinaldo, and, before he could explain how he seemed to be fighting on the Saracen side, received such a blow upon the head that he fell, unable to utter a word. Orlando, cutting his way to a spot where there was a great struggle and uproar, found the poor youth Baldwin, the son of Gan, with two spears in his breast. "I am no traitor now," said Baldwin, and those were the last words he said. Orlando was bitterly sorry to have been the cause of his death, and tears streamed from his eyes. At length down went Oliver himself. He had become blinded with his own blood, and smitten Orlando without knowing him. "How now, cousin," cried Orlando, "have you too gone over to the enemy?" "O my lord and master," cried the other, "I ask your pardon. I can see nothing; I am dying. Some traitor has stabbed me in the back. If you love me, lead my horse into the thick of them, so that I may not die unavenged."

"I shall die myself before long," said Orlando, "out of very toil and grief; so we will go together."

Orlando led his cousin's horse where the press was thickest, and dreadful was the strength of the dying man and his tired companion. They made a street through which they passed out of the battle, and Orlando led his cousin away to his tent, and said, "Wait a little till I return, for I will go and sound the horn on the hill yonder."

" 'Tis of no use," said Oliver, "my spirit is fast going, and desires to be with its Lord and Saviour."

He would have said more, but his words came from him imperfectly, like those of a man in a dream, and so he expired.

When Orlando saw him dead, he felt as if he was alone on the earth, and he was quite willing to leave it; only he wished that King Charles, at the foot of the mountains, should know how the case stood before he went. So he took up the horn and blew it three times, with such force that the blood burst out of his nose and mouth. Turpin says that at the third blast the horn broke in two.

In spite of all the noise of the battle, the sound of the horn broke over it like a voice out of the other world. They say that birds fell dead at it, and that the whole Saracen army drew back in terror. Charlemagne was sitting in the midst of his court when the sound reached him; and Gan was there. The Emperor was the first to hear it.

"Do you hear that?" said he to his nobles. "Did you hear the horn as I heard it?"

Upon this they all listened, and Gan felt his heart misgive him. The horn sounded a second time.

"What is the meaning of this?" said Charles.

"Orlando is hunting," observed Gan, "and the stag is killed."

But when the horn sounded yet a third time, and the blast

was one of so dreadful a vehemence, everybody looked at the other, and then they all looked at Gan in fury. Charles rosē from his seat.

"This is no hunting of the stag," said he. "The sound goes to my very heart. O Gan! O Gan! Not for thee do I blush, but for myself. O foul and monstrous villain! Take him, gentlemen, and keep him in close prison. Would to God I had not lived to see this day!"

But it was no time for words. They put the traitor in prison, and then Charles with all his court took his way to Roncesvalles, grieving and praying.

It was afternoon when the horn sounded, and half an hour after it when the Emperor set out; and meantime Orlando had returned to the fight that he might do his duty, however hopeless, as long as he could sit his horse. At length he found his end approaching, for toil and fever, and rode all alone to a fountain where he had before quenched his thirst. His horse was wearier than he, and no sooner had his master alighted than the beast, kneeling down as if to take leave, and to say, "I have brought you to a place of rest," fell dead at his feet. Orlando cast water on him from the fountain, not wishing to believe him dead; but when he found it to no purpose, he grieved for him as if he had been a human being, and addressed him by name with tears, and asked forgiveness if he had ever done him wrong. They say that the horse, at these words, opened his eyes a little, and looked kindly at his master, and then stirred never more. They say also that Orlando then, summoning all his strength, smote a rock near him with his beautiful sword Durindana, thinking to shiver the steel in pieces, and so prevent its falling into the hands of the enemy; but though the rock split like a slate, and a great cleft remained ever after to astonish the eyes of pilgrims, the sword remained uninjured.

And now Rinaldo and Ricciardetto came up, with Turpin, having driven back the Saracens, and told Orlando that the battle was won. Then Orlando knelt before Turpin, and begged remission of his sins, and Turpin gave him absolution. Orlando fixed his eyes on the hilt of his sword as on a crucifix, and embraced it, and he raised his eyes and appeared like a creature seraphical and transfigured, and, bowing his head, he breathed out his pure soul.

And now King Charles and his nobles came up. The

Emperor, at sight of the dead Orlando, threw himself, as if he had been a reckless youth, from his horse, and embraced and kissed the body, and said: "I bless thee, Orlando; I bless thy whole life, and all that thou wast, and all that thou ever didst, and the father that begat thee; and I ask pardon of thee for believing those who brought thee to thine end. They shall have their reward, O thou beloved one! But indeed it is thou that livest, and I who am worse than dead."

Horrible to the Emperor's eyes was the sight of the field of Roncesvalles. The Saracens indeed had fled, conquered; but all his paladins but two were left on it dead, and the whole valley looked like a great slaughter-house, trampled into blood and dirt, and reeking to the heat. Charles trembled to his heart's core for wonder and agony. After gazing dumbly on the place, he cursed it with a solemn curse, and wished that never grass might grow in it again, nor seed of any kind, neither within it nor on any of its mountains around, but the anger of Heaven abide over it forever.

Charles and his warriors went after the Saracens into Spain. They took and fired Saragossa, and Marsilius was hung to the carob-tree under which he had planned his villainy with Gan; and Gan was hung and drawn and quartered in Roncesvalles, amidst the execrations of the country.